Fundamentals of Total Quality Safety Management and Auditing

Fundamentals of Total Quality Safety Management and Auditing

Editor:

Jacinta Austin

ArclerPress

www.arclerpress.com

Fundamentals of Total Quality Safety Management and Auditing

Editor: Jacinta Austin

© 2017 Arcler Press LLC
708 3rd Avenue, 6th Floor
New York
NY 10017
United States of America
www.arclerpress.com

ISBN: 978-1-68094-498-3

Library of Congress Control Number: 2016951400

About the Editor

Jacinta Austin

Jacinta obtained her International Business degree from Griffith University 2012 and a Postgraduate Certificate in Business from University of Southern Queensland in 2014. Her interested is in business and marketing. Jacinta is currently studying a Master of Business (Marketing) from Queensland University of Technology.

Contents

List of Contributors

Miguel Blanco Callejo
Universidad Rey Juan Carlos Spain

Erika Alves dos Santos
Fundacentro/Ministry of Labour and Employee,, Brazil

Roland Iosif Moraru
University of Petroşani Romania

Jarmo Heinonen
ABB Full Service® Business Unit Finland

Mika Raassina
ABB Full Service® Business Unit Finland

Nick Moss
ABB Full Service® Business Unit Finland

Jan Emblemsvåg
STX OSV AS, Norway

Marin Andreica
Department of Management, Academy of Economic Studies, Bucharest, Romania

Stere Farmache
BSE, Bucharest, Romania

Madalina Ecaterina Andreica
The National Scientific Research Institute of Labour and Social Protection, Bucharest, Romania
Dept. of Economic Informatics and Cybernetics, Academy of Economic Studies, Bucharest, Romania

Octavian Stroie
Department of Audit, National Authority for Scientific Research, Bucharest, Romania

Jesús E. Martínez Marín
Technical University of Catalonia Department of Nautical Sciences & Engineering Rideport: International Network of Port & Coast's Experts Spain

Bruna Galdorfini Chiari
Faculdade de Ciências Farmacêuticas, UNESP - Univ Estadual Paulista, Departamento de Fármacos e Medicamentos, Laboratório de Cosmetologia – LaCos, Araraquara, Laboratório de Cosmetologia, São Paulo, Brazil

Maria Gabriela José de Almeida
Faculdade de Ciências Farmacêuticas, UNESP - Univ Estadual Paulista, Departamento de Fármacos e Medicamentos, Laboratório de Cosmetologia – LaCos, Araraquara, Laboratório de Cosmetologia, São Paulo, Brazil

Marcos Antonio Corrêa
Faculdade de Ciências Farmacêuticas, UNESP - Univ Estadual Paulista, Departamento de Fármacos e Medicamentos, Laboratório de Cosmetologia – LaCos, Araraquara, Laboratório de Cosmetologia, São Paulo, Brazil

Vera Lucia Borges Isaac
Faculdade de Ciências Farmacêuticas, UNESP - Univ Estadual Paulista, Departamento de Fármacos e Medicamentos, Laboratório de Cosmetologia – LaCos, Araraquara, Laboratório de Cosmetologia, São Paulo, Brazil

Štefka Gorenak
Faculty of Commercial and Business Sciences, Celje, Slovenia

Elizabeth A. Cudney
Missouri University of Science and Technology, USA

Cassandra C. Elrod
Missouri University of Science and Technology, USA

Víctor Reyes-Alcázar
Andalusian Agency for Health Care Quality Spain

Antonio Torres-Olivera
Andalusian Agency for Health Care Quality Spain

Diego Núñez-García,
Andalusian Agency for Health Care Quality Spain

Antonio Almuedo-Paz
Andalusian Agency for Health Care Quality Spain

Jakob Rosenqvist
Department of Management and Engineering, Linköping University, Linköping, Sweden

Patrik Thollander
Department of Management and Engineering, Linköping University, Linköping, Sweden

Patrik Rohdin
Department of Management and Engineering, Linköping University, Linköping, Sweden

Mats Söderström
Department of Management and Engineering, Linköping University, Linköping, Sweden

Goknur Arzu Akyuz
Atılım University, Turkey

Stephen Inkoom
Radiation Protection Institute, Ghana Atomic Energy Commission, Legon, Accra, Ghana

Fereshteh Farzianpour
Department of Health Management and Economics, School of Public Health, Tehran University of Medical Sciences, Tehran, Iran

Kazem Mohammad
Department of Epidemiology and Biostatistics, School of Public Health, Tehran University of Medical Sciences, Tehran, Iran

Abbas Rahimi Foroushani
Department of Epidemiology and Biostatistics, School of Public Health, Tehran University of Medical Sciences, Tehran, Iran

Samira Alirezaei
School of Health Management and Information Sciences, Iran University of Medical Sciences, Tehran, Iran

Fatemeh Manafi
Department of Health Management and Economics, School of Public Health, Tehran University of Medical Sciences, Tehran, Iran

Jianfei Leng
School of Business, Hohai University, Nanjing, China

Lingfen Zhang
School of Business, Hohai University, Nanjing, China

Madan Lal Bhasin
Bang College of Business, KIMEP University, Almaty, Republic of Kazakhstan

Giron Kamonja
School of Economic and Management, China University of Geosciences (Wuhan), Wuhan, China

Yan Liang
School of Economic and Management, China University of Geosciences (Wuhan), Wuhan, China

Muhammad Tayyab Sohail
School of Public Administration, China University of Geosciences (Wuhan), Wuhan, China

Shahzad Ahmad Khan
School of Economic and Management, China University of Geosciences (Wuhan), Wuhan, China

Olumuyiwa O. Matthew
MSc in Information Technology Management, MCPN, AMBCS, The University of Wolverhampton, United Kingdom.

Carl Dudley
Oracle Professor in Database Technology University of Wolverhampton, UK. UK Oracle User Group Official, oracle ACE Director

Maryam Abulghasemi Komeleh
Department of Accounting, Science and Research Branch, Islamic Azad University, Golestan, Iran

Mansour Garkaz
Department of Accounting, Aliabad Katoul Branch, Islamic Azad University, Aliabad Katoul, Iran

Derek Fowler
JDF Consultancy LLP UK

Ronald Pierce
JDF Consultancy LLP UK

Gilberto Santos
College of Technology, Polytechnic Institute Cávado e Ave, Imasys Research Centre, Barcelos,, Portugal

Manuel Rebelo
College of Technology, Polytechnic Institute Cávado e Ave, Imasys Research Centre, Barcelos,, Portugal

Síria Barros
College of Technology, Polytechnic Institute Cávado e Ave, Imasys Research Centre, Barcelos,, Portugal

Martinha Pereira
College of Technology, Polytechnic Institute Cávado e Ave, Imasys Research Centre, Barcelos,, Portugal

Preface

The fundamentals for quality safety management and auditing can be very different and dependant on the industry the organisation is operating in. Not only does quality safety management can be different with relation to the industry, but also the departments of the organisation, such as occupational health and safety. In addition to this, how the organisation is implementing or distributing their corporate responsibility on things such as the environment. Not only does the organisation need to look at the internal environment, but also the external environments. May organisations have implemented quality management for economic crisis for organisations and fraud within the banking industry and other industries and departments that may be effected by external influences. In addition to this, how quality management has been deployed to maintain improvement and maintain security levels within the organisation.

Also, looking how quality safety management and auditing is taking place in different areas of the world and comparing how it is implemented in places like Africa and with countries in Europe and how they are creating the foundation of quality management within different industries. When an organisation is working within products and service they need to considered the life cycle of the product or products and services'. But also look at conditions on an external basis when an organisation is looking to outsource an aspect of their organisation such as call centres. When quality safety management and auditing is needed to be taken into consideration organisation needs to look at how different countries consider the different management systems that are implemented and how they are different. These may include aspects such as risk management. Also, look at what success factors have been implemented in other industries to ensure the quality of practice are maintaining and if these success factors can be implemented into the overall fundamentals, but also looking at how the feasibility of management model, awareness and attitudes of managers. Along with the collaborative quality of management and what management practices work effectively for the organisation. With relation to auditing, may organisations have implemented these to maintain high level of security and quality control. But looking at the study on internal control auditing and what finding have come out of this and what are the effects of this and if this has an effect on quality management. These can be clearly seen in clearly in the tourism industry the cosmetic industry. With regards to the tourism industry, these can be seen with the security measures implemented at airports, airlines and hotels. With the cosmetics industry the quality safety management is needed to maintain the health and safety of consumers without having contaminated products. But also looking at how auditing is use in sustainability methodology and measurement. While looking at how auditing can maintain security levels within different database systems and the relationship between internal auditing and quality.

Editor
Jacinta Austin

INTRODUCTION

Those who are committed to Total Quality Management (TQM) often say that Safety Management is included within their philosophy. In this paper we suggest this view cannot be defended at a practical level. Safety Management shares many characteristics and techniques with TQM, but a significant 'set' of factors does not overlap. Indeed, there are conflicting needs between Safety Management and production and attempts to meet Safety Management needs through Quality Management alone will, at best, be sub-optimal and could result in complacency - a critical deficiency for safety management.

Management is the common thread. All management should seek constant improvement by implementing, recording/monitoring and controlling new processes and this applies especially to safety. TQM theorists use this generic similarity to say that Safety Management can be encompassed within their philosophy no matter what the content. That won't do. Practical TQM is essentially about the product and management of production is inherently at odds with safety as we will show below. That the concept of encompassment has no practical relevant can be dramatically demonstrated by considering the literature on TQM for the workplace - in most books safety has no mention - in a few there is a peripheral comment. If Safety Management was seems as an essential management system then it would be a mandatory part of TQM accreditation whereas, in practical quality management, extraneous or difficult areas are ignored and Safety Management seems to fall into one or other of those categories.

In the sections that follow, we lead gently into the subject by considering first some evidence for difference between the two forms of management. Thereafter, we consider and contrast the form of outputs from management initiatives in quality and safety considering the limits on any effects, where costs of failure fall and how easy it is to measure the output. We follow on from that into a more detailed consideration of the difficulties that exist in measuring safety performance in any reasonable time scale so that conventional TQM measurement/control philosophy will not work well. Finally, to show that there are significant differences in both the techniques and the ability to manage the outputs, we consider and contract in terms of quality and safety fully automated plants with those where purely manual work dominates. Our conclusions are presented dogmatically, but they are intended to inspire discussion and refutation because we consider that this subject has not been sufficiently addressed.

Measurements

Measurement of effects - quality

Typically with a product, goals are set and performance measured against them. In setting these goals the environment of use of the product is critical and the criteria might be, for example, reliability, or a match to customer needs or simply minimization of rejects internally or at the point of supply. For a physical item it should be possible to set and meet whatever level if quality is selected.

This is rather more difficult for a service industry where the critical areas are t5ransactions with people. Standards might be set, for example, in terms of speed of service, staff appearance, rate of complaint or customer perceptions becomes the independent variable. This is a problem that is shared in some respects with Safety Management, but that we feel is not adequately addressed within the standard TQM literature. Perhaps there are experiences that can be shared by safety managers and the managers of service industries. That is not to say that problems are solved - only that there is commonality of management technique, but beyond that observation we no longer consider TQM in service industries in this paper because the subject is too wide.

The basis of quality management is the setting of targets and observation of results and, by definition product quality is observable. Where the goals are defined in physical terms, therefore, the techniques of TQM should work.

Measurement of effects - safety

Safety failures on the other hand are not readily observable. The statistics of injuries may be gathered, but these are coarse, unstable measures and can only be gathered after damage has been done. Three main systems or techniques are used at present to measure industrial safety,

- *Monitoring* is generally post facto on a measure of incidents and analysis of events.
- *Audit rating systems* assess groups of management factors that are claimed or just assumed to be indicators of 'safe' working systems.
- *Detailed observation of behavior* over short timescales is used as a predictor for accident rates.

It is not clear that, in fact, any of these techniques provide information directly related to safe working that is useful in realistic management time scales. That is not to say they have no value because they are, in fact, complementary methods that all have a place in an efficient system. It is, however, true that one seldom finds all three combined or evidence that their deficiencies are understood.

Monitoring either provides statistically unstable or excessive amounts of information and, in any event, although ‹raw› statistical measures are useful for cross company or industry benchmarking, they are usually useful at all for line managers at projects or task level. Attempts to make them more stable by extending recording to incidents as opposed to accidents has been shown to introduce bias caused by the very efforts to ensure reporting and this also requires significant resources for analysis. Promotion of incidents to ‹potential› events as employed by Shell and other is, perhaps useful in providing more stable ‹targets› for management effort. It is, however, aimed at understanding of causes rather than monitoring of effect and makes a nonsense of the statistics because there is no clear link between the underlying frequency distribution of the incidents and their output effect.

Rating systems on the other hand require belief that the factors measured and controlled have a direct positive impact on safety and while some factors seem intuitively to affect safety, other have no direct relationship and, at worst, the factors themselves become goals or check lists with no impact. That may seem harsh, because systems based on ISRS or CHASE have had companies involved, but, putting it very bluntly, that may only show the impact of bringing safety into the foreground. Insofar, therefore, as ‹rating› systems seek to bring Safety Management into a record, measure and control system they fail because the measures are not directly concerned with safety. They do, however, formalize some of the management aspects and provide a framework within which Safety Management can operate. In this sense they are part of the overlap between TQM and Safety Management and their deficiencies are the deficiencies of TQM applied to safety.

Intensive observation of behavior has a firmer foundation in that unsafe behavior has clear links with incidents and accidents so that it should be possible to determine a distribution function for unsafe acts and extrapolate it to accidents given some basis for the extrapolation. The problem is the amount of resource that is required and the nature of the assessment. Only skilled observers can assure that events are being counted on an equal basis and it is unlikely that intensive observation cab be used as a measurement system by middle management - it is intended more as a control variable for overall plant use within a global safety attitudes initiative.

Quality Management

The meaning of quality was adequately presented by Hoyle who discussed the three basic quality truths: the internal and external to the organization requirements constantly change; organizational performance must be constantly changing to keep pace with requirements; quality is the difference between the standard required, meaning the stated, implied or obligatory need, requirement or expectation, and the standard achieved, meaning the performance level measured. The latter truth according to Godfrey & Juran reflects the control process that intends to provide stability and to prevent any adverse change during the operations; the control process includes the stages of defining the control subject, establishing the measurement and standards of performance, measuring the actual performance, comparing the performance measured by the standards and implementing remedial actions in cases of difference. The specific procedure is widely known as the Plan – Do – Check – Act (PDCA) quality circle. Moving from the partial quality processes implementation including the performance monitoring, the quality control and the quality assurance, to a holistic approach of quality as expressed by the contemporary establishment of Quality Management Systems (QMS) Morgan &Murgatroyd stated "TQM is a total organizational approach for meeting customer needs and expectations that involves all managers and employees in using quantitative methods to improve continuously the organization's processes, products and services", and Dale (1999) stated "TQM is the mutual co-operation of everyone in an organization and associated business processes to produce products and services, which meet and, hopefully, exceed the needs and expectations of customers. TQM is both a philosophy and a set of management guiding principles for managing an organization". One of the fundamental targets that the quality process is based on the needs of the customers, either the external or the internal ones. External customer is defined as any person that directly enjoys the product or service offered or may profit from the product success, such as company shareholders, suppliers and the society. Especially the society may in the aggregate withdraw support for an organization, protest or invoke legal action; this is mostly concerned by the regulators, who demand society's safety and protection regardless of the product's compliance to the rest external and internal customer needs. Internal customer is everyone who comprises part of the system processes, such as managers, supervisors and operational personnel; the employees are aware of their working conditions and their reputation deriving from organization's place in the market and society, and, in addition, they are a basic and variable resource that must be also satisfied in order to offer their labor. External and internal customer needs are the top priority presented with a pyramid shape the hierarchy of needs that the managers must always consider in order to lead their organization in sustainability; the physiological needs comprise the base of the pyramid, followed by the safety, social, esteem and self-actualization needs. Another classification of needs was discussed by Coletti & Early, who distinguished the perceived needs, meaning the statement of needs by customers according to their perceptions, and the cultural needs, which are mostly related to the internal customers and include job security, self and mutual respect and other cultural values. Quality policy comprises the fundamental and the high level expression of quality management requirements and commitment to continuous improvement. The policy determines the form and the nature of the quality objectives, processes etc. And must be aligned with the overall business vision of the organization (Bass & Lawton, 2009); the organization's goals, resources and activities must be aligned with the overall strategy (Godfrey, 1998). Moreover, following the highest level quality policy, mission statements must be prepared for every partial project and the project goals must be specific, measurable, agreed upon, realistic and time specific; these partial mission statements provide legitimacy since any project becomes official, and confers rights for holding meetings, requesting data, asking for employees attention and assistance etc. Interactively, quality performance reflects the organizational structure and culture; in order to achieve quality both management and operational team commitment and involvement are required. Hoyle (2007) reported two additional dimensions of quality that are directly related to its human aspects: the "business quality dimension", meaning the outward view of the stakeholders regarding the organization, and the "organization quality dimension", or "system quality dimension" declaring the inward facing view in terms of efficiency (productivity, motivation etc.) and effectiveness that is related to the proper utilization of knowledge. Consequently, it is apparent that QMS is related tightly to the management of resources, the human ones, the infrastructure resources and the working environment. Human resources include education, training, experience, qualifications and skills for any task assigned to the operational and administrative levels. The corresponding needs must be derived from the highest organizational policy; each organization shall keep records of the employees' competence in order to monitor their adherence to the basic requirements and shall manage personnel allocation and promotion; in addition, as Zhang (2000) emphasized, recognition and reward for quality improvement efforts are essential for quality enhancement. Infrastructure consists of buildings, workspace, hardware and equipment, software including documentation, literature and computer programs, and any supporting mean and device. Although the working environment includes the needs for adequate lighting, reduction of noise, temperature control and the manipulation of every physical factor that affects the personnel's comfort, these are usually included in the infrastructure area; the specific domain is more related to the psychological aspects of the environment such as staff satisfaction, trustful culture, productive communication, sense of ownership etc.

CHAPTER 1

TOTAL QUALITY MANAGEMENT MODEL TO FACE THE ECONOMIC CRISIS

Miguel Blanco Callejo

INTRODUCTION

The aim of this chapter is to describe the recent evolution of Mercadona, a leading Spanish family-owned supermarket company, that has become a worldwide benchmark in retailing industry (Blanco and Gutierrez, 2010; Ton and Harrow, 2010). The chapter presents the company and describes the 1993's top management decision of implement Total Quality Management (TQM) as well as the outstanding and rapid growth of the firm between 1995 and 2008 under that management model (Blanco and Gutierrez, 2010). The surge of the economic crisis which has its origin in the United States in the summer of 2007 started to affect significantly Spain in the second half of 2008. The crisis has had a dramatic impact in the Spanish Economy and Society declining the GDP -3.9% in 2009 and rocketing unemployment rate to 21.5% in October 2011 (INE, 2011). In September 2008 consumer spending dropped off sharply affecting Mercadona's turnover. This situation was a real challenge for the top management team and motivated a significant realignment of the company according to its management model goal: "anticipating and meeting its customers' needs". Anyway, the strength of Total Quality Management has allowed the company to face successfully this situation by refocusing in its management model and adopting innovative and pioneering initiatives in the Spanish retailing industry.

Citation: Miguel Blanco Callejo (2012). Total Quality Management Model to Face the Economic Crisis, Quality Management and Practices, Dr. Kim-Soon Ng (Ed.), InTech, DOI: 10.5772/38755.

As a supermarket chain providing basic food and hygiene products to its customers Mercadona started to suffer a sustainable client's loss in the second half of 2008. Facing the situation the company has put the customer back at the center of the company's decisions, taking only those steps that provide customer value (Mercadona, 2010; Ton and Harrow, 2010). Given this context Mercadona reviewed all its references, tightened up the product assortment and has launched a campaign to reduce its prices as much as possible "pinching pennies in all its processes" in order to provide the "shopping cart menu" to its customers, offering the highest quality products at the market's most economical prices. Mercadona's recent economic and financial results seem to show the adequacy of the firm's strategy to overcome the economic crisis and to continue firmly with its growth and outstanding development in the upcoming future.

MERCADONA

Mercadona is a Spanish family-owned supermarket company dedicated to the commercial distribution of food and hygiene products. The firm runs large supermarket (averaging between 1,300 and 1,500 square meters of retail space) following a model of local city centre stores. The 63,500 employees' company finished 2010 with 1,310 urban supermarkets representing a market share of 13.1% of the total food store retail space in Spain (Mercadona, 2010). Mercadona's objective is to fully satisfy the grocery, home cleaning, hygiene and pet product needs of its customers and their pets. The company would like to be a "prescriber" that means that Mercadona recommends to its customers the best products. Every one of the supermarkets has an ample and efficient selection that includes up to 8,000 different items which combine Mercadona's brands and other commercial brands highly recognized by the customers. This large selection of products pretends to satisfy necessities of the 4.4 million households that usually place their trust in the company every year (Mercadona, 2010).

The company name Mercadona S.A. (Initial letters from Spanish Sociedad Anónima, publiclimited company), appeared in 1977, but the company actually originated in Cárnicas Roig, a family firm owned by Francisco Roig Ballester specialized in carving and selling meat. The firm subsequently evolved into a chain of eight grocer's shops (Mercadona, 2010). In 1981, one of Francisco's sons, Juan Roig, now running the firm, along with his brother Fernando and sisters Trinidad and Amparo bought Mercadona from his parents. At that time, they had eight stores with some 300 square meters of retail space each. It was a small commercial chain of various stores, which soon began to growth in size, first in the Valencia region and then in other areas of Spain. The firm's expansion was coincident with a period of growth in the commercial distribution sector in Spain, which had various causes, in particular, the increasing concentration of the population within cities and the massive entry of women into the labor market. This growth attracted the attention of the large European distribution chains, which began to enter in the country. The strategy of these large companies was to open major retail outlets (hypermarkets), and offer low prices in particular products accompanied by strong promotions, special offers and discounts that were supported by aggressive advertising campaigns in the media (Navarro, 2005). The firms achieved low prices by putting pressure on their suppliers to cut their prices as far as possible. Customers attracted by the low prices on some products also bought other products not on special offer that yielded high profit margins (Blanco and Gutierrez, 2010).

As a consequence of this strategy, in the 1990s the food distribution sector became highly concentrated and foreign multinationals controlled a large part of the market. The competition from these firms intensified the rivalry in the industry, which was now mature, with strong competition and low margins. In 1990, Juan Roig, along with his wife, Hortensia Herrero took over control of the company. After that, in the early 1990s, Roig faced the first great challenge for the firm. As a consequence of the arrival of the International Retail chains profit margins decreased significantly all through the supermarket industry. Mercadona responded to this highly changeable and turbulent environment by adopting a similar policy to that of the large hypermarket chains. The retailer put downward pressure on its suppliers' prices and ran intensive advertising campaigns to promote its special offers every day. But the results were not as good as expected, since this was the same strategy as the big hypermarket chains'. Mercadona was selling more, but every year its profits declined1.

This was a very tricky time for Mercadona, which had to face some extremely difficult situations. Nevertheless, the President ignored tempting offers to buy the company and stuck firmly to his commitment to remain in the business. Thus, in 1993 Juan Roig decided to implement a strategy that broke radically with the dynamic of the sector: he introduced the TQM model as the basis of all its operations. This involved a strategic switch from the Supermarket industry's traditional high-low pricing with promotions to a new commercial strategy summarized in a simple slogan "Siempre Precios Bajos" (SPB, which translates as "Always Low Prices") and a culture of quality and continuous improvement (Blanco and Gutierrez, 2010; Ton and Harrow, 2010).

While its competitors continued with their massive daily advertising campaigns in the media, Mercadona immediately stopped all its advertising spending. Mercadona cancelled all its special offers, and made a commitment to its customers always to sell at the same price, and to its suppliers to remain loyal to them and maintain stable prices for years (Caparrós and Biot, 2006). This was quite a turnaround, as suppliers had previously seen Mercadona as one of the toughest negotiators. The firm's main objective was to protect itself in the midst of all this turbulence and implement an unusual and original model, novel in the commercial distribution sector: price, supplier and employee stability to achieve permanent customers. The notion was to allow the customers enjoy a Total Shopping with products of the highest quality at the lowest prices on the market keeping the motto "quality doesn't have to be more expensive" (Mercadona, 2010).

The results immediately after adopting the new model were not very promising: although the firm managed to practically double its sales from four years before, its profits were less than half. But the President stuck by his decision and firmly maintained the strategy based on the new management model. In 1995 its performance improved, and Mercadona soon entered a spectacular and unstoppable process of growth, which was mainly organic. From 1995, the focus on TQM worked well for Mercadona and between 1998 and 2008, Mercadona enjoyed double-digit growth in sales and profits. Supermarkets spread out throughout the whole country like an olive-oil spill. By the end of 2008, it was the biggest supermarket chain in Spain, with 1,210 stores and 61,500 employees (Ton and Harrow, 2010). Moreover, in recent years Mercadona has maintained a rate of new supermarket openings of nearly 100 per year (Figure 1). The growth rate in its sales of over 25% per year from 2000 to 2006 makes Mercadona the 14th fastest-growing retailer in the world, and in 2006 it was the fastest-growing food distributor in the world, after the American commercial distribution giant Wal-Mart, (Deloitte, 2007).

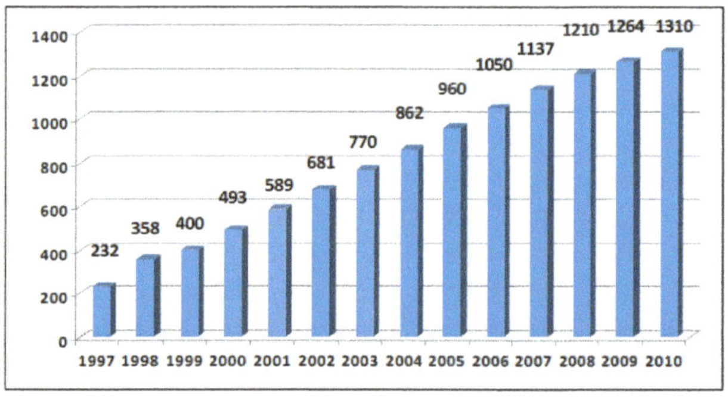

Figure 1: Evolution of Mercadona's stores

MERCADONA'S TOTAL QUALITY MANAGEMENT MODEL

Mercadona's management firmly believes that adopting and maintaining the TQM model has been critical in allowing the firm to achieve this rate of growth and these spectacular economic results. As Juan Roig, Mercadona's president stated: "Without doubt one of the greatest milestones of Mercadona was the implementation of the Total Quality Model. The involvement of all those whom we train at Mercadona in applying and developing it is doubtlessly the reason for our success" (Ton and Harrow, 2010: 2). Through this approach, management has impressed on the firm a clear orientation to satisfy the needs and expectations of all its stakeholders. On the basis of this approach Mercadona has defined five components in the firm: first, customers ("the Bosses"); second, the employees; third, the suppliers; fourth, society, and fifth, capital. All are equally important, but in that sequential order, (Mercadona, 2010). As the president of Mercadona noted "Mercadona's mission is not just to make a profit, but to make it while satisfying all of the five components" (Ton and Harrow, 2010)

Mercadona's TQM model starts from a universal premise: "to be satisfied, first you have to satisfy everyone else", (Mercadona, 2007). Thus, in the first place, Mercadona orients its entire business model towards the complete satisfaction of its customers, which the firm considers so important that internally it calls them its "bosses". In the same sense, the management is convinced that the workers – who are the people who have to satisfy the customers in the stores – must, in turn, be satisfied as well. This is why the firm, has established its own way of managing its employees, implementing policies that seek to encourage their self-realization through job security and stability, training, internal promotion and improvements in their quality of life. It is the suppliers' products that have to maximally satisfy the firm's customers, so Mercadona has established a relationship with its suppliers based on trust, cooperation, mutual collaboration and stability. Society is the medium in which the firm carries out its activities, so Mercadona feels involved with and ethically committed to its protection and development. Finally, by satisfying the needs of its customers, employees, suppliers, and society, Mercadona contributes to satisfying the expectations of the fifth component of its model, capital (Figure 2).

Despite its apparent simplicity, applying the TQM model is neither simple nor easy. In fact, one of the main difficulties is to introduce and develop programs and tools allowing the firm to satisfy each and every one of its diverse components, and at the same time, ensure that the components perceive that the firm is satisfying their needs so the firm transmits the image of a responsible and committed company. In any case, with this powerful model Mercadona has gained competitive advantages over its rivals, has been able to globally orient its strategy and organizational culture and has had adopted a coherent decisionmaking tool. So, any initiative proposed in the company must first be evaluated for its compliance with the model. The firm adopts and implements proposals only when their consequences are satisfactory to all five components, otherwise it rejects them.

Figure 2: Mercadona's Total Quality Management Model.

Orientation towards bosses' (customers') satisfaction

One of the fundamental cornerstones of the Total Quality Management Model is its orientation towards satisfying customer needs. This is why Mercadona puts the customer in a privileged position and carries out a large number of activities and initiatives to be able to care for its customers, strengthen their loyalty, and help them generate the maximum possible value from doing their shopping in Mercadona stores.

For Mercadona, the customers are at the center of its activity, since its very survival depends on their decision to shop in Mercadona supermarkets or elsewhere. Nevertheless the staff of Mercadona never spoke about their customers; they spoke of their "Bosses". Thus, the firm calls anyone who shops in its stores "boss". Under this premise, the whole organization is focused on providing an excellent service to its customers. This conception places the customer at the top of the firm's inverted organizational pyramid, and the function of the leader and the rest of the organization is to serve the customer. So, everyone's job is to provide "the Bosses" with the best quality-to-price ratio, the correct assortment of products and the highest level of service while ensuring that the Bosses could complete their purchases as quickly as possible (Ton and Harrow, 2010).

The culture of serving the customer prevailed throughout the business. Given the customer's privileged position, Mercadona's philosophy is to continually increase the "value for the customer" by maintaining its "Always Low Prices" policy and eliminating special offers, promotions and temporary discounts. A key service to "The Bosses" is keeping prices not only as low as possible but also as stable as possible (Ton and Harrow, 2010) But the philosophy not only focuses on prices. All the firm's actions are oriented toward satisfying all the customer's specifications, whether known or potential future expectations. In order to find these out, Mercadona maintains a constant and direct dialog with its "bosses", carrying out activities to collect information, opinions and needs from its customers: meetings with neighbors in neighborhoods where new stores are being opened, monographic courses on product lines, open days, blind tests, free customer service hotline, and suggestion boxes in supermarkets2. These operations require considerable economic investment from Mercadona, but the firm considers this form of contact more appropriate than big advertising campaigns in the media, which are extremely expensive and collect little information from the customers. Mercadona directly learns about its customers' tastes, the products habitual customers need, and the future trends in different lines of consumption. The firm then tries to anticipate their future needs through innovation, R&D and product improvement programs.

On the basis of the information collected and distributed, Mercadona carries out actions to increase value for the customers. The aim is to give them the chance to carry out all their shopping under the principles of "maximum quality, maximum range, maximum service, minimum cost and minimum time—always". With regard to quality, the retailer stresses the nutritional quality of its more than 8,000 products3. But quality also involves convenience, speed, comprehensiveness of service, and product variety. Product variety—the maximum range—does not mean offering a large number of brands, but rather all the products that satisfy all the customer's needs in food, hygiene, cleaning and pet food. Moreover, Mercadona aims to become a "prescriber": choosing and recommending products for their quality and minimum price. Mercadona guarantees the life and name principles for those products, guaranteeing the origin and date of packaging of the products, as well as the same name on products of the same quality. For this, the firm has designed a relationship system with the suppliers of its own-brand products4. This reduces customer insecurity, strengthens customers' loyalty to recommended products, and generates trust. With regard to service quality, Mercadona makes shopping as convenient as possible: payment by credit card, loyalty card, online or telephone shopping, home delivery, and free parking for customers. Moreover, the firm improves the convenience of the store by using a very functional design, what Mercadona calls "Ambience Stores" (Blanco and Gutierrez, 2010). From 2000, the stores are divided into six ambiance store sections (butcher, fish, bakery, fruit and vegetables, cosmetics and deli), each with its own décor and adjusted and designed depending on its marketing requirements. The stores have air-conditioning, shelves are restocked outside opening hours, products come in various packaging formats according to customers' needs, and the firm aims to minimize the time customers spend shopping. The notion behind this is to "provide value to the Bosses' shopping experience". The "Ambience stores" offer Mercadona's customers larger supermarkets with more pleasant atmospheres and a more logical product arrangement (Mercadona, 2010).

The result of this policy was a spectacular growth in the firm's sales: turnover has increased more than nine-fold in the past decade from 1997 to 2007 his growth is not only down to new store openings: the company has also increased its same-store sales considerably increasing it by an annual average of around 8% between 2005 and 2007 (Figure 3).

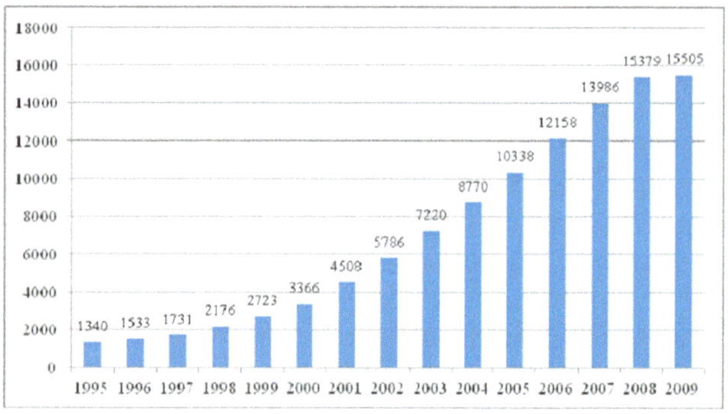

Figure 3: Evolution Mercadona sales 1995-2009 (€000s)

Orientation towards employee's commitment

For Mercadona, the orientation toward the employees is another cornerstone of the TQM model. The premise is that quality is made by people, and all 63,500 employees (67% women) need to be conscious of quality. The firm needs to achieve the commitment, involvement and/or participation of its workers by incorporating certain values that translate into concrete practices in human resources management. So Mercadona's human resources policy is based on providing its employees with stability, good working conditions, training, transparency, compensation, quality of life and opportunities for advancement (Ton and Harrow, 2010).

Within Mercadona's management, Total Quality is based on the universal premise that "in order to be satisfied, one must first satisfy others". The search for the total satisfaction of what Mercadona considers its most valuable asset, its employees is "relentless". To this end, Mercadona's human resource model is based on leadership and relies on self-realization, permanent employment, ongoing training and striking a balance between work and family life for everyone at the company. This makes it possible for the person who has to satisfy "The Boss" to in turn be satisfied (Mercadona, 2010).

With regard to staff selection and recruitment, Mercadona looks for people who fit in a quality environment. Mercadona tried to recruit store employees who would fit its carefully developed and distinctive culture. Candidates must be at least secondary-school graduates, and the selection process involves cultural knowledge and psycho-technical tests, interviews, and group dynamics. Recruiters held meetings at which they interviewed applicants, explained the job conditions, and then placed the applicants into groups where they develop a role-playing scenario. Recruiters received close to 30 applicants per opening and typically interviewed three for each position (Ton and Harrow, 2010).

Employees' training begins as soon as they join the firm with the so-called "Welcome Program". Before they start work, all employees receive 4-weeks, full-time training on the TQM model, which aims to inculcate the firm's culture and cost 5,000€ (Ton and Harrow, 2010). To aid learning the firm gives all its workers manuals outlining the main ideas of the model, plus practical exercises that are subsequently evaluated in exams and written tests. After taking up their posts, the workers receive very varied training during their time in the firm, including courses on how to use new technologies, task specialization in the supermarket, leadership, and occupational safety and health5 . The training programs are taught by staff members and evaluated internally. Moreover, they often take place in the supermarkets themselves, all of which have specially-designed training rooms. The aim of the training policy is to develop employees' skills, and the policy is accompanied by an internal promotion policy that facilitates employees' identification with Mercadona. In fact, all the firm's senior managers started at the bottom.

Mercadona has designed a simple and complete compensation policy aimed at strengthening its link with its workers and favoring their identification with the project. Part of each employee's compensation is fixed, and the other part is variable, satisfying the equity principle: "for equal responsibility, equal pay". The fixed component has only four bands, and is based on three criteria: experience, responsibility, and performance. The variable component depends on the company and each individual supermarket meeting their objectives. In any case, Mercadona pays wages above the sector average, and the firm consequently demands more commitment from its workers in exchange. The evaluation of the performance and quality that the employee shows in their work, which is carried out by the employee's immediate superior, is determinant in pay rises and promotions. It is significant that the majority of Mercadona's employees earn bonuses for meeting objectives6 .

On the other hand, jobs are designed broadly, which enhances both the firm's flexibility and the workers' employability. Each worker knows half an hour in advance what their function will be that day, and this depends on variables such as the number of customers, restocking needs, and staff available in the store. The firm has tried to standardize different types of timetable through its "standard timetable" program. All timetables have the same start and finish times regardless of the day of the week, and staff members have a maximum number of hours work per week. Mercadona workers also have a concentrated working day. In other words, they do not work the split shifts—with a long lunch break from 2 to 5 o'clock— that are typical in Spanish stores. This program also allows workers to know their timetables one month in advance and hence be able to plan their 30 days per year vacations (Mercadona, 2010).

Mercadona also aims to reconcile its employees' working and personal lives as far as possible through stability programs, additional services and benefits, as well as protect its workers to the maximum. In a sector where temporary contracts are the norm, all of Mercadona's staff has stable, indefinite-duration contracts. Moreover, Mercadona continually tries to improve its employees' working conditions. The firm offers free kindergartens in its logistics centers, pays for one month extra maternity leave, does not open its supermarkets on Sundays, and has a policy allowing workers to work in the supermarket closest to their homes. Finally, Mercadona also carries out preventive and corrective activities in the area of occupational safety and health through a culture of internal prevention that measures and actively combats accidents and illnesses. In addition, all the firm's employees have life insurance. Mercadona pays employees 100% of their wages if they are incapacitated, and the firm has measures in place to help the family if a company worker dies.

With all these actions included in a comprehensive human resources policy and in the framework of its TQM model, Mercadona has managed to considerably reduce its employee turnover and absenteeism figures, which are traditionally very high in the sector. At the same time, the firm has also raised its workers' productivity levels considerably, and consequently its own results. The following figure shows the upward trend in sales per employee (Figure 4).

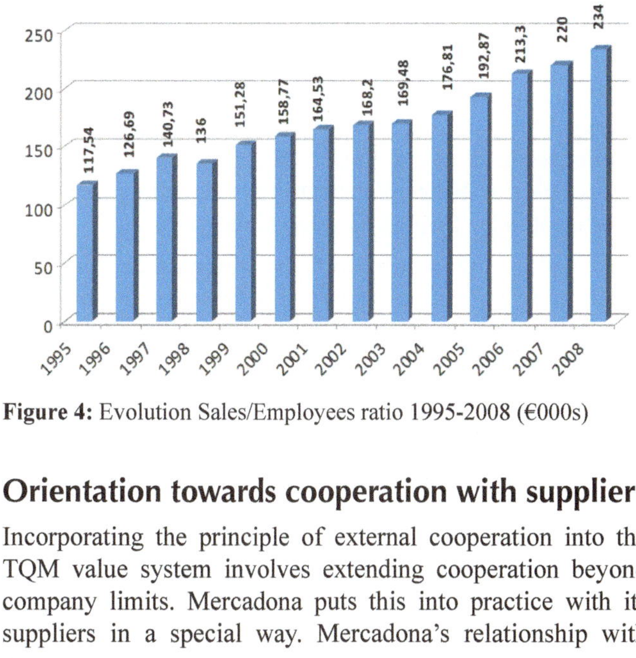

Figure 4: Evolution Sales/Employees ratio 1995-2008 (€000s)

Orientation towards cooperation with suppliers

Incorporating the principle of external cooperation into the TQM value system involves extending cooperation beyond company limits. Mercadona puts this into practice with its suppliers in a special way. Mercadona's relationship with its suppliers seeks cooperation, stability in the relationship, mutual benefits, and the sharing of training and information to improve all the business processes.

The starting point is the adoption of a model of "process management and analysis". Mercadona studies and analyzes these processes from when the products leave the supplier to when they reach the customer. The central idea is that any inefficiency in the production process will eventually reach the end-customer. The aim is to iron out inefficiencies, and to try to extend cooperation to the whole value chain and even reach the suppliers' suppliers.

Mercadona believes that in order to optimize process management it is necessary to generate a relationship of mutual trust with its suppliers. This relationship starts from the premise that the continuity of the supplier-Mercadona relationship is in the hands of the end-customer. The supplier will continue to supply Mercadona if it can respond to and satisfy customer needs. Thus, the supplier becomes a fundamental element for satisfying the customer, and according to Mercadona's philosophy, the supplier must also be satisfied with its relationship with Mercadona, generating synergies between both parties. Mercadona's suppliers share certain generic characteristics: they are partners, capitalists, and focused on adding value for the customer. They are partners because the firm establishes a relationship with Mercadona in which both parties share the objective of fully satisfying the customer. They are capitalists because the supplier risks capital in an attempt to earn profits. And what is most important, the firm must be focused on the customer. It must be able to offer value thanks to its expertise in its area of activity: carrying out R&D and innovation, and knowing the raw materials, processes and procedures of its particular business.

Given the generic characteristics of its suppliers, Mercadona distinguishes between four categories of supplier: classic, "distressed" suppliers, intermediaries, and what the firm calls "intersuppliers". Mercadona maintains a conventional contractual relationship with "classic suppliers", which supply products and services that the customers demand mainly as a result of these companies' marketing. "Distressed suppliers" are producers that have difficulty finding a market for their products. Mercadona acquires their products, and these firms' very survival depends on their sales in this supermarket chain. Working with Mercadona allows these firms to stay in business, and hence avoid exits that would have traumatic effects on the workforce. Intermediaries are agents operating between the supplier and Mercadona. The retailer believes that these intermediaries do not add value, are unnecessary and only increase the cost of the product to the customer, so it tries to avoid them.

Finally, the so-called "intersuppliers" or "integrated suppliers" (Ton and Harrow, 2010) are Mercadona's fourth category of supplier. Mercadona works with over 2,000 suppliers, of whom approximately 100 were "integrated suppliers" who supplied it home-brand products (Mercadona, 2010; Ton and Harrow, 2010). The Integrated Suppliers, manufacturers of Mercadona's brands and with which the company has a long-term mutual cooperation and commitment relationship regulated by way of a Sound Business Practices Framework Agreement and which results in "contracts for life" (Mercadona, 2010).

These firms share Mercadona's TQM-based management philosophy, and their relationship with Mercadona is long-term and indefinite, with a willingness to undertake activities jointly. Mercadona's management is committed to the growth, development and sustainability of its "intersuppliers", and the firm dedicates substantial resources to joint research and product improvement, which help improve these firms' competitiveness and their chances of satisfying customer needs. The intersuppliers products exclusively for Mercadona and take on the "Totaler" philosophy, that is, to be prescribers of products that satisfy all the needs of the customers – the "bosses". They should offer customers recommended products that figure among Mercadona's store brands that have the highest possible quality at the lowest possible price. These suppliers must satisfy some requirements in order to obtain the "intersuppliers" status. Firstly, the company owners must have "passion" for what they are doing, that is, they have to be proactive, innovative and completely involved in their business. They must also have the economic resources necessary to carry out their business goals as well as the management ability to develop them. Secondly Mercadona sought companies with stability on the stock market, as they transmit security to the relationship. Furthermore, they must be companies that have an open-minded attitude with respect to information and indicators coming from customers and the market in order to provide solutions to meet customer's demands. The candidates must also be willing to introduce the TQM model in their organizations and seek to satisfy all of its components, which include the study and modification of every aspect with the aim of improvement, guaranteeing nutritional and environmental safety, and willingness to be audited by Mercadona to verify the degree to which they fulfill the model's requirements. Finally, Mercadona requires the exclusive manufacturing of some products as a result of the relationship of mutual trust and cooperation between both companies.

The process by which a firm becomes one of Mercadona's "intersuppliers" or "integrated suppliers", which is one of the most innovative and original aspects that Mercadona has contributed to the TQM model, is long and complex, and consists of three stages. In the preliminary or approach stage, candidate firms must occupy a position of leadership and have a consolidated and reliable production system. In the second stage, the firm and Mercadona establish a relationship where they share all information—a true partnership. In the third stage, the supplier must produce in response to customer needs and starting from their expectations and demands. This is why Mercadona shares the information it obtains from its customers through various mechanisms with its suppliers, and works with them in projects to produce new products.

This is when the relationship fits perfectly with Mercadona's management philosophy, which is to try to become a "prescriber" of products for all its customer's shopping. For this, Mercadona must use the information obtained to inform its "intersuppliers" of customer needs, and the two firms must jointly develop products and services, apply the TQM model in a coordinated way, and use the value-effort model to measure each other's value generation.

Orientation towards society

Analyzing the impact of the firm's actions on its social environment is also a defining aspect of firms with a management model based on total quality. In fact, it is a principle of TQM that, by contributing to the development of society, Mercadona would increase its own potential for development. The company attempted to detect what society needed through its communication with customers, as well as through business organizations and municipalities (Ton and Harrow, 2010). Mercadona's social strategy runs a large number of initiatives seeking social advances in various aspects: education and research; improvement and care for the natural environment; programs to help people with health problems and disadvantaged people; revitalization of trade in urban areas; participation in sectorial associations of commercial distribution; and finally, creation of wealth and jobs in the Spanish agro-food sector.

In education, Mercadona participates in initiatives linking university studies with business activity, fundamentally in the region of Valencia, and runs research programs in the agro-food field. To care for and improve the natural environment, the firm has adopted the principle of behaving responsibly toward the environment incorporating "environmental productivity" (Ton and Harrow, 2010). The firm runs waste recycling programs, studies waste treatment, implements measures and global solutions aiming to minimize the environmental impact of its activities, seeks mechanisms that achieve maximum energy efficiency, and optimizes merchandise distribution systems both nationally and in the cities7.

With regard to Mercadona's assistance for social groups with health problems and disadvantaged people, the supermarket chain sells special gluten-free products for customers with celiac disease, and sugar-free products for diabetics, thereby helping these groups with their shopping. The firm has also signed agreements with public institutions to promote joint measures aimed at helping victims of domestic violence to find employment, and professional and social training programs for young people with social problems and difficulty entering the labor market. Mercadona has also contributed visibly to revitalizing and re-energizing local city-centre trade, for this, the firm has restored and re-launched traditional Spanish indoor markets situated in the city centre, putting a supermarket inside.

Mercadona participates in sectorial and wealth-generating associations such as the Spanish Association of Supermarkets (ASEDAS) and the Spanish Association of Commercial Codification (AECOC), which work in favor of the development of the commercial distribution sector. With regard to wealth creation, it is interesting to note the retailer's important and growing contribution to Spain's GDP8 its leadership in the generation of stable employment in Spain, and its substantial investment in the Spanish agro-food industry.

Finally, the most notable of Mercadona's characteristics is that the company is not content with just implementing initiatives that show its commitment and responsibility to society. The firm also strives to measure the impact of these policies. With this purpose, in 2002 Mercadona voluntarily commissioned an ethics audit from an independent association. This resulted in a highly satisfactory assessment of the firm's compliance with the requisite ethical standards, and according to the management this should serve as reference for the development of the firm's corporate social responsibility policy9. Moreover, in another external study from an independent, international organism—the report on corporate reputation that the Reputation Institute publishes annually—Mercadona has the fourth best corporate reputation in the world, behind only Lego, Ikea and Barilla10 (Reputation Institute, 2007).

Orientation towards capital

The company's TQM model also has repercussions at the level of economic-financial results and value creation for its owners. Mercadona is a family firm that is not listed on the Stock Exchange. Its stock ownership is highly concentrated: the majority of the ownership and control is in the hands of the company's President, Juan Roig, and his family.

The President argues that under the TQM model it is also "fair" to satisfy the needs of the company's final component, the capital, in other words, those people and organizations that invest their money in the firm and hence provide economic resources. This means that Mercadona also has a clear orientation toward profit maximization, as a means of satisfying its stockholders' needs and desires (Caparrós & Biot, 2006). The company's management model has the aim of offering its stockholders various advantages that they will regard as valuable, such as profitability, stability, security and minimum risk in their investment. Mercadona was focused on long – term profitability, continuous improvement in productivity and reinvestment of profits to increase equity. In line with this position, the firm's economic performance can be classed as spectacular. The company's net profits have increased more than 14-fold from 1997 to 2007, reaching €336m in 2007. Figure 6 in the next page shows the evolution in both gross and net profits after the company introduced its TQM model.

With regard to the distribution of its profits, the firm re-invests a large part of them, thereby favoring firm growth. This has allowed the firm to grow organically and carry out a spectacular expansion strategy, opening new supermarkets, warehouses and logistics centers throughout the whole country in recent years. Figure 5 shows the evolution in the firm's equity and investments. This is the result of a careful policy of profit distribution allowing the firm to strengthen and increase its equity and multiply the investments that enable growth and expansion. This has ensured that the TQM model has had positive and multiplicative effects.

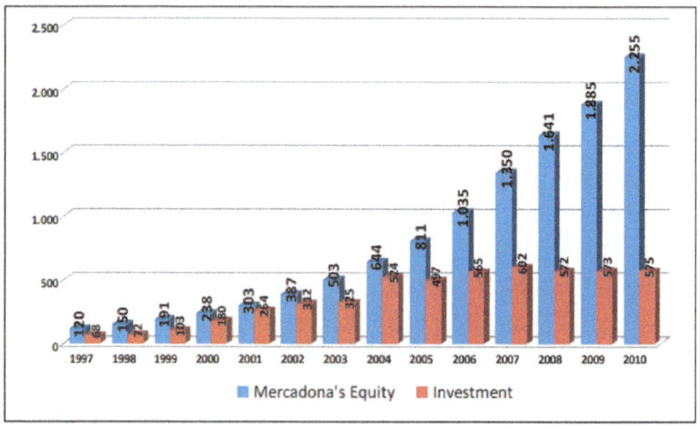

Figure 5: Evolution in Mercadona's equity and investments (€m)

The evolution in the firm's main economic indicators clearly reflects, in the words of the management, the "idealness" of the Total Quality Management model (Caparrós & Biot, 2006), and is the result of satisfying the other four components of the model: customers, employees, suppliers, and society. Continuing the current policy, as well as improving and consolidating the TQM model, should ensure the future viability of the project, confirm the trend in improved results, and increase the value of stockholders' capital.

FACING THE ECONOMIC CRISIS: THE STRENGTH OF MERCADONA'S TOTAL QUALITY MANAGEMENT MODEL

The global economic crisis, which began in September 2007 with the bursting of the U.S. property bubble has seriously affected Spain by late 2008 (Ton and Harrow, 2010). During the second half of 2008 the effects of the Global Economic crisis started to be clearly noticed in Spain. The crisis has been characterized in Spain by a high rate of unemployment, significantly above the average European rate and an important credit restriction in capital markets (Alonso and Furio, 2010). Actually, Spain has recorded the highest rate of unemployment in the European Union lately. This situation logically had a considerable impact in consumers' buying decision who tried to adjust as much as possible their budgets as well as reduced the number of transactions.

Facing such a situation, Mercadona's top management team was aware from the data from the reports tracking market's evolution that the company was starting to loss customers in its stores. According to its 2008 reports, the clients were starting to consider Mercadona "an expensive supermarket". This situation was translated into a significant reduction in Mercadona's profit that broke with an increasing trend from previous years (Figure 6)

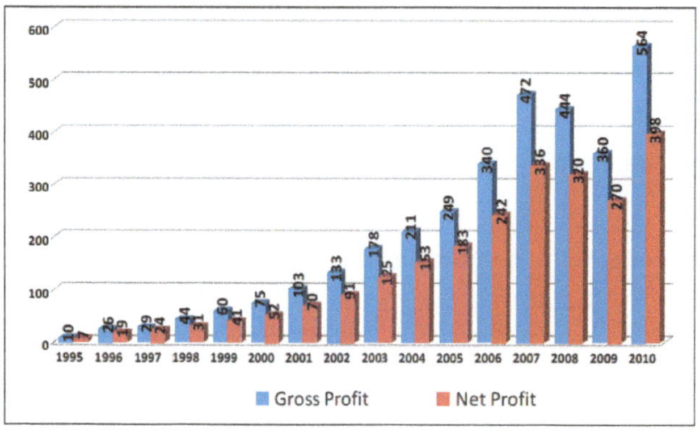

Figure 6: Evolution in Mercadona's gross/net profits 1995-2006 (€m)

Mercadona's Top Management team started to be really worried with business and profits evolution and tendency and it decided to undertake a deep strategic reflection about its business. As a result the company was able to justify the situation based in internal and external causes. Externally, the company concluded that the situation characterized by an extremely high unemployment rate and clients' difficulty to access credit, economic crisis was significantly damaging Mercadona's business. Internally, Mercadona's president noted "Based on plenty times and the belief that growth was going to last forever we had been sleepy" (Mercadona, 2008).

Taking into account this starting point, Mercadona decided to provide an answer and face that situation putting "The boss" once again at the heart of every decision the company made. Mercadona decided it had to lower its prices. Firstly, the company decided to perform a full review of the assortment of 8,000 references that it was offering to its "bosses" in the stores. Such analysis was made with the clear aim of provide an answer in line with "reduce prices" and using two criteria:

1. Did the products and commercial formats satisfy customers' needs? (Need)
2. What is the level of product turnover? (Rotation)

The analysis allowed the company to realize that it had product in the shelves which were not adding value to its customers. In 2008 Mercadona sold, for example, 72 types of milk, 112 types of juice, 100 types of coffee, carrots of every shape and size, and several types of tomato sauce. The products in some categories, such as coffee, varied only slightly (Ton and Harrow, 2010). So the company decided working to do away with anything that does not add value to the process, that raises product prices and that affects directly the grocery budgets of the customers, who "are only willing to pay for real improvements" (Mercadona, 2010).

The review was made taking into account two basic assumptions, first to eliminate everything that was not adding value to "the bosses" and, second, trying to discover everything that improving quality and product safety was, in fact, adding value. As a result of the analysis, the company was conscious that it had numerous products and commercial formats in basic and highly consumed product like milk, fruit juices, coffee and tomato sauces as well as in cleaning and hygiene products that were not satisfying customers' needs and consequently they are not adding value to the clients.

According to the analysis performed, the company decided to eliminate 800 products of the assortment, being half of them "recommended" Mercadona's branded products. The products eliminated were shown to the media in the conference press when the president presented Mercadona's 2008 results (Figure 7).

Figure 7: Some of the references eliminated by Mercadona's shelves

Once the analysis had been made, the company decided to realign its strategy again with TQM model and under one of the basic assumption of its competitive strategy, "Reduce Prices". Mercadona's top management team focused the strategic review as a return to "Total Quality Management model" and to the core activity of the firm "to be storekeepers".

The idea was to satisfy clients demands and needs with "a cart will all the needed products with the best quality and with the lowest price, prescribing them the best relationship between quality and price for each product and giving them the option of being right in their shopping decisions". Mercadona named that cart "the shopping cart menu" (Mercadona, 2008:7).

The notion of "Shopping cart menu", as a complete assortment of products that allows the company to satisfy all the clients' needs is the answer from a basic commercial learning made by Mercadona. The client was not worried by the individual price of each one of the different products that were in the cart on the contrary he was worried for the final price of the whole cart (Figure 8). Given that basic assumption, if the company is able to reduce the price of the whole shopping cart, it will be perceived as the supermarket chain cheaper in the market, which, in an environment characterized by the economic crisis will attract an increasing number of clients.

Figure 8: Mercadona's 2008 Annual Report Cover

So, Mercadona designed in 2008 a complete program of actions oriented to reduce the price of the shopping cart for its clients. The program considered a full review of both Mercadonas' products and business processes with the aim of eliminate all the elements that were adding cost without adding value to clients. After the businesses process review and the subsequent implementation of more than 600 hundred innovative initiatives the company saved more than 500 million euro cooperating with its "integrated suppliers". Between the most outstanding initiatives of cost reduction it was a sound action the elimination of trays, fixed weight and plastic in the packing of fruit and selling them loose implied a saving of 0,35 euro per Kilo which along 2009 was translated in an annual total save of 175 million euro (Mercadona, 2009).

As a result of this program and under the principle of "Back to basics" (Volver a la sencillez), Mercadona started to lower the price of the products effecting directly the reduction in the price of the raw materials, going to an efficient assortment and reducing firm profit but increasing the volume of products sold. The idea was that through the lower cost in the businesses processes the company was going to have lower prices and higher sales (Ton and Harrow, 2010). In this context the company is not defining economic objectives but quantity or volume of products sold objectives. In order to do this, it has defined a new measure from the kilo and liter sold the "Kiliters" according to which it has defined its objectives.

The result of this strategy has been a reduction of 10% in the prices in Mercadona's supermarkets along 2009 (Mercadona, 2009) and a 14% drop in prices since 2009 (Mercadona, 2010). According to Mercadona's estimates it has meant a monthly household average spending reduction of 60 euro and of 720 euro per year for its customers (Mercadona, 2009). The search for excellence in each and every one of Mercadona's processes allowed the company to offer its customers savings in excess of 700 million euro in 2010 stemming from a 4% price reduction in the "Shopping Cart Menu". If the company adds the 1,500 euro in savings in 2009 and which continued to pass on in 2010 the total savings was 2,200 million euro in 2010. None of this would have been possible without the proven dedication of the company's integrated suppliers and the commitment of its employees (Mercadona, 2010).

CONCLUSION

This chapter shows that the total quality management approach has oriented Mercadona's management model and helped the firm to achieve spectacular economic results and a profitable and outstanding growth (from 1995 to 2007) as well as face successfully a challenging situation of economic crisis (from 2008 to 2011). The key aspect of the model is the high consideration awarded to its five components, as well as the orientation of the whole company toward satisfying their needs and expectations.

The chapter shows that Mercadona's top management decision to orient the company's entire management towards satisfying customer needs was correct. But the chapter also shows that the company cannot achieve an optimal management of customer needs without also satisfying the needs of the firm's other stakeholders. Thus, Mercadona's human resource management implements initiatives that strengthen employees' commitment to and involvement in the firm's project. The firm has installed a policy of cooperation, trust and mutual collaboration in its supplier management, which ensures that the products on the supermarket shelves match customers' requirements and specifications more closely and could be adapted in case the economic situation required that. Nor does the firm ignore the social and economic context in which it operates. This can be seen both quantitatively in terms of the creation of wealth and value, and qualitatively in terms of its ethical and environmental commitment with Spanish society and citizens. Finally, with regard to the capital, the economic results of the model are spectacular and have catapulted the company to a position of leadership among Spanish supermarket chains and a competitive advantage that its rivals will find difficult to match. In fact its competitors are currently reacting by imitating its management model and copying some of its initiatives and policies.

So, Mercadona offers the lowest prices in Spain, and its operational performance exceeds that of comparable Spanish and foreign chains. In 2008, Mercadona's sales per square foot was 60% higher than that of France's giant Carrefour, and more than twice that of an average U.S. Supermarket. Sales per employee were 18% higher than that of other Spanish supermarkets that disclosed financial information that year and more than 50% higher than U.S. supermarkets (Hanna, 2008).

The difference is Mercadona's Total Quality management model (Table 1), as Mercadona's president noted is "the reason for our success" (Ton and Harrow, 2010:2).

Table 1: Mercadona's Total Quality Management Model

The boss	– *Promoting dialogue and direct communications with our "Bosses"* – *Maximum quality at the lowest price: Recommended Products.* – *A return to basics so as to reduce prices with a quality, efficient selection.* – *Shopping Cart Menu: The highest quality and lowest priced Total Shopping on the market.* – *Closeness and proximity.* – *Innovation across the board oriented toward their needs (product, technology, concept and processes).* – *Always Low Prices (SPB): Price stability, without sales or promotions.* – *Prescription: to inform "The Boss" and recommend those products with the best price to quality ratio on the market.*
The employee	– *Stability (permanent contract), professional development and promotion from within.* – *Fixed responsibilities. Employees carry out their functions in the same position and changes are avoided; this facilitates employee specialization so that they can do what they know best: satisfy "The Boss."* – *Work and Family Life Compatibility by, among other measures, not opening on Sundays.* – *Human Resources management model based on individual and collective leadership.* – *Permanent dialogue.* – *Profit sharing.* – *Necessary and continuous training for the conduct of their job functions.*
The Supplier	– *Stability/Contracts for life.* – *Long-term agreements, communications and transparency in the relationship.* – *Bolstering productive activity to promote development and wealth.* – *R&D plus 'double I' (Research and Development plus Innovation, supported by Investment).* – *Promoting innovation and process optimization so as to offer the product with the best price quality ratio on the market.*

The Society	– *Commitment to the social and economic development of those areas in which we have an established presence.*
	– *Social productivity:*
	  ○ *Produce more with fewer natural resources.*
	  ○ *Sustainable transport.*
	– *Striving to "be invisible" in the setting where we carry out our activity.*
	– *Permanent dialogue, active participation and closeness.*
	– *Training and reporting on the company's Model and on activity and decision planning.*

The Capital	– *Constant and sustainable growth.* – *Reinvesting profits.* – *Innovation as a factor in competitiveness.* – *Focusing on the long term.* – *Increasing productivity through reengineering and process standardization.* – *Building our relationships on commitments*

In any case, the above describes an outstanding example of the successful application of the TQM model in the highly competitive, mature commercial distribution sector. Reading this chapter should encourage managers to consider the implementation of this model in other sectors of activity, although clearly, and as the literature observes, firms will need to make certain adjustments to the actions and policies depending on their particular industry (Wicks, 2001) and geographical area (Lagrosen, 2002). Proof of the feasibility of introducing this model in other industries and sectors comes from the fact that the model has spread sucessfully to some of Mercadona's intersuppliers or "integrated suppliers". Indeed, some of these have achieved even better results and growth rates than the supermarket chain itself (Blanco and Gutierrez, 2010).

Finally, Mercadona's Total Quality management model, thanks both to its feedback mechanisms and its great capacity to adapt to environmental and dramatic economic changes, is guaranteeing the future of the firm, even in a challenging economic situation like the one that Mercadona is currently facing in a country with an unemployment above 20% and a significant difficult to access credit. In spite of the recession, the company has managed to prove that it can "move forward and grow in difficult times" increasing the turnover, creating jobs and boosting company's productivity (Mercadona, 2010). The strength of Total Quality Management Model and the tight links that create between firm's stakeholders has allowed the firm to effectively and efficiently respond to the lost of clients caused by the economic crisis in 2008 transforming the crisis from a threat to firm survival to an opportunity to increase its market share and consolidate its competitive advantage over competitors.

ACKNOWLEDGEMENT

This chapter has been supported by Project ECO2009-10358 of Spanish Ministry of Science and Innovation (Spain) and Catedra Iberdrola for Research in Business Management and Organization.

REFERENCES

1. Alonso, M.; Furio, E. (2010). La economía española del crecimiento a la crisis pasando por la burbuja inmobiliaria, Cahiers de civilisation espagnole contemporaine, Vol 6, Available from http://ccec.revues.org/index3212.html
2. Blanco, M.; Gutierrez, S. (2010). Application of the Total Quality Management Approach in a Spanish Retailer: The Case of Mercadona. Total Quality Management and Business Excellence, Vol.21, No.12, (December 2010), pp.1365 – 1381
3. Caparrós, A. & Biot , R. (2006). 15 x 15, quince días con quince empresarios líderes. Fundación para la Comunidad Valenciana - Escuela de Dirección de Empresas del Mediterráneo (EDEM), Valencia, España
4. Deloitte (2007). Global Powers of Retailing 2006, New York, USA
5. ÉTNOR (2003). Informe de Auditoría Ética. Fundación para la ética de los negocios y las administraciones, Madrid, España
6. Hanna, J. (2010). How Mercadona Fixes Retail's "Last 10 Yards" Problem, Research&Ideas, Harvard Business School Working Knowledge, Cambridge, MA.
7. INE (2011). Instituto Nacional de Estadística (National Statistics Institute). Data available from http://www.ine.es/
8. Lagrosen, S. (2001). Strengthening the weakest link of TQM – from customer focus to customer understanding. The TQM Magazine, Vol.13, No. 5, pp. 348-354.
9. Mercadona. (1999-2010). Mercadona's Annual Reports. Tavernes Blanques, Valencia, España
10. Navarro, R. (2005). Los nuevos burgueses valencianos., La esfera de los libros, Valencia, España
11. Reputation Institute (2007). Global Rep. Track Pulse 2007. Reputation Institute, New York, USA
12. Ton, Z.; Harrow, S. (2010). Mercadona. Harvard Business School Cases. 9-610-089. Cambridge, MA, USA
13. Wicks, A.C. (2001). The Value Dynamics of Total Quality Management: Ethics and the Foundations of TQM. Business Ethics Quarterly, Vol.11, No.3, pp. 501-536.

CHAPTER 2 QUALITY MANAGEMENT FOR OCCUPATIONAL SAFETY AND HEALTH

Erika Alves dos Santos

INTRODUCTION

What quality management and scientific information can do for an organization will hardly depend on how it is applied in the workplace. Excellence seeking is an inherent practice to most organizations regardless its branch of activity. Loss prevention and market gains are usually presented as a justification for that. In consequence, quality management is closely linked to capital gain, and that is why enterprises apply high investments in this field. What is not explicit in this scenery is that all of this is also linked to scientific information and its correct dissemination. On the other hand, it is not a secret that market share, competitive advantage and profit are directly proportional to how informed one organization's leaders are about their business. In this context, it is pertinent to say that information is money, especially considering its high costs. It is also not a secret that information generates information. It means that the more widespread, more refined information gets, according to the spiral of knowledge that will be discussed ahead. So, the major input that can culminate in findings that may contribute for Science advancement is scientific information. However, two of several potential impediments to accessing and exploiting this vast field are resource scarceness and high costs of information access, and the scenery is the same in occupational safety and health (OSH) field. The barriers faced by OSH professionals during the information retrieval process, especially those derived from scientific experiments, generate the need for reflection on ways of promoting the intellectual capital turnover among professionals and this encourages the development of research instruments that enable the access to scientific information by the OSH community.

On this way, the Internet contributes significantly, whereas the virtual space favors fluidity, agility and possible reduction of communication noise between researchers, due to the possibility of real time communication, and that promotes the knowledge growing and also the improvement of security practices in the workplace. The significant increase in the volume of publications disseminated in the Internet without any criteria of quality and reliability of data is the result of the internet popularization, which contributed to the appearance of barriers in the selection of relevance information, and in certification of the legitimacy of presented data, particularly in OSH, in which information is scarce in relation to other areas of human knowledge.

An alternative to minimize the impacts caused by noise in information flowing is the creation of specialized virtual environments, called open archives (OA), which enable direction of the information to a target audience, promote break of bureaucratic practices in processes of documents publishing, provide interoperability between systems and communication in the scientific community besides promoting multidimensional ways of accessing studies made available by such routes.

Therein, the utilization of digital repositories of information under the philosophy of information spreading applied to the open archives initiative may be considered as an alternative to promote the intellectual capital turning as well as scientific communication among researchers. The initiative in question is presented as a strategy to support management of

Citation: Erika Alves dos Santos (2012). Quality Management for Occupational Safety and Health, Total Quality Management and Six Sigma, Prof. Tauseef Aized (Ed.), InTech, DOI: 10.5772/46103.

health and safety at work, together with quality management tools PDCA and 5S.

KNOWLEDGE MANAGEMENT AND SCIENTIFIC INFORMATION IN OCCUPATIONAL SAFETY AND HEALTH

Among the barriers to information access it is important to highlight the linguistic obstacles that may difficult or even make inaccessible the consult to relevant studies, generally published in expressive international journals. These factors justify the promotion of technical and scientific exchange in order to form a professional experiences exchange network, that may assist OSH professionals in achieving satisfactory results on reversing the current degrading situation of working conditions, that are still found in several branches of professional acting.

Information is crucial to the effectiveness of OSH management system, however, in many situations, the information necessary for effective interventions are not available, restricted, for example, by temporal contingency. [...] The evaluation of the OSH management system is a systematic examination of its functionality and effectiveness in order to produce consistent information that may assist in decision making processes for the conception of new strategies to promote the improvement of OSH performance [1].

Engineering, Medicine, Law. All of these and the other fields of human knowledge exist because of information. It is also true that professional acting in any area offer occupational hazards to workers. Some more intense, some less so, but the fact is that occupational safety and health must be the basis of any professional activity, be at the office, or in heavy industry, so that the worker physical and mental integrity is always preserved.

Basically, two kind of information concern to OSH: prevention to accidents and occupational diseases and rehabilitation of occupationally sick or injured workers. The first one has proactive characteristics, while the second one seems to be reactive. An active posture allows the company to preview and prevent negative events, like an occupational accident, for example, and by means of this, save money or decrease spending, considering the expenses that the organization may no longer employ in professional rehabilitation. This means that the costs used in the prevention of occupational accidents and diseases should be treated as investments rather than as expenses.

Once the organization have identified the risks and opportunities in a pro-active way, the manager enables the tools to prevent or mitigate risks, maximize opportunities and reduce or eradicate harmful events to the employee and to the organization as a whole in consequence.

The burden of adopting a reactive posture is to expose the company to a totally vulnerable situation, in which it may not have enough time to any reaction in an emergency situation, staying at the mercy of events.

Scientific and technical activities are the fountain from where flow technical and scientific knowledge that will be transformed, after registered, into technical and scientific information. But, on reverse, these activities only exist, and become real against this information. Information is the Science sap. Without information, Science can not develop and live. Without information research would be useless and there would not be the knowledge [2].

Manage means to carry on business affairs, finance and human resources administration, what also implies to watch out for occupational health and safety. The purpose is common to all: to lead a particular activity or a group of them, to the achievement of one or more targets, which may vary according to the organization goals. Therefore, a range of compliances should be reached, and in case it does not occur, losses certainly will come, in most situations, with dimensions and impacts may vary from case to case. These factors highlight the importance of management and know-how to take advantage of all available resources, always keeping in mind the organization goals to perform tasks with the best coefficient of cost-effectiveness relationship. Management has the function to “build organization that work” [3], and to work, all sectors must maintain a synergy, so, one single action has the strength to move a whole, like a set of gears. By the way, this is the recipe of success which is unknown by so many companies. It is important that workers feel important to the organization and that their work has a real value to the company. As a returning, the worker would receive determination, and motivation, not only merely driven by obligation or interest (or duty) of economic nature. He will feel pleasure to work.

In the industry, machines and equipments receive a special treatment, with periodic reviews and replacement of components. The same way, the employee also requires some care from the organization, like the workplace adjustment and maintenance, for example. After all, the worker is the one who holds the most valuable asset of the organizations: the intellectual capital. The employee is the “keeper and guardian” of the organizational wealth, which is the knowledge. So, the same way a machine demands periodic reviews, small (or not so small) repairs, and even “vacations”, the worker demands satisfactory work conditions as well, so it will be made the most of his potential efficiency. Psychological sphere certainly is very important in an occupational safety and health management plan. Considering that most part of the day of an employee is spent in his professional activities, the manager should also value the maintenance of a healthy work environment, both in physical and mental aspects. Many practices may be adopted in this sense: a good interpersonal relationship, relaxation techniques, profits sharing, regular meetings with the teamwork to identify their needs, and also the encouragement of reading and sports practicing are some valid measures for achieving a healthy work environment.

The adoption of such measures, linked do scientific communication may assist OSH professionals in developing management tools that support the employee in a large-scale way, providing better working conditions and health, both physically and mentally. In this case, information has the role to complement the knowledge of professionals who are responsible for zealous for workers’ health and safety, besides giving wide publicity to the good practices adopted in this regard. Trainings, technical visits, lectures, simulations and other forms of professional improvement are also widely successfully applied. Added to appropriate information flowing, and also the valorization and respect for the worker, which may be made visible even in supplying adequate individual and collective protection equipments, the workplace may become a place that provides pleasant and well-being that may also contribute to occupational accidents and diseases prevention.

Occupational accidents, as well as any other accidents are unwanted events, unforeseen and which are generally accompanied by physical and / or material damages. Avoiding accidents and occupational diseases is the major concern of OSH professionals, and also a duty for any citizen. Appearing of occupational diseases, due to noise, high temperatures, radiation, exposure to chemical substances, and so on, is one of the greatest concern to hygienists [4]. An effective prevention program results in declining of occupational accidents and diseases rates and also declining of repair and consequence(s) of a possible accident [5].

This way, information sharing is crucial. A seemingly routine situation for one organization may be considered a risk task for one company which may already have had the unpleasant experience of an occupational accident as a result of that activity. Information like this should be as most widespread as possible (even though the company's name is preserved) to prevent other similar accidents from happening in other plants, or other organizations. However, the fear of intellectual overcoming, the organizational culture or even the fear of exposing thoughts to academic criticism sometimes keep the OSH professionals from starting an occupational hazards prevention discussion with other professionals.

Generating wealth and improvements from intangible assets is precisely the task of knowledge management, which is defined as a "new way of working, a new organizational culture, in which the environment and values allow to generate the necessary motivation for learning, sharing or transfer and application of knowledge [6]." In proportion to the knowledge becomes an essential and strategic asset, organizational success depends more and more on increasing the company's ability to produce, gather, store and disseminating knowledge [7]. Thus, it falls to the company to promote knowledge sharing among the work team, and consequently the intellectual capital turning within the limits of their own plant. This point by itself is already a plausible justification for building an institutional repository of scientific information. Managing knowledge in organizations is to provide conditions for this knowledge to be constantly produced, codified and shared across the enterprise. Facilitate the interactive knowledge flowing in the organization, adding value to information and distributing them correspond to the role of knowledge management, transforming knowledge into competitive advantage [8].

However, for knowledge to be effectively converted into competitive advantage, it must be subject to application and transmission in the company. This conversion takes place through the transformation of tacit knowledge into explicit knowledge and tacit knowledge again and so successively until the results are tangible enough to satisfy, or preferably exceed the organization needs and expectations.

Tacit knowledge is acquired individually by each person, through courses, readings, lectures, or even the professional experience. The access to this knowledge depends on some factors, including the potential ability of explanation of the person who holds it. Another factor is the "ways of doing things": each person develops their own way of working, aiming to make it easier and more comfortable. However, such procedures and techniques generally are not found in books, journals, films, or any other type of informational support, because this kind of knowledge only can be acquired through professional practice and experience.

On the other hand, explicit knowledge is available everywhere, to whom it may concern. So, explicit knowledge is more perceptible than tacit knowledge in an organizational environment. That is the case of books, journals, newspapers, magazines and so on. Explicit knowledge is what one can transmit in a formal and systematic language. It is the knowledge that can be registered in books, guides, or be transmitted by electronic mail or hardcopy [9]. In fact, information in general corresponds to explicit knowledge. Implicit knowledge is a more recent knowledge that serves to describe a knowledge that, though it has not been documented, it is likely to be. It is the knowledge one keeps, and is able of transmitting be in a more or less assisted way. Indeed this is the knowledge that can be made explicit, but has not been yet. For example: the way between one's home and his workplace is registered anywhere, but this person can draw a map or explain someone how to get there. This knowledge is implicit: it is not registered, but it can be, if there is one's will to do so. On counterpart, tacit knowledge the one that everyone keep, and have no conscience of that. It is personal, acquired through practice, experience, mistakes and successes, it is difficult to be formulated and transmitted in a formal way. A cake recipe (explicit knowledge), for example, can generate totally different results, depending on the experience and sensibility of the person who makes it. That happens because of the act of making a cake also involves a tacit knowledge, which is personal.

The conversion of tacit knowledge into explicit and vice versa, as in a cycle, promotes besides the human capital circulation and socialization, also the opportunity of renewal, acquisition of new knowledge, and promotes the improvement of the whole set of information already gathered. This information exchange cycle provides an intellectual capital spin, which encourage the socialization of generated knowledge, as well as the investigation and the reflection towards new knowledge creation [10]. The authors propose a model of knowledge conversion, what became known as knowledge spiral.

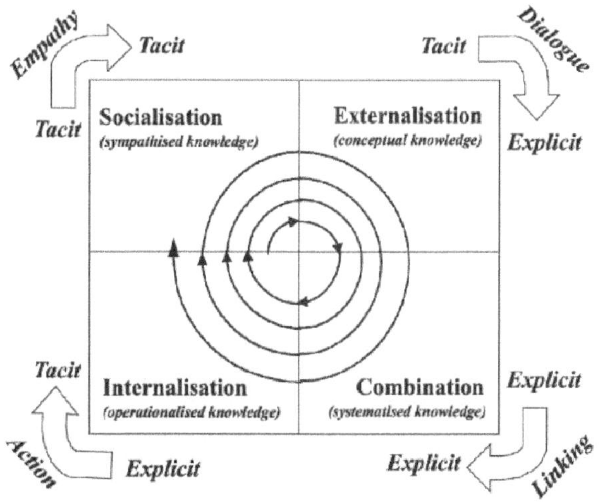

Figure 1: The knowledge spiral [10]

According to the model proposed by the authors, the process of acquiring knowledge passes through four stages:

Socialization (tacit knowledge to tacit knowledge):

Observation and also the practice are ways of transmitting knowledge through socialization. In this process, there is much experience exchange, what is the big shot to knowledge acquisition. Trainings, brainstorming, and even one's own professional experience can be mentioned as examples of knowledge socialization.

Externalization (tacit knowledge to explicit knowledge):

Externalization is the highest point of knowledge transmission. It is when occurs the encoding of tacit knowledge into explicit knowledge, so that other professionals can use such information, and convert them back into tacit knowledge. One of the tacit knowledge characteristics is precisely the verbalization high difficult degree. Scientific papers publicizing is a way to facilitate the transmission of this kind of knowledge.

Combination (explicit knowledge to explicit knowledge):

New ideas, new question and projects are designed in this stage. Explicit knowledge is confronted with another explicit knowledge. The result of that is the development of new information. Combination is very present in meetings, discussions, be in person, or by Internet, phone call, or even during a report, or even any other document reading.

Internalization (explicit knowledge to tacit knowledge):

The conversion of explicit knowledge again into tacit knowledge occurs during internalization process. This is when acquired information is absorbed and right after, converted into knowledge.

Each time the cycle is completed, it should be restarted. Each restart is a higher degree of information complexity, specificity and consistency. Scope is also amplified as well, and may start with a single person and after expand across boundary of people, departments, sectors, units and companies. And information gets more and more improved and specific, until its holder becomes an expert in such question. To enable creation of organizational knowledge, tacit knowledge accumulated needs to be socialized with other members of the organization, and that gets another spiral of knowledge started again, as in a cycle with no end [8].

knowledge creation is divided in five main phases:

- The sharing of tacit knowledge;
- The creation of concepts;
- The justification of the concepts;
- The construction of an archetype and;
- The spread of interactive knowledge [10].

At the phase of tacit knowledge sharing, occurs the socialization, when information is shared through out the company. The creation of concepts corresponds to the phase in which there is conversion of tacit knowledge into explicit knowledge, as a new concept (externalization). In the third phase, justification of the concepts, the company evaluates and decides whether the new concept proceeds or not, and if there is continuity, archetypes are constructed and may generate new prototypes of products services and so on. The last phase, which corresponds to the interactive dissemination of knowledge, is responsible for systematic sharing of applicable information, in extra organizational sphere. This phase is extremely important for OSH management once this field of study focus is to promote welfare and protect worker's physical and mental integrity, while performing their work tasks. The capital gain and the competitive advantage originated from this process, although are both desired and very well seen, are consequences of the knowledge spiral cycle completion. The interaction of one company not only with the other ones, but also with the academic community, may bring great benefits in the sense of human capital acquiring, whereas active professionals in the labor market not always have the opportunity to research and publish new knowledge. So, the scientific community which traditionally carries out this task has much to contribute to the dissemination of research results, and by consequence, to the OSH management inside the companies, reaching, this way, until the shop floor, which can be considered the apple of OSH's eyes.

Any shop floor workers' tacit and explicit knowledge that the company makes use is very healthy to the organization as a whole. Even though experts develop great theories, the more accurate knowledge is held by the employee, which is the one who knows each single part of the processes in depth. As time passes by, working activity becomes an automatic process for a person, due to one's high intimacy level with the activity in question, and this relationship creates bonds that only the familiarity and the professional practice can establish. The "best and more efficient way of doing things" only can be indicated by someone who realizes it frequently.

Facing this, the interaction between the company and the employee is indispensable for the organizational learning to put foward tangible and satisfactory results, though it is also required the employee engagement, in order to be open to new experiences, new information and so on.

Relations with other organizations in the ambit of OSH can increase the spin of the spiral of knowledge, what can bring benefits for all involved in this process, because in contradiction to mathematical laws, knowledge gets multiplied when shared, and may become applicable to other areas like management risk, for example. Once there is a failure that may lead to an occupational accident, it is not enough only to fix it, but it is also necessary to warn the whole working team about the occurrence, for it not to be recurrence, avoiding any occupational accident, regardless its proportions. From the moment that there is the transmission of this kind of information, it becomes part of the knowledge of each single person of the working team, and that makes the likelihood of repeating the same incidence decrease. Through knowledge, companies become more effective and efficient in the use of their scarce resources. On the other hand, without knowledge they become less efficient and effective using resources, and fail, at last [7].

One of the factors that may contribute to accident preventions in an industrial plant is adopting a good quality management system. In contrast, quality is not put in practice without access to information. The efficiency is nothing more than the top of a set of information, arising very often from unwanted incidents, which are responsible for the generation of lessons learned, applied to a specific process, providing satisfactory results in order to improve products and processes. Considering these points it is interesting to stimulate investments in quality management and knowledge management, which is responsible for bringing up the tacit knowledge and experience of the workers, who usually hide valuable data for management in general. This fusion, in fact can bring great benefits to the organization in its various aspects.

THE BENEFITS OF THE FUSION BETWEEN QUALITY MANAGEMENT TOOLS AND KNOWLEDGE MANAGEMENT

A quality management tool is a methodology to improve processes using as less financial resources as possible, optimizing the working processes, increasing production, and also profit, by rational use of space, time and material and human resources.

Quality management tools are widely applied in organizational processes, and generally provide positive results. After all, quality is a crucial factor for optimization of processes, resources using, and the entire operation of an organization. The knowledge management benefits may be enhanced through the use of the resources suggested by instruments of quality management.

Organizational Knowledge Management and PDCA Cycle

Organizational learning is a prerequisite for an organization existence. Or it is an organization that learns, or it will be condemned to failure soon. Considering the specificity of OSH field, the professional responsibility of monitoring the evolution in the industry becomes even greater and must be observed by each one involved in this knowledge area. However, for a company to learn it is necessary its employees learn first. In this sense, it is interesting to create policies to incentive the human capital acquisition aiming the organizational growth and improvement of processes in a larger sphere. The policy to stimulate education and multiply knowledge is important for the organization and in most cases, spending on research and development are usually recovered at short term, through improvements achieved by this process. This justifies high investments that developed countries apply in research development. So, a permanent cycle of knowledge acquirement provides to the organization the potential to achieve better results, exceeding expectations and achieving goals. The tasks improvement and staff expertise are merely consequences in this scenery.

One of the tools applied in this sense is the PDCA cycle, defined as method of managing for processes or systems. That's the way of achieving the goals assigned to the products or enterprise systems [11]. The word goal is the result of a junction between meta + *hodos*, that means a path to the goal. Thus, it is possible to affirm that the PDCA cycle is a way to achieve a goal [11, 12].

As the organization itself, all knowledge in any field of knowledge is like a living organism, constantly in change. Advances in Science and technology has created an scenery in which there is a need to create new ways of doing work, new strategies, new work tools and/or adapt existing ones to the new reality imposed by XXI Century. Each one of these items should function orderly among themselves, like a gear. So, all the processes of the larger organism, the organization as a whole, are able to flow correctly. Therefore, it is necessary to domain of some essential data for the proper functioning of this system. These data are often not found in books, or in the scientific literature, but in each employee's own experience, the tacit knowledge. In this sense, knowledge management assumes the role of contributing for each employee's intellectual qualifications to be always aligned to the mission and vision of the company which must include the promotion of safe work, and therefore, the occupational accident prevention.

Dissociating theory from practice is impossible, whatever is the activity about to be developed. Theory, due to hard studies, is the main responsible for the facilities and conveniences that can be observed specially on factory floor, as the machine protection and tasks automation, for example. Therefore, as business management, management in OSH knowledge should also be part of a continuous improvement process, like PDCA.

Conceived by Walter A. Shewhart in the 1930s at Bell Laboratories in the United States [12] and applied two decades later by the quality expert W. Edwards Deming (that's why PDCA cycle is also known as Deming Cycle) in statistics and sampling methods using, the PDCA method is recognized as a process of improvement and controlling that should be familiar to the employees of an organization to be effective [13, 14] CENTRO DE TECNOLOGIA DE EDIFICAÇÕES, 1994). Basically the PDCA cycle can be defined as

A method that aims to control and achieve effective and reliable results in the activities of an organization. It is an efficient way to provide processes improvement. It standardizes quality control information, avoids logical errors in its analysis and makes information easier to understand. It also may be used to facilitate the transition to a management style directed to continuous improvement [15].

The procedure proposed by PDCA implies constant evaluation of the entire system, enabling the early detection of possible failures or improvement points. This ideology makes necessary to conduct detailed audits at all stages of work. Each time the proposed cycle (plan, do, check and act) is completed, occurs the continuous improvement and then, improvement of knowledge of those involved with the activity in question, by consequence. In fact, the PDCA cycle is a total quality management method, which may (and should) also include the prevention of occupational accidents and diseases.

Whereas the world is constantly evolving, even activities performed satisfactorily are subject to improvements that must be pursued as incessant searching process for an unreachable perfection. That is called continuous improvement. Whenever it does not occur, the consequences are certain: occupational accidents are potentialized along with their indices of severity, losses and damages.

Occupational accidents do not happen by chance. They are just a materialization of a sequence of failures, whether human or not (although machine or mechanical failures also can occur due to human errors) which in most cases could have been avoided.

It is common for us to accept as true when the newspaper disclose, even before the experts report conclusion, that the origin of a fire was a short circuit in electrical installations. It is such an often cause, which examples are innumerable, that not even is necessary to wait a long time for the confirmation that was foreseen by journalists from interviewing experts and testimonials of the users of the hit building. [...] What is not always demonstrated for the population is that the referred short circuit was not a surprise occasioned by an uncontrollable phenomenon, but the last breath of an installation that was agonizing. Fires, originated by electrical causes start, general rule, in overloaded circuits, without proper protection and maintenance, and handled by curious laymen covered up by "economic professionals" that seek by "the lowest price" the technical solutions for problems that should have been the cause for specialized diagnosis [16].

Failures, that not always culminate in accidents, but in near-misses, may be product of several factors, among which the lack (or insufficiency) of safety audits and knowledge domain by operators responsible for the activity that has any kind of inconsistency. The set of failures, combined with temporal factors may culminate in industrial accidents. Therefore, improvement must always be pursued by the organization, regardless its maturity level or any other factor.

The cycle proposed by PDCA requires constant evaluation of the whole system, in order to detect any possible failure, in anticipation of the occurrence of inconvenient and undesirable situations. Under this ideology, it is made necessary to conduct accurate audits at each single stage of the work. So, it will always be found new (and better) ways of doing the same things in a more efficient and safety way. Following the cycle Plan, Do, Check and Act (PDCA) is a way of promoting continuous improvement and thus, improves also the knowledge of everyone involved with the activity in question. Moreover, PDCA cycle is a method of total quality management, what also includes occupational safety and health management.

So, PDCA cycle is basically composed by four phases [12]:

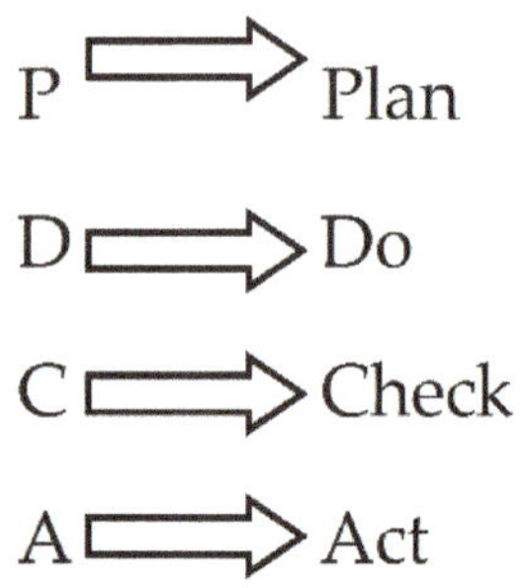

PDCA – P: Plan

The planning phase comprises the step in which all activities are outlined having the company's mission and vision as a point guide, besides other documents that may concern, like standards for example. Planning should point all the parameters of the activity, how it should be executed, financial, material and human needed resources, deadlines and all the information about the characteristics of the planned action, as in a project itself.

It is also in planning phase that are often identified needs hidden by the routine or even by convenience. Goals and methods of reaching them are all defined in this phase. Basically planning phase consists on the development and delineation of the project scope itself. That is why this is the proper moment to identify organizational weaknesses and strengths and develop strategies to convert weaknesses into strengths and strengths into points of excellence.

PDCA – D: Do

To do is to put into practice all that was planned in planning phase (P). It is like preparing a cake (do phase) following the instructions of a recipe (planning phase). This is the moment for training and educating employees, besides implementing all practices according to the project scope. Simultaneously, it can be a pre-audit, when positive and negative points of the plan should be identified and registered as a way of ensuring that all objectives previously established will be achieved in its fullness. This information also will be useful during the phase of checking the implemented actions.

PDCA – C: Check

Checking is the phase which most involves indicators and performance metrics, and comprises the comparison between planned and achieved results. Audits, processes analysis, evaluations, and satisfaction surveys are very common at this stage of the PDCA cycle. No inconsistency founded means the satisfactory following of the cycle. Otherwise, it is time to start the next phase: Act.

PDCA – A: Act

If the results are as expected, nothing should be done until the moment that any inconsistency is detected, when it is necessary to perform corrective measures to bring the project back to the scope initially established. However, besides implementing corrective actions, acting phase also may be in order to standardize processes that worked well, as a manner of registering information that can be used as stepping stone in similar situations. This phase corresponds to the PDCA cycle completion.

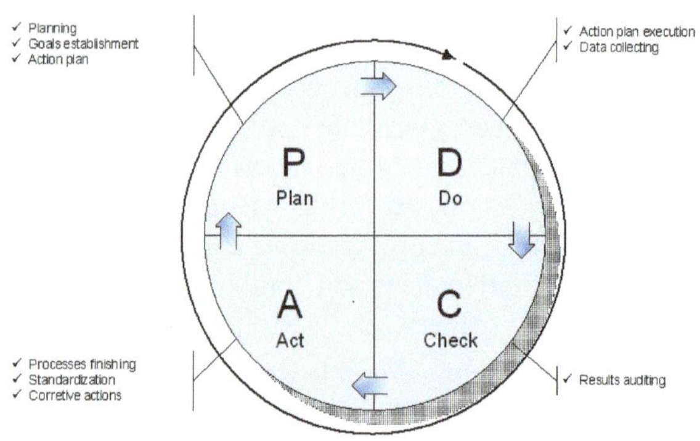

Figure 2: The PDCA cycle [12]

Once all those phases are concluded, PDCA has completed its cycle, which must rotate clockwise, following the sequence of the proposed activities. The most the cycle is completed, the greater the knowledge accumulated by the whole teamwork, in the same way that the rates of quality also will tend to be increasingly towards to excellence.

PDCA cycle is designed to be a dynamic model. The completion of a cycle will flow back in the beginning of the next cycle, and so on. Followed by the spirit of continuous quality improvement, the whole process can always be reviewed and a new process of change can be started [12].

The optimization of processes, reached through the PDCA cycle, promotes a reduction in costs and increasing productivity, what means creating new products, with less use of resources, which yields competitive, once production becomes higher than the competitors'. Likewise, the rate of complexity of information is growing each time the PDCA is fully completed. Each time the process is completed, the involved processes presents indices of improvements, which are represented by the numbers 1, 2, 3 and 4, according to figure 3. The closer to the top of the ramp are the improved processes, the better will be the indexes of maturity of the organization. Andrade (2003) points out that the lessons learned in a PDCA cycle application can be used in a second, third, fourth application (...) that can be more complex and daring, and so on.

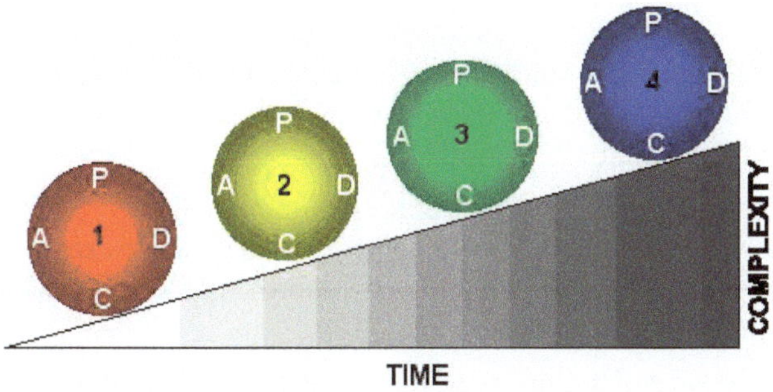

Figure 3: The improvement ramp [17]

The roll of information gathered can be a valuable instrument for the OSH management community, for the moment it is made available for public consultation as a data source of best practices, it may help managers to think globally and act locally. This way, the healthy and safe workplace will not just consolidate into one organization, but in all Brazilian industrial fabric.

There are several instruments for improving the quality of products and processes within an organization. Another instrument that can also be used together with PDCA to optimize the quality of work live is 5S.

Quality Management According to the 5s Process

Designed in Japan in 1950 by Kaoru Ishikawa [18], 5S is a method of quality management which aimed to delineate efficient and effective techniques to reach costs reduction, optimization of material, technological and human resources, and also combat waste [19]. It is an educational process, which is often applied as a basis for other management instruments.

The 5S program is a philosophy of work that aims to promote the discipline in the company through awareness and responsibility all to become the workplace a pleasing, safe and productive place.

The Program was named after five Japanese words that synthesize the five steps of the program. They are: Seiri, Seiton, Seisso, Seiketsu, Shitsuke [20].

The goals are to transform the environment of organization and the attitude of people, improving the quality of life of employees, and also reduce costs, waste and raise institutional productivity [18].

The 5S method may imply the improvement of other functions, not directly related in this process, such as production (acquisition of new equipments and adoption of new processes and systems), quality (standards application), human resources (adoption of new organizational policies), as well as hygiene, safety and environment (changes in management process, audits). For this reason, as well as any other innovation within a company, the implementation of 5S requires a detailed analysis on the budget funds to certify that financial aspects will not be an obstacle for the complete implementation of this instrument.

Another point to focus on is the possibility to be applicated simultaneously to other quality management tools, such as the Kaizen method of continuous improvement, safety, environment and quality management tools (NBR ISO 9001, NBR ISO 14001 and OHSAS 18001), Six Sigma, as well as PDCA Cycle itself. It demonstrates that 5S method is an extremely flexible tool that can be combined to other management instruments, what potentizes the results that can be reached by this method.

So, 5S acts in three organizational aspects, which are divided into 5 phases: physical aspects (Seiri, Seiton, Seiso), standardization aspects (Seiketsu) and behavioral aspects (Shitsuke). Each one of the five phases of the method is represented by a sense as follows [21]:

Sense of Use and Disposal (SEIRI)

The sense of use and disposal awakens the workers consciousness to keep in the workplace only what is really necessary for the development of their functions. This provides to the worker a clearer, more accessible and easier to clean workplace, and increase visibility to the material actually used. Furthermore, this practice promotes the evacuation of areas previously occupied by unnecessary materials. Thus there may be an increase in productivity, reduction on bureaucracy processes, and prevention of unnecessary purchases.

The methods applied for materials disposal can be diverse: once separated all the unnecessary material, this can be transferred to other sectors, or returned to the warehouse, sold or donated for recycling entities, or even be disposed as trash, that also should be classified as common or toxic.

Sense of Ordering and Arrangement (SEITON)

For each material, its proper place. The ordering sense recommends that once separated all the useless material, the remaining should be sorted in the workplace, preferably in the closest place to where its use is more frequent, location to which it should be returned as soon as it is not being used anymore. This provides benefits, for example the rationalization of the space designated to material storage, the encouragement of creativity, quickness, and facility in finding documents and objects. This reduces physical efforts and emotional distress in searching for not founded objects, besides preventing occupational accidents that possibly may be caused by a disordered workplace.

Cleaning Sense (SEISSO)

Machine, equipment and any work tool including the workplace itself, must be kept clean and organized. The duty of maintaining hygiene in the workplace is not the sole responsibility of the cleaning crew, but also an obligation of each one of the employees. Cleaning makes the environment becomes more pleasant, and transmits the image of excellence in organization's products. And again, a cleaning workplace is less susceptible to the occurrences of occupational accidents, for example, a fall caused by a slipping way.

Sense of Health and Hygiene (SEIKETSU)

Personal hygiene is also essential as well as mental health and life quality in general. The good maintenance of employee's health is like an organizational intangible asset, as a prerequisite for the execution of any task in the company. However, this sense requires an holistic view that permits the manager to extend the meaning of health and hygiene also for the issue of OSS. The ergonomic adequacy of the workplace, the adoption of relaxation techniques, and even the aesthetic and disposal of the workplace are factors that must be considered in this way. As results, it can be achieved higher levels of team motivation, facilities in human relationships, dissemination of the positive image of the sector and also its employees, favorable working conditions to health, and also the occupational accidents and diseases prevention.

Sense of Self-Discipline (SHITSUKE)

The last and most individual sense is the sense of self-discipline. This corresponds to the regulator sense, which creates in a company's workers the awareness for the accomplishment of the four previous senses. This provides a natural implementation of all recommendations, the discipline, the moral and ethics, the cultivation of good habits, the promotion of participative management and also the ensuring of the quality of life at work.

The 5S program implementation may provide more efficiency and safety at workplace. The disorganization and lack of asepsis may be considered factors that may culminate in occupational accidents and diseases. The waste generates financial losses. The sense of using and ordering allow a better use of space, and finally, self-discipline, as the name suggests, promotes the discipline among the employees toward a policy of awareness in the use of the company resources. And what is more interesting in this process is that its cost of implementation is considered relatively low.

In fact, 5S may be integrant part of PDCA cycle. Both focus on quality management: 5S, aims to improve the quality of the processes and workplaces, while PDCA focus on strategical and managerial issues, although there is no restrictions for PDCA to cover some areas of 5S.

Both PDCA and 5S are quality management tools which may provide great benefits to an organization. It is also pertinent to point that, the implementation and management of both tools can be much more complex than it seems in this discussion. However, it is also important to consider that discussing these tools in a deeper point of view is not the primary objective of this discussion. These quality management tools were chosen and mentioned because they were considered useful in the sense of promoting the generation of information that may be applied in other workplaces or even other enterprises, through the association with a system of scientific information sharing among all of them. The management of safety and health at work can also be considered a quality management process, once it cares about quality of life at work, quality of safety processes, quality in the workplace, and so on. That does justify the association between quality management and OSH.

THE FUSION BETWEEN CYCLE PDCA + 5S = ORGANIZATIONAL BENEFITS?

Increasing the quality and productivity while promoting quality of life, simultaneously with competitiveness: that is the great challenge of the manager / entrepreneur of the XXI Century. Whatever are the tools used to improve the quality of the work process within industries, there will be tangible benefits for OSH management.

An OSH quality management process may improve the systems applied in the worker safety and health:

As the organization adopts the audit protocol over time, it has the opportunity to experience the evolution of the performance of the OSH management system as well as the opportunities for improvement.

As it knows the opportunities of improvement, it becomes possible to develop an action plan focused on more expressive and efficient results, continuously improving the performance of the OSH management system [22].

Whatever are the instruments used to improve the quality of the work process within the industries, there will be tangible benefits to the OSH management. Equally, information systems also have their importance in this issue, since they are responsible for storage and make available case studies, which may be useful in identifying diverse points susceptible to improvements in organizational processes as a whole. Case studies, in particular, play a fundamental role in order to disseminate best practices applied by one organization, so other organizations also may be inspired in these cases to promote process improvement and quality of life at the workplace. Nevertheless, they have the potential to get the OSH professionals together, and promote the ongoing discussion about emerging issues in order to promote the prevention of occupational accidents and diseases.

The knowledge is available, the techniques, methods and tools exist and their use has proven results. At the same time, those who study the accident issue in a deeper way probably concluded that the best results only can be obtained from the holistic vision, both of the issue, and specially of the man. Innovating is a need! Dare to actually move toward a more efficient accident prevention which, at last, means to save lives, suffering, reduce costs, increase quality and productivity [23].

Information systems also have their importance in this regard, once several case studies are deposited and published there. These papers are valid to assist in identifying issues for the further improvements in organizational processes as a whole. Information management also is associated to knowledge to management quality [24].

In times when the quality, competitiveness and transparency are considered on determining an organization market share, there is too much to be explored about knowledge management inside the organizations, once explicit knowledge represents a very small portion of what the organization knowledge worth actually. It is also important to invest in capital for the intellectual training of employees in managing occupational safety and health at work. The worker is the most value asset of any organization because it is him who holds the most needed resource to maintain the business "health and force": the human knowledge.

Information, quality, organizational management, OSH, financial returns. Isolated, each one has its particularity, but applied together, these instruments converge to the establishment of organizational improvement programs, which benefit not only the client, but mainly the worker, who is responsible for the final product existence. The value of a worker for an organization is incalculable. Each time a life is lost, it is not only a worker who is not part of the staff of an organization anymore, but also a member of society, whom keeps a range of knowledge, which may still have not been disseminated. In this case, besides the worker, the organization loses a valuable intangible asset: the knowledge.

Effectiveness and efficiency of organizational improvement are linked to innovation to the method applied to available information sources and to the speed and flexibility which they apply, in addition to personal motivation, leadership practiced by the direction of the organization, and the relationship between the organization and stakeholders [25]. That justifies the importance of disseminating knowledge at most. The proposal is that the OSH and knowledge management are convergent in order to ensure that the quality management as a whole, not just the final product, may present strengths to provide better working conditions for workers, being subsidized by the provision of technical-scientific data from both tacit knowledge, and other professionals experience.

The availability and use of scientific information in an organization environment are fundamental to the process natural and safe flowing. And this safety may be built jointly by several professionals, through scientific dialogue, exchange of experiences and joint reflection. Accidents will always happen but if at least one live is saved by something that has been read somewhere, every effort will have been valid [26].

The principle proposed by Maguire seals the proposed link between scientific information and OSH management, and emphasizes the need to reflect on the creation of tools that enable scientific exchange among peers. The Open Archives Initiative (OAI) philosophy adds up this cause, in making available as much information as possible, specially the gray literature (thesis and dissertations, reports and other documents) which usually hold the results of observations, experiments and empirical reflections that may contribute to the OSH management.

THE INTERNET AS A SOURCE OF DATA IN OCCUPATIONAL SAFETY AND HEALTH

Among the many emerging communication forms, the one which excels at terms of enabling the information transferring is the Internet, which is defined as a set of academic, scientific, commercial, and military interconnected networks, which communicate with each other through the use of a common protocol Transmission Control Protocol / Internet Protocol (TCP/IP) [27]. The authors highlight the facilities offered by the Internet to the scientific community like its globalization power, the immediacy of production, release, update and access to published information, the hypermedia capability (hypertext and multimedia), that makes it easy to search and access information as well as the volume of data gathered at relatively low cost, in addition to the possibility of interconnecting users, to eliminate barriers in the geographical, temporal, political, social spheres among other barriers to information transferring.

From the moment information has its value recognized, in the sense of being able to aggregate power to its holders, it became essential to generate resources to facilitate the information flowing among scientific community. The Internet has emerged in this scenery as a tool to add value for produced work, and increase visibility not only for presented results, but also to their respective authors and institutions. The creation of research groups besides the facilities offered by the virtual space, such as discussion groups and even electronic mail, narrowed the relations and facilitated access to the author of recently published works and this generates and enriches the scientific discussion, favoring the maturation of the collective intellectual thought [28].

The advent of Internet assured conditions for significant changes in ways of communicating among people, both in regard to communication media, and also the speed of data transferring.

The virtual ambient offers to the researcher agility in processes of production, evaluation, publication and validation of the essays. In printed media, the communication flows slowly, since the entire process of developing a new publication, which involves reviewing, formatting, graphics constructions and other activities related to the completion of the research are made prior to its publicizing. On the other hand, in digital environment, the processes of review and validation of works, through scientific proof, may be done jointly with the target audience of the work, accelerating the process of information transferring. Thus, the high levels of formality in contact with authors, give way to interactivity since a simply electronic mail replaces the content of an official letter, which could take several days to reach the final destination. The Internet enables immediate and direct contact with members of the community to close relations between scientific researchers.

It is true that the Internet being a network of networks with services of electronic mail and thematic discussions in group facilitates the informal communication between researchers in different areas of Science & Technology. And when one think that informal channels are essential to work at levels of great value added to the information, because they are useful in decision making and allow the creation of strategies from unpublished information, one can have an idea of the value of the communication network [28].

It is worth an interesting comparison between the virtual environment, and the typical scenario of scientific events such as symposiums, conferences, and discussions, exchanges of experiences, and other considerations that both enrich and add value to the collective intellectual thought. The scientific dialogue promoted in digital media, is like an extension of the shared moments of reflection, always present in scientific events, round tables, sessions of questions, debates etc... In this sense, the authors refer to the facilitation of informal communication, once at a conference or other event of this nature, there is the establishment of a direct dialogue between authors and the target audience of your statements. The virtual space in a way, also promotes this feature, since once that there are two computers connected to the Internet, the communication between them can be directly established at any time. A dialogue is formed since there is a transmitter who sends a message to a receiver, who decodes and process the sent message, and generates a response for the transmitter, who assumes the position of receiver at this moment, while the receiver, passes to be the transmitter. It is also true that this not always happen be due to the unavailability of the receiver, be due to human or technological failures in the moment of message sending, but this, not necessarily consists a barrier to scientific dialogue.

Even so, the Internet can be considered a way of direct communication between two or more people which may offer great benefits to the scientific community, when applied properly. By using this computer network, the scientific debates which are usually made in scientific events, are able to extend for an indefinite period, rather than being limited to the 15 or 30 minutes generally reserved for complaints in events. With this, the author-reader interaction enables the clarification of one or another aspect addressed in the work that deserves a greater detailing, creating opportunities for the improvement of qualitative indices of the work presented, since any failure or passages that deserve special attention, will certainly be raised by the community members. Thus, a particular work is no longer individual, but will incorporate the collective thought, expressing the opinion of a community on a given topic.

The consensual opinion of the scientific community, which is one of the most fundamental standards of Science, is that the works should be disseminated by their respective authors [27]. The act of publishing enables that a research result be recognized as scientific truth, through validation of theories presented [29].

Interestingly, the publication and dissemination of information are essential to the development of new studies, since previous publications may be considered as inputs for the development of new studies as a way of providing greater credibility, validate, demonstrate and emphasize the new data submitted. Thus it is formed a scientific dialogue among different authors, which is precisely what makes possible the verification of the premises presented, and encourages the generation of new studies, and instigate researchers to explore emerging topics in their respective areas of expertise.

In this context the Internet is presented as the support which receives such a dialogue, which can also be called scientific debate, giving continuity to the information cycle which is responsible for the generation and improvement of human knowledge. Just as in other areas of knowledge, in occupational safety and health the Internet is a powerful tool while helper and source of research in professional forming, or continuing education in OSH, specially in remote, poor and less assisted geographical areas.

Additionally, the option of publishing in electronic format offers various facilities, both to the author of the study, and the information units, that later will incorporate such publication to their collections, with possibility of eliminating decisive processes of production and dissemination of knowledge that includes the best way of providing, acquiring and disclosing information, how much to spend, and so on. The stages of the publishing process is generally lengthy and costly - factor of impediment to the publication of works for many writers - is broken, since the cost of publication in digital format are lower in relation to the printed publication, not to mention validation activities, which in this case are made collectively by the entire scientific community, speeding up the improvement of publication process, and covering topics since from formatting and standardization until wording and content revision.

From the viewpoint of the information user, the greater and most social visible benefits and probably the most relevant ones provided by digital publishing are:

- The possibility of simultaneous access by multiple users to the same document;
- The facilities of handling, transporting and transmitting data;
- The possibility in converting the digital media in a printed document;
- The versatility of the media;
- The possibility of breaking down temporal, geographical and linguistic barriers.

The benefits of electronic communication are numerous and surrender itself a new research. The trend that has been the cause of controversy among scholars is that the volume of information produced in analog format, (paper) decrease significantly. Many publishing companies and other organizations are already producing their journals only in electronic format, which generally corresponds to the CD-ROM or online versions. Besides the benefits discussed, the fact brought the rationalization of physical spaces for storage, cheapening of resources for conservation of material, since the digital media tends to be more resistant to decay in relation to the paper. All this, not considering that traditionally, printed periodical publications only can be accessed inside the information units dependencies, with no possibility of home loan, which can cause potential complications or even impossibility of consulting the material by the researcher. Such restrictions do not occur with electronic publishing, since its contents can be duplicated for another media, and transported for consultation in another location, without making the original document unavailable for immediate consultation in its unity of origin.

From the moment in which the publications are available exclusively in electronic format, there is an increased risk of excluding many people from the scientific discussion, considering all these people that has no access or are not familiar with the digital environment, and thus the whole purpose of facilitating access knowledge, promote scientific integration, and provide visibility to published researches is inversely reached.

A possible solution to this situation may be to provide equipment connected to the Internet in educational institutions, both public and private, with monitors for guidance on access to information. However, the fact is that even though these facilities are available, they are not sufficient to eradicate the digital exclusion. The reasons are diverse, ranging from disinterest of the public to the lack of available equipment. Considering the global trend, driven by globalization, which initiated the computerization era, it becomes necessary to establish a national policy to encourage the generation and use of electronic information, so that the country can keep up with advances worldwide, regarding to the development of information retrieval systems. On the other hand, although the scientific information does not reach 100% of the public involved, managers often have easy access to these kind of data. It is up to them so, to consult such information and transmit them to their whole staff, so that scientific language is properly converted to the worker understanding, which constitutes the focus on OSH management.

However, the fact that the information is available does not mean that it will be accessed and converted into knowledge for further practical application, when applicable, as a way of promoting the advancement of OSH, and consequently the welfare of the worker. Thus, the OSH class institutions, together with the units and information professionals, play a crucial role in order to highlight and promote the use of this vast material, which stores the inputs to the construction of knowledge, and also provides support to the professionals of the area for such actions to achieve remarkable and satisfactory results. This responsibility increases from the moment that is considered the fact that the OSH institutions are the main producers of information on this subject. So, a new necessity arises, besides an encouragement for computerization, creation and scientific knowledge communication. The investigative spirit must be something inherent to the researcher, so that he must feels the need for seeking information involuntarily, and do not expect something to emerge that bring it to him. Hence the need to develop the instinct of independence in these professionals to have greater autonomy to act in terms of information searching and scientific expression.

In this sense, knowledge management plays a key role considering the need to promote the scientific informational capital turnover allowing the maturation processes of knowledge management within organizations. The benefits offered by the Internet allow the process of information transfer to increased speed and efficiency to ensure the safety of workers more effectively, reducing the rates of occupational accidents.

According to tables 1 and 2, official statistical data from the Brazilian Ministry of Social Welfare (Ministério da Previdência Social – MPAS) indicates that from 2008 to 2010, Brazil has registered over 700.000 occupational accidents a year, resulting in more than 8.000 deaths. Important to remember that these numbers do not correspond to reality, once that underreporting is still a problem faced in the workplace. Statistics themselves, better than any other data, justify with great skill the necessity of reflecting on the working conditions not only in Brazil, but all around the world, and, above all, the need for developing effective tools in reducing these rates.

Table 1: Number of occupational accidents registered by Brazilian Ministry of Social Welfare, from 2008 to 2010 [30]

Number of occupational accidents registered by Brazilian Ministry of Social Welfare, from 2008 to 2010														
Total number (with and without CAT registered)			With CAT** registered											
	Total with CAT registered			Cause of the accident										
		Typical acciden***			Commuting Accident****			Occupational diseases						
2008	2009	2010	2008	2009	2010	2008	2009	2010	2008	2009	2010	2008	2009	2010
755.980	733.365	701.496	551.023	534.248	525.206	441.925	424.498	414.824	88.742	90.180	94.789	20.356	19.570	15.593

** CAT (Comunicação de Acidente do Trabalho) is a form that the company must fill in to communicate to the INSS (Instituto Nacional de Seguridade Social / National Institute of Social Security - Brazil) a work accident, which occurred with an employee, with or without removal, until the first working day following the occurrence, or immediately, in case of death, under penalty of fine.

*** A typical accident is the one with happens during the execution of a professional activity.

**** A Commuting accident is an accident occurring on the habitual route, in either direction, between the place of work or work-related training and:

(i) the worker's principal or secondary residence;

(ii) the place where the worker usually takes his or her meals; or

(iii) the place where he or she usually receives his or her remuneration;

which results in death or personal injury

Table 2: Number of occupational accidents in Brazil, by consequence, from 2008 to 2010 [30]

Number of occupational accidents in Brazil, by consequence, from 2008 to 2010							
Years	Total	Consequence					
		Medical assistance	Temporary disability			Permanent disability	Deaths
			Total	Less than 15 days	More than 15 days		
2008	774.473	105.249	653.311	317.702	335.609	13.096	2.817
2009	752.121	103.029	631.927	306.900	325.027	14.605	2.560
2010	720.128	97.069	606.250	299.928	306.322	14.097	2.712

Achieving development is a virtually impossible task if at least the minimum conditions to preserve the physical and mental integrity of the worker are not observed. Therefore, work, health and safety are three components that must walk and advance together. From this perspective, the Internet can be applied as an instrument that enables and facilitate the scientific information flow and also the OSH intellectual capital turning, especially in underdeveloped regions, where the levels of exploitation and misinformation are higher.

So, the Internet can be considered an efficient tool for communication and dissemination of organizational knowledge, which assists in the process of homogenization of knowledge among employees of an organization. Information is essential to any organization, including all its workers, be from top management, be from shop floor, and emphasize the need for rapid access to data to reach the open market, competitiveness and also quality [31]. For this it is necessary to reveal the way in which information technology interact with organizations, since according to the literature, it is by this process that occurs cultural changes what includes the interlocutors behavior, which yet can involves business results, motivation and well-being of employees.

Information technology is a powerful tool to maximize the number of people reached, especially in shop floor, where can be found workers that have all the conditions to opine on a subject, resulting in new ideas, aiming to optimize ways of working and even getting better relationships among the staff. It is up to OSH professionals, to recognize the resources applied by information technology as a tool for OSH management in Brazil, so there will be a really valid and visible contribution the worker point of view.

- It should be generated by means of empirical thinking;
- It must be liable of understanding and proof;
- It must be formerly communicated to scientific community.

The most common form of communicating scientific information is by written communication (publication of books, articles, essays and so on) or by oral communication (informal conversation or oral presentations in events like congresses, seminars, symposiums and so on). Which one is better in OSH field is a hard question, because it depends on several factors, including the nature and complexity of information to be transmitted. However, written media is still the easier way to access scientific information, once participation in scientific events may become unviable due to geographic limitations or even budgetary restraints. So, an alternative to overcome these barriers to information access is to create information systems designed to store, preserve, disseminate, and promote access to intellectual output of the scientific communities around the world, preferably in an open access ambient, to overcome another barrier to scientific information: its costs.

Considering the opportunity of promoting collective thinking on OSH and the conveniences offered by digital age, some reflections emerge in order to build and encourage the use of instruments that allow scientific communication flowing. Therein, the Open Archives Initiative (OAI), coupled with the proposed mechanisms for quality management, emerges as an instrument with high potential for promoting a healthy and safe work environment for workers, overcoming geographic, temporal, and possibly linguistics barriers, facilitating access and dissemination of information.

So, scientific information reliability and validation is based on three points:

DIGITAL INFORMATION ACCESS RESOURCES UNDER THE OPEN ARCHIVES PHILOSOPHY

Success and professional recognition are the targets of any professional, but only can be achieved against great deeds. For that, the main additive is a good quality information made timely accessible. Precisely for this reason, information has been increasingly valued and pursued by all professionals.

The society has watched to an informational explosion along the last few decades, both in qualitative and quantitative aspects. Many facts should have collaborated to it, for example, the need of publishing, to get or to maintain a job [2]. This is a common practice in the academic world. However, regardless of the reason, information is there, everywhere, To Whom It May Concern. Once available, information has to be communicated, for it to have its worth, and to achieve its objectives. Internet has contributed significantly for that, as an effort to facilitate the access for information, and communication processes among scientists and researchers, that is, the scientific society, defined as a social group formed by of individuals whose profession is scientific and technological research [2].

But how do these scientific communities work? By the same way that did the primitive societies: by donation system. Scientists transfer their knowledge spontaneously and gratuitously to the scientific community, without expectation of receiving any economic compensation in return [2].

However, the existence of use and production of information become useless, if whomever may need it do not know about its existence or cannot retrieve it, whatever the reason. Just for this not to happen, any effort towards making information available to as many people as possible is valid. Thus, facing the scenery described, arises the incentive to free access to scientific information that

as already extensively reported in the literature, is both the result: (a) of a reaction of researchers to the business model of scientific journals commercial publishers (and their increasingly high prices for [...] signing and (b) increasing awareness of the impact caused by availability of scientific papers free from access barriers. The motto of the worldwide movement in favor of the Open Access search results, therefore, is the wide and unrestricted dissemination of the researches supported by public resources [32].

Considering that information can play the noble task of generating and disseminating knowledge, which through an empirical combination (scientific communication), may culminate in the development of increasingly effective tools for building and maintenance of healthy and safety work environments, any expenses for this purpose, either with job training (input) or with the access and dissemination of information (output) should be considered as an investment.

Facing this, the Open Archives Initiative may be applied as a tool for adding value to quality management in OSH, while providing information, including successful reports, which may be adapted and possibly applied in the workplace, aiming to promote better working conditions for workers.

Open archives (OA), which can also be considered an information quality management tool, are seen as an innovative concept designed to provide the text as quickly as possible, promoting and popularizing free access to electronic publications, so that there is a weakening of the monopoly detained by the publishers upon any scientific publication until then [33]. The OA established a set of standards that enable interoperability between different digital repositories, which [34], are defined as a form of storage for digital objects that have the ability to maintain and manage material for long periods of time and provide proper access. Becoming the main forum for dissemination of scientific results and discussions [35].

Digital repositories of information are information systems which are intended to storage, preserve, disseminate and promote access to the intellectual output of the various scientific communities around the world. The main features are the extensiveness of public access, the variety of documents regarding to form and content, including aspects of interdisciplinary and preservation of digital data stored in there, and also the storage of this kind of informational support, that dispense the formation of the traditional printed collections, that demands above all, physical spaces for the accommodation of the archived material. However, the differentiating feature of open archives is the ability to provide simultaneously, freely accessible documents, using the philosophy of self-archiving, and also more restricted documents, made available only to a select audience, such as researchers engaged in a specific educational institution, for example. This way, digital repositories may present both interfaces: one widely and opened accessible, and another one, more restrict, gathering both the philosophy of free access, and the digital repositories philosophy itself. The policy used in the process of adding new documents collection ever assembled determines the repository as open archive, or digital repository. In the first case, the name refers that the information access is completely open, allowing the authors to remove or alter documents already posted whenever they found it convenient. In digital repositories, instead, access is restricted to a specific community, such as university professors or researchers from an institution.

Since digital repositories are constructed within the philosophy of open access, the final user of this kind of information source is able to search, copy, print, and also send a document to another researcher besides the possibility of using the full text documents in other discussions, since the source and authorship is indicated. The data reliability is ensured through quality policies that establish minimum standards of quality of the archived information. A way of applying this sense is to have a specific judging commission, which should be responsible for examining the papers submitted for publication before making them available in the network.

The popularization of the Internet contributed to the depreciation of the degree of reliability of the data available in there, since anyone that dominates some basic features of information technology are able to add and/or change data on the network, inserting new documents and information that are not always reliable or truthful. The thematic digital repository under the philosophy of open archives, however, can mitigate such effects, recovering the initial principle of scientific communication in digital format, which is to facilitate the scientific information exchange between professionals.

Usually maintained by renowned institutions, thematic repositories adopting the philosophy of open archives gather in one place plenty of documents on a specific issue. That saves the researcher free time, and eliminates the need of displacement until an information unit or a library to have access to such data. Therefore, rather than the researcher looks for information, the opposite is what happens: the information comes to the table of the researcher, through a computer, bringing with it the backing of the institution responsible for its authorship.

The establishment of the open archives initiative in Brazil, may contribute to the breakdown of the barriers to access to OSH information, and also promote joint reflection between the members of the scientific community. The self-archiving, defined mechanism that allows the authors to submit or deposit their papers in a digital repository [36] besides being a way of democratizing forms of publication and access to scientific information, is also a way of promoting the continuing debate about a subject among scholars. The contribution to the construction and sharing of knowledge in this scenario becomes an automatic process, in order to contribute significantly to the evolution of science and improvement of various forms of labor relations in the OSH context.

OSH INFORMATION MANAGEMENT IN SÃO PAULO CITY, BRAZIL, UNDER THE PROFESSIONALS PERCEPTION

During the year of 2008, Santos realized a study (presented as a master dissertation) in the south area of São Paulo City, in Brazil. The objective of this study was to detect the perception of the OSH professionals regarding to the availability of scientific information in occupational safety and health, and ways of accessing it, in their perception. It was also investigated the perception of the OSH professionals about how OSH scientific information and the maintenance of a healthy working environment could contribute to increase quality indicators, and consequently the organizational profits, that corresponds to the managers and stakeholders main interest.

It was randomly selected 23 organizations of the south area of São Paulo city, which OSH professionals were interviewed. 52% of the studied population consisted of safety technicists, while safety engineers consisted 21% of the total sample. The profile of the selected community was characterized predominantly male (82.6%), ranging in age from 36 to 50 years and over 10 years experience in the area.

The analysis of the answers to the 17 questions questionnaire that was applied to these professionals indicated that there is still a great job to be done to improve OSH information access and application in companies in São Paulo. It was found that the virtual environment for research is not yet fully exploited by the respondents, which is a fact that arises some concern to OSH managers, considering all the benefits of this knowledge transfer resource.

With regard to the worker welfare, the results clearly show that access to information is essential for safety processes improvement. Workers physical and mental health protection depends largely on access to the occupants of senior professionals have to the scientific information in general. According to respondents, cross-check between one and another company is very important in order to improve techniques and processes to assist in decision making or problem solving.

The study results also showed the need to promote the practice of OSH management as a means of protecting workers, and not as an inspection agent with punitive power to those who fail to comply with its recommendations. The worker must have a different view of safety at work, as well as professionals working in the area. Therein, integration and awareness of employees through information once again revealed itself effective. Information by itself is not the key to all problems solving, but it may be a major step in building and maintaining the ideal working environment. Data exchange among companies provides the sharing of experiences, improvement of processes and support in the prediction of harmful events, the accident itself.

The initial premises, which were confirmed at the end of the study, indicate that the philosophy of dissemination of scientific information used by open archives is considered by the interviewed professionals as a support tool for OSH management. Regarding the attitude of these professionals, the acceptance of this new form of dissemination of scientific information is plausible, although the reliability and familiarity of the public with digital instruments of research is relatively low, what creates the need of promoting the scientific culture, which stirs up both production and sharing of information, and above all, the scientific papers publication.

The discussion emphasized that scientific information can be viewed and used as a support tool to OSH management in general, which is considered a pillar to occupational safety and health management. An information resource would help professionals in the area, be in decision making processes, be in technical aspects. Allied to the mechanisms for quality management, benefits are enhanced with the possibility of achieving significant results to organizations.

FINAL CONSIDERATIONS

It is important to establish the alignment of the alliance among scientific information, quality management and occupational safety and health. This combination, stands for the interests of OSH professionals, workers (including shop floor), and managers. OSH professionals, through the access of information are able to improve their professionals skills and apply methods of accident preventions never experienced before, or experienced in other organization, while quality management tools, like PDCA and 5S may help them to evaluate the adopted measures, making easier the identification and correction of any fail, and also to provide a clear, organized and healthy work environment, through the 5S recommendations. Workers, may enjoy a better (friendly) work environment, ergonomically correct, cleaned and organized job stations, not to mention the perception of the importance of him and his job to the organization, and also the improvement of occupational hazards management, once a suitable working environment reduces the chances of the occurrence of occupational accidents. For the organizational manager, all of this represents profits increasing. Once the OSH professional has conditions to offer a proper workplace in the organization, the worker is able to produce more, and more efficiently (profit). The worker, less susceptible to occupational accidents, requires less spending with medical assistance and rehabilitation costs (profit). Conscientious use and disposal of organizational raw material, also represents saving money (profit). PDCA also has its contribution in this sense through the provision of the constantly evaluation of the production process, what allows the organization to keep a continuous evaluation and improvement process, towards excellence, which may represent the conquest of market share (profit).

Increasing production and quality indicators, decreasing occupational accidents, using raw material properly (including human resources), and all of this supported by scientific information, meet the interests of any organization manager which is profit. In this scenery, the effective use and application of scientific information and communication may be considered as one of the major challenges, to be reached by occupational safety and health professionals. Since OSH is a branch of knowledge that deals with human life, comfort and safety become priority issues in order to provide the quality of work life, especially in activities that exposes the worker to occupational hazards, which risks both safety and even the workers lives.

However most needed material goods, we must not forget the following: ALL OF THIS EXISTS FOR THE MAN. And he can not have his health unprotected. The workplace control is obligatory. This is a matter of morality. If the work does not contribute to your happiness, it will be a huge and lamentable loss [37].

In work accidents field any kind of adaptation must be unacceptable. After all, a worker who is mutilated by an occupational accident, hardly will to adapt to society and the workplace in order to carry out their routine activities. The accident scene will never be erased from his memory. Neither compensation, (no matter the value) nor any other social benefit will aid the psychological trauma of an injured worker, or replace the activities of which he was deprived as a result of an accident. Therefore, it is inadmissible to use the term adaptation when it is related to safety and health at work, since the health and integrity of the employee is an acquired right that must be respected by the employer.

Knowledge attracts money, while the converse is not true. Whereas the non-conformities in the workplace may culminate in damages to the organization, investments in the development of the intellectual capital and management knowledge should be priorities to the organizations and be considered as support tools for managing health and safety at work.

Quality management should promote effective changes in the workplace, and these changes should reach and invigorate in all working environments, so that the workers lives, which represents the strength of a nation, be respected and preserved.

ACKNOWLEDGMENT

Special thanks to Dr. Simone El Khouri Miraglia (Universidade Federal de São Paulo - Unifesp), master's advisor of the autor, whose dissertation entitled "Gestão da saúde e segurança no trabalho: uma análise sobre arquivos abertos", has led to this paper, and also to Fundacentro, for financing this study.

REFERENCES

1. D. Barreiros, Gestão da segurança e saúde no trabalho: estudo de um modelo sistêmico para as organizações do setor mineral. [thesis]. [São Paulo]. Universidade de São Paulo, 2002
2. F. Y. A. Le Coadic, da. Ciência, 2nd. Informação, Rio. ed, Briquet. de Janeiro, de , Lemos; 2004
3. Silva JPC, Machado, FO. A qualidade como estratégia empresarial: um estudo conceitual. Ingepro. 2011, 3:35-46. [cited 2012 Feb 10]. Available from
4. https://ojs.ingepro.com.br/index.php/ingepro/article/view/473/388.
5. J. O. Magretta, é. que, e. gerenciar, administrar, Rio de Janeiro: Elsevier; 2002
6. M. Braga, acidentes. Prevenção de, ou. investimento, Cipa. custo?, 2007Oct; 28(355)92.
7. Silveira AA. A gestão do conhecimento como ênfase na aprendizagem organizacional: um estudo de multicaso no contexto bancário. [dissertation]. [Itajubá]. Universidade Federal de Itajubá, 2004. [cited 2012 Feb. 23] Available from
8. http://adm-net-a.unifei.edu.br/phl/pdf/0031263.pdf
9. D. A. Almeida, F. Leal, A. F. Pinho, et al.Gestão do conhecimento na análise de falhas através de sistema de informação. Produção. 2006Jan./Apr. 1617188
10. Pereira FCM. O Processo de conversão do conhecimento em uma escola de atendimento especializado. Enc. BIBLI: R. eletrônica de Bibl. Ci. Inform. 2005 20. [cited 2011 Nov. 9] Available from
11. http://www.encontrosbibli.ufsc.br/Edicao_20/3_mafra_pereira.pdf.
12. Centro de Referência em Inteligência Empresarial. Gestão do Conhecimento. [cited 2012Jan. 4] Available from:
13. http://portal.crie.coppe.ufrj.br/portal/main.asp?ViewID=%7B32E72BC9-F838-4577-AF25-A5803179DF22%7D.
14. I. Nonaka, H. Takeuchi, Criação de conhecimento na empresa: como as empresas japonesas geram a dinâmica da inovação. Rio de Janeiro: Campus; 1997
15. Campos VF.Gerenciamento da rotina de trabalho no dia-a-dia. 7th. ed. Belo Horizonte: Desenvolvimento Gerencial; 2001
16. Andrade FF. O método de melhorias PDCA. [thesis]. [São Paulo]. Escola Politécnica da Universidade de São Paulo, 2003. [cited 2012 Feb. 14] Available from
17. http://www.teses.usp.br/teses/disponiveis/3/3146/tde-04092003-150859/.
18. R. Souza, G. Mekbekian, Metodologia de gestão da qualidade em empresas construtoras. EdUSP. Anais do ENTAC93: encontro nacional de tecnologia do ambiente construído: avanços em tecnologia e gestão da produção de edificações. 1993127131
19. Centro de Tecnologia de Edificações.Sistema de gestão da qualidade para empresas construtoras. São Paulo: SINDUSCON; 1994
20. Parceria do Distrito Industrial em Ciências Ambientais. Ciclo PDCA. [cited 2010May 22] Available from:
21. http://www.pdca.org.br/.
22. Mattos RP Eletricidade: perigo de morte. Cipa.2007283339091
23. Unlimited Learning Resources.The Deming Cycle (PDCA). [cited 2012Feb 13]. Available from:
24. http://www.4ulr.com/products/productquality/deming_cycle.html.
25. I. P. E. M. O. programa, . esses, from. [cited, 2012Mar. 20] Available from:
26. http://www.ipem.sp.gov.br/3emp/5esses.asp?vpro=abe.
27. F. Gomiero, Os cinco sensos do combate ao desperdício. [cited 2011Sep 20]. Available from:
28. http://www.janelanaweb.com/digitais/gomiero24.html.
29. PUCRS. Programa 5S. [cited2011Nov 5]. Available from:
30. http://www.pucrs.br/feng/5s/capa.php.
31. ANVISA. O Método 5S. Brasília: ANVISA; 2005. [cited 2010 July 15]. Available from:
32. http://www.anvisa.gov.br/reblas/procedimentos/metodo_5S.pdf.
33. Amaral. M. Garcia, Auditoria como instrumento de avaliação do desempenho do sistema de gestão da saúde e segurança no trabalho. Anais do SIMPEP. 2005
34. H. Couto, limites. a. Rompendo, é. neurolinguística, técnica. uma, aplicação. com, prevenção. na, de acidentes, Proteção. 199811793839
35. Hékis HR et al.Estratégia para crescimento através da gestão da qualidade alinhada com a gestão da informação e do conhecimento: um estudo de caso em

uma empresa do ramo da construção civil em Natal/ RN. Ingepro.3.111Cited 2010Aug. 10]. Available from:

36. https://http://ojs.ingepro.com.br/index.php/ingepro/article/view/427.

37. 3038Penabad AA et. Al. Consideraciones para la mejora de los sistemas de gestión de la calidad en la Industria Biofarmacéutica. Vaccimonitor. 2010. 19.30-38. [cited 2011 May 5] Available from

38. http://redalyc.uaemex.mx/src/inicio/ArtPdfRed.jsp?iCve=203415359006&iCveNum=15359.

39. R. Maguire, Safety cases and safety reports: meaning, motivation and management. Hampshire: Ashgate; c2006

40. E. L. Silva, E. M. Menezes, M. A. Bissani, como. Internet, comunicação. canal de, científica, Inf. & Soc.: Est. 2002121290320

41. V. R. H. Araújo, I. M. A. Freire, Internet. rede, canal. como, na. de comunicação, da. perspectiva, da. Ciência, Informação, Transinformação. 1996824555

42. L. A. A. Velho, e. Ciência, público. seu, Transinformação. 1997931632

43. Brasil, Ministério da Previdência Social. Anuário estatístico da Previdência Social. Brasília; 2010. [cited 2012 Fev 22] available from

44. http://www.mpas.gov.br/arquivos/office/3_111202-105619-646.pdf.

45. A. M. Rosini, A. Palmisano, Administração de sistemas de informação e a gestão do conhecimento. São Paulo: Thomson; 2003

46. Baptista AA, Costa SMS, Kuramoto H et al. Comunicação científica: o papel da Open Archives Iniciative no contexto do acesso livre. Enc. Biblio: R. Eletr. Bibliotecon. Ci. Inf. special edition, 2007. [cited 2010, Aug 26] Available from

47. http://journal.ufsc.br/index.php/eb/article/viewFile/1518-2924.2007v12nesp1p1/435.

48. R. Triska, L. Café, abertos. Arquivos, da. subprojeto, Digital. Biblioteca, Brasileira, Ciência da Informação. 2001

49. C. L. M. Viana, Arellano. Márdero, M. Shintaku, Repositórios institucionais em ciência e tecnologia: uma experiência de customização do Dspace. [cited 2010Mar. 22] Available from:

50. http://eprints.rclis.org/archive/00005563/01/viana358.pdf.

51. Machado M. Open archives: panorama dos repositórios. [dissertation]. [Santa Catarina]: Universidade Federal de Santa Catarina, 2006. [cited from 2012 Jan 10] Available from

52. http://www.tede.ufsc.br/teses/PCIN0015.pdf.

53. H. Kuramoto, científica. Informação, um. proposta de, modelo. novo, o. para, Brasil, Ciência da Informação. 200635291102

54. I. F. S. O. Saad, insalubridade. adicional de, a. após, N. nova, R-, Revista ABHO de higiene ocupacional. 200651314

CHAPTER 3

CURRENT TRENDS AND FUTURE DEVELOPMENTS IN OCCUPATIONAL HEALTH AND SAFETY RISK MANAGEMENT

Roland Iosif Moraru

INTRODUCTION

Occupational safety and health (OHS) like all facets of business, needs to be properly managed. A company's OSH system helps ensure effective control of OHS risks and continual improvement in OHS performance, prevent work-related illness or injury and to achieve compliance with regulations and standards.

The goals of this chapter are 1) the identification of effective practices, processes and structures in OHS risk management, and 2) using a simple framework to draw together what is known of good and bad practice in this area, particularly in deciding what rules should be explicitly formulated and imposed. We argue that there is an urgent need for the formulation and implementation of a new management framework for occupational hazards; one that is appropriate for the new economic and occupational structure of work. The overall objective is 1) to underpin observations, 2) illustrate typical characteristics of the current situation and 3) indicate directions that could lead to solving these new safety problems. We suggest that this task should initially involve stepping back and revisiting the frame of reference in which the protection against occupational injury is viewed.

In approaching the issue, the chapter, first, attempts to provide a succinct mapping of the environment of occupational risk, through a brief examination of its historical dimensions.

Based on a thorough literature review, the major role of the ISO 31000:2009 standard is emphasized. Given that risk management is an adaptive process and that risk assessment is merely one of its features, the question is what can risk managers do to make their activities more credible and acceptable? A section is devoted to benchmarking organizational practice and risk treatments. This focus also raised the discussion of drawbacks and pitfalls of risk ranking methods. The chapter pays special attention to developing a new understanding of the participatory approach and closes with a comparative analysis which seek further explanation of approaches to occupational health and safety risk management based on two kinds of epistemological assumptions existing in the field, namely constructivism and positivism. This work should assist those practitioners, researchers and other stakeholders within industry who are interested in assessing and managing the existing OHS risks in their organisations, with the intention of identifying the priority areas for focussing improvement effort.

RISK MANAGEMENT: THE NEED FOR AN EVOLUTIONARY AND MULTIFACETED APPROACH

Regardless of the type and size, any organization faces risks that can affect the achievement of its goals. Therefore, acquiring a coherent system of concepts and rules, generally accepted nationally and internationally, becomes essential for the public and private sector today, regardless of their nature. The approaches to safety seem to put emphasis on management functions, guidelines, industry standards, quality principles, to establish the safety management system, as outlined bellow.

Premises and brief history

All the activities of an organization involve risks and risk management is the foundation of the decision-making,

Citation: Roland Iosif Moraru (2012). Current Trends and Future Developments in Occupational Health and Safety Risk Management, ISBN: 978- 953-51-0571-8

considering the effects of uncertainty on the objectives. Companies that have applied risk analysis and management for many years also recognize that the change to a "culture of prevention" via "systematic and comprehensive risk management" involves a journey (Hudson, 2003). The model shown in Figure 1 suggests that a move towards an integrated risk management system is multifaceted and evolutionary. As pointed out by (Joy and Griffiths, 2004) the key for success is for companies "to select the method that is designed to suit their needs". They also need to understand the challenges related to risk management of the company. Stakeholders must understand where important decisions are requiring risk to be systematically considered, as well as the current status of their culture or systems, so the next step can be triggered.

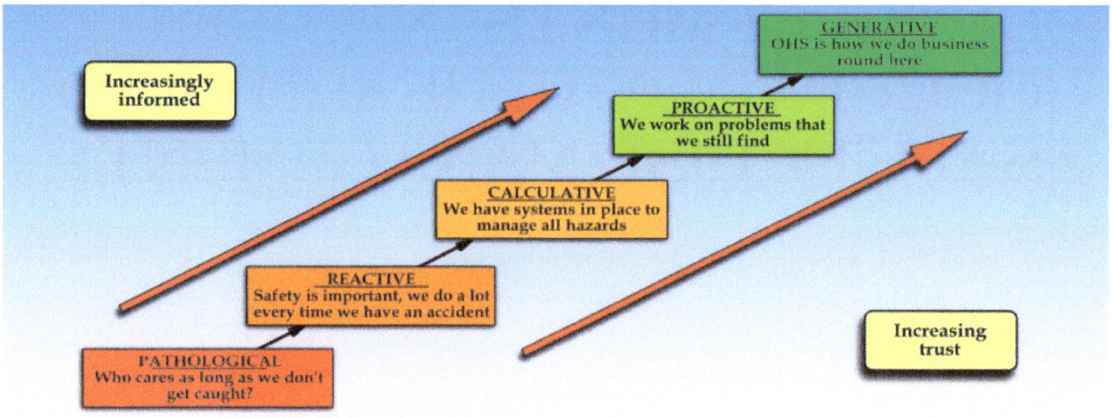

Figure 1: Multi-faceted and evolutional journey toward risk management (Adapted from Ayers, 2007)

A discussion of the major challenges related to development of causal models of organizational safety performance and a set of principles to address them have been presented by several authors in separate publications, see for example (Bourrier, 1998; Haines et al, 2002; Reason, 1995). The conceptual models proposed for organizational safety performance are naturally heavily influenced by the particular theoretical perspective adopted and the objectives chosen for the model. For example, literature on safety culture (Cox and Flin, 1998) and safety climate, such as (Zohar, 1980; Zohar and Luria, 2004) focuses primarily on the psychological causes of safety, with perception survey as the main measurement method. On the other hand, safety management literature including (Walters et al, 2005) primarily considers organizational safety structure and practices using auditing measurement approaches. Yet other disciplines (e.g. Preliminary Risk Analysis) mainly focus on direct causes of accidents such as hardware failures or operational errors, and on a common metric for measuring them (Sage and White, 1980; Reason, 1993).

The best state of health, safety and well-being for the workers and of physical and economic health for the company cannot be reached in once. Effective systems are based on the principle of "Plan – Do – Check - Act" (Deming, 1982). In OSH terms this will require to develop a policy on what is intended to achieve, then a plan of how and when it will be done, including any necessary arrangements. Next is the "doing" phase, when plans are implemented and then check that you have done what you planned to do and that it is effective in controlling risks. Any deficiencies found need to be acted upon and rectified, so that the system performance improves continually. Numerous management practices and processes include elements of risk management and several organizations are resorting to formal management processes for specific circumstances and particular risks, as depicted in Figure 2 (Smith, 2008).

Figure 2: Risk Management Process – Marsh Perspective (Adapted from Smith, 2008)

Over time, more than 60 Technical Committees and Working Groups of ISO and national standards or regulatory bodies, have addressed the risk management issue one way or another. Numerous multi-sectoral standards have been drafted, e.g. OHSAS 18001, BS 8800, FD X50-252:2006, ISO/IEC 51 guide etc or dedicated to a particular sector. While the AS/NZS 4360:2004 (published in 1995 and amended in 1999) was the most widely used global standard for risk management. Considering the need for unification, Australia proposed to set up a Working Group on Risk Management, aimed at providing practical guidance on the risk management principles for all applications, including small and medium enterprises. Before the first meeting of the Working Group, it was developed a discussion document, based on AS/NZS 4360:2004 (Standards Australia and Standards New Zealand, 2004), using the terminology of ISO/IEC 73. The 20 delegates from 12 national standards associations attended the first meeting held in September 2005 in Tokyo. The following Working Group meetings were held in Sydney (February 2006), Vienna (September 2006), Ottawa (April 2007), Sanya (December 2007), Singapore (November 2009). Voting began on May 25, 2009 and ended in July 25, 2009; in November 2009, the ISO 31000 standard was issued.

In order to better highlight the evolutionary and multifaceted character of the risk management conceptual models, a brief comparison of AS/NZS 4360 and ISO 31000:2009 standards is performed in the following section.

AS/NZS 4360 and ISO 31000:2009: A comparison

Basically, we can argue that ISO 31000 is the natural successor to AS/NZS 4360:2004 and although the comparative analysis of the two standards is not the purpose of this work, we consider necessary and useful to highlight the differences. The main elements are shown in Table 1 and the basic terms are defined in Table 2.

Because we are describing a holistic process, the scope of this section is greater than that of some documents which deal with limited scope of the topic. In particular, many texts deal only with the analytical processes of risk assessment, and omit the management and organizational aspects of their implementation. The steps of the risk management process which are often omitted are 1) establishing the context, 2) monitoring and review, and 3) communication and consultation. This trend is particularly valid for the field of OHS risks.

Table 1: AS/NZS 4360:2004 and ISO 31000:2009: Differences regarding the main constituents

Elements	AS/NZS 4360:2004	ISO 31000:2009
Application	All organizations, all risks - no exclusion. Australia and New Zealand	All organizations, all risks - no exclusion. All countries
Context for risk management	The organization's objectives	The organization's objectives
Risk Management Process („What you do?")	Core of AS/NZS 4360	Part of ISO 31000
Risk Management Framework („How you do?")	Substantially revised in 2004	Extension of AS/NZS 4360
Risk management principles	Implicitly approached, to some extent	Explicitly and clearly approached
Attributes of enhanced risk management	Not approached	Annex to ISO 31010:2010

Table 2: AS/NZS 4360:2004 şi ISO 31000:2009: Basic definitions

Term	AS/NZS 4360:2004	ISO 31000:2009
Risk	The chance of something happening that will have an impact on objectives	Effect of uncertainty on objectives
Risk management	The culture, processes and structures that are directed towards realising potential opportunities whilst managing adverse effects	Coordinated activities to direct and control an organization with regard to risk
Risk management framework	Set of elements of an organization's management system concerned with managing risk	Set of components that provide the foundations and organizational arrangements for designing, implementing, monitoring, reviewing and continually improving risk management processes throughout the organization
Risk management policy	Not defined	Overall intentions and direction of an organization related to risk management
Risk management plan	Not defined	Document within the risk management framework, specifying the approach, the management components and resources to be applied to the management of risk
Risk management process	The systematic application of management policies, procedures and practices to the tasks of communicating, establishing the context, identifying, analysing, evaluating, treating, monitoring and reviewing risk	Systematic application of management policies, procedures and practices to the tasks of communicating, consulting, establishing the context, identifying, analyzing, evaluating, treating, monitoring and reviewing risk

The ISO 31000:2009 Standard is aimed at harmonizing the risk management processes. It is not a substitute for the existing standards, but a a top-level generic document providing a unified and coherent approach of the risk management principles and framework. Its purpose is to contribute to mutual understanding amongst stakeholders rather than provide guidance on risk management practices.

Any application or private sector requirements, brings its particular perceptions and individual criteria and, therefore, one of the key features of the standard is to include "establishing context" as the initial stage of the process, step that allows to "capture"the criteria diversity and complex nature of risks involved in each case. A brief outline of the major requirements of the standard is now needed to highlight its usefulness within the OHS risk management.

Snapshots from ISO 31000 standard "Risk Management – Principles and guidelines for implementation

The aforementioned standard emphasizes how the organization should understand the specific context in which risk management is implemented throughout the organization, at all levels and in every moment of its existence, to allow:

Fosterage of proactive, rather than reactive, management;

- Awareness of the need to identify and address risks throughout the organization;
- Improvement of opportunities and threats identification;
- Compliance with relevant legislation and international standards;
- Improvement of corporate governance and stakeholder confidence;
- Solid base of planning and decision making processes;
- Better control systems, learning and organizational resilience, operational efficiency, safety and health, loss prevention and incident management;
- Effective allotment and use of resources.

To be effective risk management must become an integral part of governance, management, reporting processes, policies, philosophy and culture of the organization. As stated in Clause 3 of the standard, the risk management: a) creates value; b) is an integral part of organizational processes and part of decision making; c) explicitly adresses uncertainty; d) is systematic, structured and timely; e) is based on the best available information; f) is tailored; g) takes human and cultural factors into account; h) is transparent and inclusive; h) dynamic, j) iterative and responsive to change; k) facilitates continual improvement and enhancement of the organization (ISO, 2009).

The general framework (see Clause 4 of the standard) supports the organization to effectively manage risks, applying risk management process on different levels, in the specific context, at a given moment. This clause describes the necessary components of a risk management framework and how they inter-relate, as illustrated in Figure 3. The process involves the use of logical and systematic methods for continuous communication and consultation, defining the context for identifying, analyzing, evaluating and treating risks, as well as monitoring and reviewing risks. It includes activities described in the standard through requirements 5.2-5.6, as shown in Figure 4.

In the spirit of this new standard, one may decide to review the foundations of existing processes and practices regarding the OHS risk assessment and management. While it is not specific to a particular industry or sector, the standard can be applied to any organizational entity regardless of the type and nature of the risks. Despite this, the standard is not about promoting uniformity in risk management, because the design and implementation of the framework and management plans should take into account the specific needs of the organization's particular objectives, structure, operations, processes, functions, projects, products, services, goods, and specific practices employed. Some areas, as in OHS, are requiring regulatory criteria that reflect an „aversion" to the predominantly negative consequences of risk. Resorting to the approach proposed in the standard proposed enables the identification and application of such criteria. We argue that the standard supports organizations to comply with legislative requirements and international standards while increasing the performance of the organization. Unfortunately, this argument is not currently possible to qualify as the standard is so new that little reliable empirical research on its usefulness has been conducted.

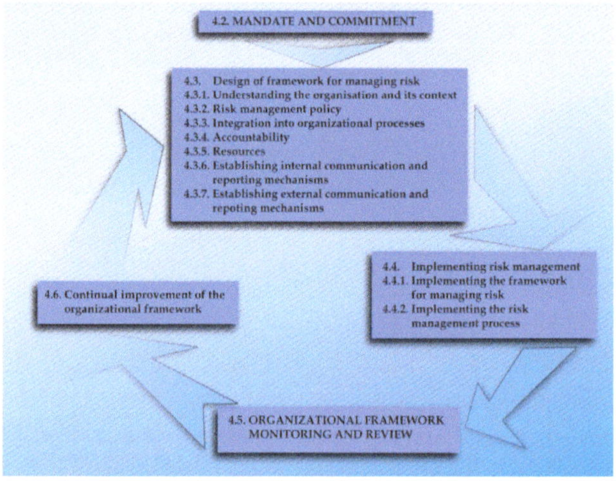

Figure 3: Components of the framework for managing risk (Based on ISO 31000:2009)

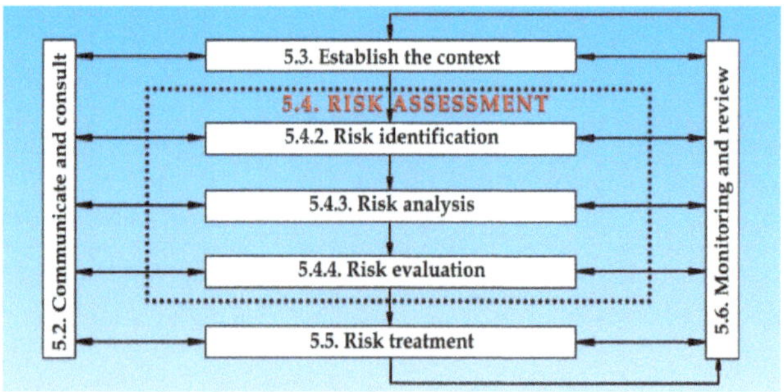

Figure 4: The risk management process (Based on ISO 31000:2009)

Assessment of workplace risks is the foundation of a company's OHS risk management. Yet it is surprising how little literature there is about 1) how to conduct risk assessments effectively, 2) how to decide what methods and rules are needed, 3) how to prepare and formulate them and 4) how to promulgate them and ensure they stay appropriate. As such, we are now focusing on the practical application of the risk assessment process, representing a resource for getting up to speed quickly on the different options available and the means to introduce and implement risk management.

CURRENT TRENDS AND CHALLENGES IN OHS RISK MANAGEMENT

Risk assessments are vital support to decision-making process. Risk assessment supports the design review process by providing the underlying analysis on which safety decisions can be made. Risk assessment methods are being deployed in many industries, and the momentum is likely to continue. Although the level of sophistication in risk assessment processes varies the general risk assessment process applies both across and within all industries.

Occupational risk assessment: Benchmarks for the organization's practice

Modern risk assessment began over three decades ago, with applications in the military and nuclear power (Theys, 1991). In the late 1970s it gradually expanded, and was applied to a vast array of chemical risks. Applications to engineered systems, and in particular infrastructure, are common; examples are given by (Lave and Balvanyos, 1998). Blockley (1992) also devotes a number of chapters to civil engineering topics (e.g. design codes or risk assessment in structural engineering), and several infrastructure-engineering applications (e.g., dam safety, marine structures).

According to ISO 31000:2009 standard, risk depends both on the probability or frequency of an adverse outcome, and also on the severity of that outcome. Risk has similarly been defined generally as "the potential for realization of unwanted, negative consequences of an event" (Moraru and Băbuţ, 2010). More quantitatively, in (Sage and White, 1980) risk is defined as "the probability per unit time of the occurrence of a unit cost burden", and state that it "represents the statistical likelihood of a randomly exposed individual being adversely affected by some hazardous event". Thus, risk has been defined at many different levels of detail. The usage of of the word risk ususlly has negative connotations and risks are regarded as something to be minimized or avoided. The aforemetioned standard recognizes that activities involving risks may lead to impacts that can be positive as well as negative. The processes described herein can be used to exploit opportunities for enhancing organizational outcomes as well as reducing negative consequences.

Risk treatment efforts to achieve acceptable risk must work within the real world constraints of feasibility, practicality and cost. A practical solution to achieving acceptable risk is a good faith application of the hierarchy of controls within the risk assessment process. The number of methods aiming at assessing the risks is definitely greater than the number of methods aiming at preventing them.

In Romania, since 2006, when the new Occupational Health and Safety Act (Romanian Parliament, 2006) have stated that the risk assessment is compulsory, several approaches were in use but only one method is extended in application. It appears as obvious that a large number of practitioners are resorting to a single method, without considering the great variety of working systems and conditions which are requiring specific approaches and techniques. Methods are used to rank risks and to define priorities for actions - which is desirable - but often this is done by neglecting the analysis of the elements defining these risks and the means of improving the situation. The accident risk management should be seen as the process of providing recommendations on whether to accept or resolve potential consequences of hazards associated with a given activity. It is neither a "science" (in that it provides a precise prediction of future events), nor just "common sense" or "something good managers have always done". It resorts to systematic procedures and specific techniques to analyze safety and occupational health factors, design and construction of equipment, and other situational hazards. As highlighted by Pasman (2009), for this process to be effective, the company culture must be willing to embrace the risk assessment process, and cultural acceptance stems from management leadership. Engineering design needs to change to include the risk assessment process to more effectively move safety into design.

Guidance on how to most effectively introduce the risk assessment process to an organization, and how to conduct them thereafter can be extracted from different sources, but the most valuable information source remains the practical experience gained by effectively performing the risk management. Practical guidance should be provided for Romanian companies get started and make progress in the risk assessment process. Topics addressed include: 1) the time to complete an assessment, 2) forming a team, 3) what to expect, 4) when to stop a risk assessment, 5) what to do in cross industry situations, 6) when to revise an existing risk assessment, 7) making changes to the protocol and 8) results of risk assessment.

When adressing the tool issue, „risk ranking matrix" is the term that describes how risks are ranked in the first instance, employing a method-specific tool. There are many variables, factors and combinations that must be considered in selecting an appropriate tool for further analysis, as that presented in Table 3. The different variables that are used to rank risks are requiring a proper understanding, and the three most common types of risk ranking systems are 1) qualitative, 2) semi-quantitative and 3) quantitative. Given the subjective nature of rating risk, risk scoring systems will likely continue to emerge and proliferate, as users refine and improve their risk assessment process.

This diversification of methods should be considered healthy, due to the variety of working circumstances requiring specific approaches. In time, convergence to one or a few risk scoring systems may occur, as efforts to harmonize and standardize risk assessment methods are made. This process will require some time, particularly in developing countries, as Romania, where the legal compliance is nowadays seen as the main requirement, instead of considering performance as main goal. There is also considerable resistance to creating risk assessment documents from the legal community primarily, due to product liability concerns and economic and financial restraints.

However, good engineering practice, continuous improvement and risk management requirements, all push for documenting processes. Documenting the risk assessment process is required or recommended by every guideline, standard or technical description of risk assessment. There are many risk ranking systems in use, each offering its strengths and weaknesses. This variation reflects the great diversity of opinion on risk assessment. Some of the most significant differences between risk assessment methods used today involve how risk is assessed. As mentioned before, there is a continuum of risk ranking systems from qualitative to quantitative that effectively address a variety of risk assessment applications. Very few benchmarks use quantitative risk ranking systems. However, there is no indication that any particular risk ranking system is better than another for all applications.

Table 3: Matrix helping to identify hazard assessment method classes. Action Guide

Occurrence	Severity			
	Catastrophic	Major	Minor	Negligible
Frequent	A	A	A	C
Probable	A	A	B	C
Occasional	A	B	B	D
Remote	A	B	C	D
Improbable	B	C	C	D

Risk level	Analysis
A	➢ Detailed and quantitative
B	➢ Semi-quantitative
C	➢ Qualitative
D	➢ Not required

Based on the above-mentioned benchmarks, the following principles directed towards practical risk assessment improvement can be stated:

- *Minimize the use of labels*: the use of labels to describe portions of the risk assessment process should be minimized. The terms used in assessing risk were until the issue of the ISO 31000 Standard very confusing. There existed confusion, or at least no common understanding, as to the meanings of the terms of risk assessment, risk analysis, risk estimation, risk evaluation. Efforts at harmonizing, standardizing or even communicating were severely hampered by the past confusion and different uses of the term „risk assessment" and others. The practitioner trying to conduct a risk assessment does not care about terms or labels. He just wants to know what he need to do to complete an effective risk assessment. Extra terms detract from this objective. Unnecessary terms that add no value should be removed from the risk assessment process. Labels that provide no value only add confusion.
- *Simplify the risk assessment process*: the steps of the risk assessment process should be written using active verbs rather than labels or titles. The steps of the risk assessment process need to be simple and straightforward, and provide the reader very clear direction on what he needs to do.
- *Adopt "risk assessment process" as overall term*: the term „risk assessment process"should be adopted to describe the overall process of identifying hazards, assessing risk and reducing risk. The terms "risk analysis", "risk assessment", "risk estimation" and others have different definitions depending on the industry using them. The two most frequently used terms to describe the overall risk assessment effort are "risk assessment" and "risk management".
- *The risk assessment process goal involves risk treatment*: there is no point in assessing the risks of a system, design, process or product, unless one plans to perform risk reduction. The risk reduction effort is always completed even though not every residual risk requires further risk reduction (the risk may already be acceptable). This implies that risk reduction is a necessary part of, and should be included in, the overall risk management process regardless of the term used to describe that overall process.
- Adopt the risk assessment process flow chart, as it is given in clause 5 of the ISO 31000 Standard;
- *Subjective judgment needs to be accepted:* subjectivity is a necessary part of risk assessment. Even in quantitative risk assessments subjective judgment occurs. However, the subjectivity does not diminish the value or credibility of the risk assessment process. Safety is not an absolute state, but a relative one. Engineers, safety practitioners and decision makers need to become comfortable with subjectivity, and recognize that the subjective risk assessments do offer value.
- *Accept uncertainty*: uncertainty enters risk assessment as assumptions, estimates and subjective judgments and lack of precise information. Even in quantitative assessments there often remains substantial uncertainty. Performing a risk assessment does not create the uncertainty. Uncertainty is, and should be accepted as, an integral part of the risk assessment process.

With experience, the risk assessor learns which assessment tool is best for investigating a certain type of activity. The qualities of a good risk analysis are:

- Clear, concise, and a well-defined method that a reviewer or reader can readily understand.
- Orderly and consistent in systematically reviewing the activity or system for risk.
- A closed loop where the assessor reviews each risk control for its impact on the other risks and their controls.
- Objective in that reviewers and users can understand and verify each step of the assessment.

Paradoxically, one of the most important advantages of some risk assessment methods is meanwhile a handicap: a numerically expressed risk assessment. Of course, an approach based on figures allows prioritization, but will not be able to consider certain major aspects, such as ergonomics and psychosocial risks. Certain methods are difficult to apply, or even impossible, for chronic intoxication risk assessment, mental or physical fatigue assessment etc. In the following section, we review the relevant strengths and drawbacks of risk ranking methods, in particular the so called Kinney Method.

ADVANTAGES, LIMITATIONS AND SUBJECTIVITY IN RESORTING TO THE KINNEY METHOD OF RISK RANKING

As outlined by Honings (2000), there is already a significant time lapse since the introduction of the Kinney method, and also to other similarly structured methods, self - denominated as risk „quantification" methods, are used on large scale in the field of OHS. The goal is nonetheless to analyze, rank and prioritize the risks identified in working place. At the present, more and more experts in the field are developing a criticism in relation to the limits, pitfalls and disadvantages of this category of methods (Koob and Malchaire, 2003), which we further denominate as "Kinney–type". They are increasingly considered as incompleted, non-reliable and detaining a strong subjective character. Other experts are refining their opinions, suggesting the resort to this kind of methods only as complementary or informational tools (Main, 2002; Schwartz, 2002).

The Kinney method was first introduced in USA, being proposed by G.F. Kinney and A.D. Wiruth in a technical document of Naval Weapons Center in California, see (Kinney and Wiruth, 1976). Initially aimed at explosion risk prevention in military industry, the method was rapidly adopted in Europe, with immediate success.

We argue that, indeed, the method can be used in the risk analysis stage, but, considering the specific estimation pattern, it rather evaluates and ranks the risks in order to prioritize them. According to this method, the risk (R) assessment, is achieved considering three parameters: 1) the probability (P) of an accident or damage occurrence, 2) the exposure at risk frequency (F) and 3) the gravity (G) of the induced consequence (see Figure 5.a). The probability of the damage occurring during the exposure to a risk factor describes the accidental, stochastic and uncertain character. Kinney has defined 7 probability classes, to whom he allocated certain numerical values (see Figure 5.b). The exposure frequency expresses the time lapse in which the worker is exposed to the risk factor action; this component is estimated by one of the 6 classes, described in Figure 5.c. The size of damages is expressed by 5 gravity classes, highlighted in Figure 5.d.

Unfortunately, if the evaluation is performed by a single individual, the process will be a flawe. Therefore the need for a multidisciplinary team is obvious. Afterwards, but only after the completion of this first identification phase, will be imagined and developed the risk propagation scenarios. Based on the context setting, the numerical values will be assigned to probability, frequency and gravity; the risk level will be obtained by multiplying these three factors. The value obtained allows then to frame the risks into 5 levels, according to Figure 5.e. If the method is applied by a working team, it is strongly recommended that all the risk values are retained, an average value to be computed, discussed and interpreted within the group session.

The use of the Kinney-type methods can offer seriously differing results, for the same working place or system, if the individuals composing the team are different from one case to another. The practical use of Kinney-type methods indicates that a misuse can lead to a variable risk factor list and diverging scores, according to the competency and expertise of the assessor. On the other hand, even if the figures obtained can be useful in increasing the awareness, the quantification is limited. It gives only the appearance of a mathematical evaluation, without really having the rigour of such an approach.

Table 4 comparatively illustrates the advantages and limitations of Kinney-type methods. However, despite their inherent limitations, Kinney-type methods do possess some advantages, such as accessibility, simplicity in use and fitness for training and teaching workers basic concepts, such as probability, frequency and gravity, in a qualitative manner. Also, these methods can be ideal sensibilization tools for the workers and staff members.

It can be asserted that the main drawback of Kinney-type risk assessment methods is their subjective character. The results, expressed in figures, have a quite low representativity and do not allow the user to compare different working places or enterprises. However, as far as certain aspects are not disregarded or neglected, these methods are sound.

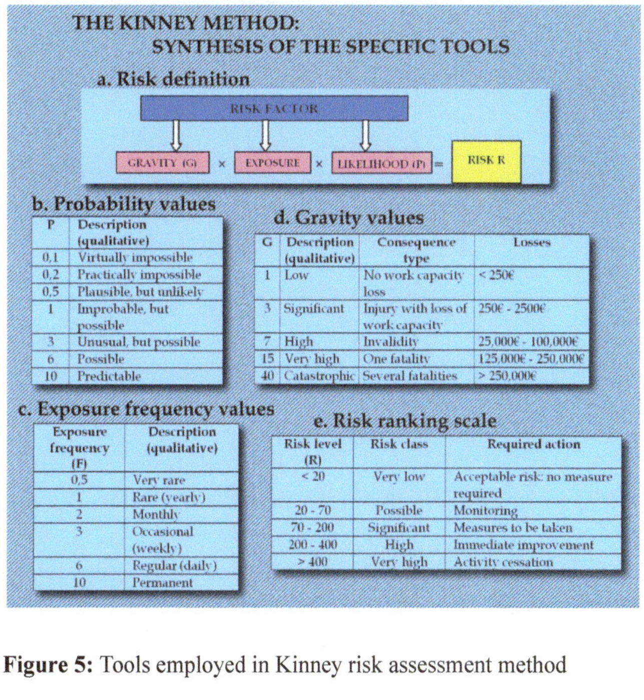

P	Description (qualitative)
0,1	Virtually impossible
0,2	Practically impossible
0,5	Plausible, but unlikely
1	Improbable, but possible
3	Unusual, but possible
6	Possible
10	Predictable

G	Description (qualitative)	Consequence type	Losses
1	Low	No work capacity loss	< 250€
3	Significant	Injury with loss of work capacity	250€ - 2500€
7	High	Invalidity	25,000€ - 100,000€
15	Very high	One fatality	125,000€ - 250,000€
40	Catastrophic	Several fatalities	> 250,000€

Exposure frequency (F)	Description (qualitative)
0,5	Very rare
1	Rare (yearly)
2	Monthly
3	Occasional (weekly)
6	Regular (daily)
10	Permanent

Risk level (R)	Risk class	Required action
< 20	Very low	Acceptable risk: no measure required
20 - 70	Possible	Monitoring
70 - 200	Significant	Measures to be taken
200 - 400	High	Immediate improvement
> 400	Very high	Activity cessation

Figure 5: Tools employed in Kinney risk assessment method

Table 4: The Kinney method: Advantages and limitations

Advantages	Limitations
Numerical	Random data
Simple in use	Cost
Risk ranking	No guarantee for risk identification quality
Allows to assess the prevention-protection measures efficiency	Subjective method (high variability of results)
Risk acceptability evaluation	Unable to council the diverging risk scores
Establish if measures are required	Confusion hazard: P, F and G inaccurately defined
Education, information, reflection	False safety feeling
Employer or financial manager persuasion	Lack of rigour: how the scores differences are interpreted?
-	Applicable just for certain risks (not psychosocial or occupational illnesses, etc)

If traditional risk management approaches have focused mainly on actions to counter hazards, modern methods are promoting actions of prediction, simulation, forecasting risk, reducing the reactive function and enhancing the preventive one. As outlined in previous work (Moraru and Băbuţ, 2010 ; Moraru et al, 2010), risk management is no longer a narrow, limited approach, targeted exclusively to restrict or control the negative effects of potential events.

Controls development and decision-making in the risk treatment stage

Risk treatment involves selecting one or more options for risk control and implement these options through an iterative process. Figure 6 shows the sequence of phases which, in its entirety, guides risk treatment stage of the risk management process.

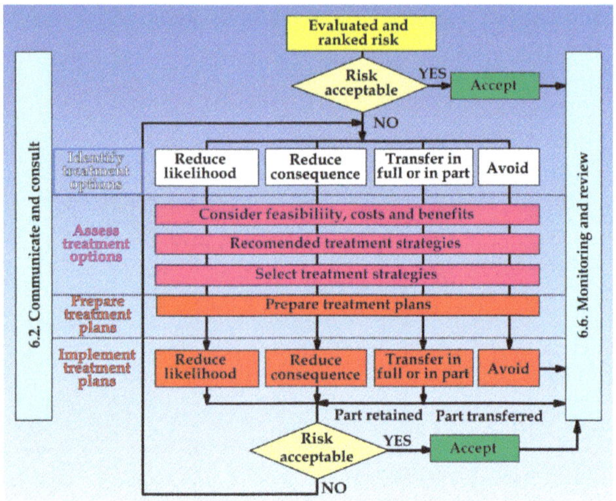

Figure 6: The structure of risk treatment stage (Adapted from AF-NOR, 2006)

After assessing each hazard, the assessor develops one or more controls that either eliminate the hazard or reduce the risk (likelihood or consequence) of a hazardous incident. A key element of the risk decision is determining if the residual risk is acceptable. The decision maker, based upon the level of risk associated with the mission, must compare and balance the risk against mission objectives. If the the risk level is too high, he or she can direct the development of additional controls or alternate controls, or can modify, change, or reject the course of action.

When developing controls, it is important to try to implement controls based on the mitigation order of precedence (ISO, 2009; Moraru, Băbuţ and Cioca, 2010;). The mitigation order of precedence is a prioritized ranking of methods for instituting countermeasures and controls, ranked by effectiveness in reducing the risk associated with an identified hazard. The mitigation order of precedence is discussed below.

- *Design to eliminate hazards*: the most effective method of controlling a hazard is to eliminate it from the system or equipment, by making fundamental changes in the design, process, system, equipment or task. Each situation must be viewed considering not only the hazard being addressed, but also the total situation. An excellent control used in another situation might seem appropriate, yet when viewed holistically in the context of the current task it not only does not work, but also introduces new hazards.
- *Incorporate safety devices*: when the hazards cannot be designed out or eliminated from the process, system or equipment, then safety devices need to be incorporated.
- *Provide warning devices*: warning devices are passive. While they provide notification that a hazardous situation exists, they require the operator to react to a given situation.
- *Develop procedures and provide training*: procedures rely upon the operator executing them. This requires initial training as well as periodic training, to ensure that the operator understands the "why" and the "how" of the procedures. They should be trained in 1) what the hazards are, 2) how to recognize the hazards and 3) what the control procedures are. If they do not understand the consequences, they are less likely to follow procedures. When implementing procedures certain factors need to be considered prior to their development, as those outlined in Table 5.
- *Selection, development and evaluation of controls*: a good understanding of the risk mechanisms facilitates effective development, selection, and prioritization of risk countermeasures and controls. The idea is to brainstorm as many controls and countermeasures as possible.
- *Decision-making:* this involves deciding which countermeasures to use, and in some special situations, requirements may dictate that the hazard and the risk be accepted due to constraints placed on the mission,

process, system, or equipment. However, when the hazard is not eliminated or controlled to tolerable limits, the organization's top management needs to decide about the acceptability of the risk based upon mission requirements. Supervision ensures that deviation from standards, complacency, or violations of policies and risk controls are not allowed to threaten safety and health of the workers (U.S. Department of Army, 2010)

The process for treating risks should be integrated with other planning and management activities at the programme, project or team level. It is important to try to link plans at this level to the corporate strategic plan where possible.

The employee must thus be the main actor - and not only the object - of prevention. This means that participation - and not only consultation - of the employees is indispensable. The successful implementation of OHS standards requires the process to be integrated into the activities of managers and supervisors at all levels of the hierarchy as well as the active participation of employees. The 'key considerations' concerning the strength of a participatory approach in the dynamic context of occupational risk management are described in Section 4, ahead of the review.

Table 5: Training procedure development: questions to address

Issue	Questions to adress
Targeted working group	What is the structure of the team? What is the at-risk team? How large is the team.
Intervention	Are the reasons for application clearly defined? Are the results repeatable?
Outcome measurement	How do we measure the effectiveness? Have measurable goals and objectives been established?
Implementation process	What are the implementation issues? Are there unresolved issues and questions?
Developing training	What factors to address in the training? How to address those factors? Does the employee need new knowledge to do the procedure? What is that new knowledge?
Leadership	Leadership must supervise their operators to enforce the standard operating procedures. If leadership does not place value and importance on them, operators will not value or implement them.

INTERVENTION STEPS IN DYNAMIC OHS RISK MANAGEMENT: THE PARTICIPATORY APPROACH

In the last decade, an increasing attention was given to participatory approach of occupational health and safety risk management (Honings, 2000; Maclagan, 1999; Malchaire, 2007, St. Vincent et al, 1998; Walters and Frick, 2000; Walters et al, 2005). By "workplace", we generally understand, in a restrictive way, the place and the conditions in which a worker has to perform a stereotyped task (Moraru & Băbuţ, 2010).

This concept seems now out-of-date and, in the new forms of work organization, the operators work in a group of workplaces, that we will call a "work situation", where they interfere the ones with the others, as depicted in Figure 7. Moreover, the behavior, satisfaction, quality of work and well-being of any worker do not depend only on the physical factors of his working environment, but also on the work organization, the responsibilities and the collective relations. The collocation "work situation", firstly introduced by (Malchaire 2007), refers to all the aspects, physical, organizational, psychological or social of the working life (Cioca and Moraru, 2010), that are likely to have an influence on the health, the behavior and the well-being of the employee, see Figure 8.

A quite realistical assumption is that knowledge from what really occurs in the work situation is decreasing from the employee to the expert. On the other hand, qualification in health and safety increases in the opposite direction (Malchaire, 2007). It thus appears logical to consider that the two sets of knowledge - about the work situation and about the principles of the well-being - are complementary. What remains is to organize a cooperation in an interdisciplinary way. Many risk assessments by OHS practitioners or external experts, are undertaken in a given time span, on a specific problem often extracted from its context. This is why they may have very little positive effects, especially if workers are not involved directly in the process.

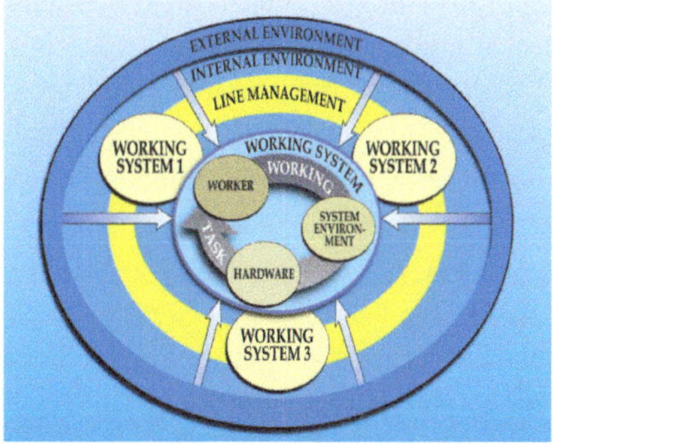

Figure 7: Graphical representation of a hypothetical working situation

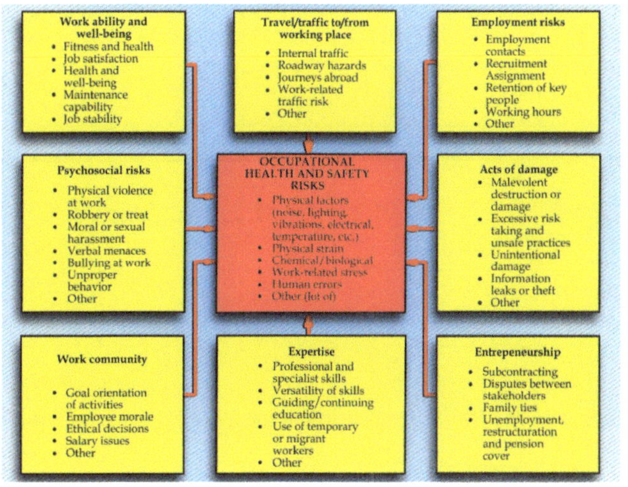

Figure 8: The complex and multifactorial landscape of OHS risks

But workers participation is only effective if the qualification of the employees concerning their work situation, and their integrity are explicitly recognized (Haines et al, 2002). The employee "sees" his work situation like a whole and not like a set of distinct and independent facts: he is "being well" or not, he enjoys his job or not. In addition, all aspects of the work situation are inter-related: the noise influences the relations between the people; the technical organization between workstations influences the risks for musculoskeletal disorders; the division of the responsibilities influences the work content, the accidents, etc.

The prevention approach consists in seeking the most effective means to reduce the risk, by acting on one or several of its components: elimination of the risk factor, reduction of the exposure, increase of the reliability of the work system. It is thus essential that the analysis of the risk be not simply a recording of its components, but consisting of a careful analysis of the reasons of the exposure, the circumstances of this exposure, the severity of the consequences and the most useful means to reduce them. The final quantitative evaluation of the risk is consequently secondary, the most important thing being to study the components and the details on which it is going to be possible to act. Rather than speaking about risk assessment, it is thus more appropriate to speak about risk management.

Although all the problems are inter-dependent, it is neither realistic nor possible to solve all of them at once. Considering the Swiss-cheese accident model (see Figure 9) and the spirit and structure of the Sobane strategy (see Figure 10), developed by Malchaire (2007) the first stage (called Screening) consists, for example, in replacing a defective tool, improving the ventilation system or modifying a hierarchical relation. Even if such a simple measure is essential, it is not sufficient because the primary latent causes were not eliminated and the situation can return to the initial defective state.

The second stage (Observation) can consist in reexamining the general work organization, the institutional links between people or in rearranging the operating area. Perhaps a third stage will relate to the workers training (Analysis): vocational training to perform the tasks, education to their well-being, leading them to recognize themselves the problems, to manage them directly as they arise, bringing the employees to a degree of self-management of their health, safety and well-being to work. Maybe a next stage (Expertise) will relate to the culture of the company, the integration of the concerns of well-being in the overall management of the company.

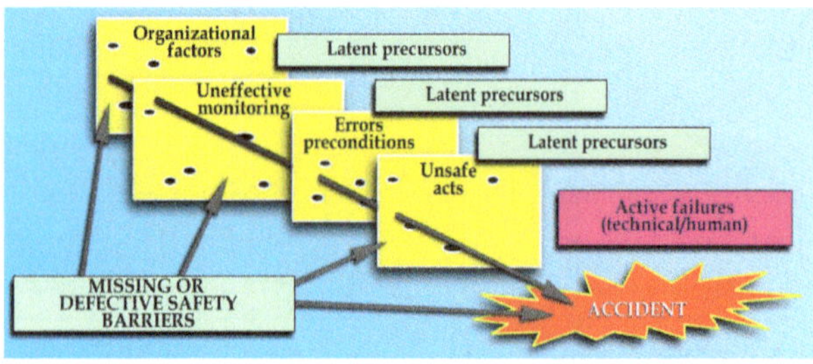

Figure 9: The Swiss cheese accident model (Adapted from Reason, 1993)

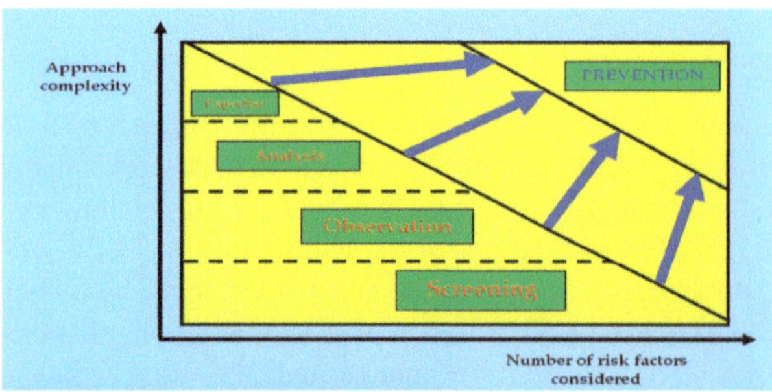

Figure 10: General layout of the Sobane risk management strategy (Based on Malchaire, 2007)

The knowledge, information and data necessary during the first steps relate primarily to the work situation. Knowledge in ergonomics, medicine and safety is certainly desirable to select the good tool or to ventilate more effectively, but is less essential than the knowledge of the work situation. This first step must therefore be carried out as close as possible of the work situation and its output will be especially a function of intimate knowledge of what occurs in the course of time in this work situation.

Conversely, at a more advanced step of the process, the problems require more qualification in work organization, training or management. The analysis must be finer, more specific and requires tools and competences that only OHS practitioners generally have. According to the step, the necessary competences will thus rather be those of an OHS practitioner or of the workers themselves, these remaining the main actors of the prevention, for whom and by whom prevention is implemented.

In our attempt to highlight the future trends in OHS risk management, we will focus in the next section on two epistemological assumptions existing in the field, presently valid in complex socio – technical systems. Epistemological issues determine how we see the world and is hence of fundamental importance. Our aim is to emphasize that contrary to common beliefs, the positivism and the constructivism are complementary and not competeing.

TOWARDS COMPLEMENTARITY OF POSITIVISM AND CONSTRUCTIVISM IN OHS RISK MANAGEMENT

Risk management within complex socio - technical systems must be subordinated to the objectives that form an integrated, coherent system and converging to the overall objectives, so that levels of activity to be mutually supportive (Emmet and Hickling, 1995). Operational safety techniques in use did not appear, indeed, though it seems paradoxical, until during the Second World War, with the emergence of complex systems, which encompass a large number of components. The '60s have brought new techniques for identifying risks, following the deductive or inductive approaches. In the '70s, great efforts have been made to assess risks to populations near nuclear facilities, being developed many scenarios of accidents related to equipment failures and/or operational errors. In the following decades, methods and techniques of risk assessment and control were widely spread in various industries and now enter new sectors (health, food, water treatment, etc.), including in Romania, following the harmonization of the national legislation with the European Union.

As depicted in Figure 11, technical risks are related to the main features of operational safety. Technical risk control covers all methods, means, analysis, procedures and measures applied throughout the life cycle, to remove or render acceptable the identified risks.

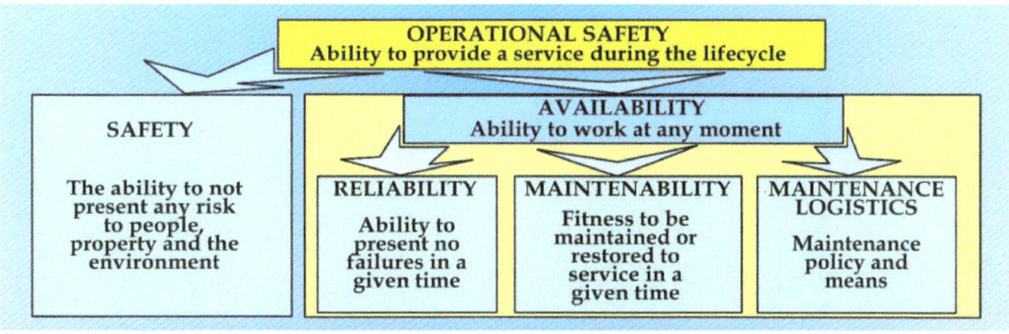

Figure 11: Operational safety components within a complex socio - technical system

As discussed before, the omnipresence of uncertainty about the reliability of data used, adopted measures to limit or minimize the consequences likely to materialize, the degree of subjectivity of the assessments are rending particularly difficult a precise formalization of applied assessment and decision – making procedures. Moreover, we find very often that the existing level of expertise itself is an area of experimentation. Most times, between policy makers and technicians, OHS practitioners and economists, there is a fundamental degree of independence. For various reasons, one can minimize the real risks, for example by overpricing available technological level, leading to a dogmatic extreme reaction (by ignoring his own ignorance) or because of reasons that we might euphemistically call "inconspicuous". Precaution and prevention is a step fall in anticipation of risk. Precaution can be understood as extending prevention methods applied in the field of uncertainty. Precaution and prevention are thus two sides of prudence that is required to reduce the occurrence of situations likely to cause losses to humans, property and environment.

Until recently, the safety of complex systems were addressed in a manner called "positivist" (Journe, 1997), which is to control risks during the design stage. Developed specifically by engineers and ergonomists, this approach considers technology as 1) a real phenomenon ("ontological principle"), 2) having an existence outside the subject that one observes and implements (principle of objectivity"), 3) having a fixed operation and successful law of his own ("wired universe principle"), 4) which leads to an optimal solution ("single optimum principle") (Le Moigne, 1990 b). It is considered that the reliability and safety of a system can be developed by acting on technology, on the working environment and on the proper definition of procedures to follow. The human factor is often identified as "the weak link" element, which reduces overall system reliability, as "a black box capable of unpredictable and irrational behaviour, the origin of the errors, failures and shortcomings" (Journe, 1997). The operator has only a small margin of action or response to an organizational and technical reality which is external to him, because it was set a priori by those who designed the system.

Following the serious incidents that have occurred mainly in the nuclear field (e.g. Three Mile Island in 1979, Chernobyl in 1986 etc), there have been strongly emphasized the limits of such an approach. Due to the ever increasing complexity of systems studied, it becomes obvious the impossibility to predict all possible accident scenarios.

A complementary approach, called "constructivist" was therefore proposed (Le Moigne, 1990a; Theys, 1991, Journe, 1997). This one, considers technique as 1) a construction ("principle of the built universe"), 2) including the subject which tries to control it, through the intermediate of his own representation ("projection and representation principles"), 3) having a complex operation that can not be broken down into simple, independent elements and 4) which can only lead to more or less satisfactory solutions ("principle of intelligent action"). This approach leverages operators role in the complex socio – technical systems reliability and security, seeking to benefit as much of their intelligence and capacity to respond to new situations. Founded on "safety culture" and developing the spirit of initiative within organizations, at the opposite of the quasi-military discipline required in the positivist tradition, this approach gives the central role to the individual and is subject of the "organizational communication" (Zohar, 2010).

In opposition to the positivist conception, the constructivist approach considers that the reliability is, above all, a social and organizational construction, which is the final output of the symbolic representations that operators develop together, in action. From this perspective, safety conditions lies, particularly, in organizational and human variables. This organization's ability to remedy failures would be particularly related to a clear definition of each individual's role and a strong personal responsibility. We argue that this approach can be extended to any kind organization, even to small and medium enterprises, to properly manage the OHS risks, following a conceptual model as the one described in Figure 12.

Safety is considered both as 1) a non-event because the result of a safe state is invisible through nature (nothing happens when the situation is under control) and 2) a dynamic state because a seemingly stable system conceals intense internal activity, requiring vigilance and anticipation capacity of the operator. Thus defined, safety is an issue of interaction, development and management of the representations that will give a sense to the situations experienced by operators. It is obvious that, from this perspective, the role of safety culture and climate is ever increasing.

In this constructivist approach, risk control means, above all, the operators ability to anticipate and recover abnormal situations. It requires the skill of the actors to understand the environment in which they work, based on their own experiences, the meaning of various stimuli perceived. It is the product reached through cognitive operations and not the result of a pre-existing sense, independent of themselves. The constructivist approach also put emphasis on the performance of involved actors and the role of everyday communication; it considers communication as part of a process of organizational structure. We would like to outline that this is also consistent with ISO 31000:2009 standard.

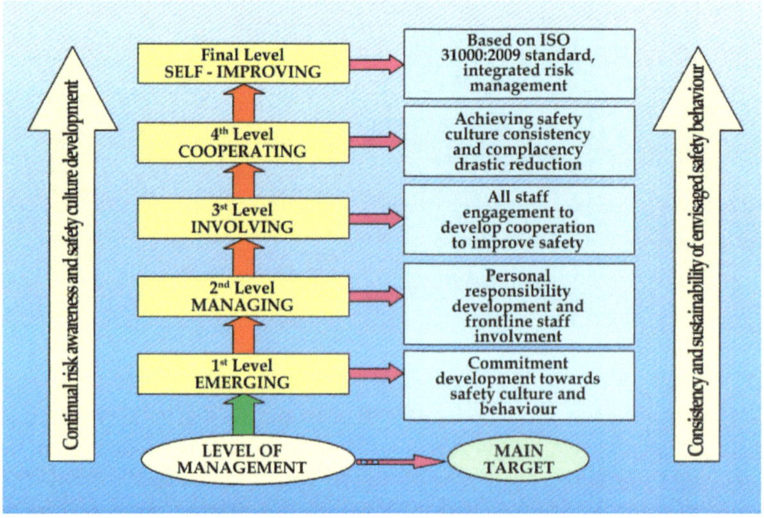

Figure 12: A constructivist conceptual model for OHS risk management

On the other hand, there is always an unexplored ethical dimension over and above the list of causes of occupational accidents. This can result in a cascade of bad decisions being taken at the organizational, human and technical levels, which cause tragic accidents, often with loss of human life. To manage risks properly, it will not only be necessary to develop techniques but also to develop processes, at the personnel level as well as at the organizational level, which will take human nature into account. There is indeed a real difficulty to forecast the operator's representations and reactions, in a context that develop a growing public distrust in the complex high-risk organizations, such as for example nuclear power plants. Positivist and constructivist visions of operational safety, which initially appeared in an opposite, even irreconcilable, may be complementary, we believe, in the minds of some players, including designers of new systems that would like to associate quality in design with operators professionalism, to limit risks to a level still untouched.

CLOSURE

This paper reviews the main strands of literature and proposes a framework of steps in good OHS management. It offers a number of suggestions of good practice and illustrates a number of the dilemmas. It also considers that the approach based on ISO 31000:2009 Standard is of paramount importance and may represent a step forward to managing safety, but may not be enough to address the management of risk effectively. There is a need to adopt a systemic approach to safety management. Systemic may be defined as trying to see things as a whole and attempting to see events, including failure, as products of a working of a system and, within that, see fatality/injury/property loss, etc as results of the working of systems. Companies that have applied risk management for many years recognize that the change to a "culture of prevention" via "systematic and comprehensive risk management" involves a journey.

On the other hand, risk assessment and risk management should be described more fully, recognizing that some companies are currently going well beyond the minimum level of practice that is described here. From this perspective also, we consider that the ISO 31000:2009 Standard can be seen as a milestone. Risk management should try to change everyone's mind set toward proactive, empowered, systems oriented thinking. Risk management should become a continuous process of learning from past experiences.

What is extremely important in seeking to achieve effective risk management is an ongoing consolidation of an organizational culture of risk. Risk management is incompatible with attitudes such as "leave it, that goes like this too", "someone else looks after, I shouldn't worry", "we shall live and see", "devil is not quite so black as it seems", "this is a fatality" etc. Risk management is the assumed accountability. This is the difficult problem in the way of implementing effective risk management and not learning the terminology and techniques.

Learning from the past is crucial in making progress. Yet, there are obstacles of various nature such as 1) human factors, 2) technical complexities of how to store and retrieve information, restraints to knowledge management, and last but not least 3) policy and decision making in view of cost–benefit. Over the last decade, wide interest in the role of behaviour has led to the development of numerous safety climate tools and behavioural modification programmes. It must be emphasised that behavioural approaches should not be seen as the panacea for all safety problems. Behaviour modification is not an alternative to sound safety management policies, systems and procedures. However, when these are well established and functioning effectively, behaviour modification can play an important role in achieving further improvements in safety performance.

Also, the move towards continuous management and learning demands participation from employees. Often, however, initiatives are imposed from above. Creativity and initiatives from the shop floor to improve are stifled in such a climate. A different approach is required to encourage further improvement.

This next step involves taking action to ensure that the behaviours of people at all levels within the organisation are consistent with an improving safety culture Once rules become more conceptual and goal-oriented, rather than prescriptive, this cannot work. Nor can it work if the technology is changing or there are many abnormal situations to be coped with. It is hard to have an expert around all the time to make up new rules or modify old ones. The only other alternative is to delegate the rule-making and changing to the work group. Participatory methods are increasingly utilized in improving risk management of work and workplaces. The merits of these methods are widely recognized as a means of promoting initiative of local people and achieving workable solutions. A notable merit is that they contribute to improving various forms of workplaces in their diverse conditions. The influence, though still low, of constructivism allow actors to assign a contextual re-creation and permanent interaction capacity with the working system. Unfortunately, we find that this vision strikes with numerous and powerful resistance, both inside and outside the organization.

The in-depth analysis of the dynamic policy of risk management resulted in proposing a participatory strategy whose purpose is 1) to gradually approach the work situations, 2) to coordinate the cooperation between employees, management and OHS practitioners and 3) to arrive faster and less expensively to effective prevention.

If we put together all of the trends sketched in this chapter, they add up to an improvement in the way OHS is, or should be, managed compared to a decade ago. With an increasingly complex structure of society, trade and industry, communication, political and administrative systems, technical systems and technological change etc, it is getting more and more important to relate to different ethical and political arguments to keep an image of being in control and for being trusted. There is a need for developing a mechanism for a path between the positivistic and rational choice founding of risk assessment and the richness of perceptions and judgements of risk issues. The best answers to risk issues are reached by exposing risk assessments and decisions to intelligent debate, criticism, and amendment by the scientific community and the workers likely to be affected by the risk.

The preliminart conclusion of this work is also an outlook to the future. Although there are many signs of renewed interest in questions regarding OHS risk management , the road to a more full implementation of "premises for risk management" is long and there are many obstacles. One of the main issues to be resolved is how to decide on differing levels of risk depending on the nature of the activity and the importance or benefits of the activity for society.

REFERENCES

1. Association Francaise de Normalization, AFNOR, (2006). Management du risque – Approche globale, ISBN 2-12-169211-8, Saint-Juste-la-Pendue, France
2. Ayers, G. (2007). Encouraging meaningful and effective consultation about occupational health and safety (OHS) in the construction industry: a recognition of workforce competence. Retrieved June 2011 from: http://web-safety.com/kosha/SY38-03.pdf
3. Blockley, D. (1992). Engineering Safety, McGraw-Hill, London, UK.
4. Bourrier M. (1998). Elements for designing a self-correcting organisation: examples from nuclear plants. In Hale A.R.& Baram M. Safety management: the challenge of change. Pergamon. Oxford.
5. Cioca, L.I. & Moraru, R.I. (2010). Psychosocial Occupational Risk Management, (in Romanian), "Lucian Blaga", Publishing House, ISBN 978-973-739-924-3, Sibiu, Romania
6. Cox, S. & Flin, R., 1998. Safety culture: philosopher's stone or man of straw? Work & Stress 12 (3), 189–201.
7. Deming, W.E. (1982). Out of the Crisis, Center for Advanced Engineering Study, ISBN 0- 911379-01-0, Cambridge: MIT Press
8. Emmett, E. & Hickling, C. (1995). Integrating Management Systems and Risk Management Approaches. J. of Occupational Health and Safety – Aust. NZ , 11(6), 617–624
9. Haines, H., Wilson, J.R.,Vink, P. & Koningsveld, E. (2002). Validating a framework for participatory ergonomics. Ergonomics vol 45, nr. 4, pp. 309-327
10. Honings, C. (2000). Complémentarité des méthodes Kinney et d'analyse participative des risques, Travail & Bien-être n°5, décembre 2000, pp. 29-32.
11. Hudson P.T.W. (2003) Aviation safety culture. Journal of Aviation Management, issue 3, 27–48.
12. ISO (2009). ISO 31000:2009 Risk management -- Principles and guidelines, International Organization for Standardization, Available from: www.iso.org
13. Journe, B. (1997) Positivisme et constructivisme dans la gestion de surete et de la fiabilite des centrales nucleaires, Constructivisme et Sciences de gestion, Lille, 23 octobre.
14. Joy, J. & Griffiths, D (2004). National minerals industry safety and health risk assessment guideline, version 3, March, MCA and MISHC, Australia, Retrieved November 2008 at www.planning.nsw.gov.au.
15. Kinney, G.F. & Wiruth, A.D. (1976) Practical risk analysis for safety management, Naval Weapons Center, California, SUA.
16. Koob, J.-P. & Malchaire, J. (2003). Fiabilité de la méthode Kinney d'analyse des risques, Essai sur un chantier de pose de conduites enterrées, Université catholique de Louvain, Unité Hygiène et Physiologie du Travail.
17. Lave, L. B. & Balvanyos, T. (1998). Risk Analysis and Management of Dam Safety, Risk Analysis, Volume 18, , pp. 455-462.
18. Le Moigne, J-L. (1990a). Epistemologies constructivistes et sciences de l'organisation, în Martinet, A.C., Epistemologies et Sciences De Gestion, Paris, Economics.
19. Le Moigne, J-L. (1990b). La modelisation des systemes complexes, Paris, Dunod.
20. Main, B.W. (2002). Risk Assessment is Coming. Are You Ready? Professional Safety ,47(7) , pp. 32–37
21. Maclagan, P. (1999) Corporate social responsibility as a participative process, Business Ethics: A European Review, Vol. 8 (1), pp. 43-49.
22. Malchaire, J. (2007). Stratégie SOBANE et guide de dépistage DEPARIS, Service public fédéral Emploi,

Travail et Concertation Sociale, UCL, Retrieved September 2010 at www.sobane.be

23. Moraru, R. & Băbuț, G. (2010). Participative risk assessment and management: a practical guide,(in Romanian), ISBN 978-973-677-206-1, Focus Publishing House, Petroşani, Romania

24. Moraru R.I., Băbuț G.B. & Cioca L.I. (2010). Adressing the human error assessment and management, Archives of Mining Sciences, Vol.55 (2010), No.4, pp.873-878.

25. Pasman, H.J. (2009). Learning from the past and knowledge management: Are we making progress? Journal of Loss Prevention in the Process Industries vol.22, pp.672–679

26. Reason, J. (1993). L'erreur humaine, Paris: Presses Universitaire de France

27. Reason, J. (1995). A system approach to organisational error. Ergonomics, vol. 38, nr. 8, pp. 1708-1721.

28. Romanian Parliament (2006). The 319/2006 Act on Occupational Health and Safety, Oficial Monitor of Romania, Part I, nr. 646/26.07.2006

29. Sage, A. P. & White, E. B., (1980). Methodologies for Risk and Hazard Assessment: A Survey and Status Report, IEEE Transactions on Systems, Man and Cybernetics, SMC-10(8), pp. 425-445.

30. Swartz, G. (2002). Job Hazard Analysis. A Primer on Identifying Hazards. Professional Safety, 47(11), pp. 27–33.

31. Smith, D (2008). Implementing the new BSI code of practice on risk management (BS31100) in the Public Sector, ALARM Scotland Conference, Bournemouth, Retrived July 2011 from : http://www. theirm. org/ events/ documents /IRMNoSGroup DougSmith PresentationNov08.pdf

32. St.Vincent, M., Chicoine, D.&Beaugrand, S. (1998). Validation of a participatory ergonomic approach in industries in the electrical sector. Int J Ind Ergonomics, vol. 21, pp. 11-21.

33. Standards Australia & Standards New Zealand (2004). Risk management, AS/NZS 4360/2004 Available from https://infostore.saiglobal.com/store

34. Theys, J. (1991). Conquete de la securite, gestion des risques, Paris: L'Harmattan, p.279-298.

35. U.S. Department of Army (2010). Safety Mishap Risk Management, DA-PAM 385-30, Retrieved August, 2011 from http://www.apd.army.mil/pdffiles/p385_30.pdf

36. Walters, D, & Frick, K. (2000). Worker participation and the management of occupational health and safety: reinforcing or conflicting strategies? Cht.3, in Systematic occupational health and safety management; perspectives on an international development (ed by Frick, K., Jensen, P., L., Quinlan, M., & Wilthagen, T.), Pergamon, Amsterdam.

37. Walters, D., Nichols, T., Connor, J., Tasiran, A. C. & Cam, S. (2005). The role and effectiveness of safety representatives in influencing workplace health and safety, Health and Safety Executive, Retrieved April 2011 from http://hse.gov.uk.research/rrhtm/rr363.htm

38. Zohar, D. (1980). Safety climate in industrial organizations: theoretical and applied implications. Journal of Applied Psychology 65/1980, pp. 96–102.

39. Zohar, D. & Luria, G., (2004). Climate as a social-cognitive construction of supervisory safety practices: scripts as proxy of behavior patterns. Journal of Applied Psychology 89/2004, pp.322–333.

CHAPTER 4

A SAFETY ENGINEERING PERSPECTIVE

Derek Fowler and Ronald Pierce

INTRODUCTION

Safety is a viewpoint. By this we mean that safety is not in itself an attribute of a system but is a property that depends on other attributes and on the context in which the system is used. The question that arises (and which we will attempt to answer in some detail) is which attributes of a system determine whether it is safe or not, in its context of use.

Throughout this chapter, the term *system* is used in the widest sense - ie it includes not just the technical elements (equipment) but also all other elements - eg the human-operator and operational procedures - that necessarily make up the complete, end-to-end system.

We will start by attempting to dispel what seems to be a not-infrequent misconception (also reflected in some safety standards) that safety is mainly dependent on reliability (and / or integrity, depending on one's definition of the terms - see section 3.1 below). This we feel is important for those readers who may have had some previous exposure to areas of safety engineering in which this view is held and will lead to the inescapable conclusion that we need a broader view of system safety than is sometimes taken.

Next we will establish some basic safety concepts firstly by defining key terms, and then by considering two distinct categories of safety-related system and seeing how the system properties determine safety in each case.

Finally, and for the most part of this Chapter, we will explain how the broader approach to safety works and show that it is closely linked with (not 'special and different' from) systems engineering in general.

Citation: Derek Fowler and Ronald Pierce (2012). A Safety Engineering Perspective, Systems Engineering - Practice and Theory, Prof. Boris Cogan (Ed.), InTech, DOI: 10.5772/32113.

"SAFETY IS RELIABILITY" – DISPELLING A MYTH

[Leveson, 2001] in a review of major software-related accidents and the implication for software reliability, presents compelling evidence that software reliability had never been the cause of such disasters - on the contrary, in every case investigated, the software had performed in exactly the manner that it was designed to. The problem was that the software was designed to do the wrong thing for the circumstances under which it "failed" (or, as in the case of Ariane V, for example) was used for a purpose (ie in a context - see above) different from that for which it was originally designed. Professor Leveson quite rightly, therefore, poses the question as to why, in most software safety standards, so much emphasis is placed on processes to improve software reliability whilst not ensuring also that the resulting systems actually perform the intended function – ie allowing them to be what one might call "reliably unsafe". This same misconception is prevalent also at the system level in, for example, European Air Traffic Management (ATM) - see [Fowler, 2007].

We can illustrate the problem by considering the simple, everyday example of a car airbag for which, for the sake of this discussion, we wish to make a case that it would be safe.

If we were to simply follow a failure-based process - ie focus on how reliable the airbag needs to be in order to be 'safe' - we would start (at the wrong point, as we will see shortly) by identifying the hazards[1] presented by the airbag. Such hazards are those caused by the airbag's two main failure modes: failure to operate when required, and operating when not required. We would then use a risk classification scheme to derive safety requirements that specify the maximum frequency with which those failures could be allowed to occur and from that we would deduce more detailed safety requirements which limit the frequency with which the causes of the hazards could be allowed to occur.

Even if the results were valid, they would lead us only to:

- an understanding of how reliable the airbag needs to be - so that it operates when required; this would, however, not give any assurance that, when it did operate, the airbag would actually protect the front-seat occupants from death or serious injury in the event of a collision, and

- the totally irrational conclusion that putting an airbag in a car would only increase the risk of death or serious injury to the front-seat occupants, because of the finite (albeit small) possibility that it would operate when not intended to!

Of course, what is missing is any evidence of a positive safety contribution from the airbag - only the possibility of actually being killed / seriously injured by it - without which we would have no case for fitting one.

If instead we were to take a more rational view, we would start from the position that in the event of, say, a head-on collision without an airbag there is a very high risk of death or serious injury to the driver (and other front-seat occupant(s)) of a car. This risk we can call *pre-existing* because, by definition, it is inherent in driving and has nothing whatsoever to do with the airbag – indeed it is to mitigate this risk that we are intending to fit the airbag in the first place. So, the more rational approach would be to:

- firstly assess how effective the airbag would be when it did work – ie by how much the *pre-existing* risk from driving would be reduced by the airbag - and what properties of the airbag determine the amount of this reduction; and then
- assess the *system-generated* risk, induced by airbag failure

Thus, given the correct set of functional properties – eg shape, location, strength, compressibility, sensitivity to 'g' forces, speed of deployment etc – as well as adequate reliability and integrity, our safety case should show that the airbag would make a positive contribution to the reduction in the identified pre-existing risk that is very much greater than the system-generated risk due to airbag failure. This would be a much more balanced, and rational conclusion than what emerged above from considering only airbag failure.

SYSTEM SAFETY – BASIC CONCEPTS

Definitions

This section defines the safety terms that are used in the rest of this chapter. In most cases, as there is no single, universally accepted definition, the ones given below have been adapted from those in Part 4 of international functional-safety standard IEC 61508 [IEC, 2010] and, if not actually used by, should at least be understood in, any safety-related sector.

- *Harm* death or serious physical injury or damage to the health of people, or serious damage to property or the environment
- *Hazard* a situation, state or event that may result in harm2
- *Risk* combination of the frequency of occurrence and severity of harm
- S*afety* freedom from unacceptable risk
- *Reliability* the ability of a system / element to provide a long period of continuous delivery of an intended service (or function) without failure
- *Integrity* the ability of a system, under all stated conditions, to provide all the services (or functions) required by the users, with no unintended or un-commanded services (or functions)
- *Failure* termination of the ability of a functional unit to provide a required function or operation of a functional unit in any way other than as required

Risk acceptability

The ALARP principle

Risk may, in extremis, be either so great that it would be intolerable under any circumstances or so small as to be insignificant and therefore may be discounted altogether. In practice, however, risk will usually fall somewhere between these two extremes and the ALARP principle requires that any risk shall be reduced to a level that is as low as reasonably practicable, bearing in mind two factors: the benefits resulting from its acceptance, and the costs of any further reduction. ALARP is described in more detail in IEC 61508 [IEC, 2010], Part 5, Annex C; other standards and practices use different acronyms such as ALARA (USA) and SFAIRP (Aus). In the UK, the ALARP principle has a specific legal connotation and expert advice should be sought before applying it! [Ladkin, 2008].

A practical way of specifying what tolerable risk is, and in some cases applying the ALARP principle, either qualitatively or quantitatively, is the so-called Risk Classification Scheme (also known as a Hazard-Risk Index).

Risk Classification Schemes

Risk Classification Schemes (RCSs) are used in a number of industry sectors. Their form is as variable as their usage but a typical example, from the ATM sector [EUROCONTROL 2010], is shown in Figure 1.

An RCS is typically set out as a matrix, in which the severity of possible outcomes is mapped against the frequency with which the outcomes might occur.

		Severity Class			
Probability per flt hr		1	2	3	4
Frequent	$P>10^{-4}$	A	A	A	B
Probable	$P<10^{-4}$	A	A	A	C
Occasional	$P<10^{-5}$	A	A	B	D
Remote	$P<10^{-6}$	A	B	C	D
Improbable	$P<10^{-7}$	A	C	D	D
Extremely Improbable	$P<10^{-8}$	B	D	D	D

Figure 1: A Risk Classification Scheme

In this ATM example, the severity of outcome ranges from Class 1 (an accident involving death and/or serious injury[3]) to Class 4 (the lowest level of safety-significant incident) and, in practice, would be explained by detailed descriptions and illustrative examples. The frequency of outcome is shown both qualitatively and quantitatively, as the probability per flight hour (or per operating hour). The grid is populated with the tolerability / acceptability of the risk and, in this example, includes the ALARP principle[4] as follows:

- Risk Class A is defined as intolerable
- Risk Class B is tolerable only if risk reduction is impracticable or cost grossly disproportionate to improvement
- Risk Class C is tolerable if cost of risk reduction would exceed the benefit of improvement
- Risk Class D is defined as broadly acceptable

An RCS should be tailored to the purpose and function of the system or service concerned and the risks and benefits involved. It would normally be published in the Safety Management System for the organization responsible for the operation, and be approved by the relevant safety-regulatory authority. It can be used in one of two ways:

- for safety monitoring of an on-going operation (see section 6.5 below) - in this case the achieved risk can be compared with what is tolerable / acceptable according to the RCS, and / or
- for *a priori* safety assessment - in this case the severity of each potential outcome is assessed and the required maximum frequency of occurrence, in order to achieve an acceptable (or at least tolerable) level of risk, is obtained from the RCS.

One of the main attractions of RCSs is that they are relatively simple to use - and therein lies a potential problem, unless each user it careful to check the following:

- at what level in the system hierarchy, and within what scope, the values apply
- where the probability / frequency values used in the scheme came from and whether they are appropriate and (still) valid
- how the aggregate risk can be deduced from analysis of individual hazards, in restricted segments of the total system
- what allowance needs to be made for pre-existing risk - see also section 3.3.3 below.

The significance of some, if not all, of these 'health warnings' should become more apparent in the subsequent sections of this chapter.

Safety-related systems and their properties

Safety-related systems – General

Consider the two types of safety-related system (SRS) shown in Figure 2. Case (a) is a system - say, a complete nuclear power plant - which simply provides a service into its operational environment. Because the service in the case of a nuclear power plant is the provision of electrical power then, from a purely safety viewpoint, we do not care whether the service is provided or not. What we do care about are the hazards (eg radiation leakage), and the related level of risk, that a failure internal to the system might present to its operational environment (and to the people therein).

Case (b) is quite different. Here we have, first of all, a set of hazards that already exist in the operational environment. If, for example, the System was our car airbag (see section 2 above) then these hazards (and associated risks) would be those (*pre-existing*) hazards / risks inherent in driving a car, and the operational environment (from the airbag's perspective) would be the whole car.

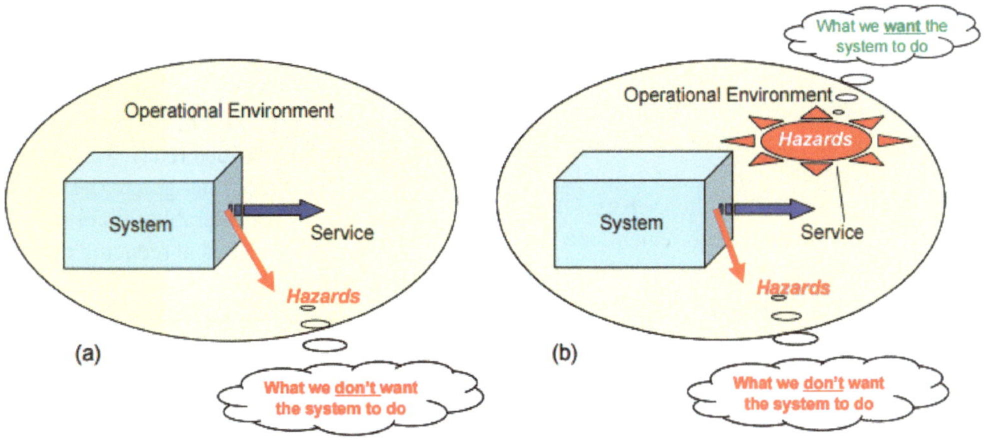

Figure 2: Two types of Safety related System

As we will see in more detail in section 3.3.3 below, what is very important about Figure 2 is that for case (b) the mitigation of *pre-existing* hazards / risks (ie what we want the system to do) and the inevitable introduction of *system-generated* hazards / risks (ie what we don't want the system to do) depend on entirely different properties of the system.

Before that, however, we will introduce IEC 61508 [IEC, 2010], probably the most widely accepted, international standard on the functional safety of systems.

IEC 61508

IEC 61508 has a particular model of how SRSs influence the real world that is based on the concept of the *Equipment under Control* (EUC) which itself is regarded as the hazard-creating system[5] and for which SRS are designed in order to mitigate those hazards [Pierce & Fowler, 2010]. Since IEC 61508 is a generic standard, to be adapted for application to a wide range of specific industry sectors, it has no particular view on the nature of the EUC, which could be a nuclear reactor, a chemical plant, an oil rig, a train, a car, or an aircraft etc[6].

The standard then defines two types of SRS that are intended to mitigate the hazards and risks associated with the EUC:

- *Control Systems* (eg a railway signaling system) which provide *Safety Functions* that are designed to maintain continuously a tolerable level of risk for the EUC, and
- *Protection Systems* (eg an automatic train protection (ATP) system or car airbag) which provide *Safety Functions* that are designed to intervene when they detect a hazardous state developing within the EUC and/or its Control System(s), and put the EUC / its Control System(s) into a safe, or at least safer, state[7].

As far as a Control System is concerned, the hazards and risks associated with its EUC are clearly *pre-existing*, since they are caused by the latter not the former. Similarly, the hazards and risks associated with the combination of an EUC and its Control System(s) are pre-existing as far as a Protection System is concerned.

With this concept, an SRS (Control and/or Protection system) is put in place to reduce the pre-existing risks to an acceptable level. IEC 61508 refers to this as *Necessary Risk Reduction* but does not actually stipulate what is "acceptable", this being left to local or national considerations, including legal frameworks, for the applicable industry sector.

As we will see in section 3.3.3 below, safety integrity requirements on Control Systems are usually expressed as probability of failure per operating hour, whereas for Protection Systems they are usually expressed as probability of failure on demand. In either case, the target probability will of course depend on the level of the pre-existing risk. The objective of the SRS for Control and Protection systems is *risk control* and *risk reduction* respectively[8].

In both cases, IEC 61508 is quite clear that the safety functional requirements (specifying functionality and performance of the Safety Functions) must be completely and correctly identified before the SRS can be designed. This requires hazard and risk analysis of the EUC not (initially at least) hazard and risk analysis of the SRS(s) themselves. Once the safety functionality and performance requirements of the Safety Functions have been identified, the tolerable failure rates of the Safety Functions can then be identified, and the Safety Integrity Level (SIL) for each Safety Function established[9].

Safety properties

We can build on our simple example of a car airbag to explain more generically, and develop, the above principles since it can readily be seen that an airbag fits Figure 2 case (b), and the IEC concept of a Protection System, very well. Figure 3 shows the risk, in the Operational Environment (or EUC), with and without an SRS – ie R_U and R_A respectively. As we saw for the airbag in section 2 above, the safety case for the SRS depends on its making a (much) bigger positive contribution to safety when operating as intended (ie the *success* case as represented by the green, right-to-left arrow) than any negative contribution caused by its failure or incorrect / spurious operation (ie the *failure* case as represented by the solid red, left-to-right arrow).

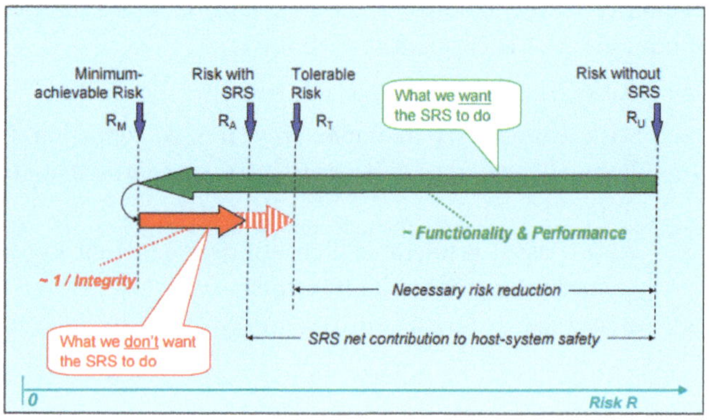

Figure 3: Risk Graph for a Safety-related System

There are a number of very important points to note about this diagram:

- R_U has nothing to do with the SRS – ie it is the pre-existing risk, as above
- R_M is the theoretical minimum risk that would exist in the complete absence of failure / spurious operation of the SRS – it is not zero, because there usually are some accident scenarios for which an SRS cannot provide mitigation[10]
- since R_M is defined as the risk in the absence of failure, it must be determined only by the functionality & performance of the SRS, as explained in section 2 above
- the risk increase R_A-R_M is caused entirely by failure / spurious operation of the SRS - thus it is the system-generated risk and is determined primarily[11] by the reliability & integrity of the SRS
- the safety case for the SRS is based on showing that $R_A \ll R_U$
- if we now introduce RT, the maximum tolerable level of risk, then an interesting conclusion emerges: given that R_T is fixed (eg by a regulatory body), then the maximum tolerable failure rate of the SRS - ie a function of the length of the extended red (l-r) arrow (R_T-R_M) - depends on the length of the green (r-l) arrow (R_U-R_M); in other words, the tolerable failure rate depends on how successful the SRS is in reducing the preexisting risk in the first place
- overall, R_U-R_T fits the IEC 61508 definition of Necessary Risk Reduction
- if, as we desire, $R_A-R_M \ll R_U-R_M$ then the overall risk actually achieved (ie R_A) is much more sensitive to changes in the length of the green (r-l) arrow (ie to changes in functionality and performance) than to proportionate changes in the length of the red (lr) arrow (ie to changes in reliability & integrity).

We can also see from Figure 3 that in the limit that R_M approaches R_T, so the integrity required of the SRS approaches infinity! This raises further important questions regarding the origins and use of traditional risk-classification schemes, which are often are based entirely on R_T and do not take any account of R_M in setting tolerable failure rates for a system. As we saw in section 3.2.2 above, RCSs generally model only the system's negative effects on safety, not its positive contributions and, therefore, to get a more complete picture of where risks lie in a system we need to turn to more sophisticated forms of risk modelling.

Risk modelling

One of the systems engineering techniques that is commonly used for the static modelling of risk in a safety assessment is Fault Tree Analysis (FTA) [IEC, 2006b]. This is illustrated, for a very basic Protection System, in Figure 4.

An accident would occur if one, or both, of two conditions occurs, as follows:

- firstly, the (pre-existing) hazard occurs and the consequences of the hazard are not mitigated; in this case, if the hazard were never mitigated, then the accident rate would be the same as the hazard occurrence rate – ie the hazard occurrence rate would be the pre-existing risk (R_U) defined in Figure 3. The situation that the hazard is not mitigated could arise because Protection System either: operates but is not effective; or fails to operate
- or secondly, the Protection System operates spuriously (eg when it is not supposed to, or in a way different from what was required) and the consequences of this (system-generated) hazard are not mitigated.

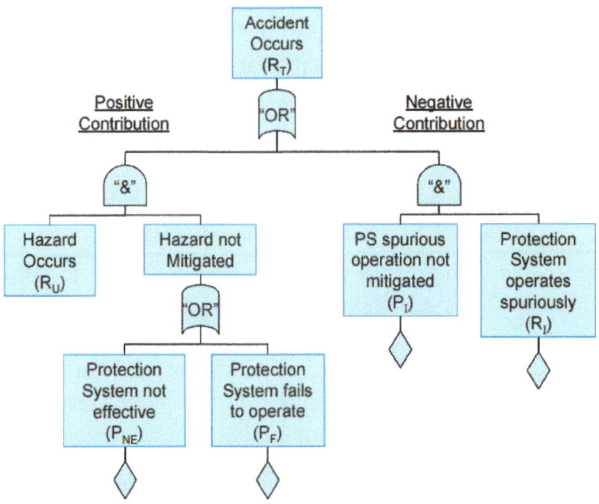

Figure 4: Simple Accident Fault Tree - Protection System

It is the presence of the external input R_U that distinguishes Figure 4 from Fault Trees in general, and it is this that enables the computation of both the positive and negative contributions to safety.

It should be noted that a simple failure (to operate) of the Protection System is shown on the *success* side of the model rather than on the *failure* side - corresponding to shortening the green arrow on Figure 3 rather than lengthening the red arrow. This would be valid for our airbag if driver behaviour were not affected by the knowledge that the car had an airbag - because the risk of airbag failure would simply be the same as not having an airbag at all for the period of the failure. However, if drivers drove less carefully and / or faster in expectation that the airbag would always protect them in the event of a head-on collision then the consequences (and therefore the risk) from failure of the airbag to operate when required would be correspondingly greater - in this case the effect of the failure would better be shown on the failure side of the model. The latter case is an example of what is very common in safety-related environments, especially where humans are involved, and requires extra care to be taken when incorporating such loss-type failures in a risk model.

In practice, risk models are much more complex than the simple illustration in Figure 4. Their uses range from a discrete safety assessment of part of an overall system up to developing a risk model for an entire operation. An example of the latter use, from the ATM field, is EUROCONTROL's Integrated Risk Picture (IRP) [Perrin & Kirwan, 2009]. As a complete model of both positive and negative contributions to safety, the IRP has proved to be a much more powerful tool, in the management of functional safety, than a simple RCS (see section 3.2.2 above) and can be used in many different ways including *a priori* safety assessment, safety monitoring and safety-strategy formulation. Such models are used also in some parts of the nuclear and rail industries but, to the authors' knowledge, not in other industry sectors at the moment.

REQUIREMENTS ENGINEERING – THE KEY TO SAFETY ASSESSMENT

Capturing, and then satisfying, a complete and correct set of safety requirements is as fundamental to any *a priori* safety assessment as requirements engineering is to systems engineering in general, as explained below.

Requirements capture

Some crucial issues regarding requirements capture can be expressed through the simple, but rigorous, requirements-engineering (RE) model shown in Figure 5. This model has been adapted from [Jackson, 1995], in the introduction to which Dr Jackson sums up the requirements-capture problem perfectly, as follows:

"We are concerned both with the world, ***in which the machine serves a useful purpose****, and with the machine itself. The competing demands and attractions of these two concerns must be appropriately balanced. Failure to balance them harms our work".*

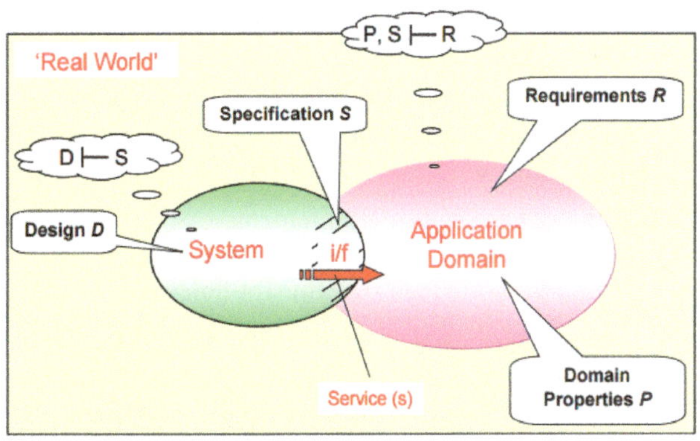

Figure 5: Jackson Requirements-capture Model - General Form

In this context, what has been said in section 2 above about the lack of a success approach in safety assessments is an example of a pre-occupation with the machine itself at the expense of considering its useful purpose (ie to reduce pre-existing risk). Figure 5 helps clear our thinking as follows.

In the Jackson model, the *system* exists in the *real world.* The part (ie subset) of the real world that influences the system, and into which the system provides a *service* through an interface (*i/f*), is known as the *application domain. Requirements* are what we want to make happen in the application domain[12] and are defined in that domain - not in the system.

A *specification* is what the system has to do across the interface in order that the *requirements* can be satisfied - ie a specification takes an external, or "black-box", view of the system. Another way of thinking about a specification is that it contains all the shared properties between the service provider and the service user - therefore it might include things that the service user has to do, not just what the system has to do.

Design, on the other hand, describes what the system itself is actually like and includes all those characteristics that are not directly required by the users but are implicitly necessary in order for the system to fulfil its specification and thereby satisfy the user requirements. Design is essentially an internal, or "white-box", view of the system.

The formal notation in the "bubbles" in Figure 5 defines two relationships that must be shown to be true in requirements capture:

- that the specification *S* satisfies the requirements *R*. However, this can be true only for a given set of properties *P* of the application domain; therefore, if any one of these three sets of parameters is changed then satisfaction demonstration is invalidated until one of the other sets is also changed
- that the design *D* satisfies the specification S

The distinction, and relationship, between requirements, specifications, application-domain properties, and design are not merely academic niceties; rather, they provide the essential foundations for developing systems that do, and can be shown to do, everything required.

What is described above in this section applies, of course, to systems engineering in general. However, if the assertion at the beginning of section 1 is correct then it should be possible to apply the same principles to the safety perspective. By comparing Figure 5 with Figure 2 (b) we can see that there is a direct equivalence for safety, as shown in Figure 6.

The main differences from Figure 5 are limited to:

- the Application Domain is now known as the Operational Environment / EUC - merely a change in terminology
- the aspects of the Requirements of particular interest are the Safety Criteria - ie the level of safety that has to be achieved in the Operational Environment / EUC
- for safety-related systems of the type shown in Figure 2 (b) above, the *pre-existing hazards* exist in the Operational Environment / EUC [13] - therefore, the primary Requirements are for the service(s) provided by the system to reduce the associated pre-existing risks to the level defined by the Safety Criteria.

Otherwise, everything that is said in section 4.1.1 above applies to safety.

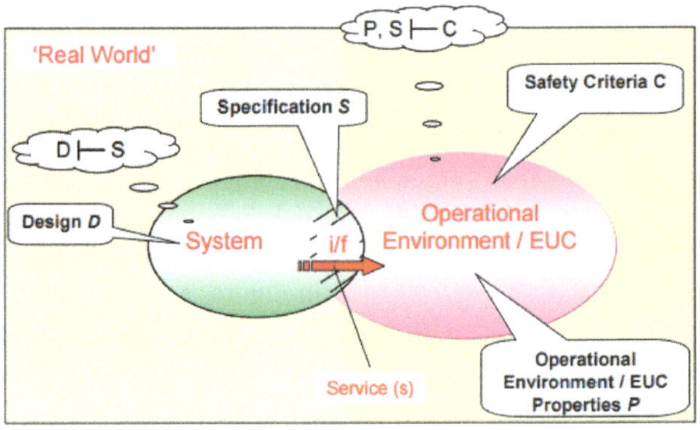

Figure 6: Safety Engineering form of the Jackson Requirements-capture Model

Safety requirements satisfaction

Implementation of the design, in the built and integrated system, involves a third relationship that must be shown to be true:

- the implementation *I* satisfies the design *D*

The validity of this relationship requires two objectives to be satisfied in implementation of the design - ie showing that:

- the required properties (functionality, performance, reliability and integrity) of the built system satisfy the requirements established for the design, and
- no emergent properties (eg common-cause failures) and unwanted functionality have been introduced inadvertently such that they could adversely affect the ability of the built system to satisfy the (safety) requirements established for the design

Because these two objectives are generic - ie apply to all properties of a system - there is no difference in principle between the satisfaction of safety requirements and the satisfaction of design requirements in general. That said, there is usually a difference in degree, in that safety requirements require a higher level of assurance that they have been captured, and then satisfied, completely and correctly.

SAFETY ASSURANCE AND SAFETY CASES

Safety assurance

Safety assurance, like systems assurance in general, relies on planned, systematic activities to provide the necessary confidence that a service or functional system satisfies its requirements (which are themselves complete and correct), in its intended environment[14]. *Assurance activities* are systematic in that they specify how the *assurance objectives* (ie what has to be demonstrated) are to be achieved, as indicated in Figure 7.

Which assurance objectives have to be achieved, and the rigour with which they have to be achieved, are often determined by assurance levels (ALs), which are based upon the potential consequences of the anomalous behavior of the system element concerned, as determined by the system safety assessment process.

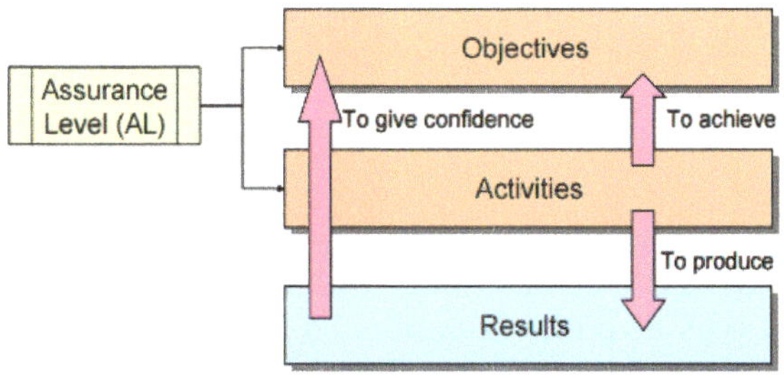

Figure 7: Safety Assurance – Basic Elements

The AL implies that the level of effort recommended for showing compliance with safety requirements increases with both the severity of the end effect of the element failure and the probability / likelihood of occurrence of that end effect, given that the failure has occurred [Mana et al, 2007][15]. The results (outputs) of the activities are then used to show that the assurance objectives have been achieved.

For high-integrity systems in particular, there is a further issue that safety assurance is often used to address and concerns the safety-integrity of system elements - software functions and human tasks, in particular. Whereas it may be necessary to specify Safety Integrity Requirements for all elements of a system in order to show compliance with a numerical Safety Criterion, it is usually very difficult to show in a direct way - through, for example, test results - that such requirements are actually satisfied in implementation. In such situations, it becomes necessary to adopt a more indirect, assurance-based approach which uses the rigour of the development processes to give confidence that the requirements are likely to be / have been satisfied. This is reflected in, for example, airborne software standard DOD 178B [RTCA, 1992] and IEC 61508 both of which are assurance based.

The problem with safety standards is that their use can become highly proceduralized, leaving open two important questions:

- where did the full set of assurance objectives come from in the first place?
- how was it decided which objectives and activities have to be done (or may be ignored) for a given AL, and how to we know that this would be appropriate for a particular application?

We can address this problem by putting safety assurance into an *argument* framework but in order to understand this we first need to look have a brief look at Safety Cases.

Safety cases

Safety assessments are often done within the context of a Safety Case which, like a legal case, comprises two main elements:

- a set of *arguments* - ie statements which claim that something is true (or false), together with
- supporting *evidence* to show that the argument is actually true.

Safety arguments are normally set out hierarchically; this is shown in Figure 8 using and adapted form of goal-structuring notation (GSN). In safety work [Kelly & Weaver, 2004], GSN is simply a graphical representation of an argument / evidence structure and usually starts with the top-level claim (Arg 0) that something is (or will be) acceptably (or tolerably) safe; this is then decomposed such that it is true only if, and only if, the next-level argument statements (in this case Arg 1 to 4) are all true. The *strategy* text should explain the rationale for that decomposition.

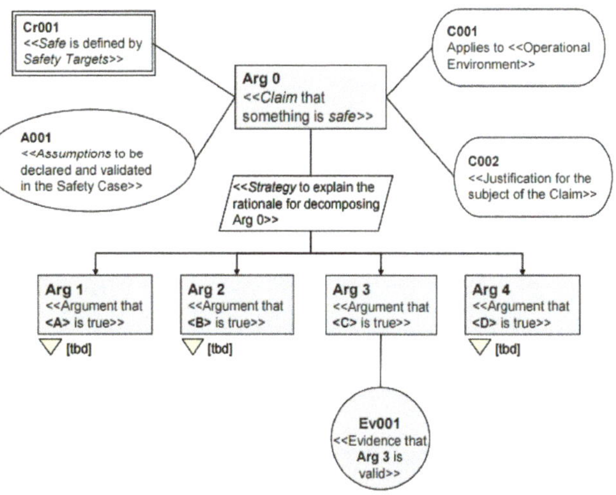

Figure 8: A generic high-level Safety Argument

The claim is supported by vital contextual information, as follows:

- what is meant by acceptably safe is defined by means of safety criteria
- the context for the claim must include a description of the operational environment for which the claim is being made - we can deduce from section 4.1 above how critical this is to the validity of the claim
- assumptions are usually facts on which the claim depends and over which the organisation responsible for the safety case has no managerial control - eg driver behaviour, in the case of our airbag
- if the claim relates to a major change to a safety-related system, it is good practice to provide a justification for that change.

The arguments would then be further sub-divided until a level is reached at which a piece of documented evidence, of a manageable size, could be produced to show that the corresponding argument statement is valid. The question is how to ensure that a safety argument is complete and rigorous – for this, we use the three formal relationships derived in section 4, as follows.

- Arg 1 - the system has been specified to be safe - ie meets the appropriate safety criteria - in the given operational environment (or EUC)
- Arg 2 - the system design satisfies the specification
- Arg 3 - the implementation satisfies the design

Then, by adding two further arguments:

- Arg 4 - the transition from current system to the new (or modified) system will be safe – ie the known risks during this process have been reduced ALARP - and
- Arg 5 - the system will be shown to operate safely in service

we have a sufficient, high-level safety argument for developing a new or modified system, bringing it into service and maintaining it throughout its operational life [Fowler et al, 2009]. Since it is the safety argument that determines ultimately what we need to demonstrate, we can use it to drive the whole assurance process as shown in Figure 9.

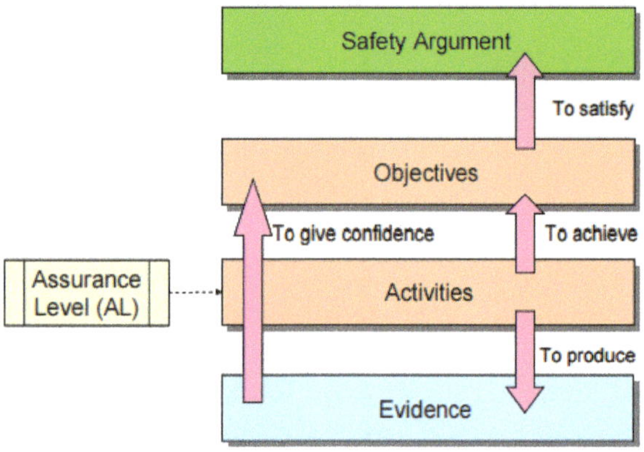

Figure 9: Safety Assurance within an Argument Framework

The key point about this diagram is that it is the needs of the argument (ie the generation of evidence) that drive the activities - not the other way around - and the lifecycle phases contain only those activities that are necessary to support the argument.

SAFETY ASSESSMENT IN THE PROJECT LIFE-CYCLE

The above assurance principles apply to the five phases of a typical project lifecycle, as shown in Figure 10.

In practice, the Safety Plan (produced at the start of a project) should set out a specific safety argument and assurance objectives – with a rationale as to how they were derived to suit the nature and scope of the safety assessment concerned - the lifecycle assurance activities to be carried out, and the tools, techniques etc to be employed. Since the Safety Case (developed during, but finalised at the end, of a project) uses the same argument, it needs only to present the evidence resulting from the activities and provide the rationale as to how that evidence satisfies the argument.

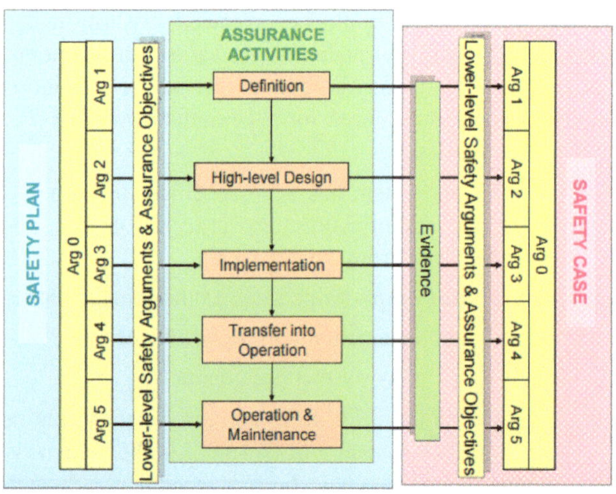

Figure 10: Overall Safety Lifecycle Process

Definition phase

From section 5, we can see that in this phase we need to show that the system has been specified to meet the appropriate safety criteria in the given operational environment (or EUC). We will use a new, innovative[16] railway level-crossing[17] control (and possibly protection) system for a planned new two-way suburban road in order to illustrate some of the points in the steps described in sections 6.1.1 to 6.1.4 below - it should be noted that the analysis presented here is not intended to be exhaustive.

Operational environment

For our level-crossing, the properties of the operational environment would need to include:

- users of the crossing - eg passenger and freight trains, road vehicles (of which 80% are cars / light vans and the rest are trucks up to 40 tonnes weight) and occasional pedestrians; exceptionally (once very 1-2 months), large slow-moving vehicles carrying abnormally heavy loads will need to use the crossing
- average length of train - 120 m
- two-way rail traffic levels - 150 passenger trains per day (mainly between 07:00 and 23:00 hours) and 10 freight trains per day (mainly at night)
- road traffic levels - 3000 vehicles per day (mainly between 07:00 and 23:00 hours)
- traffic performance - the current railway speed limit is 140 kph for passenger trains and 60 kph for freight trains. The planned speed limit for the road is 100 kph for cars, 80 kph for vehicles over 2 tonnes and 65 kph for vehicles over 7.5 tonnes
- details of the road / track layout - the geography of the area makes the construction of a bridge /tunnel prohibitively expensive[18]

Pre-existing hazards

The main pre-existing hazard is" HAZ_{PE}#1 - any situation in which, on current intentions, a road user and a train would inadvertently occupy the crossing at the same time". The use of "on current intentions" is crucial since it is describing a hazard not an actual accident. We could use mathematical modelling here to estimate the frequency with which this hazard would occur for a completely uncontrolled crossing and hence estimate the pre-existing risk.

Safety criteria

A suitable quantitative criterion would be that the likelihood of an accident involving multiple fatalities shall not exceed one per 100 years, supported by a second, ALARP criterion. However, given a possible range of outcomes of the hazard in this case, it might be appropriate to make use of a suitable RCS (along the lines of Figure 1 in section 3.2.2 above) in order also to set criteria for outcomes of lesser severity[19].

The specification

We recommend the use of the term Safety Objectives to describe the safety aspects of the specification. The reason is that it helps us remember that, in accordance with the Jackson model of section 4.1 above, what we are seeking to do here is describe, from the users' perspective, what the system must do, not to determine how the system will achieve that in its design.

First of all we need to consider the success case and assess how the pre-existing hazard is mitigated for all *normal* conditions in the operational environment - ie all those conditions that our SRS is likely to encounter on a day-to day basis - constructing various operational scenarios (eg single and multiple trains) as necessary. Two examples of a Safety Objective for this are as follows:

- SO#1 - a road user shall not enter the area defined by the crossing until its exit from the crossing is clear
- SO#2 - road users shall not enter the crossing from [say] 1 minute prior to a single[20] approaching train reaching the crossing until the train has cleared the crossing.

Note that these are genuine objectives (as above) and that the illustrative numbers would need to be verified by some form of dynamic risk modelling based on the environment described in section 6.1.1.

Next we need to assess how well the pre-existing hazard is mitigated for all *abnormal* conditions in the operational environment - ie all those adverse conditions that our SRS might exceptionally encounter - again, constructing various operational scenarios as necessary. An example of a Safety Objective for this is as follows:

- SO#n - in the event that an abnormally large / heavy vehicle (to be defined) is required to use the crossing, all approaching trains shall be prevented from entering the section of track [say] 1 km prior to the crossing until the vehicle has completely cleared the crossing.

This situation is expected to occur infrequently (see section 6.1.1 above) and therefore the system is allowed to operate in a different mode - in this case the train no longer has priority over the road vehicle - from the *normal* case. Again, some form of dynamic risk modelling could be used to determine a suitable exclusion distance for approaching trains.

Finally, we need to consider the potential failure modes of the system, at the service level. At this level, we are not concerned with the causes of failure[21], only with the consequences of failure - for which we would often use Event-tree Analysis for assessing multiple possible outcomes of a particular failure. It is important that the identification of possible failure modes be as exhaustive as possible; a useful starting point is to take each of the success-case Safety Objectives and ask the question what happens if it not satisfied. This will lead to the *system-generated* hazards, an example of which is:

- HAZ_{SG}#1 - road vehicle enters crossing that is in a *closed* state[22] (failure to satisfy SO#2).

Using the operational data from section 6.1.1 we can derive the following Safety Objective to limit the frequency of the hazard such that the appropriate portion of the tolerable-risk criterion (see section 6.1.3) is satisfied for this hazard:

- SO#n+r - the probability of a road vehicle entering the crossing when it is closed shall not exceed $5x10^{-5}$ per operating hour

Note that this illustrative figure takes account of the total number of system-generated hazards (assumed to be four in this illustration), the frequency with which road and rail traffic uses the crossing, and the providential mitigation that even if a vehicle incorrectly enters the crossing there is a significant probability that it would not actually collide with a train. Note also that the hazard occurrence rate is expressed as a frequency even though the SRS is not continuously operating - this was done in accordance with IEC 61508 because the demand rate on the SRS is relatively high (ie up to 150 operations per day).

Thus, at the end of the Definition Phase we should have a set of Safety Objectives which, if they are satisfied in the system design and implementation, would ensure that the pre-existing risk is mitigated, and the system-generated risk is limited, such that the level crossing would satisfy the specified quantitative Safety Criteria.

High-level design phase

Having derived what Jackson [Jackson, 1995] refers to as a Specification for the system, the system-development task becomes less safety-specific, and has even more common with general system-engineering principles, except for one key feature - the higher level of confidence (ie assurance) that is required in the results of safety assessment.

Design, as we have seen, is about the internal properties of the system but for this phase we restrict the analysis to a logical design, in which Safety Requirements describe the main human tasks and machine-based functions that constitute the system, and the interactions between them. An illustration, based on our 'futuristic' level-crossing control system (LCCS) of section 6.1, is given in Figure 11.

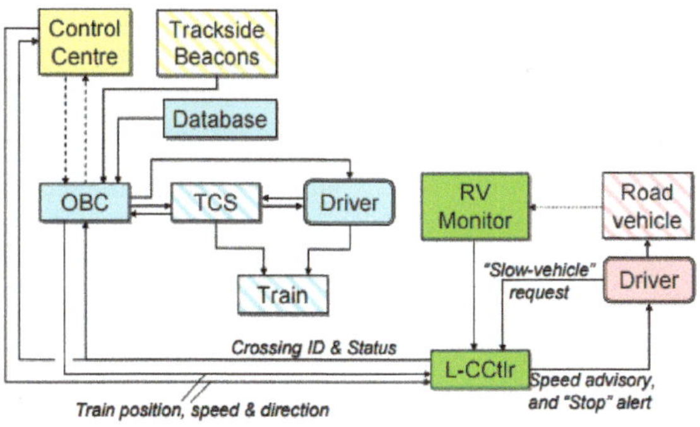

Figure 11: Example of a Logical Model

A description of this example and the way that the model works is beyond the scope of this chapter - suffice it to say that the new system comprises a fully automated Level-crossing Controller and a Road Vehicle Monitor, which detects the presence of road vehicles within the crossing area. It is to be integrated into a regionally-based "Moving Block" signalling system using Communications Based Train Control - all the train control systems including ATP, but excluding the Onboard Computer, are subsumed into the TCS box[23].

The main points to note are as follows:

- it does not show elements of the physical design[24], such as hardware, software, procedures, training etc - nor does it separately represent human-machine interfaces, these being implicit in every link between a human and machine actor
- since the machine (eg Onboard Computer) and human

(eg Driver) elements are shown separately this implies that the degree of automation in the system has been decided, at least provisionally

- the use of colour distinguishes between those elements of the end-to-end system that are in the train (blue), in the road vehicle (pink), in the LCCS (green) and are elements of external, interfacing systems (yellow). All elements that remain unchanged are shown with a striped background.

Safety Requirements capture what each of those "actors" needs to provide in terms of functionality, performance, reliability and integrity in order to satisfy the specified Safety Objectives. Whereas Figure 11 shows the actors and the way in which they interact quite clearly, the functionality that they provide is contained in the textural Safety Requirements, and the links between those functions are not easily seen. For this reason, on functionally-rich systems we often use a Functional Model, showing an abstract view of the system functions and data, as a bridge between the Specification and the Logical Design, thus increasing the confidence of the completeness and correctness of the latter [Fowler et al, 2009].

It is very important to note that making an argument for a Logical Design is not simply a matter of showing traceability of the individual Safety Requirements, for the Logical Design, back to the Safety Objectives of the Specification. This would ignore three possibilities: that the design as a whole might be in someway internally incoherent; that new failure properties could emerge at the design level that were not apparent at the higher (service) level; or that the Safety Requirements are too demanding of technology and / or human performance. Thus it is necessary to provide assurance that the Logical Design:

- has all of the functionality and performance attributes that are necessary to satisfy the Safety Objectives of the (service-level) Specification
- will deliver this functionality and performance for all *normal* conditions of the operation environment that it is likely to encounter in day-to-day operations
- is robust against (ie work through), or at least resilient to (ie recover easily from), any *abnormal* conditions that it may exceptionally encounter
- has sufficient reliability and integrity to satisfy the Safety Objectives of the Specification
- is realistic in terms of the feasibility of a potential physical system to satisfy the Safety Requirements, and the ability of validation & verification methods to demonstrate, at the appropriate time and to the necessary level of confidence, that the Safety Requirements are eventually satisfied.

By now it will (we hope!) be no surprise that to analyses, verify and validate the design from a safety perspective we use classical systems-engineering techniques, including:

- requirements traceability [Hull et al, 2005]
- Use-case Analysis [ISO/IEC, 2005] and Fast-time / Real-time simulations - for the normal, abnormal and failure scenarios
- Fault-tree Analysis [IEC, 2006b] to assess the causes of failure, "top down" , and
- Failure Modes Effects & Criticality Analysis [IEC, 2006a] to check the FTA, "bottom up".

Furthermore, since the human elements of the system have started to emerge, we can use human factors (HF) techniques such as Cognitive Task Analysis (CTA) and Human Reliability Assessment (HRA) to assess initially whether the task, performance and reliability & integrity demands which the Safety Requirements place on the human operators are at least realistic.

By the end of the High-level Design Phase we should have a set of Safety Requirements - covering the success and failure cases - that are sufficient to ensure that, if they are satisfied in the Implementation, the specified Safety Objectives would be met.

Implementation phase

We have defined the Implementation Phase such that it comprises development of a Physical Design and the realisation of the Physical Design in the built system. In making an argument for Implementation, we need to show that:

- the Physical Design satisfies the Safety Requirements for the Logical Design
- the causes or effects of any adverse, emergent safety properties (eg common-cause failures) or unwanted functionality have been mitigated in the Physical Design such that they do not jeopardize the satisfaction of the Safety Requirements
- the built system satisfies the Safety Requirements of the Physical Design (ie verification[25])
- the built and integrated system is consistent with the original qualitative Safety Objectives (ie validation).

In the physical design, we take the Safety Requirements from the Logical Design and allocate them to the elements of the Physical System, as follows:

- human tasks map on to, and provide the initial Safety Requirements for, skills, knowledge, procedures and training
- machine-based functions map on to, and provide the initial Safety Requirements for, hardware and software design
- human-machine interactions map on to, and provide the initial Safety Requirements for, human-machine interface (HMI) design.

These in turn lead to further design, Safety Requirements derivation and implementation for each of these elements and then to integration of the complete system - for further reading see [ISO/IEC, 2008b and ISO/IEC, 2008a]. The steps would follow, for example, the classical "V-model" of system development in which the safety engineer must ensure that the physical system as a whole (and its constituent parts) have sufficient reliability and integrity, and complete and correct functionality and performance, to satisfy the higherlevel Safety Requirements. These are discussed in turn, as follows.

Building reliable systems – General

The engineering of a safety related system must ensure, as a minimum, that the safety reliability and integrity requirements are met. It is useful to consider first how failures occur and what techniques can be used to reduce failure rates to meet the safety criteria. Random failures can occur in hardware of any kind due to physical degradation and wearout mechanisms; the exact time when such a failure will occur is unknown but statistical distributions can be used to predict failure rates and quantification of overall system reliability can be modelled by techniques such as FTA mentioned earlier. Techniques for making hardware elements sufficiently reliable are considered in section 6.3.2 below.

Systematic failures by contrast are caused by design defects – they will occur whenever a system enters a state in which a latent defect is revealed. Software failures are always systematic[26], but hardware designs (especially those such as computer processor chips) can also exhibit systematic failures. Methods of ensuring that software is sufficiently free of defects, such that it can meet its safety function and performance requirements with sufficient reliability and integrity, are discussed in section 6.3.4 below. The concept of a systematic failure may also be applicable to human factors - eg if a procedure is designed incorrectly.

Common-cause failures are ones in which redundant subsystems fail at the same time due to the same external events (eg earthquake or tsunami), internal causes (eg power supply failure) or due to a systematic error affecting multiple systems (known as a common mode failure). This could be a software defect or a human maintenance intervention, for example. Common cause failures in practice often limit the achievable reliability of complex systems. The general approach is to attempt to identify and eliminate sources of common cause failure where possible and also to be conservative with reliability predictions to cater for the possibility of unknown causes.

Hardware safety

The main techniques for ensuring that random hardware failures are sufficiently unlikely are use of high reliability components and redundancy. High-reliability components are expensive so redundancy is used in practice except in special circumstances (such as space applications) where repair is difficult or impossible. Redundancy simply means having two or more subsystems each of which can perform the required safety functions; if one fails then a standby can take over provided that there is some mechanism (automated or manual) to detect the failure. Further gains in reliability can sometimes be achieved by using diversity, where the standby system(s) are not identical to each other. Ideally the diversity should be both conceptual (using different physical processes or measurements) and methodological (different design methods) since this helps to reduce the likelihood of common mode failures (discussed in the next section). Part 2 of IEC 61508 [IEC, 2010], in particular, provides requirements and guidance on hardware safety techniques and measures.

Of course, we must not forget the fundamental principle that (with the possible exception of Information Systems) the functionality and performance properties of hardware is as important to safety as its reliability and integrity is - see the airbag example in section 2.

Human factors safety

HF is a topic that in the past in many industries has had only scant coverage in functional safety [Sandom, 2002]. More recently, things have improved, not the least in European ATM for which EUROCONTROL has developed the "HF Case" [EUROCONTROL, 2007].

In the HF Case, Human Factors are considered on two different levels, the System Level and the Human Performance Level. The underlying philosophy is that the design of tasks, procedures and tools must correspond to the safety requirements on both the level of the overall system as well as on the level of the individual human operator.

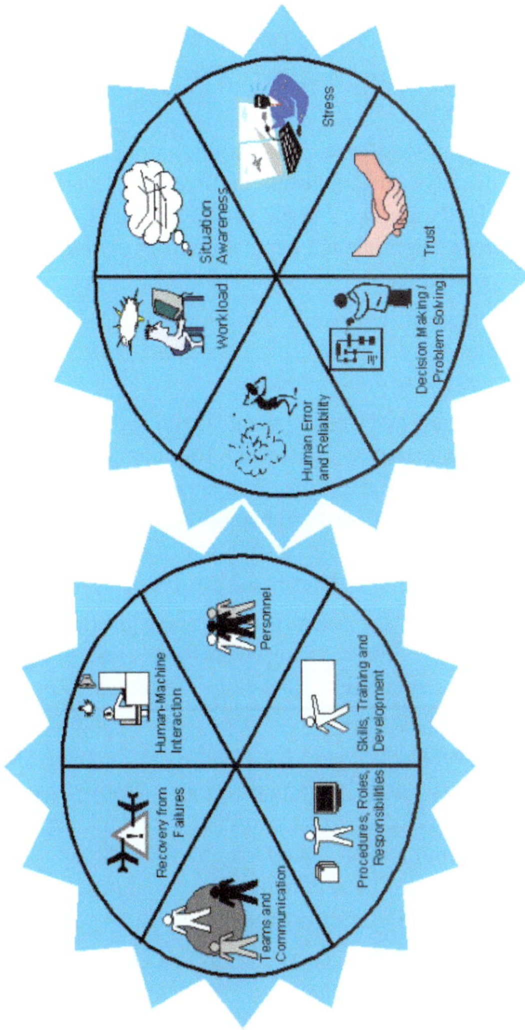

Figure 12: The HF "Gearbox"

The HF aspects can be classified into six areas at each level, and for each specific task, procedure or tool some of twelve areas may be more important than others; however, the underlying principle is that the HF evaluation should involve both levels. The resulting approach is known as the HF Gearbox, as illustrated in Figure 12.

From a safety perspective, the HF Gearbox, at the human-performance level, addresses:

- Situation awareness: the continuous extraction of external information, integration of this information with previous knowledge to form a coherent mental picture, and use of that picture in directing further perception and anticipating future events
- Workload: the degree to which the operators' mental resources are consumed by the task at hand.

- Stress: a positive or (more often) negative emotional response to a more or less demanding situation.
- Trust: the 'right degree of trust' in the equipment permits the operator to exploit the benefits of a equipment whilst being aware of its limitations
- Human error and reliability: Human reliability is the operator's capacity to execute a specific task resulting in a performance within specified limits - see section 6.2.
- Decision making/problem solving: Decision making is performing a selection between possible options in a specific situation. It can be rational / or emotional.

From a safety perspective, the HF Gearbox, at the system level, addresses:

- Human-Machine Interaction: input devices, visual displays, information requirements, alarm handling, HMI usability, fatigue, distraction and concentration, noise, lighting and general comfort as it affects human performance
- Organization and Staffing: Staff requirements, manpower availability, operator profile / selection criteria, shift organization
- Training and Development: Training needs performance / competence standards, training content, training methods and media, trainer role / responsibilities / competency, on-the-job training, emergency / abnormal-situation training, testing of training effectiveness, effects on operational task performance
- Procedures, Roles and Responsibilities: allocation of task, involvement, workload, trust / confidence, skill degradation, procedure format and positioning, procedure structure, procedure content, procedure realism
- Teams and Communication: Team structures / dynamics / relations, coordination, handover processes, communication workload, phraseology, language differences, communication methods, interference effects, information content
- Recovery from Failures: Human error potential, error prevention / detection / recovery, detection of, and recovery from, equipment failures.

It is crucial from a safety perspective that HF is not considered to be a separate activity - rather it must be fully integrated into the safety assessment and resulting safety case.

Software safety

An IEC 61508 perspective on software safety

Part 3 of IEC 61508 [IEC, 2010] starts at the point where the software requirements specification for a safety related system has been developed, in terms of safety functional behaviour and safety integrity. The system engineering approach described in this chapter should, of course, be used in deriving those software requirements in the first place.

IEC 61508 Part 3 is based on a conventional V lifecycle model for the design and implementation of software. A process-based approach is convenient for software developers who have to follow the standard, but Part 3 stresses that it is not the existence of the process itself but the evidence resulting from the application of the process which will demonstrate the achievement of safe software. The development lifecycle stages comprise:

- software architectural design,
- detailed design,
- module design,
- coding.

Verification is required after each stage, to check that the output of the design stage is a correct refinement of the input and has other necessary properties. Verification as a minimum includes software code reviews but can include other forms of analysis ranging from code complexity analysis and rigorous inspection techniques up to formal proof that the software has certain properties. Testing of the software mirrors the design, as follows:

- module or unit testing, to demonstrate that the each software module behaves in accordance with its specification
- integration test at the software design level(s) (which includes hardware/software integration testing), to show that all modules function together as intended
- safety validation testing at the software requirements level, to provide confidence that the safety function and performance requirements are met.

The stress laid by IEC 61508 Part 3 on module testing is justified by experience that software which has been well tested at the module level will usually reveal few errors during later testing, although it is a step often skimped due to time pressures during development.

Detailed techniques and measures are recommended in Annexes A and B of IEC 61508 Part 3 to support each lifecycle stage. Techniques are either Highly Recommended (HR), Recommended (R) or noted without any specific force (-). In a very small number of cases, techniques are Not Recommended. The nature and rigour of the HR techniques and the number to be applied increases with the SIL – this is common to a number of software safety standards and guidelines. However, it is not possible simply to apply all the HR techniques for a given SIL, since some may be contradictory; therefore judgement must be applied in selecting the techniques which will give the greatest benefit. If a relevant HR technique is not used, its omission must be agreed with the independent safety assessor (see below). The standard stresses that it is the combination of testing and analysis that provides the necessary confidence that the software will be safe.

Properties of the design artefact(s) are stated for each lifecycle stage as a guide to selecting and justifying the techniques and measures to be used. Properties include:

- completeness (with respect to the higher level representation)
- correctness
- ease of understanding
- freedom from intrinsic errors.

An "intrinsic" error is one which can be recognised regardless of the functions which the software is to realise – examples at the source code level could include division by zero, numeric overflow, or access via a null pointer. This class of errors typically cause run-time "crashes" and there are analytical tools which can help to eliminate such errors.

Use of pre-existing software elements (such as an operating system or communications software) is allowed, provided that sufficient evidence of reliable operation can be provided. This can include evidence from non-safety applications subject to certain conditions.

Although IEC 61508 Part 3 is based on the V lifecycle, alternative lifecycles can be used. For example, if code is generated automatically from a high-level requirements model (which is possible for some types of control applications) then the software design and coding stages can be omitted, although testing will still be required. The selection of tools to support each lifecycle stage and technique is specifically addressed in Part 3 – a tool which makes a direct contribution to the final software (such as a compiler) must be chosen and justified with greater care than one where the output of the tool is readily amenable to manual inspection and correction.

In common with Parts 1 and 2 of IEC 61508, independent functional safety assessment is required, the degree of independence depending on the SIL to be achieved. For example, a person independent of the designer is sufficient at SIL 1 whereas an independent organisation is required at SIL 4. The assessor should examine both the process itself (the selection of techniques and measures) and the products of the development (for example the test and analysis results and the backing evidence that the testing and analysis have been sufficiently thorough). It is interesting to note that independence between designer/implementer and verifier/tester is not required in IEC 61508, although it is required in other standards and guidelines for safe software.

All evidence resulting from test, analysis and field service experience must be recorded and kept under configuration management along with the design artefacts and software code– therefore, applying the standard should generate the evidence required to meet SW01 (see subsection 6.3.4.2).

A regulatory perspective on software safety

There are two main ways of gaining *assurance* that the safety requirements have been properly and completely implemented in an SRS: assurance which is obtained directly from the attributes of the product itself; and that which is obtained from the characteristics of the processes which gave rise to the product.

So what is an appropriate balance between product and process assurance, and what part should the various standards play in the achievement and demonstration of system safety? The SW01 section of the UK CAA's safety regulation CAP 670 [UK CAA] takes an objectivebased approach that provides a sensible answer to these questions27. SW01 takes an approach to safety assurance which is deliberately non-prescriptive in terms of the development process; instead, it demands arguments and evidence of the achievement of five safety assurance objectives – ie to show that the:

- software safety requirements correctly state what is necessary and sufficient to achieve tolerable safety, in the system context
- the software satisfies its safety requirements
- each software safety requirement can be traced to the same level of design at which its satisfaction is demonstrated
- software implemented as a result of software safety requirements is not interfered with by other software [that is not safety related]
- all assurance relates to a known executable version of the software, a known range of configuration data and a known set of software products, data and descriptions that have been used in the production of that version.

SW01 defines seven behavioural attributes of safety-related software, which the safety assurance must address, with equal rigour (or a valid argument presented as to why a particular attribute has not been addressed), as follows: functionality, timing, accuracy, robustness, reliability, resource usage, and overload tolerance.

In the context of requirements satisfaction, SW01 allows assurance to be offered from three different sources – ie testing, analysis (of design), and field service experience (FSE). For each source of assurance, two forms of evidence are required, for each attribute, as follows:

- Direct evidence - that which provides actual measures of the product (software) attribute concerned and is the most direct and tangible way of showing that a particular assurance objective has been achieved
- Backing evidence would relate to quality of the process by which those measures were obtained and provides information about the quality of the direct evidence, particularly the amount of confidence that can be placed in it.

Testing is restricted largely to tests of the final product (executable code) or a very close relation of it. Direct evidence is concerned with what tests were carried out and what the results showed in terms of satisfaction of the safety requirements. Backing evidence is concerned with showing that the tests were specified correctly and carried out adequately.

FSE is based on previous operational use of the software. *Direct* evidence is concerned with analysis of data from FSE and what the results of that analysis showed in terms of satisfaction of the safety requirements. *Backing* evidence is concerned with showing that the environment from which the data was obtained is sufficiently similar to that to which the re-used software will be subjected, that an adequate fault-recording process was in place when the software was originally deployed, and that the data-analysis process was adequate and properly carried out.

Analysis covers any proof of requirements satisfaction that is obtained from the design or other representation of the software, including models, prototypes, source code etc. *Direct* evidence is concerned with what the results of the particular *analysis* techniques showed in terms of satisfaction of the safety requirements. *Backing* evidence is concerned with showing that design and other representations of the software were appropriate and adequate and that the *analysis* was adequately specified and properly conducted; where *analysis* was carried out on source code, it is necessary also to show that the object code correctly translates the source code.

In general, the rigour demanded of the evidence increases as the integrity required of the software increases. However,

SW01 defined this integrity only in terms of the consequence of failure – ie it does not take account of the probability that such a failure will occur, as is the case, for example, in IEC 61508.

The way in which evidence from the three sources can be used in combination varies according to the attribute for which evidence is offered, and also depends on the integrity required of the software. As the required integrity increases, SW01 allows less dependence on a single source of evidence, and places more emphasis on *analysis* of design as the primary source of evidence.

The advantage of testing over design analysis is that it is carried out on the end product rather than on a representation of that product. On the other hand, the effectiveness of testing can be limited by problems with test coverage and with confidence levels in respect of statistical attributes of the system. For these reasons, assurance from testing usually takes second place to design analysis for the more safety-critical systems, though it is interesting to note that SW01, for example, mandates some degree of testing even where the primary source of assurance is design analysis.

As a source of assurance, design analysis has one further advantage over testing – it is available much earlier in the lifecycle and can therefore make a major contribution to the reduction of programme risk. Iterative development techniques seek to bring forward the availability of test evidence but in so doing bring with them their own problems, including a possible reduction in effectiveness of design assurance unless specific measures are taken to avoid this.

Transfer phase

The Transfer-into-Operation Phase takes the assurance process up to the point that the system concerned is ready to be brought into operational service. In making an argument for Transfer into Operation, we need to show that:

- everything necessary has been to prepare the new (or modified) system for operational service
- the process of bringing the system into service – ie transitioning from the current system to the full new system – will itself be as safe as reasonably practicable

Preparation for operational service is about showing that all the necessary operational procedures, trained personnel and technical resources are in place to operate and maintain the system and that, under conditions as close a possible to real operational service, the system / resources as a whole will meet the expectations of the service users (ie system validation). Typically, a safety case would be submitted for management approval and regulatory endorsement before transition from the current system to the new system begins. Therefore it is necessary to show beforehand that any risks associated with transition will be managed such that the AFARP criterion will be met throughout this process.

Especially in safety-critical industries that require an uninterrupted operation for 365 days per year, live system testing and the subsequent transition from the old to the new system are often hazardous. Thus a Transition Plan needs to drawn up and executed to ensure that:

- the hazards and risks associated with the transition process have been completely identified and correctly assessed
- measures have been put in place to reduce those risks ALARP
- contingency plans are in place to revert to a safe state if the transition is not entirely successful
- the old system components can be removed safely

Operational phase

The safety focus during the whole of the systems in-service life is on providing assurance of its continuing safe operation. This is vital for a number of reasons, including:

- the a priori safety assessment, covered in Arg 1 to 3, might not be complete and correct in every particular
- the system, including the equipment and human elements, might degrade in operational service
- the system will most probably be subject to changes at various times during its operational life
- the operational environment might change during the life of the system.

Thus we need to ensure first of all that the system (comprising equipment, people and procedures) will be supported so as to maintain the required level of safety. The evidence in support of this will be mainly in the form of SMS processes (and related operational and engineering procedures) and how it will be ensured that they will be properly applied - including the use of surveys and audits related to the application of those SMS processes.

Secondly, in order to provide assurance of actual safety achievement we need to show that:

- there is a culture to encourage full and accurate reporting of safety incidents
- the frequency of safety incidents will be measured against pre-defined indicators
- all reported incidents will be properly investigated
- appropriate corrective action will be taken to prevent incident recurrence.

Finally, we need to show that there are procedures in place to manage future changes to the system and / or it operational environment.

CONCLUSIONS

We started by asserting that safety is not a separate attribute of a system but is a property that depends on other attributes, and on the context in which the system is used. The misconception that adequate reliability and integrity are sufficient to ensure the safety of a system has been prevalent in, for example, the ATM sector [Fowler & Grand-Perret, 2007], but is dispelled in the specific context of software by the results of extensive research [Leveson, 2001] and more generally herein by rationale argument using the example of a car airbag.

After introducing some basics safety concepts and principles, we then showed that safety is as much dependent on correct functionality & performance of the system as it is on system reliability & integrity - the former set of attributes being necessary for the mitigation of *pre-existing* risk (inherent in the operational environment) and the latter for controlling *system-generated* risk (caused by system failure). This led to the view that what was needed was a broader approach (what we called the *success & failure* approach) to system safety assessment, a view that was then shown to be consistent with the principles underlying the generic functional-safety standard IEC 61508 [IEC, 2010] - principles that, however, are not always captured in industry-specific instantiations of this standard.

We then turned to a vital aspect of systems engineering - ie requirements engineering, some important principles of which are advocated in [Jackson, 1995] - and found direct equivalence between the derivation of the required safety properties of a system and the derivation of its non-safety properties.

Finally, we introduced the principles of safety assurance and safety cases and showed how they should drive all the processes of a safety assessment, throughout the lifecycle. Whilst emphasising the importance of ensuring that the level of assurance is appropriate to the safety-criticality of the system, we now leave it to the knowledgeable systems engineer to recognise the common processes of a system development lifecycle in this chapter and to conclude for himself / herself that safety is (with the assurance proviso) actually just a viewpoint (albeit a very important one) on systems engineering!

ACKNOWLEDGMENT

The authors would like to record their appreciation for the many very helpful suggestions made by Drs Michael A Jackson and Anthony Hall during the development of this chapter.

REFERENCES

1. European Commission, 2005, Regulation (EC) No 2096/2005, *Common Requirements for the Provision of Air Navigation Services*, published in the Official Journal of the European Union
2. Eurocontrol, 2007, *The Human Factors Case: Guidance for Human Factors Integration*
3. Eurocontrol, 2010, http://www.skybrary.aero/index.php/Risk_Assessment
4. Fowler D, Grand-Perret S, 2007, Penetrating the Fog of Safety Assessment - and Vice-versa, Proceedings of the 2nd IET International Conference on System Safety, London, UK
5. Fowler D, Perrin E, and Pierce R, 2009, 2020 Foresight - a Systems-engineering Approach to Assessing the Safety of the SESAR Operational Concept, Proceedings of the 8th USA/Europe Air Traffic Management Research and Development Seminar, Napa, USA
6. Hull E, Jackson K and Dick J, 2005, Requirements Engineering, Springer, ISBN 1852338792
7. International Electrotechnical Commission, 2006a, IEC 60812, Analysis techniques for system reliability – Procedure for failure mode and effects analysis (FMEA)
8. International Electrotechnical Commission, 2006b, IEC 61025, Fault Tree Analysis
9. International Electrotechnical Commission, 2010, IEC 61508, Functional Safety of Electrical/ Electronic/ Programmable Electronic Safety Related Systems, V 2.0
10. ISO/IEC 12207, 2008a, Systems and Software Engineering - Software Lifecycle Processes, V2.0
11. ISO/IEC 15288, 2008b, Systems and Software Engineering - System Lifecycle Processes, V 2.0
12. ISO/IEC 19501, 2005, Information technology, Open Distributed Processing — Unified Modelling Language (UML), V 1.4.2
13. Jackson M A, 1995, The World and the Machine, Proceedings of 17th International Conference on Software Engineering, IEEE, pp283-292
14. Kelly T and Weaver R, 2004, The Goal Structuring Notation – a Safety Argument Notation, http://www-users.cs.york.ac.uk/~tpk/dsn2004.pdf
15. Ladkin P B, 2008, An Overview of IEC 61508 on E/E/PE Functional Safety, http://www.causalis.com/IEC61508FunctionalSafety.pdf
16. Leveson N G, 2001, The Role of Software in Recent Aerospace Accidents, 19th International System Safety Conference, Huntsville AL, USA
17. Mana P, De Rede J-M and Fowler D, 2007 Assurance Levels for ATM system elements: Human, Operational Procedure, and Software, proceedings of the 2nd IET International Conference on System Safety, London, UK
18. Perrin E and Kirwan B, 2009, Predicting the Future: The Integrated Risk Picture, Proceedings of the 4th IET International Conference on System Safety Engineering, London, UK
19. Pierce, R and Fowler D, 2010, Applying IEC 61508 to Air Traffic Management, Proceedings of the Eighteenth Safety Critical Systems Symposium, Bristol, UK
20. Rail Safety and Standards Board - RSSB (2007). Engineering Safety Management (The Yellow Book), Volumes 1 and 2 - Fundamentals and Guidance, Issue 4
21. Reason J, 2000, http://www.bmj.com/cgi/content/full/320/7237/768
22. RTCA, 1992, DO-178B, Software Considerations in Airborne Systems and Equipment Certification,
23. Sandom C, 2002, Human Factors Considerations for System Safety, in Components of System Safety, Redmill F and Anderson T [Eds.], proceedings of 10th Safety Critical Systems Symposium, 5th-7th February 2002 Southampton, Springer-Verlag, UK
24. UK CAA, 2011, UK Civil Aviation Authority, CAP670, Air Traffic Services Safety Requirements

CHAPTER 5 RISK MANAGEMENT ON THE ROMANIAN CAPITAL MARKET

Marin Andreica, Stere Farmache, Madalina Ecaterina Andreica, and Octavian Stroie

INTRODUCTION

The Stock Exchange is a barometer of economic and financial life in any country, an indicator of world business and economic prospects. Its movement is reflected in the stock market indices that express the overall performance of the stock market or just a certain sector, and offers the investors the base of their investment decision on the markets. Therefore, the authors have proposed in this paper to summarize the results of research in order to highlight the most significant issues of the risk management on the Romanian capital market and to provide solutions to them.

The first part highlights the role of stock market indexes in describing the state of the capital market, as well as the difficulties arising on their representation in the current financial and economic crisis. In order to reduce the risk of erroneous information to investors, the authors propose a composite index that summarizes the information from other indexes on the capital market in Romania. Finally, using the Risk Grades method, the authors make a comparative analysis of the risks on the Romanian capital market with those in the Czech Republic, Poland and USA capital markets.

The second part outlines the main classes of risks that arise in the settlement of exchange transactions that dominate in the risk hierarchy of the stock operational management. After highlighting some international regulations on reducing the risk of stock trading settlement, the authors develop a broad range of solutions for reducing these risks on the Bucharest Stock Exchange.

Citation: Marin Andreica, Stere Farmache, Madalina Ecaterina Andreica and Octavian Stroie, Risk Management on the Romanian Capital Market, http://dx.doi.org/10.5772/50493

RISK ASSESSMENT OF STOCK MARKET INDEXES

The role of stock market indexes

In the economic literature, the stock exchange is often characterized as being a true "engine" of the economic life, which stimulates business activity and allows the development of large-scale investment projects. Through its existence and operation, the stock markets provide liquidity for financial assets, enabling the sale of securities previously purchased, thus turning them to money. Economic and financial crisis that has monopolized economies worldwide in recent years has had a negative impact on the development of stock markets. Thus, stock prices of large companies listed on stock exchanges fell dramatically, the liquidity of stock markets fell heavily, and on this basis, the transaction volume decreased due to the reduction of interest shown by investors and speculators. Indexes saw an overall decrease and a distortion of information provided to potential investors because of "interference" occurred in the structure of the companies participating in their training. By their developments, stock market indices are able to provide clues on the economic outlook whereas in countries with developed financial markets, leading companies have almost without exception status of listed companies. Thus, the indices themselves may be true barometers of economic development or they may be included in the calculation of aggregate economic indicators, with a high degree of complexity.

Expressing the overall performance of stock markets or simply of a sector of the market, indices allow investors to perform analysis on yields of already performed transactions or on investment opportunities that may arise in the future. The existence of indices make the analysis of various stock markets much easier, even if the different methodologies used for calculating the indices affect to some extent the comparisons accuracy [1-3].

On any stock market, the indices are a reference for each investor when assessing the quality of the management portfolio. Due to the fact that in many cases individual performance fail to exceed indices' long-term growth rate, investors and fund managers especially were tempted to build their own portfolios using the precise structure and composition of the indices.

Critical elements in building and managing indexes

A first issue to be solved when considering the desirability of launching a stock index is if you choose to use a formula in the category of arithmetic or geometric average. Since the use of geometric replication creates difficulties when the stock index would be eligible as underlying for derivatives or as a benchmark for investment fund, managers will prefer to use a formula based on the arithmetic average.

Also, the option to use weights in the calculation of indices involves an analysis of market characteristics to be described by the respective stock market index. The decision to weight the prices which is part of an index is itself a controversial:

- the supporters of the unweighted variant believe that such an index only ensures equal treatment of each stock symbol which is part of an index;
- those who appreciate more weighted index say that the only way to avoid unwanted situation in which the relative change in price of shares issued by a company small in size will influence the stock index as much value as a change in the same type of the share price "Blue Chips".

Another issue that arises is the choice of the weighting factor. In theory there may be various options for the weighting factors, but in practice have won two:

- weighting by market capitalization (or the amount of the outstanding shares);
- weighting the liquidity of the shares that make up a stock index.

In the first case there is a risk that a relatively small number of companies - which have a market capitalization way above the market average - will decide the meaning and scope of developments in practice the whole index. It is a common situation in emerging markets. Therefore, it is often set a maximum level of the share capitalization of a single symbol that can play in the total capitalization of the symbols in the composition of a stock index.

In practice, the liquidity is the most common alternative criterion to using market capitalization as the weighting factor. Attractiveness of the weighted indices to the liquidity lies in the idea that virtually any listed price of a share is a fiction as long as it materializes through a stock transaction. Therefore, prices become relevant only insofar as they are the result of a large number of transactions, which require (at least at first) the use of liquidity as a weighting factor in calculating the indices. The disadvantage of using liquidity as a weighting factor consists, however, in the presence of many differences from one day to another in the number of shares made with a specific symbol, which significantly alter its influence in the evolution of the overall index [4-5]. In principle, a stock index is a tool for measuring aggregate price developments for the symbols which compose it, the sole result of supply-demand ratio of the market and the continuing process of reassessment of the price of each symbol individually [6-8]. Therefore is needed to incorporate the adjustment coefficients in the formula for calculating an index, allowing correction of artificial effects induced by certain events on the trading price of a symbol:

- events which directly affect the trading price of a symbol: the provision of dividends, granting of rights to subscribe.
- events that influence the number of shares taken into account: the change in share capital by increasing / reducing the number of the outstanding shares, split face value, strengthening the nominal value, granting free shares (bonus issues).
- changes in the composition of a stock index: the inclusion of a new symbol, a symbol of exclusion.

Payment of the dividends or issuing of preference rights involves reducing the value of traded shares of a company, unless the subscription rights have value "zero" or negative. When providing payment of dividends and share trading, price decrease is due to reducing the company's value by the amount allocated for dividends, while the rights issue of preference allocation occurs due to the decreased value of the company on a number of shares. These decreases in market value of a share are fully balanced by increasing the same amount of portfolio investors as a result of amounts received as dividends or the sale of preference rights indices as a result of the above events has the advantage of simplicity, though in practice most indices are adjusted when there are such price changes.

- Assuming that the granting of a certain amount as dividend per share produces a decrease in the share price with the exact amount of the dividend, the adjustment procedure will require adding value to the price of the stock dividend is taken when calculating the indices. Otherwise, you can use an adjustment factor, multiplied by the share price is taken when calculating the index.

In the construction and management of indices there are other critical elements, which primarily aim to adapt to the concrete conditions of the stock market that they are going to describe. One such factor is the choice of a data base, which is preferably selected so that it does not belong to a period marked by turbulence or excessive volatility. As a general rule, the base date of an index must be chosen "in order not to overlap with a minimum or maximum market history".

The base value of an index is also an important element in building a stock index. It should be chosen so that the reporting of the current nominal value of an index value based may allow easy calculation of percentage change in that timeframe. Therefore, the most commonly used figures based on an index value are 100 and 1,000 points.

In the case of adjusted indices, selecting a large number of shares to be part of an index basket involves assuming the possibility of relatively frequent cases of adjustment, thus reducing the transparency index. Also, a too extended composition raises serious problems for managers who use index funds as a "benchmark" or which suggest as investment strategy to make investments in securities index.

If an index is used as underlying assets for the development of financial derivatives, its composition becomes more important. It is desirable that the selected symbols, especially those with high weight in the index, have a sufficiently high level of liquidity in order not to influence the price with the idea of obtaining a more favourable settlement value of futures contracts or options. The issue of settlement value of derivatives that are underlying indexes has been addressed and in terms of prices that are taken in calculating its value at the close of trading session. Intuitively, the last price recorded in a day by a certain symbol should generate and last values of stock market index. To avoid forcing the closure of certain levels of price indexes, administrators have considered closing the option that its value is determined either as the average of past values of the index calculated based on average prices in a given period time for each symbol in its composition. This concern for the accuracy of the closing price of the shares and hence the value of stock index led some stocks to decide to introduce at the end of the trading session of the tender period in which prices are determined on a multilateral basis, through a fixing algorithm.

Improvement of the management of Bucharest Stock Exchange indexes

Through the changes that were made in time upon the methodology of calculation and management of indices, the Bucharest Stock Exchange (BSE) showed that it understands their importance for the investors and the general public. However, according to the authors, there are still some aspects in the functioning of the indices in the future, as changes might occur, so that the indices calculated by the BSE to increase their representativeness and to become more attractive tools for use as benchmarks in management activity portfolio.

The first change is imposed by the profile described by the historical values of the indices. As it may be seen on Figure 1, joining the five indices calculated by BSE in the same graphic deprives us of any opportunity to make a comparison. This is obviously due to objective factors, as as BET, BET-C, BET-FI, BETXT and BETNG were launched from different basic data. Moreover, the BET and BET-C had worked in a period when inflation was very high and the national currency exchange rate at the time of their release was lower than the current one.

Therefore, it is required the denomination of all the BSE indices, so that on a specific reference date to have the same value for all indices. Bringing all indices at the same amount for a certain date, would open the way for a much easier tracking trends and comparison of their indices and market sectors they represent.

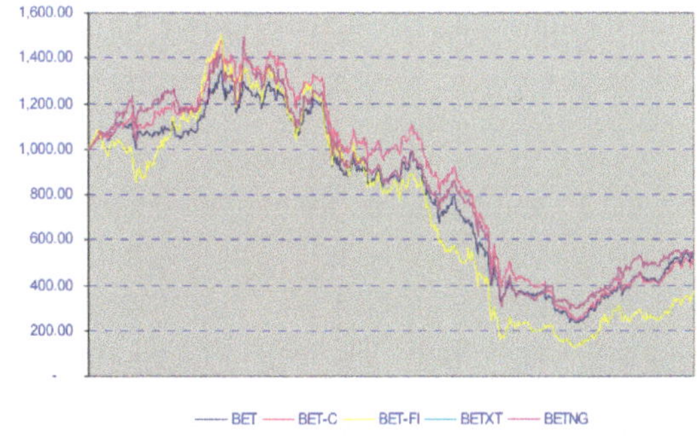

Figure 1: BSE indices (denominated) in January 2007-8 September 2009

To achieve this denomination, an important element consists in determining the reference date, which should be the first day of 2007, the day that marked the accession of Romania to the European Union, and thus integration of the regulated market operated by the Bucharest Stock Exchange in the unique European financial market.

Once the indexes are denominated, it appears the following problem consisting in identifying their new base value. Since 2 January 2007 had already established that the reference date for two of the indices BSE - BETNG and BETXT – which were then calculated for 1000 points, a value which seems to be the most appropriate and which will greatly ease the adjustment values of Historical BET index, BET-C and BET-FI. Adjusted historical series for these three indices of BSE will be as one that can be quite easily associated with the original series.

Another problem to be solved is to develop a synthetic stock index describing the overall market share in Romania, as the Bucharest Stock Exchange also calculates a number of indices for Rasdaq: RAQ-I, RAQ-II and RASDAQ-C (which is a composite index).

One of the main concerns of a stock market operator is to identify the most effective means by which information about the activities of the regulated market that he manages, reaches the participants, from potential investors or the general public. Indexes are highly effective tools in promoting or communication, and that is why special attention should always be given to their management. Regardless of the methodology used, the scope or the "brand" adopted, the indexes must reflect as closely as the stock market developments in a given period of time, and the investors and the general public should recognize this status. Therefore, we believe that the stock market in Romania would be even discussed whether to outsource the work associated with the major indexes by a specialized international company to calculate and disseminate indexes. Market indexes license is highly specialized, with a relatively small number of participants. Therefore, "rebranding" of BSE indices under the name of one of the leading players in this market (Dow Jones, FTSE or MSCI) it would significantly increase the international exposure of local indexes.

Construction of a synthetic index for the stock market in Romania

Currently, the shares of the Romanian companies are traded in two distinct market sectors (BSE - regulated market and Rasdaq), with the chance to add another market (alternative trading system). For historical, but also technical reasons, the two market sectors are currently covered by two families of indices:

- "BET index family", for the regulated market;
- "Rasdaq index family", for the RASDAQ section.

Therefore, as stated, there is not a single synthetic indicator to describe the evolution of prices in the two market segments. Furthermore, in the "BET index family" there is a composite index, BET-C that does not include in its membership the five SIF symbols. So, even the most comprehensive index of the regulated market does not include the five most liquid stock market symbols, which normally accounts for almost half of the total transactions on the BSE [9]. That is why, it is necessary to create a more comprehensive stock index, which describes the overall evolution of the quotations for all shares traded on markets and market sections administered by the BSE. A possible name for this could be ALL-X, and that structure will be an "index of indices".

Once the objective is defined and the name is established, the next step is to clarify the composition of such an index, so there is no overlap, but at the same time to remain as few "areas" uncovered as well. From the analysis of the five indices of the "BET family" and all three of the "RASDAQ family" it is very clear that the optimal variant is that the composition of ALL-X to enter the next three BSE indices:

- BET-C: reflects the price development of all companies listed on regulated market, Category I and Category II, except for the SIFs.
- BET-C is a price index weighted by market capitalization of companies in its composition. The maximum weight of a symbol in the
- BET-C composition is 20% BET-FI: reflects the overall trend in the shares prices issued by the five financial investment companies (SIF) on the regulated market. The maximum weight of a symbol in the composition of the BET-FI is 25% RASDAQ-C: includes all the shares traded on the "RASDAQ market" and follows the synthesized global trend in prices.

Regarding the topic, the fact that the Rasdaq-C index is calculated at the end of the trading session (and not in real time) also requires that the ALL-X index to be calculated with the same frequency.

Also, the type of formula chosen is relatively simple, since all three indices *(I_i)* use the arithmetic average. Therefore, the ALL-X index will use the same formula - weighted arithmetic average, as the relative importance of the three indices in the general stock market in Romania is very different, both in terms of market capitalization and liquidity of the shares in their composition. Therefore, it is necessary to use a weighted arithmetic average.

For the price index, the most frequent weighting factors ($P_{i,t}$) are either capitalization or liquidity. Since all of the three indexes found in the composition of ALL-X are capitalizationweighted price index, at least apparently the natural alternative is to use the same weighting criteria: capitalization. Moreover, the choice of the capitalization weighting factor ensures that the advantage of not requiring frequent rebalancing for an investor who decides to adopt a passive investment strategy in relation to the ALL-X index.

Through its coverage, the ALL-X index will create replication difficulties. Therefore, in its construction, the focus should be on its descriptive issues and less on the investment. Consequently, it becomes important to find a variant that takes into account the weighting of liquidity, which has the disadvantage that the index can cause daily changes without evidence of membership to undergo changes, or changes in scope than the other induced increases or decreases in the BET-C index, BET-FI and Rasdaq-C. Such a compromise version could be given to the establishment of fixed predetermined weighting factors, which remain unchanged for a defined period of two consecutive data adjustment index ALL-X (one quarter). In calculating these predetermined weighting factors, both the capitalization and liquidity will be taken into account.

The formula for calculating the determining factors will be:

$$Pi,t = \frac{Ui + Vi}{2} \qquad (1)$$

where:

U_i is the weight that the capitalization of the symbols within I_i index holds in the total capitalization of the market, at the time of reference;

V_i is the weight that the value of transactions with the symbols of the I_i index holds in the total market turnover in the reference period (quarterly).

To ensure a unified form to display all BSE indices, will opt for the next version of the equivalent representation:

$$(\text{ALL-X})_T = (\text{ALL-X})_{T-1} x \frac{\sum_{i=1,N} p_{i,T} \times I_{i,T}}{\sum_{i=1,N} p_{i,T} \times I_{i,T-1}} \qquad (2)$$

where:

$P_{t,i}$: weighting factor at time T, associated with each index in the composition of ALL-X; $I_{i,t}$: ALL-X indices, at time T (BET-C, BET-FI, Rasdaq-C).

To ensure the possibility to compare the new ALL-X index with the main stock market index, BET, the start value will be 2901.10 points and the start date will be fixed for 31.12.2008. The calculation of the weighting factor, Pi,t, will be done quarterly, on the last trading day of the final month of the quarter, and will enter into force on the first trading session of the next quarter [10].

The main advantage of building the index ALL-X is that it can be obtained a simple and effective tool to provide an overview of the entire stock market development in Romania. The index is limited to the evolution of shares issued by the Romanian companies, while any direct influence induced by the prices movement of foreign securities admitted to trading on domestic capital market was being removed from the beginning.

In the presented form, ALL-X index is defined primarily as a descriptive index and less like an investment. This deficiency can be corrected later, to the extent that the BSE will decide to use the same calculation methodology for all its indices, regardless of the section or market segment that is addressed: regulated market, Rasdaq market or alternative trading system. Moreover, in order to emphasize the character of investment, it will be necessary to modify the weighting factor (which may become the capitalization of each index), as well as the dates when its new value is calculated and effective.

To calculate the ALL-X index values retrospectively, after the release date was determined (December 31, 2008) and the reference value at that time (2901.10 points), the first step is to determine the Ui and Vi factors for the first quarterly interval (January-March 2009). To this end it will determine:

- capitalization associated to the symbols in the composition of the BET-C index, BET-FI and Rasdaq-C on the last trading sessions of December 2008, March 2009, June 2009, September 2009 December 2009, March 2010, June 2010, September 2010 and December 2010 (RON);

Table 1: Capitalization associated to the symbols in the composition of the BSE indices

Date	BET-C	BET-FI	Rasdaq-C
23-Dec-08	25,441,147,900	1,715,098,084	12,099,865,129
31-Mar-09	20,494,699,824	1,473,851,929	11,799,297,770
30-Jun-09	28,577,557,323	2,276,366,573	12,359,818,473
30-Sep-09	35,329,737,297	3,454,691,266	12,868,187,477
24-Dec-09	35,313,895,995	3,264,425,651	12,346,442,408
31-Mar-10	46,106,028,659	4,391,516,633	14,104,548,987
30-Jun-10	36,894,347,800	2,715,614,092	11,065,581,044
30-Sep-10	41,488,093,266	3,282,932,587	11,556,865,887
30-Dec-10	41,901,691,868	3,004,035,475	10,832,645,290

- liquidity (total amount in RON) associated to the symbols in the composition of the BET-C index, BET-FI and Rasdaq-C in Quarter IV 2008, Quarter I 2009, Quarter II 2009, Quarter III 2009, Quarter IV 2009, Quarter I 2010, Quarter II 2010, Quarter III 2010 and Quarter IV 2010 (RON).

Table 2: Liquidity associated to the symbols in the composition of the BSE indices

Period	BET-C	BET-FI	Rasdaq-C
Oct - Dec 2009	435,647,850.34	468,296,885.00	186,402,641.20
Ian - Mar 2009	423,175,985.74	203,780,032.70	86,885,606.44
Apr - Jun 2009	668,823,417.53	658,946,311.40	102,202,564.63
Jul - Sep 2009	600,539,594.05	728,518,117.60	94,069,608.81
Oct - Dec 2009	485,044,466.85	691,750,042.50	113,518,426.21
Jan - Mar 2010	691,952,816.70	735,425,007.50	148,602,226.21
Apr - Jun 2010	695,515,698.95	1,039,348,556.50	130,801,236.36
Jul - Sep 2010	331,670,219.85	407,212,194.50	57,407,872.87
Oct - Dec 2010	352,178,129.60	304,259,023.50	87,486,365.49

Based on the data presented in the previous tables, we will calculate the following elements:

- weights associated with each index in the total capitalization for each final quarter;

Table 3: Weights associated to the BSE indices in total capitalization (%)

Period	BET-C	BET-FI	Rasdaq-C
Jan - Mar 2009	64.81	hicag30.82	30.82
Apr - Jun 2009	60.69	4.36	34.94
Jul - Sep 2009	66.13	5.27	28.60
Oct - Dec 2009	68.40	6.69	24.91
Jan - Mar 2010	69.35	6.41	24.24
Apr - Jun 2010	71.37	6.80	21.83
Jul - Sep 2010	72.81	5.36	21.84
Oct - Dec 2010	73.65	5.83	20.52

- weights associated with each index in the total liquidity for each quarter;

Table 4: Weights associated to the BSE indices in total liquidity (%)

Period	BET-C	BET-FI	Rasdaq-C
Ian - Mar 2009	39.95	42.95	17.10
Apr - Jun 2009	59.28	28.55	12.17
Jul - Sep 2009	46.77	46.08	7.15
Oct - Dec 2009	42.20	51.19	6.61
Jan - Mar 2010	37.59	53.61	8.80
Apr - Jun 2010	37.28	55.71	7.01
Jul - Sep 2010	41.65	51.14	7.21
Oct - Dec 2010	47.34	40.90	11.76

Once the weights are determined, it will be necessary to calculate the weighting factors in the composition of each ALL-X index for each quarter:

Table 5: Weighting factors $P_{i,t}$

Period	BET-C			BET-FI			Rasdaq-C		
	Ui	Vi	Pi	Ui	Vi	Pi	Ui	Vi	Pi
Ian - Mar 2009	0.6481	0.3995	**0.5238**	0.0437	0.4295	**0.2366**	0.3082	0.1710	**0.2396**
Apr - Jun 2009	0.6069	0.5928	**0.5999**	0.0436	0.2855	**0.1646**	0.3494	0.1217	**0.2356**
Jul - Sep 2009	0.6613	0.4677	**0.5645**	0.0527	0.4608	**0.2567**	0.2860	0.0715	**0.1787**
Oct - Dec 2009	0.6840	0.4220	**0.5530**	0.0669	0.5119	**0.2894**	0.2491	0.0661	**0.1576**
Ian - Mar 2010	0.6935	0.3759	**0.5347**	0.0641	0.5361	**0.3001**	0.2424	0.0880	**0.1652**
Apr - Jun 2010	0.7137	0.4391	**0.5764**	0.0680	0.4666	**0.2673**	0.2183	0.0943	**0.1563**
Jul - Sep 2010	0.7281	0.3728	**0.5504**	0.0536	0.5571	**0.3053**	0.2184	0.0701	**0.1442**
Oct - Dec 2010	0.7365	0.4165	**0.5765**	0.0583	0.5114	**0.2848**	0.2052	0.0721	**0.1386**

Figure 2: Evolution of the ALL-X index vs. Evolution of BET index (Jan. 2009 – Dec. 2010)

The biggest weight in the ALL-X index is given by the BET-C composite index. The values of $P_{i,t}$ associated with the BET-C for the full period 2009-2010 ranged between 0.5 and 0.6 percent.

Risk assessment indices

Stock markets investors constantly face several risks, which is why researchers have focused their concerns on issues related to developing risk management improved models of assessment and management. Among the latest methods used in economic practice in assessing risk in financial markets the method Value at Risc (VaR) is required [11].

Risk Grades indicator provides a synthetic image of the risk associated with a certain financial security, a portfolio or an index. This new way of measuring volatility is based on exactly the same data and analysis as VaR, while making it possible to translate the Risk Grades estimates in terms of VaR. Furthermore, Risk Grades methodology is intended to be more intuitive and easier to use than VaR. The characteristics of the Risk Grades are:

- It is a dynamic method of measurement that adjusts to the market conditions
- Allows comparison between different investment classes, regions and different areas, is a standardized method of measuring volatility
- Allows comparison of different market indices.

The Risk Grades formula for the financial asset i is:

$$RiskGrades_{(i)} = \frac{\sigma_i}{\sigma_{base}} x100 \qquad (3)$$

where: σ_i the volatility of the financial asset "i" σbase the base volatility

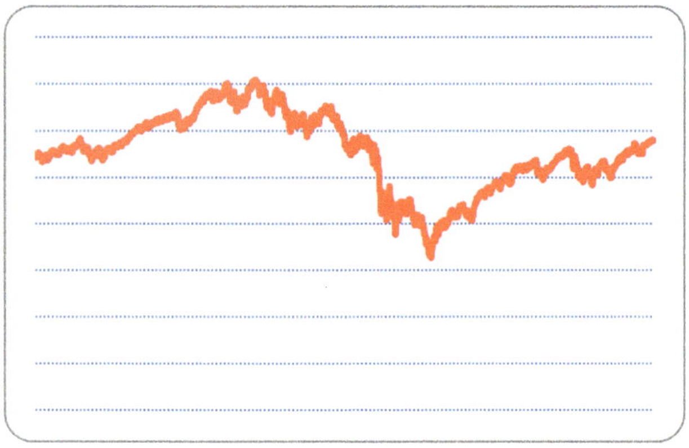

Figure 3: Evolution of DJIA between 1 Jan 2006 – 30 Dec. 2010

To determine the Risk Grades values associated to the main indices calculated by the BSE (BET, BET-FI, BET-C) it will be considered a decay factor $\lambda = 0.98$, which corresponds to a minimum number of records $n = \ln(0.1)/\ln(\lambda)$ of 113. The series of values for indexes is 1 January 2008 to 30 December 2010 and the index used as reference for determining the Dow Jones Industrial Average (DJIA) is σ_{base}.

We can notice in the above chart the negative effects of the financial crisis that occurred on the DJIA mainly by early 2009, when the North American stock market indexes registered multi-minimum (on 9 March 2009, the DJIA was calculated for 6547 points). Choosing the interval 1 January 2009 to 30 Dec.2010 for the series of values Risk Grades indices used in the calculation took into account to cover both a pronounced downward trend of the DJIA index and an increasing trend after March 9 2009.

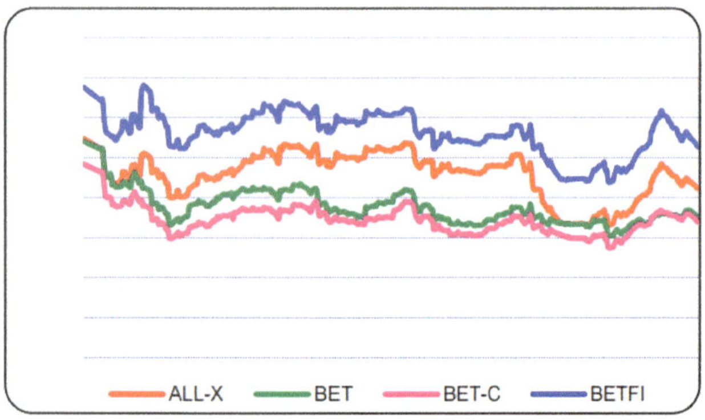

Figure 4: Risk Grades values for BSE indexes between 21 May 2009 - 30 Dec.2010

The Risk Grades values determined for the BSE indexes confirms that the Romanian capital market is riskier than the North American capital market. Besides that, as one can notice from the above chart, the Risk Grades values of the ALL-X index are consistently positioned below the BET-FI sector index and above the associated BET and BET-C.

If decay factor $\lambda = 0,96$ was chosen, the minimum number of records that we need is 228, sufficient for our purpose, consisting in comparing the risk associated with the capital market in Romania with those determined for other international stock markets or within the region.

In order to make a comparative analysis of the risks on the Romanian capital market and the main indexes of the Central and Eastern Europe we took into consideration the main indexes of Poland and the Czech Republic capital markets, meaning the WIG20 and the PX.

The WIG20 index is the underlying instrument for futures transactions listed on the Warsaw Stock Exchange and represents a modified capitalization-weighted index of 20 Polish stocks which are listed on the main market. The base value was set to 1000 points in April 16th 1994. The WIG20 index may not include more than 5 companies from a single exchange sector and limits the maximum weight of one symbol included in the WIG20 to 15%. Currently, the most important companies included in the WIG20 index are PKO BP, KGHM, DAM and Bank Pekao.

The PX Index is an index of major stocks that trade on the Prague Stock Exchange. The 5th of April 1994 was selected as the starting exchange day (a benchmark date) for the Index PX 50 and its opening value was fixed at 1,000 points. At this time the index included 50 companies traded on the Prague Stock Exchange, accordingly named PX 50. In 20 March 2006 the PX 50 index was merged with PX-D into the PX index, having now 14 symbols of the Prague stock market in its composition. The maximum weight for a stock symbol included in PX was set to 20% and from the companies included in the PX index the most important are CEZ, Comercni Banka, Erste Group Bank and Telefonika.

Figure 5: Risk Grades values for the main indexes in the region between 21 May 2009 - 30 Dec.2010

When comparing the Risk Grades values of WIG20 index of the Warsaw Stock Exchange and of PX index of the Prague Stock Exchange with those of the Romanian Stock Exchange (see figure 5), we reach a surprisingly conclusion, that the Risk Grades values calculated for the main indexes in the Central and Eastern Europe do not show major differences. Although constantly the Risk Grades values are above those associated with the WIG20 and PX index, the difference is very small [12].

RISK MANAGEMENT IN SETTLEMENT OF STOCK TRANSACTIONS

Clearing and settlement of stock market transactions

The risks managed by Institutions such as market operators, clearing houses and central depositories are not less important, but are maybe less visible to the public. It is known that stock market transactions are followed by a mutual transfer of ownership from seller to buyer, and the amount of money equivalent, from buyer to seller. Clearing and settlement take into account that transfers of financial instruments and financial funds between parties are to be performed safely and with little cost.

To prevent and to reduce the risks specific to the settlement of financial instruments transactions, direct access to clearing and settlement system is limited to those participants who meet a set of capitalization criteria, operational capacity and professional experience, which means that the settlement of an exchange transaction involves a given number of financial intermediaries. The more financial intermediaries are involved in the settlement of financial instruments transactions, the more complex is the settlement process.

Clearing and settlement stages

Clearing and settlement process begins immediately after a transaction with financial instruments is closed and goes through the following main steps:

- Confirming the terms in which the deal was closed between the buyer and seller. Confirmation of transactions can be conducted directly between parties or using a system that generates such an acknowledgment. In the latter case, the terms of the transaction can be transmitted to the central system or automatically by the trading system, or separately by each party. Although apparently it is just a formality, confirmation of transactions is a significant milestone in the process of completing a stock transaction, since it can identify in due time differences that may affect the proper functioning of the system.
- Compensation is an algorithm of obligations and / or rights accrued to the participant, after transactions were inserted in the system and confirmed. Usually, the calculation of obligations and rights of a participant can be made on a gross basis for the settlement of transactions, based on a bilateral net or multilateral net basis. Therefore, the calculation algorithm can result in one or more instructions to participants in the system that have to be respected. Only in the case of net multilateral compensation, the calculation algorithm results for each participant in only one instruction, that expresses (cash settlement level) either the obligation/ write to pay/ receive a certain amount.

The settlement itself, which is composed of:

- *Obligation to deliver securities*: falls to the seller that is part of a transaction or to the participant in the settlement that is in the position of a net debtor for a particular security;
- *Obligation to pay an equivalent amount*: falls to the buyer that is part of transaction or to the participant in the settlement with a debtor net quality in respect to financial funds.

The last stages of the settlement imply the highest financial risk throughout the process of finalizing exchange transactions, one of the main criteria that measures the performance of a clearing system and securities settlement transactions refers to the method the connection between the mechanism of transfer of securities (obligation to deliver) and transfer mechanism of funds (payment required) is made. The systems within which the permanent transfer of securities are to take place, subject to an exchange transaction, only if the final and irrevocable payment of amounts is made, fulfilling one of the main conditions to measure performance: delivery versus payment (Delivery Versus Payment - DVP). By using mechanisms that ensure DVP, one eliminates the most important component of all financial risks that accompany the settlement of transactions with financial instruments: principal risk.

Risks in clearing and settlement systems

As presented before, between the moment a transaction with financial instruments is closed and the ownership transfer certain stages are to be completed in a given time frame. The following risks are present and occur:

CREDIT RISK, implies the possibility that one side of a transaction might not honor its obligations, or after maturity, in whole or in part. Types of credit risk:

- *Principal risk*: is a consequence of time the difference between payment and delivery of securities as part of an exchange transaction. In case bankruptcy occurs between the two moments or insolvency of one parties involved in the settlement of that transaction, it is possible for one party to incur a loss equal to the transaction left unsettled. If such a risk occurs, the buyer might find itself in the position of having the financial securities acquired through market transactions paid, while the counterparty is no longer able to deliver those securities. The risk of the principal, from the perspective of the seller is described by the situation in which financial instruments have been delivered, but the buyer no longer has the opportunity to order the payment to the seller.
- *Replacement Cost Risk*: refers to a situation where before a final settlement between the parties involved in securities transaction may not be able to complete the initial negotiated market transaction settlement, thus requiring a replacement of that transaction. Thus, parties' involved in a transaction are equally exposed to loss due to the price change of the security that was object of the original transaction, the time interval between the time the original transaction (but not settled) and the transaction time for the replacing one. The buyer involved in a transaction takes over the risk associated with the replacement cost if the initial price of the transaction performed with a particular security is below the market price of that financial instrument once the transaction shall take place. Looking at the situation from the seller's point of view, the same type of risk occurs when the transaction replacement loss is concluded at a price lower than that of the original transaction. The size of the losses due to the risk associated with the replacement of a stock transaction is directly proportional to the volatility of the securities that were part of the original transaction and with the time between the date of completion of the transaction and the time of the final settlement. The shorter this time frame is, the lower the probability for the risk to materialize.

LIQUIDITY RISK refers to the situation where the seller of certain financial securities does not receive on the settlement date the amount from the buyer and thus he finds himself in a position to borrow or sell other financial assets to honor at its turn various other obligations assumed in view of collecting amounts from the original sale of securities. Liquidity risk arises in the case of the buyer as well if upon settlement it does not receive the securities purchased that were possibly involved in a transaction following the initial sale. The size of the liquidity risk is inversely proportional to market liquidity: the more liquid the market is, the lower the liquidity risk costs are. Liquidity problems have a high potential to have negative influences on the entire settlement system, especially when occurring amid high volatility of shares market and any delay in completion of the settlement by a participant thus raising concerns about solvency.

SYSTEMIC RISK refers to cascade spreading of a situation when settlement is impossible, from one participant to the clearing - settlement system to other members in the system (or all participants in the system). Institutions that operate clearing and settlement of exchange transactions are required to provide mechanisms and procedures to prevent expansion of liquidity or solvency problems from one participant to the whole system. Investor confidence in post-transaction systems is essential for liquidity growth of the stock market and is a prerequisite to entering a virtuous circle: a more liquid market significantly reduces the impact of risks that may arise in clearing and settlement system, which is reflected in increased market liquidity.

OPERATIONAL RISK implies that defective processing of transactions by participants in a settlement system, failure of transactions, fraud, disruption of communications or any other operating problems turn into financial losses.

Depending on the structure of clearing - settlement systems and transaction type, there might also be other risk categories, such as bankruptcy risks of the settlement bank, legal risk or custody risk. The probability that one or other of the above risks could materialize depends substantially on the following two main factors:

- implementation of strict procedures to control risks in the clearing and settlement of securities transactions, procedures known collectively as “risk management”;
- operation plan of the clearing and settlement system of transactions with financial instruments.

Recommendations on the clearing and settlement systems to reduce risks

Materialization of risks in clearing and settlement operations may have significant negative influences on a country’s entire financial system [13].

Moreover, given the internationalization of financial flows, where some of the affected participants in a clearing and settlement system operate simultaneously in multiple markets or operational links exist between two or more national clearing and settlement systems, this may cause contamination and spread of local problems internationally. Thus a set of recommendations was elaborated by specialized international institutions.

G30 recommendations

“G30 Recommendations” consists of a set of nine recommendations that should be implemented by all settlement systems:

- Confirmation of all transactions must be achieved by all direct participants in the market (for example: brokers/brokers/dealers and other members) in T+0. Details of all confirmed transactions must be transmitted to clearing – settlement system.
- Indirect market participants (e.g. institutional investors) should be informed on the implementation details of transactions in T +1.
- Every country should have an operational central securities depository, organized and managed so as to encourage activity of the direct and indirect market participants. The range of financial instruments eligible to be registered in the central depository must be broad. Preserving or dematerializing financial instruments should be as extensive as possible. If on the same market there are several depositors, they should operate on the basis of compatible rules and practices, in order to reduce settlement risk and to allow use of funds and make available any financial securities pledged as collateral in an efficient manner.
- Each market should be encouraged to reduce settlement risk by introducing “gross settlement in real time” mechanisms (Real Time Gross Settlement - RTGS) or by using compensation based on transactions that meet Lamfalussy recommendations.
- DVP system should be used as a method of settlement for all transactions. DVP is defined as “simultaneous dismissal, final, irrevocable and immediate securities and funds continuously throughout the day.”
- Payments related to settlement of securities transactions and using a financial instrument portfolio should target all markets and financial instruments, the adoption of the “Same day fund” Convention.
- A single cycle of implementation of the settlement should be adopted for all markets. Final settlement for all transactions should be made no later than T +3.
- Loans of financial instruments should be encouraged as a method of developing financial instruments transactions settlement. Barriers and taxes that limit loan of financial instruments should be removed.

Each country should develop a standard for messages related to financial instruments based on ISO Standard 7775. In particular, each country should adopt the ISIN coding system for securities, as specified in ISO Standard 6166.

CPSS – IOSCO recommendations

CPSS (Committee on Payment and Settlement Systems) - IOSCO (International Organization of Securities Commissions) recommendations, completed in 2001, take and develop provisions of G30 recommendations, adapting them to the important changes occurring in the securities industry in recent years, but adding new ones.

- The legal system: the settlement of transactions with financial instruments must have a solid legal framework, clear and transparent.

- Confirming transactions: Confirming transactions between direct market participants should be completed as soon as possible after the time transactions are executed, but not later than the end of the trading day (T +0). When it is necessary to confirm the transaction by indirect market participants (such as for institutional investors or global custodians), it must take place as soon as possible after execution of the transaction, preferably "T 0", but not later the "T +1".
- The settlement cycle: settlement transactions mechanisms must adopt the system by which the value date is set after a specified number of days from trade date ("rolling settlement system"). Final settlement must be made no later than "T +3". Costs and benefits of a shorter settlement cycle than "T +3" should be carefully evaluated.
- Central counterparty (CCP): costs and benefits of central counterparty mechanism should be evaluated. The introduction of this mechanism should always be accompanied by control of risk assumed by the institution which provides central counterparty services.
- Loan instruments: lending of financial instruments (REPO contracts or other equivalent transactions) should be encouraged to streamline the process of settlement of transactions. Barriers that inhibit the use of loan activities for this purpose should be eliminated.
- Central Depository (CSD): Preserving or dematerializing of securities and their transfer through electronic registration account must be used as widely as possible.
- Delivery versus payment (DVP): CSDs should eliminate principal risk by linking the transfer of financial instruments and transfer of equivalent financial funds so as to achieve delivery against payment (DVP).
- Complete Settlement: Completion settlement must take place no later than the end date of settlement. Successful settlement on the basis of a real-time settlement mechanism should be considered.
- Risk control: CSD providing credit facilities to participants, including CSDs that operate net settlement systems, should establish control of risks, ensuring at least successful settlement if the participant with the largest payment obligation can settle the payment. The best way to control risks involves the adoption of a set of measures that combine the use of collateral to limit exposure.
- Settlement money: Assets used for last payment obligation securities transactions should carry little risk or not be at all affected by credit risk or liquidity risk. If settlement scheme does not involve any use of central bank resources, measures should be taken to protect settlement system members of potential losses and liquidity constraints that may occur due to risk cash settlement agent used to complete transactions with financial instruments.
- Operational Safety: Sources of operational risk arising in the clearing and settlement should be identified and minimized by adopting an appropriate architecture for the system, through control and adoption of specific procedures. Systems must be safe and have adequate capacity. Action plans and emergency back-up should allow recovery of data and timely completion of settlement.
- Protect investors' portfolio: Entities that have custody of financial instruments must use specific procedures to ensure full protection of investors' portfolio. It is essential to have investors' portfolios protected from creditors' claims on the entity that retains custody of financial instruments.
- Access: CSDs and CCPs should have objective and transparent criteria established for participants, allowing fair and open access to the system.
- Efficiency: Without affecting operations safety, securities settlement systems should ensure efficiency in terms of costs incurred by participants.
- Communication standards and procedures: settlement systems securities transactions must use or adopt procedures and standards to facilitate communication to facilitate efficient cross-border transactions. Providing conditions for all participants to communicate in a fast, safe and clear manner is of the outmost importance for the functioning of clearing and settlement systems. It is therefore recommended for all participants in the system to know and to use standard procedures in relation to the messages content, securities identification or other participants. In cross-border transactions is advisable to use international standards: ISO 6166 and ISO15022.
- Transparency: CSDs and CCPs should provide participants enough information for them to identify and evaluate risks and costs of using services provided by the central depository and central counterparty.
- Supervision: settlement systems securities transactions should be subject to transparent and effective supervision. Central banks and capital market supervisory authorities must work together or with other authorities with competence in the field.
- Risks associated with trans-border connections between central securities depositories. The CSD that establish inter-connections with another CSD to make cross-border transactions must design and operate such connections so as to reduce specific risks of cross-border settlements. Cross-border transactions carry most of and the most complex risks that you may encounter when conducting capital market investments. Besides, the costs of performing such transactions are not reduced. To reduce risks and costs involved in carrying out cross-border transactions of financial instruments that otherwise would be borne solely by investors; institutions responsible for the successful settlement of the different countries were involved in establishing relationships to facilitate these operations. Achieving inter-connections between different systems operated by Central Depository make life easier for cross-border investors, but involves close monitoring of such risks if transferred from investors to administrators of clearing and settlement systems.

Risk management of settlement transactions at the Bucharest Stock Exchange

The services traditionally offered by stock exchanges refer to admission to the stock exchange of the issuing companies, establishing criteria for maintaining a particular security traded, disseminating for the public such stock exchange market information, especially for ensuring mechanisms to concentrate liquidity for a particular security. But continuously exchanges were directly interested in the whole building technical and institutional infrastructure to ensure safe completion and cost of transactions traded on the stock market. Therefore, some scholarships have created their own departments through which to work out the full range of post trading: clearing, settlement and registration. This was the case with the Bucharest Stock Exchange, which since the resumption of operations (in 1995) has provided all operators on the stock market clearing and settlement services [14].

For settlement of stock exchange transactions, BSE chose from the beginning a variant of Model 2 settlement, which requires multilateral clearing and final settlement of funds applied to the net basis, followed by settlement of securities traded, settlement being applied to the gross. The modular structure of the electronic system of BSE that includes trading module, clearing and settlement module and registry module allowed real-time interaction between each of these components, which provided a minimum exposure of the system to operational risk. The settlement cycle used in the stock market in Romania is "T +3" and the final settlement of funds is performed in a separate section of the national payment system (ReGIS), BSE being authorized by the NBR as a inter-banking clearing house since June 9, 1997.

This brief presentation of the clearing and settlement of BSE is only an overview of its main features without revealing all relations established between participants on the stock market from the moment the transaction was closed on the exchange floor until settlement, meaning until the buyer settles all payment obligation according to the contract and the obligation to deliver the securities according to the contract stipulations, accrued to the buyer. To facilitate understanding of information flow that constitutes the transaction settlement system on the BSE it is useful to first review the following terms:

- *Trading Report*: is that statement issued by BSE with terms and conditions of sale contracts of financial instruments concluded on the Exchange floor at a certain date, called the trade date;
- *Compensation Report*: is that document issued by BSE reflecting financial obligations and rights of company's financial instruments or custodian agent resulting from the transaction;
- *Report of Settlement*: is that document issued by the Bucharest Stock Exchange outlining duties and the pay of brokers or custodian agent, resulting from clearing transactions;
- *Settlement Banking Report*: is that document issued by the Bucharest Stock Exchange based on the settlement report that outlines the duties and financial rights of each participating bank and brokers that have an open settlement bank account;
- *Balance for final settlement*: the document issued by the Bucharest Stock Exchange, upon which BSE is entitled to introduce in ReGIS the payment instructions for settlement to be applied to the net basis.

Participants in the clearing and settlement system

Bucharest Stock Exchange is at the heart of the whole system of securities transactions settlement concluded on the stock market, interacting with each of the participants in the system:

- intermediaries: are financial investment companies (SSIF) and credit institutions that have the right to trade on the BSE;
- custodian agencies registered with BSE;
- clearing participants: banks are authorized by the National Bank as credit institutions, that have a settlement contract with BSE, ReGIS participation contract and a set up and enforce securities agreement with NBR. Intermediaries have opened settlement accounts for exchange transactions at the level of the clearing participants.
- National Bank of Romania, which is the administrator of the Settlement Express Transfer (ReGIS) system within which the clearing participants hold settlement accounts and participate in the financial settlement transactions of securities concluded with BSE.

Settlement mechanism

Information flow and all the activities leading to successful settlement is achieved over three days (T +3). Presented sequentially, the process is done through the following steps:

- After the trading session is closed, the Stock Exchange prepares the Compensation Report and the Settlement Report related to securities transactions executed by each intermediary. Intermediaries and custodians registered with BSE agents are required to confirm the next day, the contents of clearing and settlement reports.
- BSE will issue and send by fax with delivery receipt or secured e-mail to the clearing participants (settlement banks) all bank settlement reports.
- Participants in the clearing and settlement system managed by BSE are required to check the reports taken from BSE system. If participants in the clearing and settlement system managed by BSE object to the reports, they will communicate this in writing to BSE. After complaints are settled by BSE staff and reports are amended by BSE, documents and operations resume the circuit described above and the brokers modified reports, custodians and that participants will be forwarded by the BSE in the same day. If no objections are raised regarding the data presented in the reports provided by BSE, these are considered to be confirmed.
- On transaction settlement date (T+3), debtor clearing participants will confirm BSE their consent to participate in the settlement, according to the amounts recorded in the Bank Settlement Report, by fax with delivery note

or secured e-mail system. Also, participants will set up deposits equal to the net amount to be paid, in ReGIS in favour of BSE.

- Based on the final Settlement Balance, BSE will initiate the payment instruction to settle all net positions.
- National Bank will confirm to Bucharest Stock Exchange that final settlement was concluded by sending the document "Settlement report of net positions".
- After payment confirmation is received, BSE will transfer financial instruments from the sellers' accounts to the buyers, according to the concluded transactions. This will be accompanied by sending a message confirming to all clearing participants that settlement transaction was closed.

Workflow described above is one in which all intermediaries and settlement system clearing participants honor their obligations that arise from the exchange transactions. Efficiency of clearing and settlement system is checked, but especially when during the settlement cycles a situation where one (or more) of the participants in the system cannot fulfil obligations. To prevent such situations and to solve them when they manifest, clearing and settlement system of the BSE has established a risk management mechanism.

Risk management

Risks that can disrupt the transactions settlement flow have been identified both at the level of the brokers and custodian (first layer) and the clearing participants (second floor). Consequently, risk management measures are structured on two levels:

- Risk management measures managed exclusively by BSE;
- Risk management measures managed together with NBR.

The main instruments to manage risk, available to BSE are the following

- In order to limit default exposure on brokers' obligations, BSE sets through procedures a trading limit for each broker.
- To limit exposure in case of no payment, BSE ask from clearing participants and brokers to give priority to clearing and disbursement of amounts necessary to cover their debit positions.
- If it is found that upon settlement date, the participant to the clearing and settlement system managed by BSE has limited solvability to cover payment obligations, the clearing participant with whom the broker holds an account may proceed to grant credit, under an agreement signed in advance.
- If the clearing participant grants participants in the clearing and settlement system managed by BSE a loan needed to cover the debit position, the participant in the clearing and settlement system managed by BSE was in position debtor may proceed to establish a claim pledge of financial instruments existing own account, both those settled, and of the pending settlement in favor of the credit granted. Clearing participant is required to present BSE documents stating the guarantee institution. 5. If the participant does not grant credit or the loan does not fully cover the debit of participants in clearing and settlement system, than BSE shall be able to call the Guarantee Fund.

BSE applies risk management measures as presented above. However, it should be noted that enforcing trading limits to each participant and using the amounts from the Guarantee Fund are the measures with the greatest impact on the entire system thus helping BSE to control risks in the settlement system

Trading limit

The trading limit is the maximum amount limit within each of the participants on the market regulated by BSE can operate over a single trading session. This limit is calculated in real time by the electronic system of BSE, for each intermediate, being affected by each completed transaction and not by the orders entered into the system by the participant. The trading limit is determined by a calculation formula and is affected by exchange transactions concluded on their own by each participant, both on their own name and on behalf of clients.

The formula for calculating the trading limit is as follows:

$$3 \times (CIFG + CCFG + VNC) + VGB - / + VMj \qquad (4)$$

where: CIFG = participant's initial contribution to the Guarantee Fund;

CCFG = participant's current contribution to the Guarantee Fund;

NPV = participant's net equity amount, included in the "Minimum net capital and indebtedness indicators";

VGB = amount by which the trading limit may be increased as follows:

- for purchases - based on the amount deposited by the participant or his clients in the settlement account (or the accounts "clients") from the settlement bank or other banks, confirmed by presenting the statement of account or other bank documents (such as, for example, the payment order accepted by the bank);
- for sales - depending on the amount of sales declared by the participant in writing that he would perform during the trading session

VMj = value that has changed the total amount of loans to the participant and its customers and represents the more or less difference than the value previously reported by the participant. BSE will modify the participant's trading limit to this value.

During the trading session, each time a participant concludes a transaction, the Stock Exchange electronic system checks that the following formula is applied:

$$3x(CIFG + CCFG + VNC) + VGB - / + VMj >= 3x(CNCP - VNCP) + VNCI + CNCI \qquad (5)$$

where:

CNCP = are financial instruments purchased by the participant in his own name in that trading session, expressed as values;

VNCP = are financial instruments sold by the participant in his own name in that trading session, expressed as values

CNCl = are financial instruments purchased by the participant in that trading session, in his own name and on behalf of his clients, expressed as values;

VNCl = are financial instruments sold by the participant in that trading session, in his own name and on behalf of his clients, expressed as values

To determine the trading limit, participants are required to submit monthly to BSE's specialized department "Minimum net capital and indebtedness indicators statement" This statement will be sent to BSE within 10 working days from the end of the reporting month. If, during the time between two successive reports, the net capital varies more than + / - 15% compared to the last reports, the participant is required to communicate to BSE the new value immediately.

If during a day, the transactions concluded by a participant affect the relationship of inequality, the participant exceeding his trading limits, the Exchange system will not allow the introduction or modification of the exchange orders on behalf of that participant, as their execution would lead to increase his exposure, and orders that are already in the market will be suspended automatically by electronic system of BSE. Basically, if a participant that has completed operations which no longer meet the inequality relationship described above, will not be allowed to the market access till increasing the trading limit. In order to increase the trading limit is however necessary that the participant expressly requests this by sending a form by fax to BSE in this respect, also assuming responsibility for carrying out the settlement. However, the participant shall submit an estimate of the value of transactions he intends to carry out during the day when the limit was exceeded.

In time, the usefulness of trading limits and especially the formula used to calculate it attracted much discussion at the level of the stock market participants. The main criticism concerns the fact that on the right side of the relationship of inequality the sales and purchases amounts made on behalf of clients are treated similarly and influence the limit in the same way. Even if by making a sale transaction the intermediary does not assume any risk regarding the cash settlement of transactions, however the value of sales transactions made on behalf of clients diminishes daily trading limit of the participant. In fact, you can even consider that sales transactions made by a participant does not induce any risk in the entire settlement system as long as before being accepted an order of sale by the Exchange's electronic system, in the account of the seller are performed verification of the securities, subject to trading order. Considered from the perspective of market participants and given the above considerations, the current formula for calculating the limit of transaction seems unduly restrictive. Intuitively, the limit of transaction reported only net amounts paid in settlement appears to be more reasonable and would create a much closer relationship of emerging risks into achieving financial settlement to the Guarantee fund.

Guarantee fund

As required by the regulations and procedures Bucharest Stock Exchange, "The Guarantee Fund", "the Fund ", has as main objective to ensure necessary resources for proper functioning of the mechanism of settlement of exchange transactions."

Sizing the Guarantee Fund and its constituent sources represent, for any settlement system, two central problems whose solutions can be found only by reference to at least the following elements:

- Settlement model used;
- Costs of setting up such a fund guarantee, costs supported mainly by direct participants in the settlement system;
- Financial strength of the participants in the system, which is closely related to the overall stock market development;
- The value of the transactions made on the stock market;
- The performance of the compensation system (the degree of compensation), which ultimately generates the size of the exposures to settlement;
- Other regulations of risk management;
- Accepting that, in fact, financial risks are minimized and in very few cases are complete eliminated.

As explained earlier, for settling the exchange transactions, Bucharest Stock Exchange is using a variant of Model 2 Settlement (BIS classification), which requires multilateral clearing and final settlement of the funds on a net basis, followed by gross settlement of securities. For such a system, in the literature were directed two ways of determining the optimal value of a Guarantee Fund:

- For net settlement systems, there are six minimum requirements to be fulfilled. The fourth requirement of this report states that "as a minimum requirement, compensation schemes and multilateral net settlement shall be able to provide for the daily settlement, when it is impossible to honour the payment obligations by the participant with the highest exposure";
- Another opinion is that the minimum requirement to be greater than or equal to the number of days of the settlement cycle (for BSE, three) plus one, multiplied by the greater of the net debtor position recorded in a recent period of time, e.g. last two weeks.

As these recommendations suggest, the total amount of the Guarantee Fund has no absolute meaning, but must be interpreted in light of the whole system of risk management, value of transactions made on the stock market and especially the amount of exposure to settlement . These considerations were taken into account when establishing criteria for setting up and functioning of guarantee fund for settlement of negotiated transactions to BSE.

Guarantee Fund of BSE was established based on initial contributions of all members of the Stock Exchange Association (later, with the transformation of BSE in a stock company, any intermediary agent, carrying out transactions at BSE became eligible to participate in the Guarantee Fund) as well as of all custodian agents authorized by the Stock Exchange.

For the Guarantee Fund to be effective and achieve the purpose for which it was created is necessary that the component assets to have a high degree of liquidity. Therefore, in managing resources in the Fund should be prioritized the safe and liquid investment criteria, the yield obtained in the administration of the Fund represents only a secondary criteria.

CONCLUSIONS

To increase the accuracy which describes the development of the stock exchange in our country, it is necessary to build a synthetic index. Regarding the risk on the capital market, Risk Grades values determined for BSE indices show that the domestic capital market is more risky than the North American market.

However, analyzing the Risk Grades values obtained for all indexes in the region we notice that they are very close and shows that the investors are not picking up the capital market in Romania as an excessively risky relative to other exchanges in the region. It confirms the hypothesis that the main problems of the capital market in Romania are not related to demand, but derive primarily from an inadequate supply.

The risks managed by Institutions such as market operators, clearing houses and central depositories are very important, even though there maybe be less visible to the public.

Clearing and settlement services ensure that transfers of financial instruments and financial funds between the parties of an exchange transaction to be performed safely and with low costs.

In order to prevent and to reduce the risks specific to the settlement of financial instruments transactions, direct access to clearing and settlement system is limited to those participants who meet a set of capitalization criteria, operational capacity and professional experience, which means that the settlement of an exchange transaction involves a given number of financial intermediaries.

Since the highest financial risk throughout the process of finalizing exchange transactions take place in the last stage of the settlement process, an essential role is associated to the way the connection is made between the securities transfer mechanism (obligation to deliver) and the funds transfer mechanism (payment required). By using mechanisms that ensure Delivery Versus Payment (DVP), one eliminates the most important component of all financial risks during the settlement of the financial instruments transactions that is the principal risk. In order to limit the exposure to the risk of default of the intermediaries' obligations, a trading limit is set for each intermediate part.

Furthermore, the BSE requires its participants to prioritize the amounts necessary to cover their redundancy payment positions. From the market participants' perspective, the current formula for calculating the transaction limit seems unduly restrictive. Intuitively, calculating the transaction limit based only on the net amounts paid in settlement appears to be a more reasonable assumption and could lead to a much closer relationship between the risks emerging in financial settlements and the guarantee fund. Meanwhile, for the Guarantee Fund to be effective and to achieve its purpose for which it was created it is necessary that the assets within it to have a high degree of liquidity. The transition process and the recent international financial crisis have significantly affected not only the evolution of stock markets in Central and Eastern Europe, but also significantly changed the outlook for their future development.

That is why the stock market management should not only consider short-term measures in order to mitigate the crisis impact, but also to try to ensure the prerequisites for further development. The improvement of stock management in general and of stock market risks in particular, requires a medium to long-term perspective, similar to the opinions and contributions formulated by the authors in this chapter.

REFERENCES

1. O'Neill Wyss, B. (2001) - Fundamentals of the Stock Market, Mc Graw Hill Printing House
2. Smith B. M. (2003) - Global Stock Market. From ancient Rome to Silicon Valley, Farrar, Straus and Giroux, LLC, Chicago
3. Bucharest Stock Exchange (2007) – Manual for the Bucharest Stock Exchange Index, Available: www.bvb.ro
4. Stoica, V., Ionescu, E. (2002)– Capital Markets and Stock Exchanges, Economic Printing House, Bucharest
5. Anghelache, G. (2000) – Exchange and OTC, Economic Printing House, Bucharest
6. Andreica, M., Farmache, S., Andreica, R. Andreica, C. (2007) – Controversies regarding the listing of shares issued by BSE, Vol. Pro-active Partnership in Creativity for Next Generation, Polytechnique International Presses, Quebec.
7. Andreica,M., Nicolae, D., Andreica, M.E., Todor, L. (2009) – Working out forecast on the Basis of Statistical Extrapolation Principle, Economic Computation and Economic Cybernetics Studies and Research, No.2, Vol. 43
8. Andreica, M.I., Deac,V., Tipa, S. (2009) – Towards Providing Low-Risk and Economically Feasible Network Data Transfer Services, Proceedings of the 9th WSEAS International Conference on Multimedia, Internet and Video Technologies (MIV), Budapest, Hungary
9. Farmache, S., Andreica, M. (2010) – Improving Stock Management Assessment Instruments, Metalurgia International, No. 3.
10. Farmache, S. (2011)– Ways of Stock Management Improvement, Cibernetica MC Printing House, Bucharest
11. Kim J., Mina J. (2001) - RiskGradesTM Technical Document, The Risk Metrics Group LLC, New York, Available: www.riskmetrics.com
12. Warsaw Stock Exchange (2009)– Warsaw Stock Exchange Indices, Available: www.wse.com.pl
13. McAndrews J., Stefanadis C.(2002) -The Consolidation of European Stock Exchanges, Current Issues in Economics and Finance, 8(6) June, Federal Reserve Bank of New York, New York.
14. Tapking J. (2007) - Pricing of Settlement Link Services and Mergers of Central Securities Depositories, European Central Bank, Working Paper Series No. 710, Frankfurt.

CHAPTER 6

SECURITY MEASURES ON THE INTERNATIONAL TOURISM

Jesús E. Martínez Marín

INTRODUCTION

One of the most important elements of the tourism industry are the cruises. All the vessels and specially the passenger ships are considered vulnerable to the incidents came from the intentionality of the humans. As of September 11- 2001, important changes have come about in security matters, especially for the Western Hemisphere. Ports and vessels, given their vulnerability due to internationalization they represent, are the target for all kinds of terrorist attacks.

For years now the International Maritime Organisation (IMO) has been establishing measures to prevent act of vandalism, such as piracy and attacks on vessels by insurgents in conflict zones.

However, to consider a port a high-risk location which could be used to perpetrate an attack on society or the port itself is a concept that has gained strength since 9/11.

VULNERABILITY & RISK ON BOARD THE VESSELS

When we are talking about security on board, we must consider that since 2004, with the come in to force of the International Ship and Port Facility Security Code (ISPS), as an amendment to the Safety of Life at Sea (SOLAS) Convention (1974/1988), the vessels and the ports must be prepared for "detect security threats and take preventative measures against security incidents affecting ships or port facilities used in international trade".

On board the passenger's vessels, the prevention must be sometimes, even stricter, due to persons have free movement for all around the vessel. The investigations regarding this matter, comments that the prevention must go to avoid that unexpected action take place during the voyage at sea or when in port. On board the vessels, as all the transportation system, a big numbers of persons are coming on board, so the first measure is precisely avoid the access of a potential conflictive persons during the sea voyage, the problem suppose to be closed a shore before departure and attended by expert staff. (Marí R & Libran A,2003)

The problem starts when the next question came: how can be appreciated the intentionality of a person?

May be, with the experts some cases can be detected, but is impossible to control something that is just theory and the majority of the times, so it's really very difficult.

Talking about security, the protection must be for the passengers, vessel's crew, vessel, and also the personal items, that other people can damage, steal, or destroy. This risk increment when during the voyage is on board a famous or politician, due to sometimes, persons or organisations are looking for the way to affect their lives.

By other hand, the international net of terrorism, is also looking for any time to attack determinate interests, and the tourism Industry, has two main reasons for their intention:

- The Quantity of persons on board, from different nationalities.
- The very high economics impact that it has.

The prevention in all these cases, seeks to prevent any damage, making even be aborted during its planning, so they do not materialize, but once on board, should develop a comprehensive security device that protects both humans as the vessel of any threat.

All these efforts must go hand in hand with intelligence investigations, with the idea to reduce the risk to the minimum.

The vulnerability is the degree of disability that has a security system to detect incidents or threats, therefore, must be periodically reviewed and studied to provide the team in charge with the authentic information and avoid losing control at any time.

The vessels have already identified the risk on determinate matters:

Citation: Jesús E. Martínez Marín (2012). Security Measures on the International Tourism, Visions for Global Tourism Industry - Creating and Sustaining Competitive Strategies, Dr. Murat Kasimoglu (Ed.), InTech, DOI: 10.5772/37178.

- Danger at sea: damaged to the hull, stranding, sinking and collision.
- Dangers associated to the transport activity: fire, machinery's risk, marine pollution, cargo's risk and pests.

Relating to the security, the risks are determinate as follows:

- Violents actions: Terrorism, guerrillas, kidnapping, piracy.
- Antisocial Risks: robbery, theft, vandalism, robbery, fraud and scam. Attacks, assaults, sabotage, extortion, data manipulation, drug trafficking.
- Social's Problems: Stowaways, Illegal immigration..

Specifics ricks for the passenger ships & ports

According to statistics, most wanted merchant ships by the crime are, in principle, cruises. Until the fateful September 11, these ships were the sector that was growing within the travel business.

The International Association of Cruise Lines in New York, represents the world's most important lines, which also has its central headquarters in the United States even do not bear American flag.

Since 1986, cruise lines and the security forces that protect them must comply with relevant legislation required by the International Maritime Organization. These regulations specify the security measures that such vessels must be met, which include security plans, restricting access to areas of ships, systems identification and review of crew and passengers, and other measures intended to improve the security of people board. In this vein, having in mind different forms of threats that may suffer ships such as:

- Threat to the ship from the outside, both sailing and in port.
- Threat to the ship from the inside.
- Threat of use of the vessel as an instrument of a terrorist act.

To prevent external attacks in port, port authorities and port logistics operators must assume the responsibilities of comprehensive port security, hand in hand with law enforcement authorities concerned and the Port Facility Security Officer (PFSO), taking into account the vulnerability of ports in terms of security.

Ports must have service attendants, guards at the docks, which are responsible for a second access control, and all appropriate measures, and to maximize the safety of the port's facilities and ships at berth.

It is important to understand that these measures, apart from meeting the minimum requirements by international and national regulations should be tailored to each port according to their uses and customs, as they may vary substantially.

As for insider threats, legislation on the subject also specify the constant vigilance that must be on board, led by the Ship Security Officer, in collaboration with the captain and the rest of the crew, so of ensuring security along the journey.

The newly built ships and bring electronic devices installed first level, which serve to monitor different types of threats that can be found on board.

The shipping companies, shipowners and logistics operators cannot cut corners on security, because security is not a cost but an investment.

Bases on the above, the author of this chapter had made and analysis on the vulnerable areas of the Ports, involved deeply on the activity of the tourism; where the visitors are passing the time when are visiting a city.

Considering all these aforementioned areas is vital to do a study about what is happening now with these port areas, we may have some questions:

- Do they have a protection plan in case you want to do a slaughter while the room full of visitors?
- Are there any chances of an attack such facilities how are you?
- Is the International Maritime Organization in the event that these places are also vulnerable to attacks?

These and other questions have been selected to design a consultation that had being passed to port authorities, port terminals and urban management of the Port, in order to establish:

- Criteria to identify if in fact these places are threats or not,
- If the port's infrastructure are already being considered in current PFSC or not,
- If people are enjoying the entertainment at these sites may rest assured that they are protected or not,
- And most importantly if the port can guarantee the operation of the themselves, and if can attached the existence of PFSC with the leisure activities of these places (if the application if needed- i.e figure 1)

Figure 1: Port of Puerto Madero (Argentina) , Port's zone dedicated to the visitors.

With the main idea of show the real actual situation of the security on the ports, the main objectives to be met with this survey are:

- Evaluate the variables to consider in the analysis of vulnerability of the Port-Tourism relationship.
- Assess the degree of knowledge in the Ports in relation to the security of the areas in relation with the tourism.
- Evaluate the possibility of integration or cooperation between the ISPS and security of these areas.

Survey & consultation design

Based on the defined objectives and the geographical area to be covered, the design of the survey seeks to assess the information on vulnerable areas outside the ship-port interface, where tourists make life and carried out activities this important industry. For the realization of the questions have been studied the most common vulnerabilities in ports, in order to identify and assess whether the port has identified in its security plan and especially the reality on the port facilities to avoid if possible, to carry out an attack and any other threat that endangers human life, facilities, and the environment, an end to the port and surrounding citizenship.

Given the great limitation, issues of confidentiality and secrecy in security issues, the sample of experts was relatively low, however, enables setting us geographic diversity to extract important information on the different regions under the study.

Experts to choose should meet the following characteristics:

- Knowledge of system and port business.
- Knowledge and mastery of the subject regarding Puerto & tourism.
- Port Security Knowledge
- Prestige in the maritime and port industries.

Following criteria and considering the limited number of experts in the area decided to contact area 13 experts covering the following regions:

Figure 2: Map of Countries under study

Initially the study included only universe to European ports, however, thanks to the efforts made by contacting various American ports, has enjoyed the cooperation of Spain, Chile, Panama, Costa Rica, Colombia, Venezuela and Argentina, significantly expanding the geographical impact initially considered.

One aspect to consider is that the realization of this survey has been possible thanks to academic character research. Sensitive and confidential nature of the data is a major constraint when conducting surveys on impact issues such as this. On the other hand, initially, the goal of this research aimed to survey staff crews of ships, but the non-accessibility, whether for security, political or business related to the subject, made to shift the topic applying the selection criteria outlined above experts in order to make a proposal to improve the current implementation of the ISPS (Martínez J. 2011). Given these considerations, it is considered as the sampling unit each of the ports where it has been surveyed.

Consultation response

The response rate on the number of surveys sent was as follows: 80 % of response received. To perform an analysis of the implications of the results shall be analyzed in detail the involvement of each of the responses.

A level of existence of the Port Facility Security Plan, the results indicate that all ports respondents have adopted a Security Plan for the protection for its port facilities in accordance with the ISPS.

This percentage would lose significance if not analyzed according to the following result, in which 90% recognize the existence of criteria for considering an area as vulnerable. Additionally, 70% admit to turn that port areas related to the city have been considered as vulnerable according to the criteria defined by the Port Authority. As for the Passenger Terminal 60% consider that they meet the security requirements defined by the ISPS Code, which does not necessarily indicate that compliance for the rest of the tourist areas of the port.

While it is true that 60% of respondents recognized that there is compatibility between the normal routine and port security duties required by the ISPS, the remaining percentage indicated. Given that security should be met for all situations in accordance with the requirements of the ISPS is to understand which are necessary to implement measures to improve this significant percentage trying to reduce or mitigate these risks and incompatibilities. i.e figure 3.

Figure 3: World Trade Centre of Barcelona- Tourisyic Port Facility

Is important to highlight processes at when one is committed, and presents a risk, the potential field which can affect not only reduces the same but all the processes that relate to it either directly or indirectly, can be placed in a vulnerable position to the whole routine activities. In considering whether the port areas related to tourism, can represent a threat for 60% of respondents believe they can pose a serious risk to port security. This implies that a high percentage agrees to consider such areas as high risk and likely to have incidents. Once verified that we proceed to analyze the risks inherent in that area.

Based on this study is demonstrated that a large part of the ports surveyed do not have control and monitoring mechanisms for public use spaces. This aspect increases the risk in all the possible actions that can be generated through the direct action of a human being, with all the consequences that are deducted.

This factor is increased to analyze the outcome of the question, in which 70% admitted that the security of port areas related to leisure (not including passenger docks but the other areas such as shops, restaurants, etc.) is not linked to the Integrated Safety Harbor.

This leaves an open space for research and that still does not relate the safety of commercial space port (with modal interchanges of goods) to the security of other spaces that belong to the port area (such as those related to leisure and tourism).

In the same vein, there is not any control to address recreational craft (they do sea's tour on the ports) leaving totally unprotected access to other port facilities. Comparing this situation with the airport security, a loophole is evidence relevant to the detriment of protecting the safety of persons, vessels, ports and cities.

Ironically and fortunately, the majority of respondents considered independently of the previous answers that there are criteria that guarantee the safety of citizens while in the port complex. In this sense, it can be considered as a future line of research in order to identify the degree of knowledge, the real risks and possible implications of an impact on the security of visitors.

In the same context, it highlights the need for further training and knowledge about ISPS and PFSC, because none of its sections provides for the protection of the areas that are port that are intended for tourist purposes, but 80% of respondents stated that the PFSC includes contingency plans for those areas of recreational use in the event of a risk When analyzing the risk may come from the surrounding areas, 90% believe they are vulnerable and risk focus of the port and its spaces.

Is important to emphasize the vast majority recognizes that there are surveillance cameras and security devices installed in the spaces of these spaces. But when it comes to prevention, 80% recognized the absence of appropriate technological tools to prevent terrorist attacks. Considering the number of people who annually visit a port with leisure facilities, it follows that the risk in case of terrorist attack can be very large and affects a significant number of lives.

Given the existing security levels in the ISPS, realizing that the maximum level of protection enabled emergency determined in the ISPS (level 3), the response of respondents implies that 50% of the stores and recreational areas would not change their activity in the event of a terrorist threat; indeed, only 70% of cases recognizing the existence of a warning to visitors in case of a threat.

On the other hand it is encouraging that 100% of the claims that there is coordination with different agencies at the time to act in case of attack. In most cases, the National State would be in charge the security forces followed by the port authority.

Additionally only 60% of cases, the development company or manager of the port city spaces, acknowledges to be doing staff training on port security. This aspect becomes once again highlight the weakness in the field of prevention.

In the case of unaccompanied baggage or packages left that could be considered suspicious, 60% confirm that measures are implemented to manage these cases immediately if they occur.

IMPORTANT CONCLUSIONS OF THE CONSULTATION CARRIED ON TO THE EXPERTS

Attached are the main conclusions deduced from the survey:

- The existing limitation when conducting surveys on the issue of security and port security, given the sensitivity and confidentiality of the data. However the response rate case has been positive with 80% for the initial sample.
- All ports respondents have adopted a Port Facility Security Plan in accordance with the ISPS.
- Only 30% acknowledge a high level of compliance with the plan, while 70% admitted to a medium or poor compliance.
- 70% admitted to have measures on the level of surveillance and control in areas considered vulnerable. Additionally, 90% recognized the existence of criteria for considering an area as vulnerable.
- 70% said that the Port-city areas have been considered as vulnerable according to the criteria defined by the Port Authority.
- 40% of respondents recognized that there are inconsistencies between the normal routine and port security duties required by the ISPS, the same percentage recognizes not fulfill all the tasks set by the protection plan.
- For conducting drills and the existence of cooperation with state bodies, the answer is nearly unanimous. It is recognized that periodic drills and with the cooperation of state security's forces.
- In 70% of cases are considered that are protected:
    - Usage by land and sea.
    - Infrastructures.
    - Communications infrastructure and information systems.
- In terms of vulnerability / protection of areas of recreational use of the port, these are the main conclusions:
    - 60% of respondents felt that this type of port areas may represent a serious risk to port security.
    - 40% of respondents ports have mechanisms to monitor and control what people do at all times when in the port facility dedicated to recreation.
    - 70% recognized that the safety of recreational and tourist areas is not linked to Integrated Port Security.
    - 60% admit to not having control of access for people with weapons to pleasure boats moored in the harbor.
    - 90% considered that the surrounding areas are vulnerable and risk focus of the port and its spaces.
    - Paradoxically, the majority of respondents (80%) consider whether the previous replies that there are criteria that guarantee the safety of people while on this interface port and the city.
- In relation to the degree of knowledge about PFSC and ISPS requirements, a record of the need for further training and knowledge of both, since none of its sections provide for the protection of public use space and yet 80% of respondents said that the PFSC includes contingency plans for public use AREAS AT PORTS IN THE EVENT OF AN ATTACK.
- When it comes to prevention:

- o is recognized by 80% in the absence of appropriate technological tools to prevent terrorist attacks
- o only 60% of cases, the development company or manager of the port city spaces, acknowledges to be doing staff training on port security

- With regard to the parameters required by the ISPS warning if:
  - o In 50% of cases, shopping and recreational areas would not change their activity in the event of a terrorist threat at Level 3.
  - o 30% of cases have recognized a warning to visitors in case of a threat.
  - o 60% confirmed that measures are implemented to manage cases of unaccompanied baggage or packages left that could be considered suspects.
- In relation to the structural security of access and connectivity port structures, the conclusions to note are the following:
  - o Only 20% say that their land access are very well protected
  - o In terms of the anchorage and maneuvering areas Donsol 10% confirmed that they are well protected, and 60% say they are poorly protected or unprotected. The same pattern applies for the berthing areas. · The following sections present the same pattern of results. Most find that they are "sufficiently secured". Only 20% believe they are under-protected or unprotected:
  - o electrical distribution systems and computer systems
  - o cargo handling equipment
  - o commercial port facilities (specialized and multipurpose terminals)
  - o container storage area
- In the case of bridges, roads and rail access, 70% do not consider there is a good level of security. Only 30% think that is quite protected and none of the respondents considered this as "Very Sheltered"
- In terms of service vessels and equipment and protective systems and surveillance, whose authority belongs to the maritime authorities of the countries despite evidence that a higher level of protection (60% and 80% respectively), cannot be that is at the level required by the legislation.
- In the waters adjacent to ports, 50% believe they are little or no protection, 40% consider a level of protection means and a minority of 10% is considered as very secure.
- It's is very important to emphasize that analyzing information by geographic area to which the port belongs dispersion and disparity found in global responses are repeated to be analyzed geographically. That is, different aspects of different degrees of compliance according to the different areas however cannot be said that an area is "more secure" in general terms that another (Martinez, 2011).

PREVENTING MEASURES

One of the best ways to prevent more attacks and attacks on ships is precisely the training of personnel of both ships and ports, which is why the ISPS establishes the obligation to train in specific courses to the actors in this business.

These courses are instructed in basic standards of protection for each measured preventives and action in an emergency at different levels has been set in the ISPS.

Moreover, in the specific case of the cruise companies must have action protocols for any additional emergency, such as unaccompanied packages, suspicious people both in port and by ship, measures that allow the passage the crew report any approach that considers normal on board, review and inspection of security equipment.

One of the most important measures for prevention are the drills with This accomplishes several objectives:

- Passenger awareness of the importance of the security the ship
- Playing much like the real action protocols ruled the ship's security plan.
- Having the information of the reaction time and assess the possible implications and improvements to be updated immediately.
- To quantify the degree of knowledge of the crew to a contingency.

Of all the above points which I consider more important is the awareness by the crew and passengers of the importance of comprehensive security of the ship and her starring role on the detection of any possible threat.

CONCLUSION

When talking about security and the tourism industry, cruise ships take primary importance as vectors of a large number of people who enjoy the ports and cities. Ironically port cities as models adapted from "port-city relationship" are not formally integrated in the ISPS, but on the contrary, its internal regulations are protecting these people who enjoy recreational activities in a port. The threats are real; there is evidence of several bombings and attacks on the ports, as well as the intentions of terrorist networks to attack the port facilities.

The idea is not to create unnecessary alarm, but be on guard against any loophole that has the current security system, which could jeopardize the most important thing there is: human life. There are many regulations, measures, policies to protect the comprehensive security of cruise ships, ports, tourist areas of port facilities, however, no regulation, all in accordance with the needs of each port.

The standardization of regulations, to create a sense of minimum protection, however, the commitment of local authorities as extremely important, as are the real connoisseurs of the manners and customs of this place. Safety requires collaboration definitely unrestricted throughout the industry, all players are invited to contribute part of its mission to ensure security.

One of the factors that help and is very important in these cases is the existence of port and logistics communities strengthened, and that based on them, it is easier to create mechanisms of collaboration and rapid response to security forces, and regular training to help workers in the industry know how to react to any eventuality. In short, security is of utmost importance and effort depends directly on the concatenated all businesses, law enforcement, but especially each person serving in any role, this conglomeration of the tourism industry.

This proposal, based on research, has the idea of precedent among other things, show that the academic-research can and should collaborate in developing proposals that will not only focus toward the traditional trading port, but also focused on new and modern opportunities of sustainable development represents a port for the cities that surround it, which are today known as "Port Cities".

Beyond the figures, the number of TEUs or tons per year, the ports, have a great interaction with people through the tourist industry, which undoubtedly comes from the same source port. As is well known, near the ports, were located the main squares of cities and the commercial heart of time, being since ancient times, places vulnerable not only to the economies of those cities but for their people, since most daily activities of citizens were developed around the harbors.

With this concept of port cities, it takes the original sense, after the modernization of ports, resulted that these compounds develop purely commercial & logistics activities and gave him back to the city, shutting down their access, limiting visibility even of cities to the seascape.

In this sense a fundamental aspect to consider, which facilitates the proper treatment of the spaces of the tourist or recreational use of the port, is to understand the complexity and variety of conditions that have these areas for processing, which are advantageous to time for inclusion in the PFSC:

- Are limited and circumscribed,
- Not all ports have space for public use or are not qualified as such,
- Have severe restrictions
- They are marked by the topography of the sites,
- They have historical memory and architectural heritage quality and attractive to tourism.
- Meet two emblematic elements: earth and water.

With site-specific differences, worldwide socioeconomic these complexes seem to be moving toward awareness and the need to generate changes in the direction of urban policy to promote a new model of physical organization otherwise accompanying the complex conditions of social and economic development.

Thus, as port companies have led to complex social phenomena taking place transfers of activities between the city and harbor, including regional and international scope due to the nature of the tourism insight. In this line and as a result of the transformation and modernization in the scale and technology infrastructure of these complexes and the greater importance to the economy of the international relationship between touristic cities, the port territory has become one of the most evocative of urban contemporary.

This space is now preferred, has become the venue in the cities for the location of business centers, shops, residences, hotels, museums and areas of recreational and cultural events, determining a trend that is accentuated and thereby permanently, which today can be considered one of the main causes of growth and development in a large set of cities, is the weight of the transformation of their port renewal areas, so that you can even say that the hope of many cities damaged, it is precisely in the conversion of the port areas. However, after the fateful 11-S, the security measures in all aspects, were reinforced and become effective, international laws to ensure protection, first of all shipping to the United States, which immediately were taken by the most countries in the world.

With the entry into force of the ISPS, security measures are restricted only to commercial terminals, even we must recognize that higher priority is given to these measures in the traffic of any port in the world to the United States, and in some cases detracts from the Ports own security outside that territory. If we talk about the initiative CSI (Container Security Initiative), launched in 2002 by the U.S. Bureau of Customs and Border Protection (CBP), an agency of the Department of Homeland Security, in order to "increase security for containerized cargo shipped to the United States" is intended to "extend the area of external security that American borders are the last line of defense and not the first." (Martinez, 2011)

This assertion can extract multiple reflections, which confirms that these agreements were initially prioritized the protection of U.S. ports, and over time have been extended to the rest of the world so it is fair to point out that the European Union also made likewise creating the ESCS (European Supply Chain Security) and as an example, this initiative in Spain has been called the "Secure Logistics Community," which means not only bring security to the port areas but extend to all steps in the logistics chain, from supply plants to modal transfer points, as a platform for promoting and improving the security of the supply chain, which promotes trade and logistics and agile safe through compliance of international customs regulations and the application of international best practice safety in World Trade.

Understanding both the phenomenon of conversion of port, the various legislative initiatives in international port security and the results of the survey in this study, we should note the following:

- First, the great lack of knowledge beyond the Port Authority in Global Business Integration Port, i.e the entities that share services in the ports, not all know the implications and dimensions of a port as a whole, majority being the ancient doctrine that the ports were limited to commercial premises where the transfer occurred modal cargo or passengers.
- Second, all respondents felt it necessary to include public use areas in Port Protection Plans (PPP), extends the scope of the scenarios in case of increasing the level of security at the ports.
- Thirdly there were many deficiencies in the current application code itself, leaving open for future research,

improvements in implementation thereof, and in particular in relation to visitor use areas, should devise mechanisms to integrate existing security plans to unify and standardize the protection of the entire port system.

- Fourth, and related to one of the questions on which further wanted to start this research has shown that the tendency of the Port-city: USOA entertainment, catering, passenger ships, considering the domestic tourism and outside, and the Safety and Security Port System they are compatible, as long as you start developing plans concatenated without affecting any other trend, i.e that the recreational use of certain port areas will not endanger the safety enclosure, and the protection of commercial space (terminal) do not leave the city without the possibility of converting obsolete spaces in modern socio-economic complexes, which are perhaps one of their few opportunities to generate employment and wealth.

To achieve protection of the port shall:

- Define all relevant areas for port security areas including tourism and recreational use;
    - Coordinate measures for areas with different characteristics from the point of view of protection.
    - Determine an organizational structure that contributes to improving port security.
    - Establish, on whether case varying measures of the different parts of the port, changing security levels and information obtained from the intelligence services.
    - Join the developers (restorations & leisure's companies) to the Port's plans drills for increase the security.
    - Evacuation drills in port areas intended for public use.
    - Provide all areas of security cameras and create (if not exist) a security team to allow monitoring at all times human movement in these areas, with the intention of ensuring peace and enjoyment of people, which keeps the flow of tourists and customers to these spaces.
    - Placing warning mechanisms that allow citizens to inform authorities and enforcement authorities of the presence of suspicious packages or abandoned, because in these places is not always easy to access safety equipment, assessing the cooperation of citizens to prevent possible incidents.
    - In the event that citizens have ports docks with yachts, or, on the other hand, harbor tour boats travel (example in Barcelona of the Swallows), find ways to prevent access to material or armed persons suspect in these vessels, preventing water mobility take advantage of any possible threat.
    - On the other hand, we must maintain a permanent monitoring of the security of the port, based on strategic planning in order to get feedback, using their own experiences and alien to meet this objective.
    - Based on the research of the author intends to create a study commission between the Maritime and Port Authority with recreation development company of the Ports, and the authorities of the port cities, to bring all the security measures they deem appropriate under the particularity of the region-specific ports, as this will allow each port integrated PFSC, according to its specific own security measures and protection that are useful and necessary.
    - This fee must design study of specific plans added to the port facility security plan, taking a global view of the port facilities in order to achieve efficiency in following minimum security measures to protect human beings in the areas surrounding recreational or leisure of the ports.
    - It is very important that these plans be developed in conjunction with national security agencies, states and / or municipalities, depending on the territorial organization and legislation of each country, and be under constant observation in these areas as well as providing areas farthest from the technological means to respond swiftly to any threat arising in the port city, given the number of lives that travel on it.
    - In line with all previous initiatives should be developed and training plans covering all active figures involved in the port and city relations, with the aim of ensuring a proper process of prevention beyond the emergency action.

The idea is that this proposal should adhere to the Port Security Plans, being the most easily in its modification and implementation, as well as the last link in the security chain and in the face of users ports, which allows these adjustments have a direct impact on achieving greater security for citizen's ports.

It should also be included in the concept of interface to all areas within the port are being related to the enjoyment of human beings in their facilities and linked to the development of surrounding communities and the marina, and with this step legally protect these facilities, which would lead to the inclusion of various measures in the port security plan that can protect citizens ports.

To this must also update the entire platform technology security and protection of these areas, which would generate greater control of possible emergencies, and taking into account that most respondents agreed that their ports do not have the ideal technological protection can be consider that this is also an important point to be agreed improvement in the system.

Moreover, taking advantage of the entry into force of the legislation governing the voluntary audit request by the member states of IMO Resolution: A974.4, adopted on 1 December 2005, at paragraph 19 of the order of day, this regulation will allow states to voluntarily request to audit their management systems (in general) and management of maritime and port security, so that the proposed improvements will help even these audits are overcome every day better conditions, highlighting the improvements in areas that present safety and security do not understand how the citizens port security, and these areas from which you can access port facilities if included, in this way, all that can be added to local marinas with space for public uses, can be evaluated through audits, generating a feedback and evaluation process, which will at all times ensure excellence in the system.

ACKNOWLEDGMENT

I would like to give a special recognition to the experts who have contributed to this study, thanks to them, the assumptions have a theoretical level, have been confirmed including the conclusions drawn from research, can have a real information, contact live with every day of those people that live in the premises for the attention of tourism, motor development of many port cities.

REFERENCES

1. Brieze, F.(1989). Brides of Sea. Port Cities of Asia from 16th to the 20th Century. Honolulu, USA.
2. Hawkes, K. (1989). Maritime Security. Cornell Maritime Press Ed. Vol 1. ISBN: 978- 0870333958, Maryland, USA.
3. International Maritime Organisation (1993). Piracy and other crimes. News, N° 1, pp9-16 , London, UK.
4. International Maritime Organisation (2002). International Ship and Port Facility Security Code, 2003 Ed. London, UK.
5. Marí R & Libran A. (2003). Seguridad Pública en Buques de Pasaje. Universitat Politécnica de Catalunya Ed.; ISBN: 9788483016923, Barcelona, Spain.
6. MARÍ, R. (2006). Security of the Port's Facilities. ICG Marge Ed. Barcelona, Spain.
7. Martínez, J. (2009). The security of the citizen's ports. Journal of Maritime Research. ISSN: 1697-4840, Cantabria, Spain.
8. Martínez, J. (2011). Proposal to improve the effectiveness of the implementation of the ISPS code in port facilities. Ph.D Thesis, Technical University of Catalonia, Spain.
9. Scovazzi, T. (1994). Elements of international law of the sea, Tecnos Ed. Madrid,
10. Parrit, B. (1986). Violence at Sea: A Review of Terrorism, Acts of War, and Piracy, and Countermeasures to Prevent Terrorism. ISBN: 978-9284210336 . Paris, France.
11. Parrit, B. (1996). Crime at Sea: A Practical Guide. ISBN: 978-1870077323. Paris, France.

CHAPTER 7 COSMETICS' QUALITY CONTROL

Bruna Galdorfini Chiari, Maria Gabriela José de Almeida, Marcos Antonio Corrêa, and Vera Lucia Borges Isaac

INTRODUCTION

The quality of a cosmetic product, in the same way as to other kind of products, is initially defined by the manufacturer that chooses the features that a product should present. On the other hand, the quality control of a product aims to verify if all of these defined features are in accordance with the standard definitions and if it will be maintained during the shelf life of the product (Shewhart, 1980).

The quality control of cosmetics is important to ensure the efficacy and safety of products and its raw-materials. Due to the rapid growth that cosmetic industries have exhibit all over the world, efficient, low cost and rapid methods to assay cosmetics' quality control are a priority. Some current techniques used by the cosmetic industry can be applied to the evaluation of cosmetics' quality control in an efficient manner, such as: rheology, sensory analysis and small angle X-ray scattering (SAXS).

Sensory analysis is a powerful tool, since there is no equipment able to measure the human feelings. It applies experimental design and statistical analysis to obtain information about a product in relation to what people feel when use or consume a product, in other words, it is used to indicate consumer acceptance of a particular product. It can be understood as the discipline that interprets, assess and measures characteristics of a product, after stimulating people in relation to their vital senses, as vision, touch, smell and taste (Stone et al., 1992). It is widely used in food industry and recently, it has also been applied in the cosmetic industry (Almeida et al., 2008; Aust et al., 1987; Backe et al., 1999; Lee et al., 2005; Parente et al., 2005; Wortel et al., 2000).

The sensory analysis can be applied in the research and development of a new cosmetic (Isaac et al., 2012a), in controlling the manufacturing process to evaluate raw-materials quality and, even, to make possible the substitution of a raw-material of a product that is traditional in the market without changes in the product's features (Meilgaard et al., 1991; Muñoz et al., 1993).

The application of sensory analysis could be related to the product control, referring to the storage, packaging and maintenance of sensory quality in relation to time and temperature (Muñoz et al., 1993), since these factors can change a sensory attribute that the product present originally (Zague, 2008) and people who participates of the sensorial panel could realize the changes in the sensorial attributes. Another function of this important tool is to performance comparative tests between competing products.

Another tool that could be applied to evaluate cosmetics' quality control is the rheology, which studies the flow and deformation of fluids. It has been used in research laboratories and industries as a tool for characterizing ingredients and products, and to predict the performance of products and consumer acceptance.

Rheology has been widely used because, by means of this tool, the researcher can determine physicochemical properties of a product. Constructing a rheogram, it is possible to check the flow curve, evaluate if there is a yield stress and a hysteresis area, which appears to be related to the release of drugs and actives. It is also possible to construct a creep and recovery curve obtaining information about viscoelasticity of each system.

Specifically, in relation to the quality control of cosmetics, specifically, rheology can be applied to help in determining the stability of products by means of the apparent viscosity measured periodically in a determined period exposing the samples to stress conditions (high and low temperatures, solar irradiation), and to monitor the flow characteristics during the shelf life or in the stability assay of a product.

The SAXS technique have being used for the analysis of cosmetics, in order to evaluate the presence of liquid crystalline structures, called liquid-crystals, which are known to increase the stability of formulations becoming, therefore, desirable in

Citation: Bruna Galdorfini Chiari, Maria Gabriela José de Almeida, Marcos Antonio Corrêa and Vera Lucia Borges Isaac (2012). Cosmetics' Quality Control, Latest Research into Quality Control, Dr. Isin Akyar (Ed.), InTech, DOI: 10.5772/51846.

cosmetics (Makai et al., 2003). Combining these three tools, it is possible to test the quality of cosmetics with a rich range of data, and obtain a deep characterization of the system. The results contribute to determining product use, or even, they provide indication of what need to be done to develop a product with predetermined characteristics.

SENSORY ANALYSIS

Sensory analysis is defined by Piana et al. (2004) as the examination of a product through the evaluation of the attributes perceptible by the five sense organs (organoleptic attributes), such as color, odor, taste, touch, texture and noise, allowing the establishment of the organoleptic profile of diverse products, including cosmetics.

The sensory analysis was first applied to the food industry, but the high advance in other areas, such as the cosmetic and pharmaceutical industries, and the important data obtained with the sensory analysis, demanded this useful technique to describe what the consumers fell.

An important advantage of the use of sensory analysis in the quality control of a cosmetic product is that it yields a complex analysis in relation to all sensorial attributes that a product could present, it means that, the volunteer who participates of the sensorial panel is able to give information about the fragrance, the sensation, the appearance, the consistence, and other features that this person experience when use such product. The description of these characteristics by means of equipment would be an arduous work and would provide not sufficient or not valuable data when compared to the data provided by the human senses. Beyond that, the acquisition of this equipment could be of high cost when compared to the sensory analyses' costs (Ross, 2009).

The association of data obtained from sensory analysis and instrumental analysis (especially physicochemical analysis) provides great information and a more complete profile of the product (Ross, 2009).

Nowadays, there are companies specialized in perform sensory analysis of cosmetic products, and thus, they could be contracted to perform this study for cosmetic industries that don't have a sector trained to do it.

The sensorial performance of cosmetics is essential to the acceptance of consumers (Almeida et al., 2008; Fouéré et al., 2005; Lee et al., 2005; Proksch, 2005), thus, especial attention should be given to this subject.

The sensorial features of a formulation are mainly related to the raw-materials and package (Dooley et al., 2009). The raw-materials influence directly in what the consumer feels when applies the cosmetic. The emollients, for example, are raw-materials of marked influence in the tactile sense (Parente et al., 2008; Gorcea and Laura, 2010). Other raw-materials are available at the market and are commercialized to be used in formulations as sensorial modifiers. The main representatives of this kind of product are the silicones and Polymethyl Methacrylate (Ozkan et al., 2012).

The package influences in the first impression of the consumer about a product, since the first sense used to choose a cosmetic in the market is the vision. After, the smell is used too. The tact is not involved in the first purchase attitude, but it will define if a consumer will become a loyal consumer.

In this context, it is possible to verify that the sensorial features of a cosmetic are of great importance in the success of it in the market.

Thus, the sensorial analysis could help a company to define the attributes that a product should or not present beyond the characteristics and intensity of these attributes.

Another point is that these desired sensorial characteristics should be maintained during the cosmetic shelf life. To obtain that, the raw-materials used should be of good quality, the manufacture practices should be appropriate, the preservatives used need to be efficient and the formulation should be stable.

In conclusion, the sensorial analysis is an indispensable technique to help the formulator to evaluate the quality of its new product, in relation to its sensorial characteristics and to its stability, testing if the product will keep the nice sensorial feelings that transmit to the consumer during the time of use. This tool is helpful to the research and development area of a company which aims to obtain good quality products of high acceptance by the consumers. The suitable application of sensory evaluation could avoid the outlay of a company with the launching of a product in the market that was rejected by the volunteers of the preliminary study.

Currently, the sensorial analysis have gained more scientific rigor due to the need to offer to the consumers products that meet their expectations and due to the high competition between the major industries of this sector.

To perform the sensorial analysis with rigor and organization, the laboratory destined to it must have the following areas:

- A room destined to the analyst who leads the team (Figure 1a)
- A conference room (Figure 1b)
- A room for the samples preparation (Figure 1c)
- An area to the analyses with the volunteers (Figure 1d)
- The laboratory should be located in an easy access place.

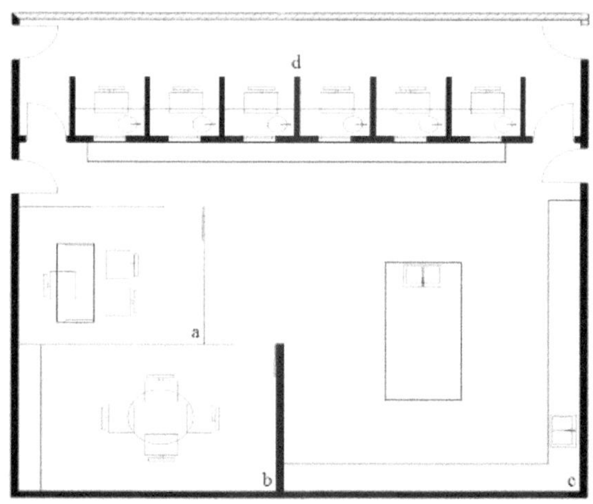

Figure 1: An example of layout of a sensorial analysis laboratory (Isaac et al., 2012a).

The area where will be performed the analyses should be divided in individual cabins (Figure 2) with a window, where the analyst must offer the samples to the volunteer, sink and faucet, to the volunteer use when necessary (Isaac et al., 2012).

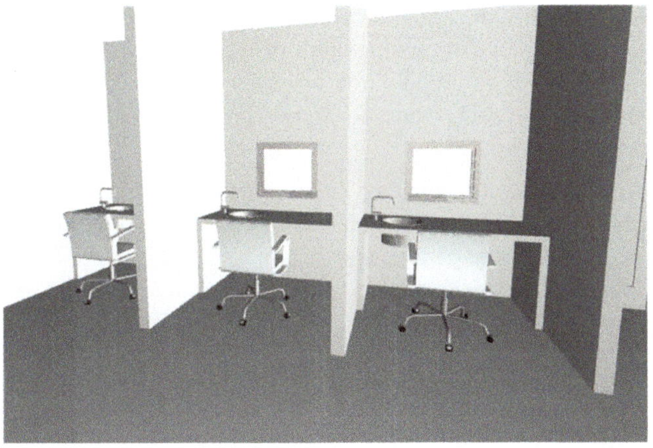

Figure 2: An example of layout of sensorial analysis cabine (Isaac et al., 2012a).

The cabins must be ventilated and odor free, to avoid interferences in the analyses. The temperature and humidity should be controled around 22 °C and at 45% of humidity (Isaac et al., 2012).

It is recommended that the walls and furniture of the rooms are colored with neutral and light colors to not disturb the attention of the volunteers and to not interfere in the attributes analyzed by the vision, such as color and appearance of the product.

The volunteers should not smoke, should be healthy, with ease of memorization and communication.

In the study, the volunteers judges could be an experienced judge or not, depending on the kind of evaluation and the answers that the professional team needs to obtain. In the case of utilization of sensorial analysis in the quality control of a cosmetic, usually the volunteers are regular users of the product in analysis, since they need to be familiarized with the characteristics of the product and have sensibility to perceive slight modification on it. When the aim of the sensorial analysis is to evaluate the acceptance of a product that should be launched in the market, it is recommended that the volunteers are potencial users of this new product, orienting the formulator to make changes in the formulation and guiding the company to evaluate if the costs of the product launch are recommended or not.

There are four different methods to perform the sensorial analysis that are most used, they are: affective, discriminative, descriptive (Aust et al., 1987) and methods to evaluate the effective of the product.

Independent of the method of sensory analysis suitable for each evaluation, the professional team should use printed questionnaires to obtain the answers from each volunteer. The use of printed questionnaires avoids the contact between the professional and the volunteers preventing that the professional is biased in his responses, beyond that, it facilitates the data collection.

In the elaboration of these questionnaires the professional team should use suitable lexicons for each class of product, for example, the lexicons used to the evaluation of lip products are different from that used for corporal lotions (Dooley et al., 2009). Some researches had developed suitable lexicons for different classes of cosmetic products (Civille and Dus, 1991; Wortel and Wiechers, 2000; Dooley et al., 2009). The manner as the volunteer is questioned is fundamental to obtain the information required from them. An inadequate formulary could invalidate a sensory evaluation. It is interesting also, that a description of all descriptors attributed to the formulation being provided to the volunteer, for example: "Thickness: Viscosity of the cream when picking up from the container", "Ease of spreading: Ease of rubbing the sample over the skin", "Absorption: Ease of absorption of the product through the skin", "Residue: Amount of product left on the skin after application" (Parente et al., 2010).

The affective methods represent the consumer opinion and evaluate how much consumers like or dislike a product. It is a quantitative method that is performed in order to know the consumers preferences (Aust et al., 1987). This technique could be applied in the development of new products and when it is necessary to replace a constituent of a formulation without loss of the product quality. It could be performed in two different ways: offering two different samples to the volunteer asking him about what sample he prefers between them or using a hedonic scale for the volunteer attributes grades of intensity of its acceptation in relation to the sample.

The hedonic scale either can be presented to the panel of evaluators in different manners, as shown inFigure 3.

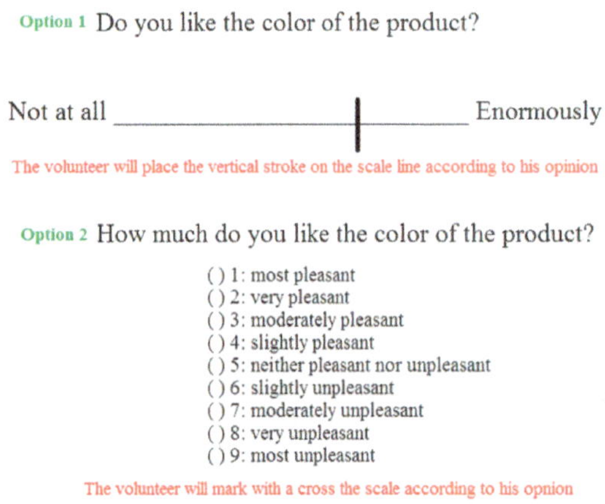

Figure 3: Examples of presentation of hedonic scale (Olshan et al., 2000; Barkat et al., 2003).

The affective methods provide quantitative data and allow more than one attribute in each sample being evaluated at the same time.

The discriminative test is better represented by the Triangular test. It allows differentiating one between three different samples and is very useful in shelf life studies and in the quality control of cosmetics. The ideal is to perform this evaluation with twelve to forty volunteers, who will receive the three samples and should indicate the different one between them (Zenebon et al., 2008).

The descriptive tests provide a broad sensory description about the product that is being evaluated (Almeida et al., 2008), helping to predict the consumer acceptance and what consumers think about such product (Almeida et al., 2006; Aust et al., 1987).

The tests to evaluate the effective of the products should be performed in true conditions of use and the volunteer may use only the product that is being assessed. These tests could be conduct by the evaluation of dermatologists, by the evaluation of volunteers, and even, by the measurement of one parameter by un equipment, such as the equipment that measures hydration, sebum and transepidermal water loss, to define if a product is really effective. Based on these clinical evaluations, a company could create an efficacy claim to the product (Wortel and Wiechers, 2000).

The sensory analysis could be also applied when a cosmetic industry needs to replace a raw-material of a commercialized product without changes in the performance of it. This replacement could be originated by many factors, such as the reduction of costs, problems with the firm who provides this raw-material problems with same raw material which causes irritation, comedogenicity or other problems that affect the consumer. In this field, the sensorial analysis helps the formulator, who proposes different raw materials as substitute, to evaluate if the consumer will notice the adaptation in the cosmetic product.

The statistical analysis is indispensable in the sensory studies. The sensory analysis data should be evaluated transforming them in scores which allows the application of statistical analysis to calculate the mean and standard deviation of the results, and the determination if the difference between the scores obtained is statistically significant. Graphics, tables and preference maps could be elaborated with the results obtained to facilitate the analysis of the data by the professional team.

The sensory analysis is especially indispensable in the industries of fragrances and perfumes, and because of that, high-resolution instrumental methods for evaluation of flavor and aroma have been developed and between them are the breath analysis via mass spectrometry (Dijksterhuis and Piggott, 2001; Ross, 2009). Instrumental measurements are thought to be objective, representing an independent fact or truth, however, the human smell sense is irreplaceable, being considered by Ross (2009) not necessarily valid because instrumental methods cannot account for the complexity of human perception.

Nevertheless, rheological studies have been applied to objectify the sensations when cosmetic emulsions are applied to the skin (Brummer and Godersky, 1999).

RHEOLOGY

Rheology is a tool widely applied in the food, petrochemical and pharmaceutical industries, but to the cosmetic industry it is incipient yet. Until now, the majority of cosmetic industries use viscometers to guarantee that the viscosity of different batches of a product is maintained.

This chapter was elaborated in order to show that many other rheological characteristics could be used to evaluate and to predict the stability of cosmetic products and could be applied to compare competing products in the market and to assay if a change in the composition will cause alterations that could be perceived by the consumer.

First, it is necessary to define the three parameters of most importance in rheology: shear stress, shear rate and viscosity. Shear stress can be defined as a force applied in an area. Shear rate is the ratio of the velocity of material to its distance from a stationary object (Naé, 1993). The shear rate can be calculated by the ratio between the velocity and the layer or film thickness. In a lipstick application, for example, with a velocity estimated in 5 cm/s and a layer thickness of 0.1 mm, the ratio (shear rate) is 5.10^2 s^{-1}. Finally, the viscosity can be defined as the resistance to flow. Thus, a viscous product presents smaller flow than others.

Concluding, rheology is the study of deformation and flow of materials under external forces. Some equations and the units of these parameters are (Naé, 1993):

$$\sigma = F / A \qquad (1)$$

Where:

σ = shear stress (Pa = $kg.m^{-1}.s^{-2}$)

F = force (N or $kg.m.s^{-2}$)

A = area (m^2)

The viscosity can be defined as the ratio between shear stress and shear rate:

$$\eta = \sigma / \dot{\gamma} \qquad (2)$$

Where:

= viscosity

= shear stress (Pa)

$\dot{\gamma}\dot{\gamma}$ = shear rate (s^{-1})

Since the unit of shear stress is Pa and the unit of deformation is s^{-1}, the unit of viscosity is Pa.s. These parameters are involved in scientific measurements of rotational assays.

Using controlled shear rate and measuring shear stress is possible to carry out rotational assays, and determine flow curves and describe the models: Newtonian or non-Newtonian and, among the last one, plastic, pseudoplastic, dilatant, tixotropic and reopetic fluids. Newtonian fluids are materials that present constant viscosity, independent of time and temperature. These materials present flow curves with proportionality between shear stress and shear rate. The Figure 4 represents the flow curve of a Newtonian material.

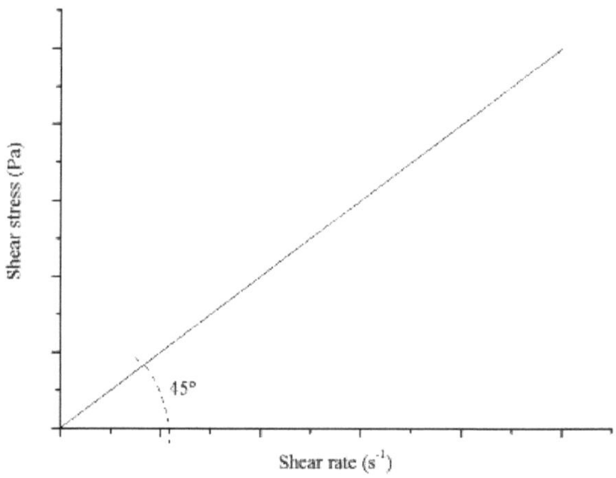

Figure 4: Flow curve of a Newtonian material.

In the case of non-Newtonians materials, this proportionality between shear stress and shear rate does not happen.

If in the beginning of the flow curve there is an increasing in the shear stress but the shear rate is equal to zero, and after to it is verified a Newtonian flow, this material is called plastic. This initial shear stress with shear rate equal to zero is called yield value and it represents the shear stress necessary for the material flow. The Figure 5 represents a plastic material. The yield value is related to the energy required to deform the material sufficiently so that they can flow. The value of the yield stress can be determined by measuring the deformation of the material as a function of the applied stress (Abdel-Rahem et al., 2005).

For non-Newtonian materials time-dependents, if the viscosity decreases with the shear rate, the material is called pseudoplastic and if the viscosity increases, the material is called dilatant. On the other hand, if the material is time-independent, it will be called tixotropic if the viscosity decreases with the shear rate or reopetic if the viscosity increases with the shear rate (Naé, 1993). When the ascending and the descending curves of the flow curve do not overlap it shows thixotropy which is a desirable feature for cosmetics and semisolid drug carriers for topical application (Lippacher et al., 2004). The Figures 6, 7, 8 and 9 represent the flow curves of non-Newtonian materials (Naé, 1993).

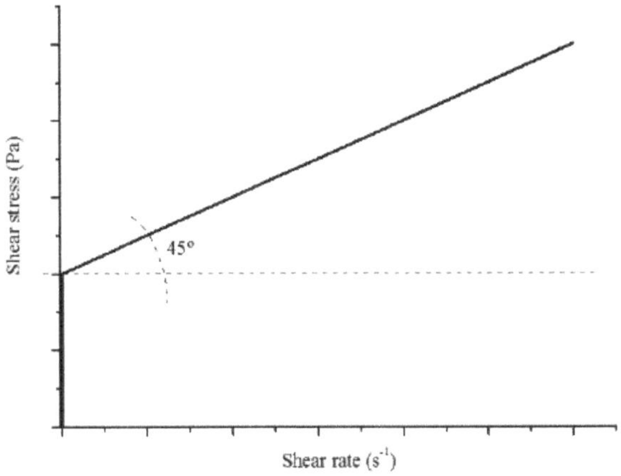

Figure 5: Flow curve of a plastic material.

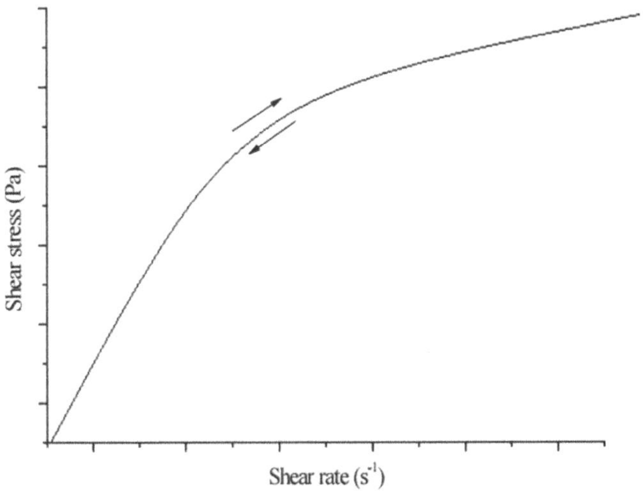

Figure 6: Flow curve of a pseudoplastic material.

For screening purposes and in the initial phases of the formulation development, the rheological tests proved to be very useful for the study of stability.

In a stability assay to determine the shelf life of a recently developed product, the formulation should be exposed to stress conditions, such as storage at -5 °C, 45 °C, and cycles of -5 °C during 24 hours followed by exposure to 45 °C during more 24 hours. This procedure is done in order to induce the appearance of instability signals in the formulations, where can be cited the darkening of the formulation, the precipitation of a constituent, the phase separation in the case of emulsions, and other signals. These stressing conditions are kept for a period around 2 or 3 months.

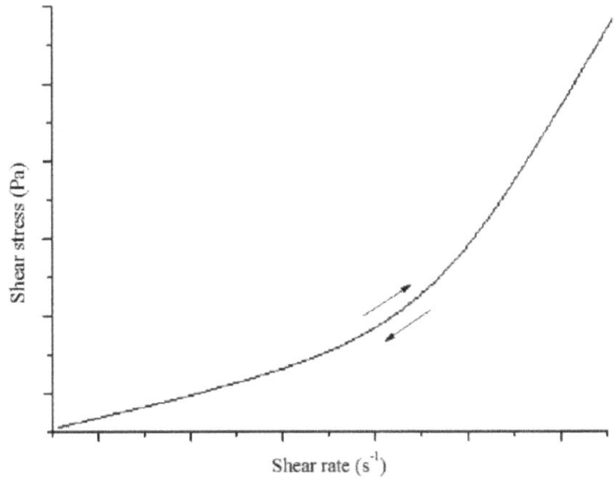

Figure 7: Flow curve of a dilatant material.

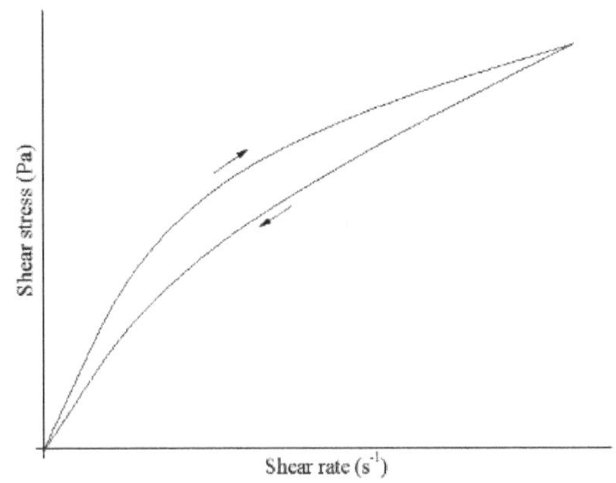

Figure 8: Flow curve of a thixotropic material.

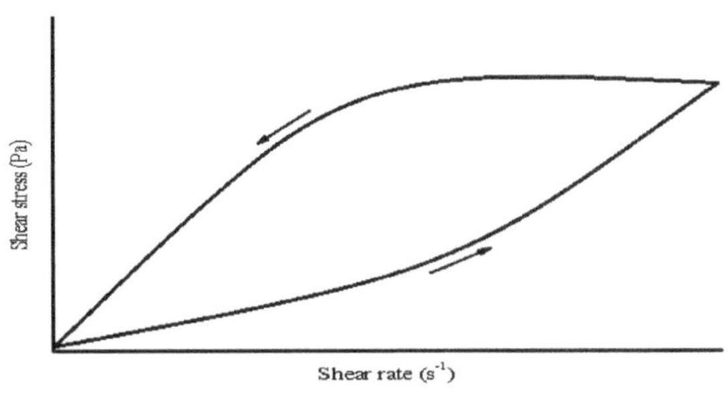

Figure 9: Flow curve of a reopetic material.

It is usually measured the viscosity of the stressed formulations periodically during the stability assay. It could be done by means of a viscometer or by using a rheometer.

With a viscometer, it is possible to carry out rotational assays or measurements by steady-state flow. On the other hand, the rheometer allows the development of oscillatory assays or dynamic measurements (Biradar, 2009).

When using an oscillatory rheometer it is necessary to carry out a flow curve assay and determine the apparent viscosity of the formulation in a defined shear rate. It is recommended to use the higher shear rate in the ascendant curve of the flow curve, since in this point the sample is in a suitable condition, it means that the formulation is not starting to flow and is not excessively sheared (Figure 10).

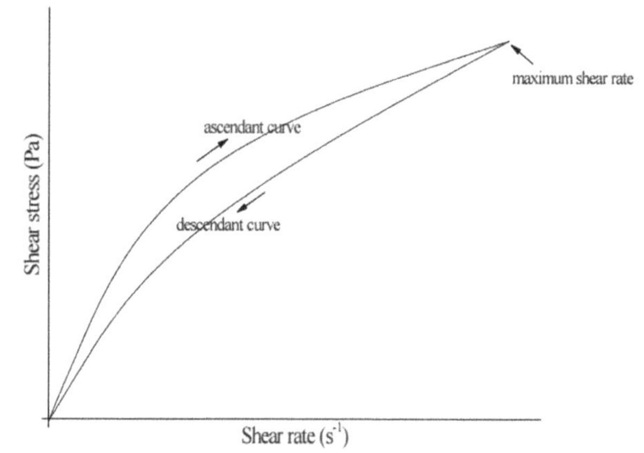

Figure 10: Example of a flow curve indicating the condition to the measurement of apparent viscosity.

In some papers, the flow curves have been plotted as viscosity as a function of shear stress instead of the traditional approach of plotting it versus shear rate because has been previously found that such curves are more discriminating and give better results for evaluation (Roberts, 2001; Samavati, 2011). After obtaining, periodically, the minimum apparent viscosity of the samples exposed to stress conditions during a period, they should be compared with the initial value, and also compared the viscosity values of the control with the samples exposed to stress conditions, which allows the verification of the increase, decrease or maintenance of this attribute of the formulations.

Further exploiting the same assay, it is possible to calculate the hysteresis area of the formulation in each flow curve performed during the stability assay. The hysteresis loop areas can be obtained through a three-step experiment: upward curve, plateau, downward (Benchabane and Bekkour, 2008) and represents a way to measure, indirectly, the spreadability of the formulation, so it is possible to define if the formulation losses or gains easiness on spreadability during the shelf life. How much bigger is the hysteresis area, higher is the spreadability.

Using the flow curve is possible to compare two samples in relation to its hysteresis area and viscosity. A simple way to verify what formulation have a higher viscosity is by simple observation of the rheogram, since the curve that forms a bigger inclination in relation to the *x* axis of the graphic is the one with higher viscosity. On Figure 12 is showed an example of it, where sample 2 is more viscous than sample 1. It happens because the tangent of the angle formed is correspondent to the viscosity of the formulation in each shear rate.

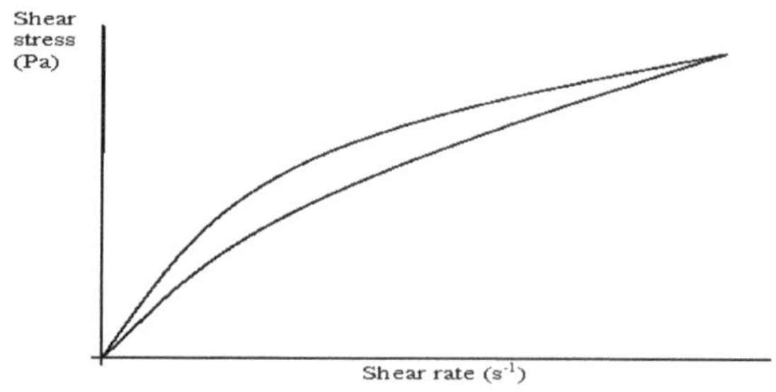

Figure 11: Flow curve with hysteresis area.

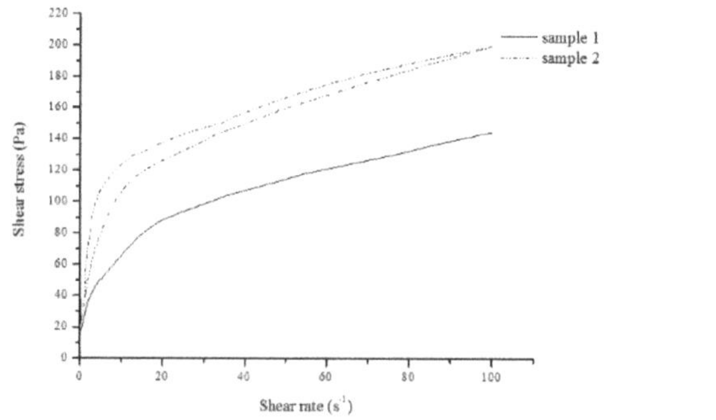

Figure 12: Comparison between flow curves of different samples (a thixotropic and a plastic fluid).

Beyond the different sensorial features caused by the differences in viscosity is known that the viscosity of emulsioned systems is one of the factors that retards or avoids the phase separation processes. The coalescence of dispersed phase can be due to the emulsifier agent and can be related to an instability because of low viscosity of dispersed phase (Corrêa & Isaac, 2012). This low viscosity can occur because of high shear stress (Samavati et al., 2011).

In general, for emulsioned systems, the continuos phase is shear thinning, which means that its viscosity decreases with the increasing on shear rate and viscoelastic, which means that it has viscous and elastic components (Tadros, 2004).

An example of the verification of differences in viscosity and thixotropy between two samples is shown on Figure 13.

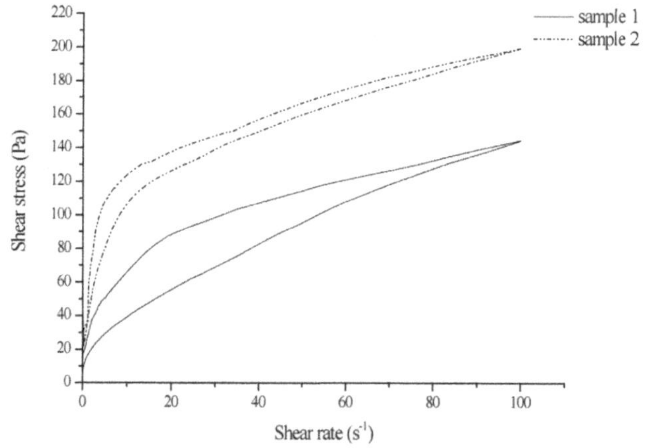

Figure 13: Comparison between flow curves of different samples.

Sample 1 is less viscous but more thixotropic than formulation 2. This simple verification gives to the analyst wide information, depending on what he needs.

Lescanne et al. (2004) studied organogels and aging properties of them. Organogels can be obtained by precipitation processes. These authors verified that, when aggregates are formed by the cooling rate, can be observed a elastic behavior, however, these aggregates can be aligned in the direction of the flow without lost the structure and when the flow is stopped, the aggregates are quickly rearranged and it inducing an thixotropic behavior. When the hot solution is introduced between the flat and the conical plates of the rheometer cell it is cooled to 5 ºC with a cooling rate of 20ºC/min, during the first hour of the gel life, it was measured the elastic properties of a gel as a function of time just after the cooling. Five minutes after its formation, the gel was submitted to a periodic stress (0.5 Pa) at a constant frequency (*f* = 1Hz). The authors showed that the shear moduli are constants and the aging phenomenon did not modify the elastic properties at least in a period of 1 h. However, when more than a week of aging is waited the samples lost most of its elastic properties.

The flow curve is a rotational assay, but using a rheometer it is possible to perform oscillatory assays too. Among the oscillatory assays are stress sweep and the frequency sweep assays.

The elastic (storage) modulus G' and the viscous (loss) modulus G" are determined as a function of frequency or stress. The elastic modulus is a measure of energy stored and recovered per cycle of deformation and represents the solid-like component of a viscoelastic material. If a sample is elastic or highly structured then the elastic modulus will be high. The viscous modulus is a measure of the energy lost per cycle and represents the liquid-like component. If a sample is viscous the viscous modulus will be high.

In the stress sweep analyses, the structure of the sample is progressively destroyed by applying oscillations with an increasing stress amplitude at a fixed frequency (Callens et al., 2003). The linear viscoelasticity region occurs over that region of strain where the complex modulus is independent of the strain (Hemar, 2000). The linear viscoelastic region is determined by the maximum stress which can be applied without affecting G' and G". Furthermore, the relative magnitude of the moduli is a qualitative indication for the structure in the sample. Two different situations can occur: G' > G" for a network consisting of secondary bonds and G' ≤ G" for a physically entangled polymer solution (Callens et al., 2003).

Frequency sweep tests are performed in the linear viscoelastic region of each sample, keeping the structure of the system intact during the measurement. By performing such small stress amplitude oscillations at a whole range of frequencies, the type of network structure can be revealed. The main difference between a network of secondary bonds and one of physical entanglements is located in the low frequency range: in an entangled network the polymers can disentangle if the available time is long enough (low frequency). In a network with secondary bonds the bonds are fixed irrespective of the time scale. This results for an entangled solution in a limiting slope of 2 for G' and 1 for G" at low frequency in a log-log plot of moduli versus frequency, while at intermediate frequency a plateau develops. For a network of secondary bonds an almost constant value of G' and G" is observed over the whole frequency range, with the value of G' exceeding that of G''(Callens et al., 2003; Madsen et al., 1998).

The stress sweep is important to evaluate the linear viscoelastic region of a sample that is a range of shear stress in which the formulation does not suffer profound alterations on it structure, being not disrupted. When a shear stress of the linear viscoelastic region is applied in an oscillatory assay, only the intermolecular and interparticle forces are being evaluated (Martin, 1993). To determine the linear viscoelastic region, the oscillating stress sweeps are carried out for the most extreme values. These measurements are used to determine where the reological properties are independent of the applied stress and the identify the critical rheological properties (Tuarez, 2011).

Knowing the values of shear stress that do not cause the disrupt in the formulation by means of the stress sweep, the analyst could perform a frequency sweep of the formulation. The frequency sweep is carried out in a constant shear stress found in the linear viscoelastic region. With this assay it is possible to evaluate the elastic or storage modulus (G') and the viscous or loss modulus (G"). The cosmetic excipients most used, emulsions and gels, are often viscoelastic samples. The viscoelastic samples when evaluated by means of the frequency sweep present G' and G" values. When the G' value is higher than G" it is an indicative that the formulation is more elastic than viscous. It is a characteristic of gels.

Emulsions which exhibits G' values higher than G" (Figure 14) are described as more stable than formulations with G" values higher than G' (Figure 15), since they tends to recovery its initial structure faster and more efficiently than the others, and are less susceptible to the gravitational forces which retards or avoids the coalescence process and the phase separation of emulsions (Alam and Aramaki, 2009). So, the G' values higher than G" in emulsions is a desirable feature, being an indicative of stability of the cosmetic system.

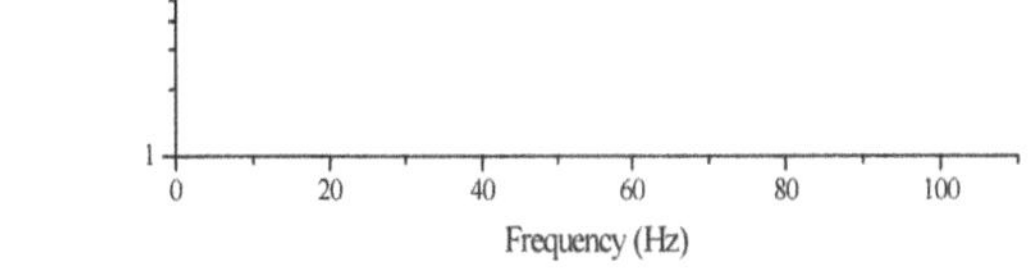

Figure 14: A frequency sweep example (G'>G").

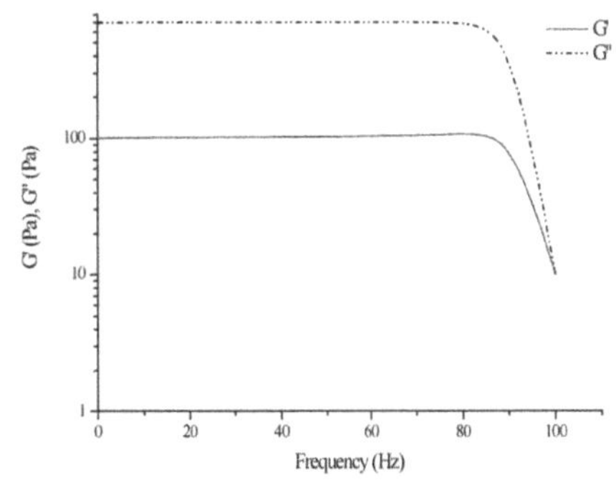

Figure 15: A frequency sweep example (G">G').

Another assay that could be conducted using an oscillatory rheometer is the creep and recovery assay. It is done by submitting the samples to a constant shear stress during a period, and after, removing this shear stress and monitoring the formulation in relation to the deformation (measured by the compliance - J) during the same period. The compliance parameter is the resulting strain divided by the applied stress (Koop, 2009; Toro-Vazquez et al., 2010). If the compliance parameter is the relationship between strain and the applied stress, the strain is dimensionless and stress is measured in Pa, then, the compliance can be measured in 1/Pa.

In the example showed on the Figure 16 the samples were submitted to a shear stress during 300 seconds, and after removing this shear stress it was monitored during more 300 seconds.

Analyzing the result obtained in the first 300 seconds is verified that sample 1 exhibited lower compliance values than sample 2, which represents a higher difficult on being deformed than sample 1. The difficult on being deformed is always linked to higher viscosity values.

In the second part of the assay, where the shear stress imposed to the sample is removed, represented in the graphic by the time 301 to 600 seconds, is verified the viscoelastic properties of the samples. Formulations that are able to recovery its initial structure or part of it exhibit a gradually decrease in the compliance values. On Figure 17 there is an example of a formulation that is not a viscoelastic sample, it means that it do not exhibits storage modulus, and is not able to recovery its structure when the shear stress is ceased.

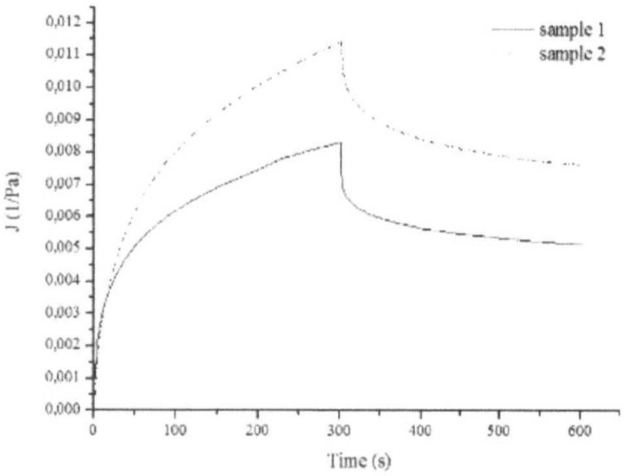

Figure 16: A creep and recovery example of viscoelastic samples.

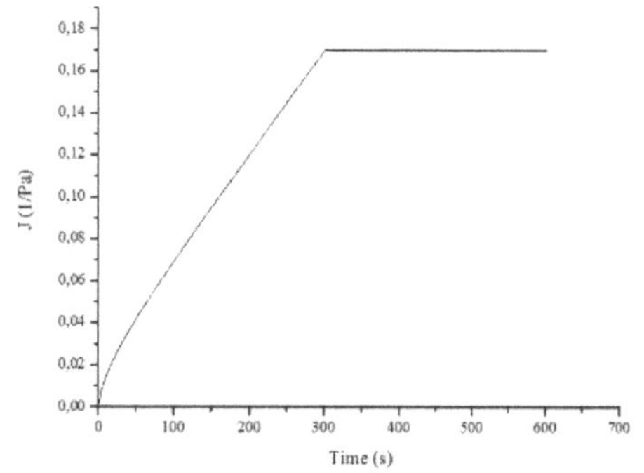

Figure 17: A creep and recovery example of a non-viscoelastic sample.

In addition, the rheology can be used to evaluate the stability over the time by dynamic and oscillatory rheological measurements (Pénzes et al., 2004; Vasiljevic et al., 2006) and the release of active principles. According to Martinez et al. (2007), the transdermal absorption of topically administered drugs depends on the rate of release and the permeability of them into the skin and also of the viscosity of the formulation (Martinez et al., 2007).

Thus, it is possible to say that different categories of products should present peculiar rheological properties inherent to its application (Gregolin et al., 2010).

In this way, the rheology can influence the diffusion coefficient, altering the release and permeation of cosmetics active substances (Welin-Berger et al., 2001; A-sadutjarit et al., 2005; Vasiljevic et al., 2006). Some authors have related the influence of rheological characteristics on the release profiles and consequently in the permeation of active substances in the skin; thus, the addition of thickening agents or attainment of a weak-gel because of physical entanglement of polymer chains must be considered in the choice of cosmetics bases (Spiclin, et al., 2003). Thus, rheology can help in the assay of release and permeation in the skin. Some studies have been published about it.

So, in a short way, the rheology is a valuable tool that helps in the quality control of cosmetics, being used in the stability tests, in the comparison between competing samples, in the comparison between an original product and a product with an alteration in a constituent, and in the development of new products, aiming to develop cosmetic with rheological characteristics which indicate stability.

SMALL ANGLE X-RAY SCATTERING (SAXS)

The use of this technique in determining the quality control of a cosmetic is closely related to the stability of the product, which could be improved with the presence of liquid crystals.

Liquid crystals are described as a state of matter between solids and liquids, it means that, they are fluid like liquids but are organized like solids, being called mesophases (Marsh, 1973; Kelker and Hatz, 1980; Müller-Goymann, 2004). These organization contributes to the highly stability of systems.

The formation of liquid crystals in emulsions could be induced by some components present in this system, such as surfactants (Müller-Goymann, 2004). So, what happens is that it is possible to find a peculiar system that is not a simple emulsion and not a genuine liquid crystal, but an emulsioned system that contains liquid crystals, commonly lamellar structures, that are formed around of the inner phase of the emulsion (Oka et al., 2008), making difficult the coalescence, flocculation and the separation of the oily and water phases, what makes the system formed more stable than a simple emulsion (Figures 18 and 19). Flocculation is defined as the formation of aggregates of droplets of an emulsion under the influence of interparticle colloidal forces which are net attractive (Dickinson, 1992) and the formation of lamellar structures avoid or prevent the occurrence of this phenomenon. The formation of lamellar structures is essential to obtain emulsified oil/water systems finely dispersed, with balanced hydrophilic-lipophilic properties, resulting in minimal interfacial tension between aqueous and oily phases, thus contributing to the stability of the system (Engels et al., 1995). Previous studies have also shown that it is possible to make correlation between SAXS and rheological analysis, since were verified that the thicker the interlamellar water layers, the higher the viscosity of the cream (Eccleston et al., 2000). Thus, liquid crystals could be responsible by the emulsion stabilization and by the increasing in the viscosity (Klein, 2002), being the presence of this structures desirable in cosmetic emulsions which could be an indicative of quality of them.

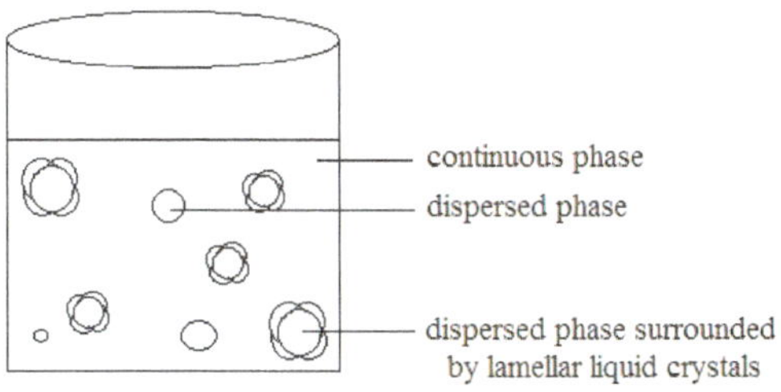

Figure 18: Scheme of a cosmetic emulsion containing liquid crystals.

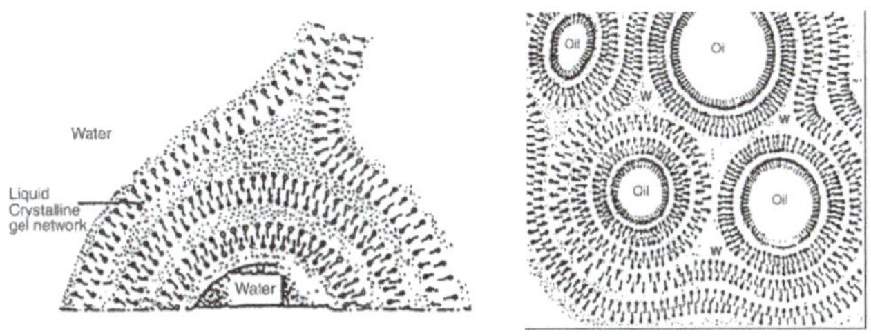

Figure 19: Schemes of the microscopic visualization of lamellar gel networks surrounding emulsion droplets proposed by Klein (2002).

This kind of structure is more commonly found in cosmetics due to the high diversity of components used in it in order to obtain a moisturizer, emollient, humectant, good sensory and, above all, stable cosmetic. In other pharmaceutical forms, usually are used a less diversified composition, which gives a system easier to understand, described as emulsion or liquid crystal, or even, a gel, a suspension, etc. The quantity of these lamellar structures, found in cosmetic emulsions, probably is dependent of three main factors: the raw-materials, the amount of it used and the process of preparation, where should be cited, the temperature and the speed of agitation.

In cosmetics, other kinds of systems could be used, such as genuine liquid crystals aiming to explore its characteristics of controlled delivery systems.

There are different kinds of liquid crystals and different classifications, but this chapter has not the function of describe them, since it have been done by many authors (Bechtold, 2005; Formariz et al., 2005; Atkins and Jones, 2006), the aim was to demonstrate the importance of these structures in the maintenance of the cosmetics' quality. Nevertheless, according to the literature data (Klein, 2002) and to our experience in this subject, it is possible to say that the lamellar arrangement is the most commonly found in cosmetic emulsions.

An initial analysis of the presence of liquid crystals in a cosmetic emulsion could be done using a polarized light microscope, but it should be confirmed and better analyzed by means of Small Angle X-Ray Scattering. When a microscope slide containing a sample of the system is studied and it presents structures that reflect the incident light, it is an evidence of the presence of liquid crystals (Figure 20). So, they should be submitted to SAXS analysis to confirm this expectation (Savic et al., 2011).

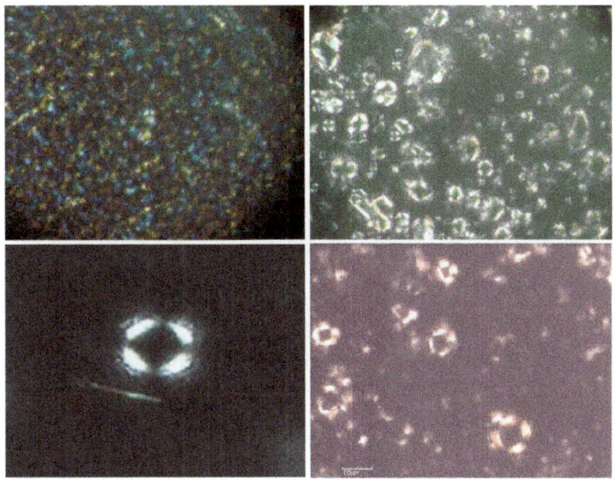

Figure 20: Photomicrographs of liquid-crystal present in emulsions evaluated by polarized light microscope.

The SAXS method requires a synchrotron light source that is formed by means of a particle accelerator, and using a monochromatic beam, that is used to irradiate the sample. After that, the scattering of the rays in small angle should be analyzed (Glatter and Kratky, 1982; Urban, 2004; Koch, 2010). Liquid crystals can be analyzed by SAXS since they are able to disperse the X-rays focused on it. In the SAXS line is used an X-rays detector and an multichannel analyzer to capture the intense of the SAXS measures (*I(q)*) in function of the modulus of the scattering vector (*q*) (Glatter and Kratky, 1982; Molina et al., 2006; Koch, 2010).

Analyzing the data obtained (Figure 19), the *d* value obtained represents the distance between the particles able to scatter the X-rays. It is calculated by the equation: $d = 2\pi / q\ max$, where *q max*, is the maximum intensity of scattering (Craievich, 2002). The relation between the *d* values obtained indicates the type of arrangement found in the system (Glatter and Kratky, 1982; Craievich, 2002;Alexandridis et al., 1998).

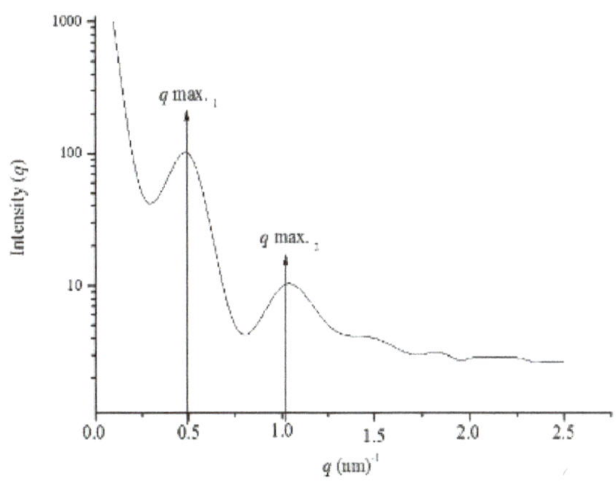

Figure 21: Hypothetical SAXS curve.

In the case of the hypothetical curve showed in Figure 19, d_1 / d_2 would result in 2, which describe lamellar structures (Alexandridis et al., 1998).

Beyond the advantages already mentioned, in a research conducted by Moaddel and Friberg (1995), the authors showed that the presence of lamellar liquid crystals in an emulsion avoids the water evaporation rate in this system, thus contributing in another way to the stability and maintenance of the cosmetic quality.

According to the advantages obtained with the presence of liquid crystals, these mesophases can be of great importance to the Cosmetic Industry in the development of very stable cosmetics and, the SAXS technique, an efficient tool to confirm the presence of these desirable structures that helps in the maintenance of cosmetics' quality control.

Camerel et al. (2003) pointed the importance in correlate the microstructure of a colloidal suspension with its rheological behavior to define its better use in industry and in life, beyond that, according to these authors there are few reports correlating these analyses.

Our research group has invested in researches to assess the stability of cosmetics (Isaac et al., 2008); evaluating of the influence of the addition of thickening agents in creams using rheological measurements (Isaac et al., 2012a); evaluating the thickeners' influence on the rheological properties of a cosmetic (Isaac et al., 2012b,c); proposing alternative methods to assay the efficacy and safety of them (Chiari et al., 2012a; Chiari et al., 2012b) and using of the sensory analysis in the cosmetics development (Isaac et al., 2012a) which, in different points of view of what was demonstrated in this chapter, also influence in the product quality.

CONCLUSION

This chapter aimed to show the facility that some simple or advanced techniques already used, sometimes to other finalities, could offer to the quality control of cosmetic products. The sensory analysis, rheology and SAXS technique have earned attention due to the important contribution that they can offer to the cosmetic area.

RFERENCES

1. Abdel-Rahem, R., Gradzielski, M., & Hoffmann, H. (2005). A novel viscoelastic system from a cationic surfactant and a hydrophobic counterion. Journal of Colloid and Interface Science, 288, 570–582.
2. Alam, M.M., & Aramaki, K. (2009). Glycerol effects on the formation and rheology of hexagonal phase and related gel emulsion, J. Colloid Interface Sci., 336, 820-826.
3. Alexandridis, P., Olsson, U., & Lindman, B. (1998). A record nine different phases (four cubic, two hexagonal, and one lamellar lyotropic liquid crystalline and two micellar solutions) in a ternary isothermal system of an amphiphilic block copolymer and selective solvents (water and oil). Langmuir, 14, 2627-2638.
4. Almeida, I.F., Gaio, A.R., & Bahia, M.F. (2006). Estimation of hedonic responses from descriptive skin sensory data by chi squared minimization. J. Sens. Stud., 21(1), 2-19.
5. Almeida, I.F., Gaio, A.R., & Bahia, M.F. (2008). Hedonic and descriptive skinfeel analysis of two oleogels: comparison with other topical formulations. J. Sens. Stud., 23(1), 92-113.
6. A-Sadutjarit, R., Sirivat, A., & Vayumhasuwan, P. (2005). Viscoelastic properties of carbopol 940 gels and their relationships to piroxicam diffusion coefficients in gel bases. Pharmaceutical Research, 22(12), 2134-2140.
7. Atkins, P., & Jones, L. (2006). Princípios de química: questionando a vida moderna e o meio ambiente. Porto Alegre: Bookmam. 3ed., p. 293-295 and 300-302.
8. Aust, L.B., Oddo, P., Wild, J.E., Mills, O.H., & Deupree, J.S. (1987). The descriptive analysis of skin care products by a trained panel of judges. J. Soc. Cosmet. Chem., 38, 443-448.
9. Backe, I., Meges, S., Lauze, C., Macleod, P., & Dupuy, P. (1999). Sensory analysis of four medical spa spring waters containing various mineral concentrations. Int. J. Dermatol., 38(10), 784-786.
10. Barkat, S., Thomas-Danguin, T., Bensafi, M., Rouby, C., & Sicard, G. (2003). Odor and color of cosmetic products: correlations between subject judgement and autonomous nervous system response. International Journal of Cosmetic Science, 25, 273-283.
11. Bechtold, I. H. (2005). Liquid crystals: A complex system of simple application. Rev. Bras. Ensino Física, 27(3), 333-342.
12. Benchabane, A., & Bekkour, K. (2008). Rheological properties of carboxymethyl cellulose (CMC) solutions. Colloid Polymer Science, 286, 1173-1180.
13. Biradar, S.V., Dhumal, R.S., & Paradkar, A. (2009). Rheological investigation of self-emulsification process. Journal of Pharmacy and Pharmaceutical Science, 12(1), 17-31.
14. Brummer, R., & Godersky, S. (1999). Rheological studies to objectify sensations occurring when cosmetic emulsions are applied to the skin. Colloids and Surfaces A: Physicochemical and Engineering Aspects, 152, 89-94.
15. Callens, C., Ceulemans, J., Ludwig, A., Foreman, P., & Remon, J.P. (2003). Rheological study on mucoadhesivity of some nasal powder formulations. European Journal of Pharmaceutics and Biopharmaceutics, 55, 323-328.
16. Camerel, F., Gabriel, J.C.P., Batail, P., Panine, P., & Davidson, P. (2003). Combined SAXS – Rheological studies of liquid-cristalline colloidal dispersions of mineral particles. Langmuir, 19, 10028-10035.
17. Chiari, B.G., Magnani, C., Salgado, H.R.N., Côrrea, M.A., & Isaac, V.L.B. (2012a). Estudo da segurança de cosméticos: presente e futuro. Revista Brasileira de Ciências Farmacêuticas Básica e Aplicada, 33(2).
18. Chiari, B.G., Martini, P.C., Moraes, J.D.D., Andréo, R., Corrêa, M.A., Cicarelli, R.M.B., & Isaac, V.L.B. (2012b). Use of HepG2 cells to assay the safety of cosmetic active substances. International Journal of Research in Cosmetic Science, 2(2), 8-14.
19. Civille, C.V., & Dus, C.A. (1991). Evaluating tactile properties of skincare products: A descriptive analysis technique. Cosmet. Toilet., 106, 83–88.
20. Corrêa, M.A., & Isaac, V.L.B. (2012). Emulsões. In:

CORRÊA, M.A. Cosmetologia: ciência e técnica. São Paulo: Medfarma, p. 337-381.

21. Craievich, A. F. (2002). Synchrotron SAXS studies of nanostructured materials and colloidal solutions. Materials Research Rev., 5(1), 1-11.
22. Dickinson, E. (1992). Structure and composition of adsorbed protein layers and the relationship to emulsion stability. J. Chem. Soc. Faraday Trans., 88(20), 2973-2983.
23. Dijksterhuis, G. B., & Piggott, J. R. (2001). Dynamic methods of sensory analysis. Trends in Food Science and Technology, 11, 284-290.
24. Dooley, L.M., Adhikari, K., & Chambers IV, E. (2009). A general lexicon for sensory analysis of texture and appearance of lip products. J. Sens. Stud., 24(4), 581-600.
25. Eccleston, G.M., Behan-Martin, M.K., Jones, G.R., & Towns-Andrews, E. (2000). Synchrotron X-ray investigations into the lamellar gel phase formed in pharmaceutical creams prepared with cetrimide and fatty alcohols. International Journal of Pharmaceutics, 203, 127–139.
26. Engels, T., Förster, T., & Von Rybinski, W. (1995). The influence of coemulsifier type on the stability of oil-in-water emulsions. Colloids Surfaces A: Physicochemical and Engineering Aspects, 99, 141-149.
27. Formariz, T.P., Urban, M.C.C., Da Silva Júnior, A.A., Gremião, M.P.D., & De Oliveira, A.G. (2005). Microemulsões e fases líquidas cristalinas como sistemas de liberação de fármacos. Revista Brasileira de Ciências Farmacêuticas, 41(3), 301-313.
28. Fouéré, S., Adjadj, L., & Pawin, H. (2005). How patients experience psoriasis: results from a European survey. J. Eur. Acad. Dermatol. Venereol., 19(3), 2-6.
29. Glatter, O., & Kratky, O. (1982). Small-Angle X-ray Scattering, Academic Press, New York.
30. Gorcea, M., & Laura, D. (2012). Evaluating the physiochemical properties of emollient esters for cosmetic use. Cosmetics and Toiletries, 125(12), 26-33.
31. Gregolin, M.T., Chiari, B.G., Ribeiro, H.M., & Isaac, V.L.B. (2010). Rheological Characterization of hydrophilic gels. Journal of Dispersion Science and Technology, 31, 820-825.
32. Hemar, Y., & Horne, D.S. (2000). Dynamic rheological properties of highly concentrated protein-stabilized emulsions. Langmuir, 16(7), 3050-3057.
33. Isaac, V.L.B., Cefali, L.C., Chiari, B.G., Almeida, M.G.J., Ribeiro, H. M., & Corrêa, M.A. (2012c) Effect of various thickening agents on the rheological properties of O/W emulsions containing non-ionic emulsifier. Journal of Dispersion Science and Technology. Available at: http://www.tandfonline.com/doi/full/10.1080/01932691.2012.695952
34. Isaac, V.L.B., Cefali, L.C., Chiari, B.G., Oliveira, C.C.L.G., Salgado, H.R.N., & Corrêa, M.A. (2008). Protocolo para ensaios físico-químicos de estabilidade de fitocosméticos. Rev. Ciênc. Farm. Básica Apl., 29(1), 81-96.
35. Isaac, V., Chiari, B.G., Magnani, C., & Corrêa, M.A. (2012a). Análise sensorial como ferramenta no desenvolvimento de cosméticos. Revista de Ciências Farmacêuticas Básica e Aplicada, 33 (in press).
36. Isaac, V.L.B., Moraes, J.D.D., Chiari, B.G., Guglielmi, D.A.S., Cefali, L.C., Rissi, N.C., & Corrêa, M.A. (2012b). Determination of the real influence of the addition of four thickening agents in creams using rheological measurements. Available at: http://www.tandfonline.com/doi/full/10.1080/01932691.2012.683759
37. Kelker, H., & Hatz, R. (1980). Handbook of Liquid Crystals, Verlag Chemie, Weinheim, Germany.
38. Klein, K. (2002) Liquid crystals and emulsions: a wonderful marriage. Chapter 26, p. 265-269. In: Skin Barrier: Chemistry of Delivery Systems. Available at: http://www.alluredbooks.com/sample_pages/skin_barr_chem_skin_deli_syst_ch26.pdf. Acessed on july, 2012.
39. Koch, M.H.J. (2010). SAXS Instrumentation for Synchrotron Radiation then and now. XIV International Conference on Small-Angle Scattering (SAS09). Journal of Physics: Conference Series 247.
40. Koop, H.S., Praes, C.E.O., Reicher, F., Petkowicz, C.L.O., & Silveira, J.L.M. (2009). Rheological behavior of gel of xanthan with galactomannan: effect of hydroalcoholic-ascorbic acid. Materials Science and Engineering C, 29, 559-63.
41. Lee, I-S., Yang, H-M., Kim, J-W., Maeng, Y-J., Lee, C-W., Kang, Y-S., Rang, M-J., & Kim H-Y. (2005). Terminology development and panel training for sensory evaluation of skin care products including aqua cream. J. Sens. Stud., 20(5), 421-433.
42. Lescanne, M., Grondin, P., D'Aléo, A., Fages, F., Pozzo, J.L., Moundain Monval, O., Reinheimer, P., & Colin, A. (2004). Thixotropic organogels based on a simple N-hydroxyalkyl amide: rheological and aging properties. Langmuir, 20(8), 3032-3041.
43. Lippacher, A., Müller, R.H., & Mäder, K. (2004). Liquid and semisolid SLNe dispersions for topical application: rheological characterization. European Journal of Pharmaceutics and Biopharmaceutics, 58, 561–567.
44. Madsen, F., Eberth, K., & Smart, J.D. (1998). A rheological assessment of the nature of interactions between mucoadhesive polymers and a homogenized mucus gel. Biomaterials, 19, 1083-1092.
45. Makai, M., Csányi, E., Németh, Z.S., Pálinkás, J., & Erós, I. (2003). Structure and drug release of lamellar liquid crystals containing glycerol. Int. J. Pharm., 256, 95–107.
46. Marsh, H. (1973). Carbonization and liquid-crystal (mesophase) development: Part 1. The significance of the mesophase during carbonization of coking coals. Fuel, 52, 205-212.
47. Martin, A. (1993). Physical Pharmacy, fourth ed., Lea & Febiger, Philadelphia.
48. Martinez, M.A.R., Gallardo, J.L.V., Benavides, M.M., López-Duran, J.D.G., & Lara, V.G. (2007). Rheological behavior of gels and meloxicam release. International

Journal of Pharmaceutics, 333, 17-23.

49. Meilgaard, M., Civille, G.V., & Carr, B.T. (1991). Consumer test and in-house panel acceptance tests. In: Meilgaard, M., Civille, G.V., Carr, B.T. Sensory evaluation techniques. Florida: CRC Press, p. 142-7, 281.

50. Moaddel, T., & Friberg SE. (1995). Phase equilibria and evaporation rates in a four component emulsion. J. Disp. Sci. Technol., 16, 69-97.

51. Molina, C., Dahmouche, K., Hammer, P., Bermudez, V.Z., Carlos, L.D., Ferrari, M., Montagna, M., Gonçalves, R.R., De Oliveira, L.F.C., Edwards, H.G.M., Messaddeq, Y., & Ribeiro, S.J.L. (2006). Structure and Properties of Ti4+-Ureasil Organic-Inorganic Hybrids, J. Braz. Chem. Soc., 17(3), 443-452.

52. Müller-Goymann, C.C. (2004). Physicochemical characterization of colloidal drug delivery systems such as reverse micelles, vesicles, liquid crystals and nanoparticles for topical administration. European Journal of Pharmaceutics and Biopharmaceutics 58, 343–356.

53. Muñoz, A.M., Civille, G.V., & Carr, B.T. (1993). Sensory evaluation in quality control. New York: Van Nostrand Reinhold, p. 240.

54. Naé, H.N. (1993). Introduction to rheology. In: Laba, D. Rheological propertie of cosmetics and toiletries. New York: Marcel Dekker, 426 p.

55. Oka, T., Miyahara, R., Teshigawara, T., & Watanabe, K. (2008). Development of novel cosmetic base using sterol surfactante. I. Preparation of novel emulsified particles with sterol surfactant. Journal of Oleo Science, 57(10), 567-575.

56. Olshan, A.A., Kohut, B.E., Vincent, J.W., Borden, L.C., Delgado, N., Qaqish, J., Sharma, N.C., & Mcguire, J.A. (2000). Clinical effectiveness of essential oil-containing dentifrices in controlling oral malodor. American Journal of Dentistry, 13, 18C-22C.

57. Ozkan, S., Gillece, T.W., Senak, L., & Moore, D.J. (2012). Characterization of yield stress and slip behaviour of skin/hair care gels using steady flow and LAOS measurements and their correlation with sensorial attributes. International Journal of Cosmetic Science, 34, 193–201.

58. Parente, M.E., Ares, G., & Manzoni, A.V. (2010). Application of two consumer profiling techniques to cosmetic emulsions. Journal of Sensory Studies, 25, 685-705.

59. Parente, M.E., Gámbaro, A., & Ares, G. (2008). Sensory characterization of emollients. Journal of Sensory Studies 2, 149–161.

60. Parente, M.F., Gambaro, A., & Solana, G. (2005). Study of sensory properties of emollients used in cosmetics and their correlation with physicochemical properties. J Cosmet Sci., 56(3), 175-182.

61. Pénzes, T., Csóka, I., & Eros, I. (2004). Rheological analysis of the structural properties effecting the percutaneous absorption and stability in pharmaceutical organogels. Rheological Acta, 43, 457-63.

62. Piana, M.L., Oddo, L.P., Bentabol, A., Bruneau, E., Bogdanov, S., & Guyot Declerck, C. (2004). Sensory analysis applied to honey: state of the art. Apidologie, 35, S26–S37.

63. Proksch, E., & Lachapelle, J.M. (2005). The management of dry skin with topical emollients: recent perspectives. J. Dtsch. Dermatol. Ges., 10(5), 768-774.

64. Roberts, G.P., Bames, H.A., & Carew, P. (2001). Modelling the flow behavior of very shear-thinning liquids. Chem. Eng. Sci., 56, 5617-5623.

65. Ross, C.F. (2009). Sensory science at the humane-machine interface. Trends in Food Science & Technology, 20, 63-72.

66. Samavati, V., Emam-Djomeh, Z., Mohammadifar, M.A., Omid, M., & Mehdinia, A.L.I. (2011). Stability and rheology of dispersions containing polysaccharide, oleic acid and whey protein isolate. Journal of Texture Studies, p. 1-14.

67. Savic, S., Lukic, M., Jaksic, I., Reichl, S., Tamburic, S., & Müller-Goymann, C. (2011). An alkyl polyglucoside-mixed emulsifier as stabilizer of emulsion systems: The influence of colloidal structure on emulsion skin hydration potential. Journal of Colloid and Interface Science, 358, 182-191.

68. Shewhart, W.A. (1980). Economic control of quality of manufactured product, American Society for Quality Control.

69. Spiclin, P, Homar, M, Valant, A.Z., & Gasperlin, M. (2003). Sodium ascorbyl phosphate in topical microemulsions. International Journal of Pharmaceutics, 256, 65-73.

70. Stone, H.S., & Sidel, J.L. (1992). Sensory evaluation practices. San Diego, CA: Academic Press.

71. Tadros, T. (2004). Application of rheology for assessment and prediction of the long-term physical stability of emulsions. Advances in Colloid and Interface Science, 108 – 109, 227–258.

72. Toro-Vazquez, J.F., Morales-Rueda, J., Ajay Mallia, V., & Weiss, R.G. (2010). Relationship between molecular structure and thermo-mechanical properties of candelilla wax and amides derived from (R)-12-hydroxystearic acid as gelators of safflower oil. Food Biophysics, 5, 193-202.

73. Tuarez, E.P., Sadtler, V., Marchal, P, Choplin, L., & Salager, J.L. (2011). Making use of formulation-composition map to prepare highly concentrated emulsions with particular rheological properties. Ind. Eng. Chem. Res., 50, 2380-87.

74. Urban, M. C. C. (2004). Desenvolvimento de sistemas de liberação micro e nanoestruturados para administração cutânea do acetato de dexametasona. 2004. Dissertação (Mestrado em Ciências Farmacêuticas) - Faculdade de Ciências Farmacêuticas, Universidade Estadual Paulista Júlio de Mesquita Filho, Araraquara.

75. Vasiljevic, D., Parojcic, J., Primorac, M., & Vuleta, G. (2006). An investigation into the characteristics and drug release properties of multiple W/O/W emulsion systems containing low concentration of lipophilic polymeric

emulsifier. International journal of Pharmaceutics, 309, 171-177.

76. Welin-Berger, K., Neelissen, J.A.M., & Bergenstahl, B. (2001). The effect of rheological behavior of a topical anaesthetic formulation on the release and permeation rates of the active compound. European Journal of pharmaceutical Sciences, 13, 309-18.

77. Wortel, V.A.L., & Wiechers, J.W. (2000). Skin sensory performance of individual personal care ingredients and marketed personal care products. Food Qual. Pref., 11(1-2), 121-127.

78. Zague, V., Nishikawa, D.O., Silva, D.A., Baby, A.R., Behrens, J.H., Kaneko, T.M., & Velasco, M.V.R. (2008). Influence of storage temperature on cooling intensity of topical emulsions containing encapsulated menthol. J. Sens. Stud., 23(1), 26-34.

79. Zenebon, O., Pascuet, N.S., & Tiglea, P. (2008). Métodos físico-químicos para análise de alimentos. Instituto Adolfo Lutz (São Paulo). On line version. Available at: http://www.crq4.org.br/sms/files/file/analisedealimentosial_2008.pdf

CHAPTER 8

QUALITY MANAGEMENT EXCELLENCE MODEL FOR ISO 26000 IMPLEMENTATION

Štefka Gorenak

Keywords: EFQM Excellence Model, ISO 26000, social responsibility, stakeholders, sustainable development

INTRODUCTION

Interest in social responsibility (SR), corporate social responsibility (CSR), total quality management (TQM), European Foundation for Quality Management (EFQM), and especially in ISO 26000 as well as their interdependence is increasing. Social responsibility is one of the most important management topics in companies as well as in other organizations in the last decade. There is a clear recognition that strategic management models are the framework for achieving sustainable growth and sustainable competitive advantages.

"The practical application of SR can be well supported by guidelines of business excellence as defined by the EFQM and includes five input and four result criteria" [1]. This changing model follows the present organizations environment, and it is reviewed every 3 years (the last version EFQM 2013). Flexibility is one of the most important factors that influence the success within global and local organizations.

The EFQM Excellence Model 2013 incorporates current key business challenges: "(1) build agility into the business; (2) greater emphasis on developing approaches; (3) more important are the accountability of leadership, governance and risk management; (4) doing the right thing is important; (5) measurement indicators; (6) criteria are now more explicit and prescriptive; (7) futuristic focus; (8) wider focus covering entire value chain; (9) greater emphasis on corporate social responsibility; (10) sustainability; (11) innovation; (12) other subtle and notable changes made are changes made in fundamental principles of excellence, changes in excellence model, changes in RADAR logic" [2]. EFQM 2013 helps organizations to manage quality successfully and operate according to sustainable determination.

"The principles and guidelines of social responsibility are outlined in the most recent release of the ISO 26000 standard, which links the principles of management with the business excellence model EFQM" [3]. The new SR definition has been implemented by International Organization for Standardization (ISO). "Social responsibility is the responsibility of an organization for the impacts of its decisions and activities on society and the environment through transparent and ethical behavior" [4].

The practice by implementation of ISO 9000 and EFQM is different; some organizations tend to implement ISO 9000 procedures first and the EFQM Excellence Model is included later. The EFQM specialists as well as the practice confirm that the most appropriate is to apply ISO 9000 and EFQM together, but it is a never-ending process. The resources limitation is sometimes the reason why organizations are not able to implement both at the same time. Moreover, we have to now that ISO 9000 (day-to-day quality standard) has limitations; on the other hand, the EFQM Excellence Model is long-term oriented (prepares organization for long-term sustainable excellence).

Social responsibility guideline—ISO 26000—was issued by a well-known authority—ISO. ISO 26000 is a CSR guideline that enables all organizations to define and implement CSR in their corporate strategy. "ISO 26000 exposes seven core subjects—human rights, labour practices, the environment, fair operating practices, consumer issues, community involvement and development [4]" in which an honest behaviour supports success; all of them are linked by two crucial concepts: (1) interdependence and (2) holistic approach. ISO 26000 is reference standard for all (C)SR topics—EFQM, SA 8000, AA 1000, ILO, ISO 14001, GRI, ISO 9001, ISO 31000, OHSAS, and EMAS.

Citation: Štefka Gorenak (2015). Quality Management Excellence Model for ISO 26000 Implementation, Perspectives on Business and Management, Prof. Vito Bobek (Ed.), InTech, DOI: 10.5772/60959.

"Business can be understood as a set of relationships among groups which have a stake in the activities that make up the business. A stakeholder approach to business is about creating as much value as possible for stakeholders, without resorting to trade-offs" [5]. Relationships with stakeholders are also very important in the educational institutions (all levels), health system, government and public sector, local communities, nongovernmental institutions, and public–private partnerships. At the same time, we can discuss about relationships with primary and secondary stakeholders. Organizations are trying to meet their own requirements as well as the requirements and expectations of their stakeholders.

Responsible competitiveness—"Businesses can compete effectively across the responsibility spectrum" [6]. The importance of corporate responsibility increases. It requires that it be integral to and supportive of broader sustainable development strategies and policies (at organizational level and governmental levels). The relationship between competitiveness and SR is not a simple one. CR can also encourage innovation, investment, cooperation, and competition. It means that organizations pay attention to ecological, social, and financial aspects of their responsibility in interaction with all stakeholders (for example, they care about their sustainable production, emissions and waste, employee safety and satisfaction, and stakeholder involvement). It is clear that responsible shareholders are important stakeholders who must support sustainable leadership orientation.

"Public policies to amplify SR practices need to be, and indeed are being, formulated in the context of this complexity at an international level, and also at regional, national, and even community levels" [7].

The purpose of this paper is to trace and define the relations between several EFQM criteria and the components of ISO 26000, total quality management (TQM), and total responsibility management (TRM) as well as interrelations between organization and its stakeholders. In the light of the analysis, the systemic and holistic approach EFQM model may be considered as a tool for the governance and implementation in the organization strategy according ISO 26000 recommendations. Socially responsible organizations focus on economic growth, stakeholder strategic management, long-term sustainable development, sustainable indicators, sustainable competitiveness, and cooperative advantages.

EUROPEAN FOUNDATION FOR QUALITY MANAGEMENT (EFQM)

EFQM was established in 1988; its members are companies and other institutions (research, education, and national organizations). "The EFQM Excellence Model is a practical tool that indicates the position of business and other organizations on excellence path and helps them to determine their shortcomings and encourages appropriate solutions" [8]. The first EFQM Excellence Model was published in 1992; it is flexible and can be implemented in large companies, SMEs, and other organizations (private and public, government, local communities, and other organizations).

"Business excellence models, particularly the EFQM Excellence Model, are being used by organisations all over the world for self-assessment, benchmarking, sharing of best practices and assessing organisations for national quality business excellence awards" [9]. From a theoretical and practical point of view, the business excellence models (particularly EFQM) have to be applicable and implementable in different types of organizations. Many countries try to encourage implementation of the organizational excellence models, like Deming (Japan), Malcolm Baldrige (USA), and EFQM (Europe).

At the same time, we would like to present the difference between ISO 9000 and EFQM Excellence Model. ISO standards have a long tradition; one of the most important standards is ISO 9000 (requires certification), which is comprehensive and exactly describes quality requirements, protocol, and how to meet all these requirements. On the other hand, EFQM Excellence Model is opened, its implementation needs creativity, but it is possible just in freedom. Furthermore, in such holistic approach, creativity and complexity go together in the EFQM Excellence Model.

"The EFQM Excellence Model is business management framework aimed at sustained wealth generation" [10]. "The EFQM Excellence Model, a non-prescriptive framework, is based on nine criteria. Enabler criteria are concerned with how the organisation undertakes key activities and results criteria are concerned with what results are being achieved" [1, 11].

The basic concepts of this model are extensive and involve results orientation. Customers are one of the main stakeholders; their satisfaction and loyalty are important for each organization. Leadership plays the crucial role; it must be the model as well as the motivator and strategic processes, which are focused on quality, stakeholder partnerships, and sustainability. Employees are one of the main stakeholders, and their involvement reflects as their contribution to innovativeness, improvement, and competitiveness. Stakeholder partnership is a long-term process and is part of the holistic and systemic social responsibility in organizations.

Furthermore, the EFQM Levels of Excellence Scheme was created to provide systemic and holistic recognition to organizations at all levels of their excellence promotion and improvement. "The main objective of the scheme are to: (1) extend recognition to organisations at every level of achievement; (2) maximize the number or organisations who are able to apply the principles of the EFQM Excellence Model for organisational improvement; (3) provide independent feedback from practicing managers to support organisations in their quest to improve and (4) provide practical products and services that help organisations achieve improved levels of excellence" [11]. Organizations practicing excellence scheme may use the EFQM Excellence Model percentages, but on the other hand, they may use percentages more suitable to their own type of organization. Additionally, we present the recommended percentage of "the EFQM Excellence Model criteria: (1) Leadership (10%); (2) Policy and Strategy (10%); (3) People (10%); (4) Partnerships and resources (10%); (5) Processes (10%); (6) Customer results (15%); (7) People results (10%); (8) Society results (10%) and (9) Key performance results (15%)" [11].

Importance of Good Leadership and Management

Leadership is similar to as well as different from management. They both involve influencing people, require working with people, and are concerned with the achievement of common goals. Organizations need people who do the right thing and who do the right things right.

Nowadays, managers must also deal with a growing international competition. "Managers, wherever they are in the organization, but particularly in the top management, need to take a long-term perspective" [12]. Transformative leaders lead by values; they are the best model for others within the organization, create and integrate vision into strategies and processes, care and make a public commitment, constantly communicate with stakeholders with the aim to avoid potential problems in the future, and encourage competitiveness and good relations with stakeholders.

The business benefits of good leadership reflect as improved business (competences, innovativeness, and proficiency) and employee performance (employee satisfaction and involvement). In addition, we want to highlight "factors identified as particularly important—commitment to management and leadership development, human resources practices that reinforce management and leadership development" [13].

How can we define good leadership and management? At the first position are core leadership and management skills. We highlight the most important effective leadership skills. "The best leaders face problems head on and have the confidence to propose sometimes innovative or difficult solutions, all managers need to be effective leaders; (1) Strategy and planning; (2) People management; (3) Budgeting & financial planning; (4) Risk management; (5) Fostering innovation and creativity—continuous innovation strategies are managed by more highly educated and better informed managers; (6) Partnership working" [14, 15].

"Improving leadership and capability management is very important, so we present 10 top tips for employers: (1) recognise that good leadership and management matters; (2) be a role model: good leadership and management starts at the top; (3) implement good working practices as a framework for good management and leadership; (4) effective leadership runs through organisations like writing through a stick of rock; (5) provide training, support and mentoring to new line managers; (6) be clear about what good management skills and behaviours look like; (7) assess your organisations' management capability at individual and organisational level and act upon it; (8) make the most of the practical tools that are available; (9) invest in your workforce routinely and as part of your business strategy and (10) be authentic about good leadership and employee engagement (adopted 30-35)" [14].

"EFQM Excellence Model is based upon 9 main dimensions and these dimensions are called criteria (input criteria—leadership, policy & strategy, people, partnership & resources and processes; result criteria—customer results, employee results, society results and key performance results (criteria are supported by sub-criteria)" [16].

The EFQM Framework for CSR is interrelated on the EFQM Excellence Model and also gives guidelines on integration of social, environmental and economic results or influences.

"The EFQM model can be described as a higher form of quality management in organizations" [17].

EFQM model refers also to CSR and ISO 26000. European Commission presented CSR definition: "companies integrate their social and environmental concerns in their business operations and in their interaction with stakeholders on a voluntary basis" [3]. Responsible organizations pay attention first to economic growth, but simultaneously they care about their environmental and societal impacts. The real sustainability-oriented winners implement higher responsibility and sustainability standards (as it is necessary according the law). Innovative social responsible organizations cooperate with all stakeholders with the aim to achieve the sustainable stakeholder synergies (excellent case are Scandinavian countries, where governments pay one of the crucial roles).

TOTAL QUALITY MANAGEMENT AND TOTAL RESPONSIBILITY MANAGEMENT

In total quality (TQ), the environment in which the organization operates is changing constantly. Management's job, therefore, is to provide the leadership for continual improvement and innovation in processes and systems, products, and services. Continuous improvement is part of the management of all systems and processes. Improvement and learning need to be embedded in the way an organization operates. Improvements are very often concentrated on customer satisfaction, products and services improvement, productivity improvement, operational performance, work processes, errors minimization, waste minimization, flexibility, responsiveness, organizational management process improvement, continuous learning (learning organization at all levels), competitive comparisons, supplier performance, employee performance, and costs and financial performance. The goal of each organization should be long-term survival; the management has very important role, and it has to focus on improvement and must be able to create a system that can produce quality outputs. Employees are one of the key factors, and from this reason, training and education can provide needed skills. On the other hand, organizations have to pay attention also to structural rationality. It includes horizontal processes from suppliers to customers (as final user or buyer of their products or services). Simultaneously, the management needs to pay attention to the so-called philosophy toward change. It means that change, continuous improvement, and learning are encouraged.

Organizations must be able to adapt to changing environment. Competition is very strong, and the winners will be just the organizations that will be able to provide sustaining total quality and total responsibility. From this reason, the critical self-assessment is needed; it should be concentrated on management and leadership involvement (all levels), products and process design (meet customer needs), product and services control (minimize defects), customer and supplier communication (cooperative relationships), quality improvement (results achieved and plan for improvement), employee participation (employee skills and their participation—quality processes), education and training (skills quality improvement techniques), and quality information (complete information about results).

"The TQM practices suggested in the EFQM Excellence Model allows firms to outperform their competitors in the results criteria included in the Model. Therefore the research published in 2007 provides a valuable benchmarking data for firms in it substantiates the EFQM Enabler's contribution to the attainment of competitive advantage" [18]. The sustainability leaders constantly involve sustainability initiatives into their processes, organizational culture, and permanent cooperate with all stakeholders. In addition, sustainability must be systemic and holistic, and the expected result is long-term sustainable competitiveness.

Responsibility management through a systemic process is called total responsibility management. It is very important to make this process explicit. In this way, managers (decision makers) understand how to manage quality and how to build constructive and responsible stakeholder responsibilities as well as relationships with them.

The linkages between more responsible practices and better financial performance and productivity come from a variety of sources and in many ways can be relate to simple good management. Some unrecognized costs can actually be reduced when responsible practices are implemented. In this way, responsibility management can be cost-effective.

TRM is very similar to TQM, where top management and customers play the crucial role. TRM pays attention to stakeholders' interests (stakeholder partnerships especially with key stakeholders). A proactive and innovative relationship with stakeholders generates improvement and permanent learning system, which contributes to the organization's growth, sustainable development, and competitiveness, as well as regions and states where they operate.

"The TRM core values include: (1) visionary and committed leadership; (2) stakeholder-driven excellence and responsible practices; (3) organisational and personal learning through dialogue and mutual engagement with relevant stakeholders, (4) valuing employees, partners, other stakeholders; (4) agility and responsiveness; (5) focus on the future (short and long term); (6) managing for responsibility and improvement; (7) management by fact, transparency, accountability; (8) public responsibility and citizenship; (9) focus on positive results, impacts and value-added for stakeholders with responsible ecological practices" [12].

Leadership (especially top management) is very important in each organization. It must be innovative and be able to include and create stakeholder partnerships. Furthermore, they have to be exemplary for the organization's values and innovative strategic management, and they should be able to manage long-term responsibility, which results also as sustainable competitiveness and sustainable development.

"The improvement and innovation elements of TRM create a significant demand for companies to broaden how they measure performance (economic, societal, and environment issues—sustainable indicators)" [19].

ISO 26000—GUIDANCE STANDARD ON SOCIAL RESPONSIBILITY

ISO 26000 is a guidance for SR and an instrument that helps organizations by systemic and holistic SR implementation. In ISO 26000, the working group involved experts from 90 countries, 40 international organizations, and stakeholder experts (customers, government, industry, labor nongovernmental organizations, services, research and academic organizations, and other organizations). Social responsibility has a long tradition, and all theories and authors pay attention to the common principles (accountability, transparency, ethical activities, and stakeholder responsibility), which have to be respected in each responsible organization include accountability and transparency.

SR core subjects according ISO 26000 are as follows: (1) organizational governance, (2) human rights, (3) labor practices, (4) environment, (5) fair operating practices, (6) consumer issues, and (7) community involvement and development [4].

Additionally, the main purpose in ISO 26000 of the concept of "SR" has been to make it simple for easier implementation in different organizations (not just in corporations). Of course, it has advantages and disadvantages and difficulties, but it is a guideline for holistic and systemic implementation in the organization's strategy. ISO 26000 is extremely important and deserves attention. Furthermore, it needs explanation for potential users, and in the near future, its review will also be needed.

Moreover, permanent monitoring of SR performance as a requirement for permanent improvement regarding SR is needed (SR tools). A disadvantage of such tools is that not all SR impact areas are relevant for all organizations. ISO 26000 again proposes that stakeholders can play and important part in the evaluation of the SR performance of an organization. Benchmarking against the objectives and achievements of other organizations (SR champions in your industry, competitors, and other organizations with which the organization wants to compare itself) can help to anticipate developments in an industry or sector and evaluate what possible changes and consequences of these changes are important for organization.

Many researches on SR have been published already. "Research conducted by Brandsma showed that 54% Dutch organizations were at the initial stage of implementing policies on SR and 15% had not taken any steps at all" [20, 34].

ISO 26000 has short history, but there are many misunderstandings that refer to potential users about the scope of guidance and its usefulness in different types of organizations. Moreover, the relationship with other standards needs explanation. Other standards like quality, environment, safety, health, and information security are in interrelation and very close to ISO 26000.

What is social responsibility? It is the variety of definitions and opinions it attracts, a feature that is both a strength and a weakness. More and more topics are being categorized under the banner of SR, which continues to inflate its meaning. Consequently, discussions about SR are confused by different interpretations because of the debate about the importance and meaning of SR—it is a dynamic concept, and its concerns change in conjunction with the development in markets and society.

The triple-bottom-line concept, introduced by Elkington, argues that paying attention to people (social justice), environment (ecological quality), and society (societal well-being or prosperity) can create economic value for organizations. Furthermore, "he argued that only those organisations that systematically align their goals with the goals of society and recognise the interdependence of the 3Ps (people, planet, profit) will be successful and survive in the future" [21].

From this reason, many developments have a role in this, such as governments and public sector authorities in many countries, especially in Scandinavian countries, which increasingly procure sustainability. CSR (or SR) has become more visible and important in the past few years for companies, governments, and NGOs alike. Many companies (especially large companies) have developed CSR strategies and report annually on successes (and failures) of these strategies—usually stand-alone sustainability reports. Moreover, citizens and (future) employees increasingly expect companies to act as "corporate citizens." The number of "green" consumers, who are inclined to buy sustainable products and services, are growing, as is the market of fair trade products.

Corporate social responsibility has a long tradition. The reason in the industrial revolution was to improve employees' health and well-being to protect their own interests.

A good illustration of this is from one of the founders of capitalism, Adam Smith (most famously known for the idea of "the invisible hand"). Smith's well-known works are An Inquiry into the Nature and The Causes of the Wealth of Nations, Theory of Moral Sentiments, and The Wealth of Nations [22, 23]. In his works, he emphasizes the importance of ethical forces in the fee-market mechanism and international trade, taking into account restrictions from a viewpoint of natural justice to prevent a dominance of amoral egoism.

In the first half of the 20th century, many authors paid attention to social responsibility of management in companies. *The Functions of the Executive* by Barnard, *Measurement of Social Performance of Business* by Kreps, and *Social Responsibilities of the Businessman* by Bowen were published [24–26].

The book on CSR written by Bowen is the starting point of the modern era regarding CSR thinking. The book discussed the observation that the largest companies are important centers of power and decision making, and that the actions of these companies affect the lives of citizens in several ways. This book notes that change is a dominant feature of life and that this change requires greater recognition and acceptance of social responsibility by business. Around the same time, some other important publications about CSR appeared, such as Management's Responsibility to Society: The Growth of an Idea by Heald and Corporate Giving in a Free Society by Eells [27, 28].

"In 1960 Davis described CSR as businessmen's decisions and actions taken for reasons at least partially beyond the firm's direct economic and technical interest" [29]. "In 1963 Maguire wrote in his book Business and Society. The idea of social responsibilities supposes that the corporation has not only economic and legal obligations but also certain responsibilities to society which extend beyond these obligations" [30]. Walton (1967) stated in his book Corporate Social Responsibilities that companies should voluntarily acknowledge and accept that they have responsibilities beyond the gates of the company [31]. In 1972, the Limits of Growth [32] described the devastating environmental effects of economic growth. The current interest in CSR also comes from other areas and disciplines—quality management, values, and ethical behaviour of organizations. McAdam and Leonard pay attention to employees and customers [33, 34]. Management models such as those of the EFQM framework also give explicit attention to CSR—and this attention is growing. EFQM perceives the social responsibility for organizations as one of the pillars of excellence, and more attention has to be paid to CSR and sustainability. The explanation for the organization area "society" illustrates that every organization does not only supply services to (members of) society but is also part of society (organization becomes aware of its responsibility for its surrounding—environment, society, and development).

There are also other authors who paid attention to CSR. "In 2005, Kotler and Lee issued Corporate Social Responsibility: Doing the Most Good for your Company and Your Cause" [35]. "In 2006, the new well-known article Strategy and Society: The Link between Competitive Advantage and Corporate Social Responsibility was published" [36]. Strategy guru Prahalad has developed the strategy concept "the bottom of the pyramid," aimed at doing business with the poor, and the well-known management guru Peter Drucker discussed CS-related issues during a large part of his career [37, 38]. "According to Friedman view, there is one and only one social responsibility of business—to use its resources and engage in activities designed to increase its profits so long as it stays within the rules of the game, which is to say, engages in open and free competition without deception or fraud—'the business of business is business'" [39]. According to Carroll, CSR has an economic, legal, ethical, and philanthropic face and points to the more strategic character of CSR—process in enterprises where ecological, economic, and social aspects are integrated in a strategic way [34, 40,41].

The development of ISO 26000 started in 2005. "ISO 26000 has ambition to be a comprehensive SR guideline that will enable all organisations to define their SR" [34]. The aim of ISO 26000 is to offer practical framework (including international conventions which are close to SR) with relevant systems (interaction with SR). The ISO organization offers several important advantages for the development of a global SR guidelines, from the perspective of the organization's objectives. ISO is one of the few organizations that is broadly acknowledger internationally. ISO will receive visibility in many organizations that already work with other ISO management systems but which have not yet engaged meaningfully with SR. "Research conducted by Brandsma in 2009 confirms this" [20]. Between 55% and 60% of the respondents that work with an ISO-certified or related management system standards are considering applying ISO 26000 in their organizations. The development of ISO 26000 has been on the largest multistakeholder process that has ever been organized. Hundreds of experts from numerous countries have cooperated in the process. The aim has been to strive for a mutual and universal basic definition, principles, working methods, and guidelines—an international standard, written in (relatively) straightforward language. In addition, the guideline is applicable to all organizations, in all countries, in all stages of development, in all sectors and does not conflict with other SR standards or demands—it has no intention of replacing these. "The ambition of ISO 26000, as a generic, overarching SR guideline, is to enable its integration with any existing SR or CSR standards" [34].

The results of the before mentioned research showed that most organizations that indicated an interest in ISO 26000 are still at an early stage in terms of SR implementation. For all these organizations, ISO 26000 is an applicable source of guidance as an introduction into SR and SR subject areas and as a guideline to structure their SR activities. Organizations that have already developed SR strategies and initiatives are more likely to apply ISO 26000 to increase the credibility of the own SR claims, e.g., by referring to the guideline in their SR communications. Moreover, ISO 26000 contains a process standard, a performance standard, a principle standard, and a basic standard, but it is not certification standard.

"ISO 26000 guideline aim is to help and support organisations, to contribute to sustainable development" [4]. Moreover, the ISO 26000 guideline highlights many aspects, and it contains advices and instructions for easier implementation in different organizations. Guidelines prescribe many requested activities and expectations, which have to be realized. Additionally, activities on SR implementation are structured, and concepts and principles are explained. SR core subjects are explained, harmonized (uniform and universal concept), and integrate ISO 26000 with other standards. It also provides the map of standards, which are in interrelation with SR and offers overview (core subjects and step-by-step implementation. Finally, the guideline reflects many SR subjects and encourages organizations (in their own context) to use them with the aim to encourage their SR activities, which reflect as their contribution to sustainable organization and sustainable society.

"ISO 26000 intends to give organisations the possibility to formulate an organisation-specific interpretation of SR, based on the SR foundation it provides. ISO 26000 crucially enable organisations to develop their own unique SR profile" [34]. This idea of an SR profile plays an important role in ISO 26000 because it characterizes a new generation of SR.

The four most important clauses in ISO 26000 are preceded by a classification of the scope of the guideline. First, ISO 26000 is applicable to all types of organization and the purpose of ISO 26000. Furthermore, it specifically states that ISO 26000 is not meant as a standard for a management system or for certification purposes. Next, the most important terms and definitions that are used in ISO 26000 are described ("terms, definitions, and abbreviated terms"). After the terms and definitions, ISO 26000 directs attention to the background to Clause 3, which includes a description of trends and developments, characteristics of SR, and the relationship between SR and sustainable development. Moreover, this clause pays attention to the relationship between ISO 26000 and the responsibilities of governments in SR. The guideline also points at the role of government in stimulating SR among companies but offers no further specific guidance on this issue.

STAKEHOLDERS INVOLVEMENT AND CORPORATE RESPONSIBILITY

Stakeholder theory has much to say about strategic management. The stakeholder perspective offers an alternative that can enhance the economic perspectives of modern strategic management. After more than half a century of research and debate, there is not a single widely accepted definition on CSR. Researchers in the field of CSR have claimed that the phrase "corporate social responsibility" has been used in so many different ideas and concepts (social performance, governance, accountability, sustainability triple bottom line, and social entrepreneurship).

Stakeholder identification and engagement—One of the general CSR principles within ISO 26000 concerns respecting stakeholders' interests. Identifying stakeholders, knowing their expectations, and enabling stakeholder engagement therefore play an important role in the guideline as they are a key to understanding, addressing, and implementing social responsibility. "Porter and Kramer add that by engaging in strategic CSR, new product offerings are likely to emerge, which are in turn benefiting both, social and environmental issues in addition to a company's long-term competitiveness" [36, 42]. Organizations engage and interact with many stakeholders (primary and secondary) with the aim to implement strategic SR processes successfully.

"Freeman et al. suggest the new vision of capitalism—stakeholder capitalism (based at six principles: stakeholder cooperation, engagement, responsibility, complexity, continuous creation and emergent competition)—founded on libertarian and pragmatist lines" [5]. Stakeholder capitalism is based on freedom, rights, and the creation by consent of positive obligations. This kind of value creation shows that on this way it is possible to make our capitalism more responsible and resilient (social nature of value creation).

For the successful processes that refer to stakeholder management, we suggest additional advices and argumentation. The organizations need better description how organizations can manage their relationships with stakeholders. The nature of relationships between different organizations and their stakeholders requires a combination of their divergent interests and ambitions. Accountability, one of key elements, includes environmental responsibility—sustainability reporting, societal demands need more attention, and political and legal trends require more regulation. Value creation is also one of the main challenges from theoretical and practical point of view—a richer description of theoretical explanation including types of measurements as well as stakeholder literature is needed. All these issues allow leaders and academics to create improved organizational practices and outcomes.

In the systemic and holistic context of stakeholder theory, there is also the opportunity to redefine the concepts that are closely related to it. These concepts refer in the literature (and researches) on business ethics, economics, public administration, finance, philosophy, management, governance, private and public sector, as well as private–public partnership and finally to local communities, nongovernmental organizations, and others. In this context, the interdisciplinary nature of stakeholder concepts needs more attention—from theoretical and practical view.

One of the general CSR principles within ISO 26000 concerns respecting stakeholder interests [4]. Stakeholders are seen as a starting point for CSR policies and fulfill an essential role in determining an organization's social responsibilities. The guideline is very clear—ISO 26000 stresses the importance of a stakeholder orientation in an organization's approach toward SR. To identify its social responsibility properly, an organization should, according to ISO 26000, understand three specific relationships [4]: (1) relationship between the organization and society—the actions and expectations that ISO 26000 specifies for core subjects and issues can assist an organization in this; (2) an organization should understand the relationship it has with its stakeholders—

stakeholder's expectations, as emphasized by ISO 26000, are not necessarily the same as expectations of society; (3) needs to be understood—the relationship with society as whole—it is always useful for an organization to consider whose or which interest certain stakeholder represents. ISO 26000 finds it important in stakeholder relationship that an organization uses its influence to encourage stakeholder to address SR.

According to ISO 26000, determining an organization's sustainability impact is the most important way to identify stakeholders (but the relevant stakeholders are not the same for every organization). Organizations should always consider the legitimacy of their stakeholder's interests, demands, expectations, and wishes. The goal of ISO norm would be to offer practical methods and tools for the identification and involvement of stakeholders with the goal of developing a substantiated basis for supported decisions. Norm can be a useful addition to several standards (the ISO proposal refers to ISO 26000, ISO 9001, ISO 14001, and ISO 10001—customer satisfaction). For any of these standards, a good stakeholder analysis is an important ingredient (complex broad process and projects with multistakeholder focus are needed as well as importance of stakeholder "sphere of influence") [34].

An organization should also be aware of the interests and needs of its stakeholders and facilitate open dialogue. Furthermore, ISO 26000 adds that the active engagement of stakeholders is based on trust and goes beyond public relations (a mutual belief that they are engaging in dialogue for the right reasons). This means that the essence of the dialogue should concern aspects that are strongly related to sustainable development and sufficiently important for the parties involved, and that the interests of all parties are clearly formulated from the start. Interaction is therefore the basis of stakeholder engagement in the view of ISO 26000, which suggests a number of methods and tools (both formal and informal; both for individual stakeholder and collective negotiations, such as stakeholder panels, seminars, conferences and workshops, roundtables, advisory committees, or internal forums). An organization is constantly interacting with its stakeholders, and it should manage these relationships and its social responsibilities well. Moreover, creating stakeholder engagement is important and offers organizations numerous advantages, but it is not one-off event, and a continuous process and periodically review of policies (activities) in the field of stakeholder engagement is needed.

Implementation is a critical area because the successful implementation of SR is clearly a big challenge for many organizations. ISO 26000 stresses that connecting SR to the culture, values and thus the identity of the organization will have a positive effect on understanding and acceptance, which in turn can facilitate and speed up the implementation process. It means that organizational change tends to be a long-term process—taking years to be realized. For each organization, it is important to indicate the most important barriers to SR implementation. The barrier to SR implementation could be, for example, lack of a clear action plan, too little time available, too little knowledge about SR implementation, too little knowledge of SR, obtaining by-in from the board, economic crisis, too little budget available, creating engagement with employees, and creating engagement with middle management, which might be eliminated by ISO 26000.

A commitment from the top of an organization is an important prerequisite to making any initiative work. According to ISO 26000, an organization should "make SR an integral part of its strategy, policy, organizational culture, structure and operations" [4]. When the board of an organization is aware of the (economic) advantages of SR in the context of sustainable development or in reaching certain ambitions of the organization, the chances for a long-term and enduring commitment increase. ISO 26000 emphasizes that commitment and understanding of SR are necessary at all levels of an organization. Furthermore, stakeholder dialogue is also an instrument to avoid and possibly solve conflicts or differences of opinion with stakeholders. Additionally, ISO 26000 provides several suggestions on how to enhance the credibility of communications and SR claims and SR report, among which are ensuring that the organization's performance as reported in its sustainability report is comparable over time, is comparable with the performance of similar organizations (in the same sector), contains explanation on why an organization does not report on certain seemingly relevant SR topics, uses eco-labels or existing SR assessment criteria, and is verified by an external third party. According to ISO 26000, "an organisation should develop mechanisms to solve conflicts or disputes with stakeholders appropriate for the kind of conflict or dispute as well as for the particular stakeholder involved" [4]. Moreover, an organization is supported to the transparent with respective stakeholders about the procedures it has in place.

Finally, to make SR a living part of an organization, a structural approach is necessary. Internal and external buy-in as well as support from top management is very important for this. SR implementation is given a lot of space in ISO 26000 and includes advice on SR communication, enhancing the credibility of SR claims and integrating SR in existing systems and structures. Implementing SR successfully depends on getting the soft side (culture, values, and engagement) right, as well as dealing with hard issues (structures, measurement, and embedding). Moreover, it should constantly benchmark performance against its stated aims and change these when and if it becomes necessary as developments inside and outside the organization evolve.

SUSTAINABLE BUSINESS EXCELLENCE AND SUSTAINABLE COMPETITIVENESS

The sources of a nation's (nowadays also regional's or local's and organization's) prosperity is competitiveness. In the global world, it is difficult to compete successfully. Innovativeness and especially SR are two of the most important factors for large or small payers at the global or local market.

SR is important to competitiveness, and placing SR within the strategy seems very important. SR should be the core activity, and it means that the stakeholder expectations regarding SR are in focus at the same time. SR strategy (reflects organization's values and mission) includes relations with stakeholders, measurement (indicators—ecological, social, and financial aspects—according Global Reporting Initiative are recommended) as well as SR reporting. Each organization should focus SR efforts on market, regulatory, and operational actions. In last decade, organizations recognize the importance of SR and care about their impacts on their ability to compete successfully. Organizations, especially large and medium sized, must be able to create innovative strategies for SR.

Simultaneously, we would like to highlight some barriers to innovative SR and sustainable excellence, and one of them is insufficient organizational capacity to incorporate SR know-how. Decision makers in organizations do not build the bridges with their stakeholders and are limited in SME's resources for SR. Furthermore, there are also practical and theoretical limits (stakeholder selection and interpretation).

"SR of creative people, their co-workers and stakeholders are one of the most influential groups. Tolerance for diversity brings talents and makes investment in technology worth, while the 3T model (Florida 3T Model—Talent, Technology, Tolerance) makes the difference between the most successful and other regions" [19].

"The concept of business excellence is deeply rooted in TQM (Rehder and Ralstons's in 1984—Baldrige criteria the first TQM model). In 1991, the EFQM Excellence Model was developed by the European Foundation of Quality Management to promote quality throughout Europe" [43].

Moreover, it significantly contributes to its competitiveness as whole as well as to competitiveness of organizations and regions or local communities where they operate. Competitiveness is a very complex and long-term process. Nowadays, it is better to discuss about sustainable (responsible) competitive advantages.

The EFQM Excellence Model is very complex, and from this reason, it is very important for each organization to recognize the key aspects or findings. First, business excellence influences short-term and long-term sustainable competitive advantages and performance and awards support competitiveness. Strong competition is one of the reasons why organizations try to improve performance and in this way contribute to sustainable development. The excellence model helps organizations to implement the core values and concepts of excellence in organizations at macro- and microlevels. Furthermore, organizations need assistance with benchmarking, and the most important is learning from the best practice (case studies).

Professional approach to benchmarking is needed. "Some projects fail because 25% had received not training in benchmarking; 30% do not use a benchmarking methodology; 30% do not develop a project plan e.g. poorly defined aims, stakeholder not identified etc. and 35% do not undertake a cost/benefit analysis. The best practice benchmarking is the most powerful type of benchmarking" [43]. Furthermore, business excellence and benchmarking provide the path of success in future.

Long-term oriented and responsible organization pay attention to the development of excellence and SR model because they are working on it in order to improve the competitiveness and sustainable cooperation (its own competitiveness and competitiveness of the local community or region where they operate). "The EFQM business excellence model can serve as an example of integration and as a system of the improvement of an organization's operational success of the basis of the integration of the models and leadership standards" [44]. Scandinavian countries are very often mentioned as a world known leaders in CSR or SR and sustainable development. The concept of "creating shared value" has Scandinavian origins, where institutional and cultural factors play important role and particularly these factors promote CSR, SR, and sustainability. "The recent phenomenon of movement from implicit to explicit CSR in a Scandinavian context and what this may entail" [45]. Stakeholder engagement encourages a cooperative approach to business and other operations.

EFQM EXCELLENCE MODEL AND ISO 26000 IMPLEMENTATION

"EFQM Excellence Model is a practical tool providing various advantages from the perspective of empirical research just like other quality awards" [18].

The EFQM Excellence Model is very useful. It has practical value, meaning it is a practical-oriented model, and we can highlight few of the most significant advantages. The model is permanently revised and updated in these activities, and EFQM consultants are involved because their contribution is significant. EFQM Excellence Model is very complex and needs systemic and holistic approach, and from this reason, it provides a large and comprehensive set of subcriteria and sometimes even sub-subcriteria to explain the precise meaning of any criterion.

Comparison with others, especially with the best organizations (leading organizations in their fields—benchmarking), is very important for each organization. Different award models are helpful for comparison between organizations, as well as a good case on how to achieve the responsible competitive advantages and cooperative relationships with all stakeholders.

The crucial role plays leadership that cares about responsibility for developing infrastructures, as to achieve desirable and requested results. For example, in ecological and social influences, one of the main stakeholders is the employees, and their satisfaction is very important and financial results (not just profit for shareholders but also satisfaction and cooperative relationships with all stakeholders).

Using EFQM model, organizations have the support of a performance excellence framework founded on the SR principles to develop sustainable approaches on for business excellence for people, planet, and profit. Each organization has to include SR as part of its strategy, but these approaches have to be measured continuously, and the results have to be reviewed and improved as necessary.

ISO 26000 is contemporarily not certifiable, but the review is necessary. It should be reviewed periodically, perhaps parallel with EFQM Excellence Model. Improvement should be included in the next version (EFQM is good example). In the near future, ISO 26000 should be transformed (step by step) from suggestions and advices to a certifiable management system. We forecast that the market (private and public organizations) will speak on this challenges (the Scandinavian countries are an excellent case; results confirm the right orientation). The initiatives related to ISO 26000 increases, and use of the guideline for contractual purposes grows. The need for a certifiable social management system (SMS) will become clear in near future. The last revision in EFQM Excellence Model has been realized in 2012. Global economic environment and stakeholder requirements are changing constantly and organizations. In the future trends, the convergence of international SR standards and other standards, including EFQM Excellence Model, the management of costs related to the implementation of SR, and the opportunities for innovation in large organizations, SMEs, and other organizations are expected.

CONCLUSIONS AND FUTURE RESEARCH

"The EFQM Excellence Model 2013 real challenge for organizations will be to become agile and flexible so as to act swiftly to attain and retain its leadership in the global and local market place" [11]. We hope that organizations will recognize and understand their key business challenges and value in EFQM 2013 (manage quality and achieve sustainable excellence).

Sustainable excellence is a long-term process. From this reason, the suggestions according ISO 26000 must be more explicit for different types of organizations (companies, local community management, education at all levels, and other organizations), including indicators as well as reporting. All companies (large- and medium-sized companies) and other organizations from developed countries and BRIC countries should report about their sustainable activities each year. It means that they should use the indicators recommended by ISO 26000 and Global Reporting Initiative. Furthermore, ISO 26000 recommendations, later certification (step by step), and legislation are needed. ISO 26000 certification will be a long-term process, and in this way, the implementation process will be encouraged, comparable between different types of organizations and even different industries. We forecast that the market will speak on this issue. As initiatives related to ISO 26000 increase, and the use of guideline for contractual purposes grows, the need for a certifiable social management (CSM) system will become clear.

How and when to implement the EFQM Excellence Model? In organizations that have introduced the Quality Management System (QMS—ISO 9001), it should already be the next step. Contemporarily, quality philosophy, like TQM, TRM, ISO 26000, and EFQM, requests ISO 9001, which is an excellent basis for the implementation of the EFQM Excellence Model (sustainably oriented according ISO 26000, including indicators and reporting).

On this way, the EFMQ implementation period is relatively short. It provides recommendations that help organizations to evaluate organization quality management level (additional subcriteria and sub-subcriteria are recommended). EFQM Excellence Model leads organizations to continual quality improvement, higher quality, sustainable stakeholder management, sustainable cooperative advantages (or competitive advantages) at local, regional, or global market, and increase the sustainable organizational culture.

The outcomes of this overview represent an innovative contribution to the development and potential implementation aspects, discussion, and conformation. Furtherance of theories is important in studying SR (or CSR), TQM, TRM, EFQM, ISO quality standards, ISO 26000, sustainable excellence, and indicators. Literature review (theoretical and empirical base) and debate on TQM, SR, EFQM, and ISO 26000 are still included.

The aim of this study is to highlight the characteristic features, systemic, and holistic ISO 26000 implementation according EFQM, to present the available theoretical frameworks for quality and SR-oriented models, and to compare them to published researches, which pay attention to sustainable models is achieved.

"Finally, we want to draw attention to the Scandinavian contest and encourage the field of strategic management to shift its focus from achieving a competitive advantage toward achieving a cooperative advantage" [46]. In the context of SR (or CSR) according EFQM, ISO quality standards, and ISO 26000, we will discuss about sustainable cooperative advantages or sustainable cooperative excellence in the future.

Future research might also analyze the EFQM and ISO 26000 in different organizations, including their specifics as well as barriers by implementation, measurement, and reporting (in large MNCs, medium-sized companies, government, local community management, educational organizations at all levels, health system, and others). Additions and concretization of ISO 26000 and EFQM especially for SMEs and recommendations for other organizations (in public sector) are needed.

REFERENCES

1. EFQM. Assessing for Excellence: A Practical Guide for Self-Assessment. EFQM, Brussels. 2003.
2. Thaiwanai, S. The EFQM 2013 Model Changes, Implications for Organizations [Internet]. 2013. Available form: http://www.exin-libary.com/Player/3-knowledge/efqm_2013_model_changes_ implications_ for_ orgzn_1.pdf [Accessed: 2015-03-20]
3. Commission of the European Communities. Green Paper: Promoting a European Framework for Corporate Social Responsibility. COM 366 final. 2001. Brussels: Commission of the European Communities.
4. International Standard Organization. ISO 26000 [Internet]. 2010. www://iso.org./ISO discovering_ iso_26000.pdf [Accessed: 2012-01-21]
5. Freeman RE, Harrison JS, Wicks AC, Parmar BL, DeColle S. Stakeholder Theory. Cambridge: Cambridge University Press; 2010. 434 p.
6. Cruz, LB, Boehe DM. How do leading retain MNCs leverage CSR globally? Insights from Brazil. Journal of Business Ethics. 2010; 91(2): 243–263.
7. Aßländer MS. Corporate social responsibility as subsidiary co-responsibility—macroeconomic perspective. Journal of Business Ethics. 2011; 99(1): 115–128.
8. Nabitz U, Klazinga N, Walburg J. The EFQM Excellence Model: European and Dutch experiences with the EFWM approach in health care. International Journal of Health Care. 2000;12(3): 191–201.
9. Jayamaha NP, Grigg NP, Mann RS. Empirical analysis of the Baldrige Criteria as both an organisational performance measure and a theoretical model. Measuring Business Excellence. 2011;15(1): 20–33.
10. DeDommartin A. ISO 9001: 2000 and the EFQM Excellence Model [Internet]. 2003. file:///C:/Users/

Uporabnik/Downloads/p.18,%20Viewpoint%20(2).pdf [Accessed: 2015-03-22]

11. EFQM [Internet]. 2013. http://www.efqm.org/efqm-model/fundamental-concepts [Accessed: 2015-03-29]
12. Waddock S, Bodwell C. Total Responsibility Management. Sheffield: Greenleaf Publishing Limited, Sheffield; 2007. 192 p.
13. McBain R, Ghobadian A, Switzer J, Wilton P, Woodman P, Pearson G. The Business Benefits of Management and Leadership Development. CMI and Penna.
14. Leadership & Management in the UK: The Key to Sustainable Growth [Internet]. 2012. Available from https://www.gov.uk/government/uploads/system/uploads/attachment_data/file/32327/12-923-leadership-management-key-to-sustainable-growth-evidence.pdf [Accessed: 2015-03-30]
15. Lal K, Dunnewijk T. Entrepreneurship and Innovation Strategies in ICT SMEs in Enlarged Europe (EU 25). Working paper. The Netherlands: UNU-MERIT. 2008; No. 016.
16. Uygur A, Sümerli S. EFQM Excellence Model. International Review of Management and Business Research. 2013; 2(4):980–993.
17. Gašparik J, Gašparikova V, Ellingerova H. Improvement of Quality Management Level in Construction Company Using EFQM Model. DOI 10.5592/otmcj.2014.1.5. Research paper. 2014:949–957.
18. Santos-Vijande ML, Alvarez-Gonzales L.I. International Journal of Business Science and Applied Management. 2007; 2(2):21–41.
19. Gorenak Š, Bobek V. Total responsibility management indicators and sustainable development. International Journal of Sustainable Society. 2010;2(3):248–264.
20. Brandsma M, Moratis L, Cochius T. Motivations for and Potential Barriers of ISO 26000 uptake in the Netherlands. Rotherdam: CSR Academy; 2009.
21. Elkington J. Cannibals with Forks—The Triple Bottom-line of 21st Century Business. Oxford, UK: Capstone Publishing; 1997.
22. Smith A. An Inquiry into the Nature and Causes of the Wealth of Nation. London: W. Strahan & T. Cadell; 1776.
23. Smith A. The Theory of Moral Sentiments. Indianapolis, IN: Liberty Classics; 1759, 1976.
24. Barnard C. The Functions of the Executive. Cambridge, MA: Harvard University Press; 1938.
25. Kreps T. Measurement of the Social Performance of Business. Palo Alto, CA: Stanford University Press; 1940.
26. Browen H. Social Responsibilities of the Businessman. New York: Harper & Row; 1953.
27. Herald M. Management's Responsibility to Society—The Growth of an Idea. Business History Review. 1957; 31(4): 375–384.
28. Eells R. Corporate Giving in a Free Society. New York: Harper; 1956.
29. Davis K. Can Business Afford to Ignore Social Responsibilities? California Management Review. 1960;2(3): 70–76.
30. Maguire JW. Business and Society. New York: McGraw-Hill; 1963.
31. [31]Walton CC. Corporate Social Responsibilities. Belmont, CA: Wadsworth Publishing; 1967.
32. Meadows DH, Meadows DL, Randers J, Behrens III W.W. The Limits to Growth—A Report for the Club of Rome's Project on the Predicament of Mankind. New York: Universe Books; 1972.
33. McAdam R, Leonard D. Corporate social responsibility in a total quality management context—opportunities for sustainable growth. Corporate Governance. 2003;3(4):35–45.
34. Moratis L, Cochius T. ISO 26000: The Business Guide. Sheffield: Greenleaf Publishing Limited; 2011. 206 p.
35. Kotler P, Lee N. Corporate Social Responsibility: Doing the Most Good for Your Company and Your Cause. Hoboken, NY: John Wiley; 2005.
36. [36]Porter M, Kramer M. Strategy and society—the link between competitive advantage and corporate social responsibility. Harvard Business Review. 2006; December: 78–92.
37. Prahalad CK. The Fortune at the Bottom of the Pyramid: Eradicating Poverty through Profits. Upper Saddle River: Wharton School; 2004.
38. Drucker PF. Management Challenges for the 21st Century. New York: Harper Business; 1999.
39. Friedman M. The Social Responsibility of Business Is to Increase Its Profit. New York: Times Magazine. 1970; 13 September.
40. Carroll AB. A three-dimensional conceptual model of corporate performance. Academy of Management Review. 1979; 4(4):497–505.
41. Carroll AB. Corporate social responsibility: evolution of a definitional construct. Business & Society. 1999; 38(3):268–295.
42. Porter M, Kramer M.R. Creating shared value. How to reinvent capitalism and unleash a wave of innovation and growth. Harvard Business Review. 2011;90 (1/2): 62–67.
43. Mann R, Adebanjo D, Tickle M. Development of business excellence in Asia—an exploratory study. International Journal of Quality & Reliability Management. 2011;28(6): 604–627.
44. Rusijan B, Castka P. Understanding ISO's 9001 benefits and research through an operations strategy framework. Managing Global Transitions. 2010; 8(1): 97–118.
45. Stand R, Freeman RE. Corporate social responsibility and sustainability in Scandinavia: an overview. Journal of Business Ethics. 2015; 127:1–15.
46. Strand R, Freeman RE. Scandinavian cooperative advantage: the theory and practice of stakeholder engagement in Scandinavia. Journal of Business Ethics. 2015;127:65–85.

CHAPTER 9

CERTIFICATION AND INTEGRATION OF ENVIRONMENT WITH QUALITY AND SAFETY

Gilberto Santos, Manuel Rebelo, Síria Barros, and Martinha Pereira

INTRODUCTION

According to Wright [1] certification of products and processes began during the 1960's in the manufacturing industry, as a tool to control and assure the quality/conformity of products and services provided by suppliers to customers/consumers. Thus, the series of ISO 9000 was published first time, in 1987 and it was been created with a flexible character, to be reviewed periodically. Later, were published others normative references, which highlight the ISO 14001 in 1996 and OHSAS 18001 in 1999. This was also, the natural sequence of the certification processes in the organizations, i.e., began with the certification of quality management systems (QMS) followed by the environmental management systems (EMS) and after for the Occupational Health and Safety Management System (OHSMS). Hence, a high percentage of organizations with an EMS, in accordance with the ISO 14001, had also implemented, a certified QMS, in accordance with ISO 9001. At first the implementation of a QMS was particularly relevant in high demanding activity sectors, like the automotive and aeronautical industries, but it has rapidly extended to every activity sector, becoming a common requisite of any company worldwide and a factor of competitiveness and survival. Due to the increasingly demanding environmental legislation in developed countries, companies nowadays are required to seriously take into consideration not only environmental aspects associated to the production chain itself, but also to the life cycle of their products.

They are forced to implement suitable EMS to manage the environmental issues as for example at the level of the prevention and reduction of wastes. Consequently to promote and protect environment in a sustainable way. This is a particularly important issue for small and medium-sized companies (SMEs), which are considered to make up the vast majority of business in Europe)[2]. They are quoted as contributing 70% of global environmental pollution, with the majority coming from the manufacturing sector [3]. Thus, following both the Rio Conference in 1992 and GATT (General Agreement on Tariffs and Trade) negotiations, international standards have become important for succeeding and for getting access to the markets; at the same time, there has been an increase in the interest of environmental management. Such regulatory and competitive pressures have caused firms to take into consideration the environmental issues within their own production and market plans. Many firms have attempted to seek an effective environmental management system. These have led to implementation and development of the ISO 14001 standard for assessing environmental management processes. Today, all over the world, many firms are seeking ISO 14001 certification [4]. Thus, improved environmental management in the industrial sector is required to protect the environment, protect human health and property, and to satisfy environmental requirements associated with international trade [5]. In a sense, the value of the ISO 14001 certificate, as a proof of environmental performance, is a combination of the supplier's environmental ambitions, the advancement of supply chain practices of the customer and the ambitions of the certification bodies [6]. On other hand, according to Casadesús [7] and others authors, the interest shown by organizations and other entities linked by the implementation of environmental management systems (EMS), especially the family of ISO 14000 standards and the EMAS regulation in Europe, has grown spectacularly all over the world in recent years, even though a certain saturation has been detected in some countries. Thus, the implementation and management of all economical, environmental and social aspects within a company is gradually becoming a crucial requirement for any business and has become a widespread phenomenon around

Citation: Gilberto Santos, Manuel Rebelo, Síria Barros and Martinha Pereira (2012). Certification and Integration of Environment with Quality and Safety, Dr. Sime Curkovic (Ed.), InTech, DOI: 10.5772/48414.

the world [8]. Large companies are increasingly requiring this management policy from their suppliers, establishing specific requests and performances that small and medium enterprises (SMEs) often find extremely difficult to accomplish. On other hand, there are many organizations which, either because of the demands of the market itself or because of other internal motivations, have implemented different Management Systems alongside their EMS.

In fact, although no reliable references on this matter have been found, it is quite plausible to think that the great majority of ISO 14001 – registered companies are also certified in accordance with the ISO 9001 standard [9]. Thus, quality management philosophy and methods have been imported into ISO 14001 from ISO 9000. As a result, it is not surprising that measurement and evaluation are enshrined as important hallmarks of an effective EMS. According Curkovic [38], a companys ability to reframe learnings from total quality management (TQM) is crucial to the successful implementation and use of environmentally responsible manufacturing (ERM) -based systems and procedures.

Generally speaking, this component of the EMS is considered effective when the contents of review meetings are well communicated, the focus of meetings is on improving the system, findings (i.e. about noncompliance, from various statistical charts, and audit results) are reported honestly, and corrective actions follow [10]. In some cases, the similarities between QMS and EMS systems can facilitate the integration of the two related management systems [11]. The people that work in environmental management and at the same time are members of quality teams, assure that quality management goes hand-in-hand with environmental management. The actions that are carried out to achieve quality are, in many situations, the same actions necessary, for example, to achieve effective environmental management. In line with this, ISO 14001 has become compatible with the ISO 9001. Consequently, the integration of environmental issues (including environmental protection and pollution prevention in the management of organizations through the implementation of an environmental management system) allow acquiring a deep insight of the most important environmental aspects associated with its activity, and identifying the processes that need to be improved through the implementation of effective environmental measures [12]. On other hand, according Curkovic [38] TQM focuses on waste as it applies to process inefficiencies, whereas ERM focuses more on pollution in the form of air emissions and solid and hazardous waste. Because the two concepts share a similar focus, it makes sense to use many of the TQM tools, methods, and practices in implementing an ERM-based system.

Moreover, human resources are the most valuable resource of any company or country, but not always the most valued. Thus, the greatest asset of any organization, any region or any country, are people and their know-how [13]. Therefore, among others, another system to be implemented in the organizations is the OHSMS. Thus, according Fernández-Muñiz [14], several fields are showing increasing interest in safety culture as a means of reducing accidents in the workplace. The literature shows that safety culture is a multidimensional concept. Hence, nowadays, companies that search greater profitability and better organization implement the quality systems, aiming at a reduction of defective products and lost time, searching for the loyalty of customers and searching for excellence. The progressive implementation of ideas and techniques related with the quality management is one of the clearest demonstrations of organizational innovation in the industry in the last decades. From the standpoint of the risk prevention literature, it has been argued that the use of advanced quality management systems help reduce accident rates because quality management methods are based on the principle of prevention rather than corrective actions. Hence, the concept of an OHSMS has become common over the past 20 years [15]. The people that work in safety management and at the same time, are members of quality teams, assure that quality management has a great relationship with risk management.

More than ever, today, is in question the business sustainability of the organizations and the focus should be placed far much more than financial results. These results will not verify if that focus does not prioritize also, the satisfaction, balanced, integrated and growing of the customers and others relevant Stakeholders, that are clearly and objectively the employees for example [16]. But according to the ISO – IMS publication [17], a common objective of management system standards is to assist organizations to manage the risks associated with providing products and services to customers and other stakeholders. On other hand the management system of the organizations is frequently split into a number of parts or sub-systems, which must be managed separately with relative independence. These parts or sub-systems of an organization's management system reflect the different needs and expectations of the stakeholders. Many organizations use standards, such as those related to quality, the environment and safety, among others, to manage certain aspects of their performance.

Within this framework, in order to have quality and excellence in products (or services), as well as in the management of the companies that manufacture and provide them, it has become imperative for the companies define and implement quality, environment and safety management system, according to ISO 9001, ISO 14001 and OHSAS 18001 standards, respectively. At the same time the companies must also improve and optimize, continually, these management systems to allow them to true added value for the companies and their stakeholders [16].

The following questions may arise: How can these three management systems be integrated? Can they be integrated? According to Santos [18] this is a problem that the most developed companies started to experience some time ago, and it has been discussed by various authors, that we highlight: McDonald [19], Arifin [20] and Bernardo [21] among others, who provides a summary of the degrees of integration according to some authors, and Labodová [22], who reported on the implementation of integrated management systems using a risk analyses based approach. Thus, according with the ISO 72:2001 Guide [23], the experience with management system standards issued by the ISO shows that there exist a number of common elements, which can be arranged under the following main subjects: policy; planning; implementation and operation; performance assessment; improvement and management review, as stated by Santos [13].

Related to the integration of management systems, Karapetrovic [9] states that there are many organizations that implement different management systems, either as a result of market demand either for internal reasons. During the combined audits in accordance with ISO 19011 [24] for Quality and/or Environmental Management Systems audits, it can be observed that the integration of the systems is implemented in a partial way by the integration of procedures by phases.

When it is observed that it exist similar procedures, those are adapted to the two systems, for exemple, quality and environment, and jointly audited. However, the manuals still individually separated. As stated by Santos [25], although an audit be integrated / joint, named as by "combined audit", the respective reports are often kept separate so that any nonconformities detected in one of the systems do not implicate to stop the other system that complies with the respective standard. This could implicate the loose of clients, which would be a backward step for the company, and is considered one of the obstacles to a quicker integration. Suditu [26], associates to the integration of management systems internal motivations and corresponding benefits, by dividing them into: 1 - Organisational – improvement of the quality of the management by downsizing of three departments into one and reducing barriers between individual systems; 2 - Financial – reduction in auditing costs; 3-Employees – increased motivation, awareness and competences; 4 - External motivations and corresponding benefits, by dividing them into: Commercial – competitive advantage, improved market position, gain of new clients and satisfying current ones; Communication – improved image of the organisation, improved relationships with Stakeholders and evidence of legal compliance; In fact, significant differences in these areas have not been found, and it is fairly plausible that the vast majority of companies certified under ISO 14001 are also certified under the ISO 9001 standard, according to Santos [13].

Therefore, a new necessity has emerged in organisations, namely to integrate these systems into a single IMS - Integrated Management System and we cannot forget the fact that the environmental improvement of the product must be considered in relation to the impacts on Quality & Health and Safety, as mentioned by Jørgensen [27]. Therefore, the idea of an IMS - Integrated Management System consists of establishing correspondences and to combine two or more independent management systems, for example in accordance with ISO 9001, ISO 14001, and OHSAS 18001. Evidence of this can be seen in table A.1 - of the annex A - of OHSAS 18001:2007 [28]. Despite having their origins in different aspects of company performance, the Quality, Environment and Safety Management Systems have a lot in common, as mentioned by Fresner [12] and Block [29], among other authors. The integration of these management systems is a path that can be followed, and the ISO 19011 standard - Guidelines for auditing management systems [24] is a good example of the future. According to Santos [13] the future lies in the integration of these management systems, managed by only one multidisciplinary team with training and skills in several areas, thereby economizing both financial and human resources.

The Portuguese industry, mainly, consists of Small and Medium Enterprises (SMEs), which activity and performance are crucial factors for the country development. SMEs provide 75% of the total labour force employed in industry, trade and services. According to the website of the Ministry of Economy and Innovation [30] SMEs are responsible of 99.5% of national business, generating 74.7% of employment and held 59.8% of sales nationwide. They are the basis of Portuguese economy. A good example of Management Systems Certification and Integration in Portugal is represented inFigure 1.

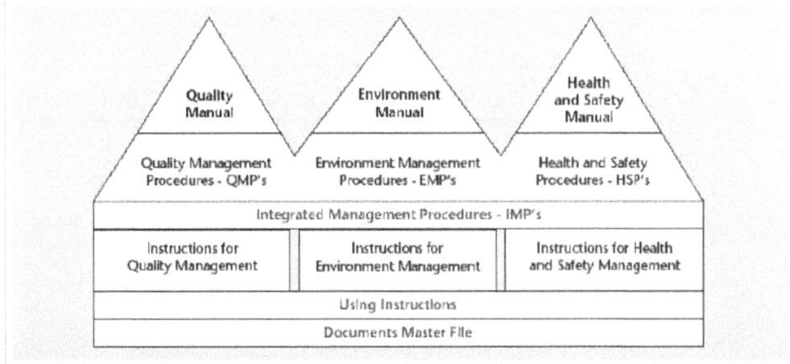

Figure 1: Documental structure of the Integrated Management Systems at Kupper & Schmidt [13]

For a long time, the only Foundry in the country to have its Quality, Environment and Health and Safety systems certified was Kupper and Schmidt, a SME that supplies exclusively the automotive industry and exports about 98% of its production to the European and American markets. Just a few years after starting its activity the company had its Quality System already certified by the main customers. In 1997 it was certified according to ISO 9002 standard, in 1998 by QS – 9000, in 1999 by VDA 6.1, and in 2001 by ISO/TS 16949 standards. In 2000 the company focused in Environment, and got the certification according to ISO 14001 standard. Since 2002 the company has its OHSMS certified according to OHSAS 18001 [31]. Presently, the company runs an Integrated Management System in what concerns to management procedures, operating instructions and documentation.

The objective of this work was to contribute to characterize the situation about the Integration of Environment with Quality and Safety in the Portuguese companies, as well, highlight the benefits obtained with the certification and integration and show that, it is a path to sustained success.

METHODOLOGY

In the last years there has been a significant increase in the number of Portuguese companies certified in Quality, Environment and Health and Safety. Some of them have a degree of integration of such systems which are not known. In order to make such characterization a survey based on a questionnaire was carried out in several Portuguese SMEs.

The questionnaire was sent via e-mail or delivered personally in hand, explaining and justifying its main objectives and it was organized in five sections, according to Table 1. Both qualitative and quantitative answers were asked, depending on the nature of the question and the available data to give an accurate response. The questionnaire was sent by e-mail together with a cover letter describing the objectives of the research and including some answering instructions to 300 SME with a certified quality management system. 162 companies were located in the centre region of Portugal (including Lisbon area), 114 in the northern region (including Oporto area) and 24 in regions located south of Lisbon. According to the data available from the "SMEs Portugal Association" this distribution is proportional to the location of SMEs within the Portuguese territory [32].

80 companies answered the inquiry, but only 46 have been validated, thus representing the sample size of the Portuguese territory. From those 46 companies, 20 (43%) were from the Trade/Services activity sector, 17 (37%) from the Industrial sector, 5 (11%) from the Electricity/Telecommunications sector and 4 (9%) from the Construction area (Figure 2).

Table 1: Main sections and question main topics of the questionnaire [13].

Main Sections	Questionnaire main topics
General Description of the Company	Number of employees; Volume of business; Branch of activity; Main products and markets; etc.
QMS	Year of ISO 9001 certification; Main reasons for Quality certification. Main difficulties; Main benefits that arose from certification (new costumers, image, competitiveness, business increase, quality improvement, customer satisfaction, products innovation, organization improvements, etc.); Main drawbacks; Quality tools that the company uses.
EMS	Year of ISO 14001 certification; Main reasons for Environmental certification; Main difficulties; Main benefits that arose from certification (waste reduction, waste destination, environmental costs reduction, etc); Main drawbacks.
OHSMS	Year of OHSAS 14001 certification; Main reasons for Health and Safety certification; Main difficulties; Main benefits that arose from certification (reduction of the number of accidents, productivity increase, absenteeism, etc);Main drawbacks.
IMS	Running independently or integrated; Degree of integration (integrated systems, what is integrated, reasons for integration, management structure, etc); Main benefits of integration (cost reduction, management simplification, etc); Main difficulties; Main drawbacks.

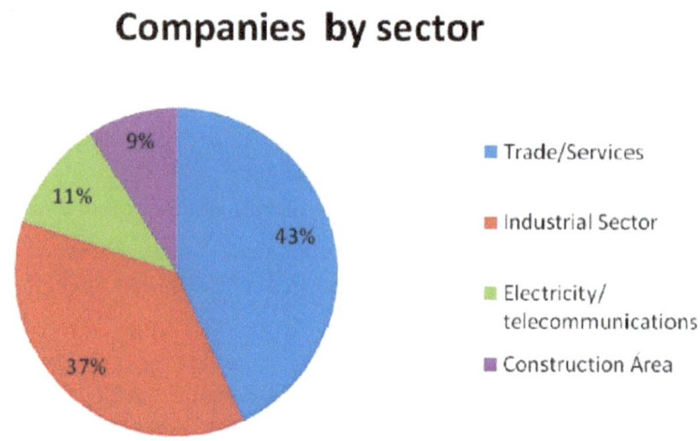

Figure 2: Distribution of participating companies by sector of activity

About 80 questionnaires were received. The main criteria for validation were to be a SME, to have the ISO 9001 QMS certification and to have answered the main questions completely. Thus, only 46 were completed properly. Data was worked and some results presented [13 ; 33]. However, it is known that there are SMEs with other certified systems, among them the EMS. An additional criterion was to have the ISO 14001 EMS certification. Initially, 12 SMEs (26,1%) fulfilled such criterion but later, 5 questionnaires was completed what totalized 17 SMEs (36,9%). This was the sample for SMEs with EMS certified. Also initially only 7 SMEs (15,2%) had the OHSMS certified according OHSAS 18001. Later it was completed and validated more 5 questionnaires, which totalize 12 SMEs (26,1%) with the OHSMS certified according OHSAS 18001. This is the sample for SMEs with OHSMS certified.

Once the information has been collected, the next step consisted of the analysis and interpretation of data. An *Excel* file has been created with the collected data, and then exported to SPSS (Statistical Package for Social Sciences). SPSS is powerful software to support statistics, which provides complex statistical calculations. However, due to the small sample size, two obstacles came up: knowing what statistical test to use and to interpret correctly the results from calculations. Thus:

1. Statistical techniques - It was used primarily to inductive and descriptive statistics: average, frequency plots, the principal component analysis, cluster analy-

sis and statistical inference to find the important conclusions about the population inferred from analysis of the sample, bearing in mind the limitation its reduced size.

2. KMO and sphericity test of Bartlett›s - the KMO and Bartlett test are two statistical procedures that allow measuring the quality of the correlation between variables. The Kaiser-Meyer_Olkin (KMO) is a statistic test that varies between 0 and 1 and compares the zero-order correlations with the partial correlations observed between the variables.

3. Internal consistency Cronbach›s Alpha - Cronbach›s Alpha is commonly used to measure internal consistency of a group of variables (items). It can be defined as the correlation that is expected to get between the scale and other scales used the same hypothetical universe with an equal number of items that measure the same characteristic.

4. Cluster analysis - is also a technique of exploratory multivariate analysis that allows to group variables into homogeneous groups or to compact one or more common characteristics. Each observation belonging to a particular cluster is similar to all others belonging to that cluster, and is different from the observations belonging to other clusters. We chose to use the method of cluster analysis to detect groups in the original variables, the issues where the sample was small, and the principal component analysis had not reached a conclusion. The analysis of the survey was directed to the most relevant items of the questionnaire.

The principal component analysis to data was applied with the help of SPSS, which allows an investigation of the multivariate structure, and a better interpretation of data. The internal consistency of the subject is given by Cronbach›s Alpha index which was applied to the 19 selected variables, considering 5 analysis components, which was 0.901. As this value was greater than 0.7, the responses were considered as trustworthy and free of errors. [33]. On this context, we used punctuation 4 for "Greater Impact", 3 for "Impact", 2 for "Little Impact" and 1 for "No impact". The resume of results of this work was published in the Journal of Cleaner Production [13].

Moreover, it was made a case study. The investigation was developed in business environment at an Portuguese Company - the Itron – Portugal, that over the years has been adopting, in whole or in part, gradually and individualized standards or specifications of different Management Systems, relevant to the ISO 14001 (Environmental Management Systems) ISO 9001 (Quality Management Systems), OHSAS 18001/ NP 4397 (Safety and Health Management Systems). While it is imperative to assess the perception of employees of the Company on the structuring, implementation and evaluation of the integration model and its validation in a real work environment, it was developed an internal research supported in an inductive approach in the context of the investigator›s experiences with the object and the environment of the study.

The technique used to evaluate the contributions to the structure of the model proposed of IMS_QES was the internal investigation by questionnaire to the Collaborators of the company. The total population was 160 employees which are the organization structure of the different branches and levels. The sample that was considered - 49 employees, represent around 30.62% of the total Collaborators. 42 Collaborators answered to the questionnaire which is an overall reply rate of 86%. This rate represents a strong adherence, at all hierarchy levels of the Organization.

In a first phase, the model was developed supported on the Lean philosophy, in order to the simplification and consequent resolution of problems and gains in efficiency of existing management systems in the company (referred as Sub-systems), which along the years were adopted gradually, but individualized and often isolated between to each other.

Were considered four main questions and for each of them several topics as described in the table 2.

Table 2: Main sections and question main topics of the questionnaire used on the investigation [34].

Main Sections	Questionnaire main topics
1 - Importance of motivation factors for the implementation of the IMS_QES.	• Improving the image of the Company • Rationalizing and optimizing the management of the resources (financial, material and human) • Facilitating the management of the three components for the Sustainable Development of the Organization and of the Business • Increasing requirements of the Costumers • Competitive advantage and strategic vision of the Business • Natural evolution of the Management Systems in the Company • The continual improvement of Quality, Environment and Safety Management Systems involves their integration
2 - Stakeholder influences on the performance and evolution of an IMS-QES	• ITRON Group - Orientations and evolution of QES and Sustainability policies • Customers, competitors, insurance companies, suppliers and official QES entities • Financial institutions • Local Management group and Collaborators
3 - Main Internal difficulties for the development of the IMS-QES model and its implementation	• Deficit of human and material resources due to the strongly competitive environment and costs reduction; • Resistance to change • Diversity of products and services vis-a-vis Customer's requirements and legal and other requirements • Do not explicitly fit in the objectives and priorities of the ITRON - Portugal • Lack of internal competences in Integration Management Systems • Do not exist an international standard for the integration of Management Systems
4 - Potential benefits resulting from the implementation of the IMS-QES	• Elimination of conflicts between individual Systems, and consequent resource optimization, namely human resources; • Elimination of several organizational waste including at the level of bureaucracy associated to the sub systems Quality, Environment and Safety • Common management policy, objectives, goals and KPIs - Key Process Indicators related to QES performance • Improvement of the internal and external image of the company in the aim of the QES issues • Involvement and consolidation, by ALL employees, of a continual improvement culture, attitudes and values of global QES scope • Reduction of the number of internal and/or external audits and to Suppliers • Improvement at the level of coordinated and integrated management of the Risk associated to the Safety of People, Infrastructure, Environment, and Products • Greater employee valorization and motivation • Integrated management of several components of Sustainability in a Global Market; • Improvement of the partnership relationships with Suppliers of goods and services;

The resume of results of this work of investigation performed at Itron - Portugal, was presented at the International Symposium on Occupational Safety and Hygiene SHO 2012 [16].

SURVEY RESULTS

The first system that was certified in majority of the companies was the QMS. When this system was consolidated, then the EMS was certified. Only when this system was consolidated, companies certified the OHSMS which has started quite recently. After the three certifications, they started in a staggered way to develop integrated procedures to integrate two systems (quality and environment or safety), and whenever possible, the three systems (quality, environment and safety) [13 ; 25].

This has been, more or less, the general rule that Portuguese SMEs have adopted, fact that was confirmed by the number of certifications, where the quality stands out in the first place (QMS), followed by environmental certification (EMS) and finally the safety certification (OHSMS).

However, we know that some companies have adopted another rule in sporadic cases. After the certification of quality according to ISO 9001, common procedures have been designed for the Environmental Management System (EMS) and the Occupational Health and Safety Management System (OHSMS) at work certification, which worked as the embryo for the implementation of a set of Integrated Management procedures [13].

The Main Benefits That Companies Have Gained From QMS Certification

Certification is certainly a strategic option for developing organizations in the sense of a wiliness to improve and gain market share. With the reality of the growing number of certified companies, it is important to analyze and quantify the benefits that companies have gained from the certification of their quality system.

Considering the descriptive analysis of responses and the analysis of each item separately, it can be concluded that certification of QMS led companies to improve their internal organization, to make it easier the access to information, improved the internal evaluation of the management systems (namely through continuous audits in time) and had a beneficial effect on the company image, as depicted inTable 3.

Table 3: Aspects of the company management where QMS had the greatest impact/benefit [13]

	Major Impact	Impact	Little Impact	No Impact
Internal Organization of the company	72%	22%	6%	0%
Continuous assessment through internal audits	54%	44%	2%	0%
Company image	52%	46%	2%	0%
Ease of access to information	44%	39%	15%	2%

It is clear from Table 3 that these were, in fact, the major benefits of QMS certification. 72% of the companies referred that the major achievement was in their internal organization, and only 6% have referred that certification had little impact on this particular aspect. 52% of the companies stated that their image was improved as a consequence of certification. The basis for these statement was the increase in the number of new or potentially new customers, the drastic reduction of customers rejections and increase of customers satisfaction (evaluated not only by the decrease in the number of rejections, as well as by the increase in the sales volume for those same customers and the increased satisfaction with the overall quality of the products). Moreover, any company reported to have not felt some sort of impact in any aspect of their management structure, as inferred by the results presented in column "no impact" of Table 3.

The Main Benefits Gained From the EMS Certification

In what concerns to EMS certification, the main reasons referred for certification have been environment promotion and protection, improvement of the company's image on this field, improvement of life quality inside and in the surroundings of the enterprise and a marketing strategy, with particular relevance for the first three. The main benefits of EMS certification were classified as having had major, relevant and low or any impact in several fields. Those fields where a major impact of certification have been detected were environment protection (evaluated by the decrease in the amount of residues and disposal costs), better integration of the company in the community, rationalization of natural resources, implementation of recycling techniques (and consequent decrease of costs related to raw-materials acquisition), legislation compliance and consequent decrease of penalty costs. Those companies with non-certified EMS refer to lack of investment support, high implementation costs when compared with the foreseen benefits of certification, or irrelevant environmental risks associated to their activity as the main reasons for their non-certification option/decision.

The Main Benefits That Companies Have Gained From the OHSMS Certification

The main benefits that companies have gained from the OHSMS certification were: "Improvement of working conditions" clearly took the majority with 91.6% of the responses. Another important question with great impact was "Ensuring compliance with legislation" with 83.3% of responses. Legislation exists which must be fulfilled and most of Portuguese SMEs with certified OHSMS fulfill that legislation work; another strong question was "Notice to workers about the risks and dangers at work" and 75% of the SMEs responded affirmatively. Hence, it can be concluded that there is "better internal communication for workers about the risks and hazards" when an OHSMS is implemented and certified.

THE INTEGRATION OF MANAGEMENT SYSTEMS (QUALITY, ENVIRONMENT AND SAFETY)

More than ever, today is in question the sustainability of the organizations and the focus should be placed far beyond the financial results. These will no longer verify it is not prioritize also the continual satisfaction, balanced, integrated and growing of the customers and other stakeholders taking as benchmarks for orientation and acting the dimensions of sustainability - economic, environmental and social and too the organizational and operational factors of the competitiveness. There exist a set of management system standards that apply to any type of organisation and activity. Others will certainly be created. These standards like as: NP EN ISO 9001:2008, NP EN ISO 9004:2011, NP EN ISO14001:2004, OHSAS 18001:2008/ NP 43397:2008, NP EN ISO/IEC 17025:2005, SA 8000:2001 /NP 4469-1:2008, NP 4457:2007, ISO 31000:2009, ISO/IEC

27001:2005, NP 4427:2004, PAS 99:2006, cover a wide array of different disciplines, aims and activities of organisation and operation of the Enterprises including the interfaces and satisfaction of all theirs stakeholders. In itself, this fact leads to a greater perception and awareness of challenges and brings sustainability to businesses, with which Organisations face a fiercely competitive global market in which the only thing that does not change is change itself [34]. Several of these standards, having been published recently, require that a lot of supplementary effort first be put at the level of the learning process needed considering the route that must be taken by organisations towards full implementation, which should be carried out in a balanced manner with added value.

In this context, Quality, Environment and Safety Management Systems certification have a great impact in companies, at internal, external and operational levels. The certification of these Management Systems includes many common procedures that can be run in an integrated basis, as illustrated in Figure 3.

In fact and according to the ISO – IMS publication (The integrated use of management systems standards) [23], a common objective of management system standards is to assist organisations to manage the risks associated with providing products and services to customers and other stakeholders. On other hand the management system of the organisations is frequently split into a number of parts or sub-systems, which must be managed separately with relative independence. These parts or sub-systems of an organisation's management system reflect the different needs and expectations of the stakeholders. Many organisations use standards, such as those related to quality, the environment and safety, among others, to manage certain aspects of their performance.

The synergy that an Integrated Management System (IMS) can offer have driven organizations into higher levels of performance at a cost lower than that associated to independent certification management systems. The simple schematic Figure 3 represents the vision of an IMS, suggesting that they have common information and procedures and at same time others standards, used in the companies, are involved in the organization and functioning of them.

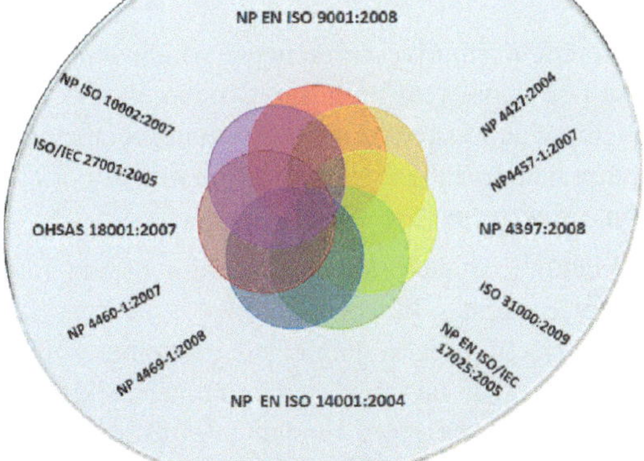

Figure 3: Integration - a route towards sustained success [34]

Integration can be achieved at different levels, leading to partially or fully integrated systems. A partial integrated system keeps their manuals separated using, as far as possible, integrated procedures. A fully integrated system is based in a single manual that integrates unified management systems requirements.

Integration of Quality, Environment and Safety Management Systems are known to have potential benefits over the companies' efficiency. Moreover, integrating IMS-QES enhances organizational performance. Thus, in a team, all employees contribute to the mission and to the defense of the values of a unique organization, bringing up the overall development of the company, thus improving the image of the organization. However, an unsuitable integration process can bring additional problems, like increased strictness, inefficiency and even professional and cultural conflicts. Thus, a careful reflexion about the way to start and run an integration process is crucial.

Similarities between the Management System Standards Which Enhance the Integration - Matrix of Compatibility of the Requirements and of Support to the Integration

One of the activities that forms part of the scope and objectives of the case study to which we have paid particular attention is the compatibility of the requirements of the standards, in context and framework of the characterization of the company's situation, backed up by an analysis of these standards. According to the Table 4 this compatibility represents, at our understanding, the starting point for consequents activities of integration, simplification and optimization, to achieve a level of the strictly necessary and consequently the three subsystems - QMS, EMS, and OHSMS are integrated to the maximum extent possible.

The ISO defines as principles of Quality Management: Customer focus; leadership; involvement of people; process approach; system approach to management; continual improvement; factual approach to decision making and mutually beneficial supplier relationships. According to the ISO Guide 72:2001, anyone drafting these and other management standards must take into account that the corresponding management systems must consider the following phases of the PDCA cycle - *Plan, Do, Check, Act*: Policies and principles; planning; implementation and operation ; performance assessment. Within this framework, taking into account the structuring of standards - management responsibility/planning; resource management; product realization/operational control and measurement, analysis and improvement, on the matrix of the Table 4 we have shown the requirements of the ISO 9001, ISO 14001 and OHSAS 18001 (NP 4397:2008), as well as we have established correspondences, made them compatible with each other and associated with the phases of the PDCA methodology - "Plan-Do-Check-Act". With this matrix, we aim to orientate and align the organizational structure of the company in the same direction, while at the same time creating a structured and useful work referential to support an effective alignment and correspondence of the Sub-Management Systems of Quality, Environment and Safety with consequent compatibilities between each other, for consequent implementation of the IMS-QES. From this matrix we can also, at the same time, to made a correspondence with the Deming Cycle, in this circumstance for the Integrated Management System, as well as a set of stages (1.1; 2.1...2.4; 3.1...3.7; 4.1...4.6 and 5.1) associated with each other these phases of the PDCA cycle, according to Figure 4.

Table 4: Matrix of compatibility of the standards requirements and of support to the integration of the Sub-systems [16 ; 34]

PHASE I - PLAN	ISO 9001	ISO 14001	OHSAS 18001
1 - INTEGRATED MANAGEMENT POLICY			
1.1 - Management commitment Continuous improvement	5.1 5.3 8.5.1	4.2	4.2
2 - PLANNING			
2.1 - Identification of: product requirements, aspects, impacts, hazards and risks and their assessment	5.2 7.2.1 7.2.2	4.3.1	4.3.1
2.2 - Identification, access to and updating of legal requirements and other requirements of Stakeholders		4.3.2	4.3.2
2.3 - Definition of objectives, targets and Programmes of QES management and improvement	5.4.1 5.4.2 8.5.1	4.3.3	4.3.3
2.4 - Definition of the plans of response to emergency situations	8.3	4.4.7	4.4.7

PHASE II - DO	ISO 9001	ISO 14001	OHSAS 18001
3 - IMPLEMENTATION AND OPERATION			
3.1 - Resources, organizational structure, roles, responsibilities and authority	5.1 5.5.1 5.5.2 6.1 6.3	4.4.1	4.4.1
3.2 - Training, awareness, competence and qualifications	6.2.1 6.2.2	4.4.2	4.4.2
3.3 - Communication, participation and consultation of the Stakeholders	5.5.3 7.2.3	4.4.3	4.4.3
3.4 - QES Management System documentation	4.2.1	4.4.4	4.4.4
3.5 - Control of documents	4.2.3	4.4.5	4.4.5
3.6 - Product realization Operational control	7.1 to 7.5.5	4.4.6	4.4.6
3.7 - Operationalisation of contingency plans.	8.3	4.4.7	4.4.7

PHASE III - CHECK / PHASE IV - ACT	ISO 9001	ISO 14001	OHSAS 18001
4 - CHECKING AND CORRECTION			
4.1 - Performance monitoring and measurement of processes and products	7.6 8.1 8.2.3 8.2.4 8.4	4.5.1	4.5.1
4.2 - Evaluation of compliance	8.2.3 8.2.4	4.5.2	4.5.2
4.3 - Incident investigation	—	—	4.5.3.1
4.4 - Non-conformities; corrections; corrective and preventive actions Control of nonconforming products	8.3 8.4 8.5.2 8.5.3	4.5.3	4.5.3.2
4.5 - Records Control	4.2.4	4.5.4	4.5.4
4.6 - Combined Internal QES Audits	8.2.2	4.5.5	4.5.5
5 - MANAGEMENT REVIEW			
5.1 - Critical analysis and combined QES Management System review	5.1 5.6.1 5.6.2 5.6.3 8.5.1	4.6	4.6

CONTINUAL IMPROVEMENT OF THE IMS_QES

Model of Development of the IMS-QES Based On Deming`S Cycle (Plan-Do-Check-Act)

The continuous improvement of the global performance of a Company shall be an objective always present in the development of the IMS [34]. The Company should therefore potentiate for each stage: Plan, Do, Check, Act, a careful and methodical analysis of the differences that effectively can be observed in terms of standards requirements under clauses equivalent involved and for each phase and each stage of development of the IMS-QES, according to the model of Figure 4 to ensure its compliance and evidence of it, in full conformity.

First of all, the definition, approval and communication of the Integrated Management Policy, a common requirement to the different normative references, which must take into account and be consistent with the Mission and Vision of the Company, these supported on a strategy and specific objectives which in turn, support the implementation of that policy and its consequent effectiveness.

The planning of activities in the aim of the Integrated Management System - Phase I (Plan) - is perhaps the most important [34]. In fact, a neglected planning will lead to inefficiencies that can be translated into potential deviations to the objectives. It is therefore fundamental to invest resources and expertise at this stage, via a thorough and careful work, in order to respond effectively to all requirements arising from the involved standards and others applicable requirements in this phase of the planning of the IMS [34].

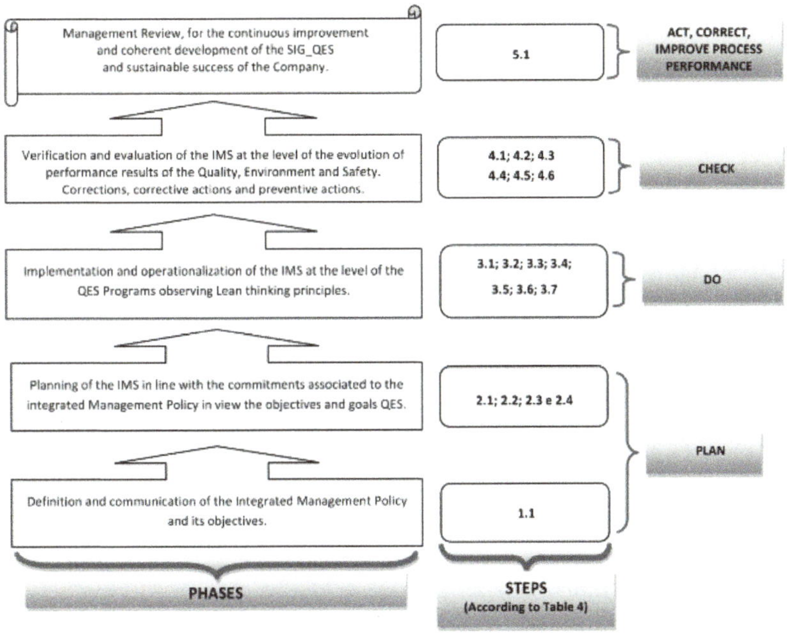

Figure 4: Model of development of the IMS-QES [16 ; 34]

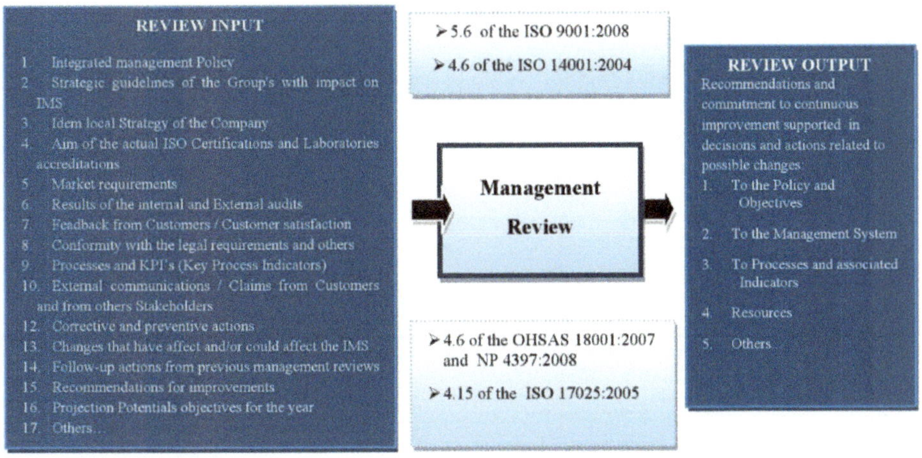

Figure 5: IMS-QES - Management Review - Standards, inputs and outputs [16 ; 34]

Following is the Implementation and Operation - «Do», the Company should, in this Phase II - Do - promote, the «Make / Do» in coherence with the pre-planned. Corresponds mainly to clauses: 7 - Product Realization, of ISO 9001 - and 4.4 - Implementation and operation of the NP 4397 and ISO 14001 and in the case of ISO 9001 should be considered associated with the product realization, other complementary clauses, particularly in context of resource allocation (6.1, 6.2, 6.3, 6.4) and management commitment (5.1, 5.5.1).

In the Phase III - Check, we identified six steps (4.1 to 4.6) designed to meet the requirements of clauses: 8 - Measurement, analysis and improvement of ISO 9001, 4.5 - Checking of the ISO 14001 and OHSAS 18001/NP 4397. With the exception of step 4.3 - Investigation of incidents resulting from a specific sub-section, the 4.5.3.1 - Incident investigation, the OHSAS 18001/NP 4397 has no correspondence in the ISO 9001 and ISO 14001.

At the end, in the Phase IV - Act, we identified the step 5.1 - Critical analysis and review of the Management System, which refers to the requirements of clauses: 5.6 - Management review of the ISO 9001 and 4.6 - Management review of the ISO 14001 and OHSAS 18001/NP 4397. The Management review process can be done in an integrated manner [34]. It requires, in itself, a very careful preparation face, particularly, to the level of various information that supports the inputs, as is schematized in Figure 5.

The continuous improvement of the global performance of organizations must be always a present goal in a perspective of sustainability [34]. The development Model of the integration of the Management System of Safety and Health at Work with the Quality Management Systems and Environmental Management at the Company should therefore to potentiate, for each phase: Plan, Do, Check, Act, a careful and methodical analysis of the differences that effectively are observed at the level of normative requirements under the equivalent clauses and for each step of their development as the advocated model of integration.

The compatibilization of the normative requirements supported by an analysis of similarities, of the normative referentials of Management Systems, which promotes the integration and it›s formatting on a Matrix of compatibilization of the requirements and of support to the integration of the referential - NP EN ISO 9001:2008, OHSAS 18001:2007 / NP 4397:2008 and NP EN ISO14001:2004, establishing correspondences, matching them with each other and associate them, according to ISO Guide 72:2001, the following phases of the methodology *PDCA - Plan, Do, Check, Act*: Policy and principles; Planning, Implementation and Operation, Performance Evaluation, Improvement, Management Review, is one of the activities that in the aim and objectives of the integration model was given special attention in context of characterization and framework of the situation in the Company. That compatibilization constitutes, the starting point for subsequent activities of integration, simplification and optimization, to a level of the strictly necessary and consequent integration maximized as desired of the three sub-systems – the EMS, the QMS and the OHSMS in context of strong competitiveness [34].

As can be expected, there are several difficulties involved with implementing an Integrated Management System (IMS). However, Beckmerhgeni [35] points out that *"the management systems implemented separately in an incompatible way results in costs, an increased probability of faults and errors, duplicated efforts, the creation of unnecessary bureaucracy and a negative impact near the Stakeholders, particularly Employees and Costumers"*.

The integration of the Environmental System supported on the ISO 14001:2004 with the Management Systems of Quality - ISO 9001:2008 and Occupational, Health and Safety - OSAS 18001:2007 represent real added value both in the present and, fundamentally, for the future, not only for the Company, as well as for a whole range of Stakeholders.

Environmental management in organizations is therefore a fundamental process for an more and more integrated and responsible management of sustainability [34]. Aims essentially, an efficient resource management, consumption, wastes and effluents, the use of cleaner technologies and compliance with applicable environmental legal requirements for protecting and promoting environmental and pollution prevention.

An Environmental Management System (EMS) is translated in practice in a continuous cycle of planning, implementation and operation, checking, analyzing and improving of the actions that drives an organization to continuously improve their environmental performance, covering a wide range of issues, including those with strategic implications as well as of competitiveness. The ISO 14001:2004 [36] is integrated in a family of standards developed by the ISO in the fields of Environmental Management according to Table 5.

The ISO 14001:2004 describes the requirements that an EMS of an Organization must meet in order to help the Organization to manage the impact of their activities on the environment, bringing advantages that are considered of high relevance to the promotion of continuous improvement in environmental performance of the Organization and to the prevention of pollution, taking into account the socio-economic surroundings. It allows an organization to develop and implement a policy and objectives, taking into account legal requirements and other requirements that the organization subscribes, and information about significant environmental aspects which the organization can control and influence. While a reference for an EMS, the ISO 14001:2004 contains guidelines that enable their implementation and the requirements that can be objectively audited for certification.

Today, the success of an organization goes through Sustainability [34]. According to ISO 9004:2009 [37], the sustained success of an organization is considered the result of its ability to achieve and maintain their long-term objectives that pass unfulfilled, in a consistent way, the needs and expectations of its Stakeholders, in a balanced and long-term as well.

Furthermore the fact that, in turn, other normative references of Management Systems, namely the ISO 14001 and OHSAS 18001/4397 NP, are valuable auxiliaries in the evolutive management of Organizations and, hence, on the three strands of its Sustainability: the Economic, the Social and Environmental. In fact, today Quality, Environment, Safety and Occupational Health are fundamental pillars of the Sustainable Development and therefore should be considered at the level of the management activities and of strategic planning of Organizations that want to take a leadership role, at present, but fundamentally in the future.

Table 5: ISO Standards in the fields of Environmental Management [34]

SERIE	CONTENTS	STANDARDS
ISO 14000	Environmental Management Systems	- ISO 14001:2004 – Environmental management systems – Requirements with guidance for use - ISO 14004:2004 – Environmental management systems – General guidelines on principles, systems and supporting techniques - ISO 14005:2010 – Environmental management Systems - Guidelines for the phased implementation of an environmental management system, including the use of environmental performance evaluation. - ISO 14006:2011 – Environmental management Systems - Guidelines for incorporating ecodesign
ISO 19011	Audits to Management Systems	- ISO 19011:2011, Guidelines for auditing management systems
ISO 14020	- Environmental label	- ISO 14020 - Environmental Labelling: General Principles - ISO 14021 - Environmental Labels and Declarations: Self-Declaration Environmental Claims, Terms and Definitions - ISO 14022 - Environmental Labels and Declarations: Self-Declaration Environmental Claims, Symbols - ISO 14023 - Environmental Labels and Declarations: Self-Declaration Environmental Claims, Testing and Verification - ISO 14024 - Environmental Labels and Declarations: Environmental Labelling Type I, Guiding Principles and Procedures
ISO 14030	Environmental performance evaluation	- ISO 14031:1999 - Environmental management -- Environmental performance evaluation - Guidelines
ISO 14040	Life cycle assessment	- ISO 14040:1997 - Environmental management -- Life cycle assessment -- Principles and framework - ISO 14041:1998 - Environmental management -- Life cycle assessment -- Goal and scope definition and inventory analysis - ISO 14042:2000 - Environmental management -- Life cycle assessment -- Life cycle impact assessment - ISO 14043;2001 – Environmental management – Life cycle assessment – Life cycle interpretation
ISO 14050	Understanding of Terms and Definitions	- ISO 14050:2002 – Environmental management – Vocabulary.

Table 6: Summary of the benefits and impact grade characterization that companies obtained with certification of the management systems (Adapted of [13])

Q M S	100% are certified by ISO 9001			
	Reasons for certification	Very Important	Empowering knowledge workers	Business benefits
			Better Quality of the products	Improvement of company image
		Important	Pressure from customers	Community relations
	Benefits	Major Impact	Improvement of the company image	Ease of access to information
			Internal organization of the company	Continuous assessment through internal audits
		Impact	Better productivity and profitability	Deadlines
			Cost reduction	Number of defects / complaints
			Competitive position	Satisfaction of internal and external customers.
		Little Impact	Absenteeism	Product innovation
	Tools	Most commonly used	Surveys	Charts (graphics)
			Sheets of data collection	
		Less used	Scatter diagram	Cause and effect diagram
	Difficulties		High certification costs	Difficulties to change company's culture
			Difficulties to motivate personal	
E M S	36.9 % are certified by ISO 14001			
	Reasons for non-certification	Main reason	Lack of investment support	A form of marketing
		Secondary reason	Benefits do not outweigh the costs	Investments are high
		Less Relevant	Environmental risks are low	
	Reasons for certification	Very Important	Progress but always protect the environment	Raising public
			Improved quality of life inside and outside the company	
		Important	Obtaining an asset in terms of marketing	
	Benefits	Major Impact	Environmental protection	Rational use of natural resources
			Business image in the community	Recycling
			Ensuring compliance	Prevention of environmental risks
		Impact	Clear, organized work environment	Waste generation
			Awareness of employees in environmental issues	
		No impact	Insurance costs	Costs of raw materials and equipment
			Ability to obtain financing at low interest rates	
	Drawbacks		Overall costs increased on the early stages of certification.	
	Main Difficulties		High certification costs	Difficulties to change Company's culture
			Difficulties to motivate personal	
O H S M S	26.1 % are certified by OHSAS 18001			
	Reasons for non-certification	Main reason	Investments are high	Certification is seen as a cost and marketing
		Secondary reason	Benefits do not outweigh the costs	

		Less Relevant	Risk of accidents at work are low	
	Reasons for certification	Very important	Eliminate or minimize risks to workers	
		Important	Improving the organization with the reduction of accidents at work	
		Less Important	Rate of absenteeism due to occupational diseases	
	Benefits	Major Impact	Improvement of working conditions	Better internal communication
			Improvement company image.	Ensuring compliance with legislation
		Impact	Less number of accidents	Reduction in cost of accidents and occupational diseases
		No impact	Dissemination in the media of data on safety and health of the company	
	Drawbacks		No drawbacks have been referred	
	Main Difficulties		High certification costs	Difficulties to change Company's culture
			Difficulties to motivate personal	Increase bureaucracy
			Management difficulties in the early stages of certification	
IMS	Main Benefits		Management costs reduction	Unification of internal audits
			Reduction of bureaucracy	Better definition of responsibilities and authority
			Easier compliance of legislation	Increased performance and efficiency
			Improved external image of the company	Better and easier communication system.
			Improved organization	Simplified management systems resulting in less confusion, redundancy and conflicts in documentation
			Increased employee training	Optimized resources(financial and humans)
	Drawbacks		One problem on a single system affects the overall management system	Initial costs increase associated to an increase in non-conformities;
			Initial higher organizational problems	Continuous update of every documentation with negative impact in the management activity itself
			Complex organizational system	Incompatible concepts between systems
	Main Difficulties		Long time to implement the integration process	Insufficient integrability of the standards
			Deep changes in the management system due to operational changes	Difficulties to implement systems integration
			High difficulty associated to training and changes in the organization methods and culture	Higher difficulty and cost to implement all systems simultaneously when compared with individual implementation

Also in this context of Sustainability, the integration of the EMS whith others management systems is, nowadays, a strategic decision of the organizations, influential of its competitiveness and continuity in the Market, fostering a better and increasing satisfaction of all Stakeholders, increasing the image and brand reputation near them [34]. Are too examples of adavantages of the integration, also highlighted by the survey respondents: the elimination of conflicts between individual systems with optimization of Resources; the improvement at the level of the Coordinated and Integrated Management of the Risk associated to the Safety of the Persons and Company Assets, Environment and Quality of the Products; the reduction of the number of internal and/or external audits and audits to Suppliers and spent time versus associated costs; the creation of added value for the business through the prevention and/or elimination of several types of operational and organizational wastes.

Summary of the Benefits and Impact Grade Characterization That Companies Obtained With Certification and Integration of the Management Systems

The three standards ISO 9001, ISO 14001 and OHSAS 18001 have a common underlying principle: continuous improvement based on Deming`s Cycle (Plan-do-Check-Act) [16 ; 34]. According to Labodová [22], basically one PDCA approach governing the aspects of quality, environment and safety, consistent with clear priorities, shows hot spots in companies, makes it easy to focus procedures and responsibilities on important areas.

According to the survey, 100% of the companies of the sample had their QMS certified. 36.9 % of these companies had also their EMS certified, and only 26.% had OHSMS certification. In Table 6, a summary of the main benefits, classified according to their impact relevance, as well as the main reasons for the three certification systems is presented. Moreover, the main factors that justify the option for non-certification of EMS and OHSMS of the remaining companies are also presented. The main factors that justify the option for non-certification of QMS are not presented, since every company participating in the survey had their QMS certified. Are also presented the main benefits, drawbacks and difficulties what concern Integration of Management Systems.

CONCLUSIONS

The theoretical fundamentation was supported on the concepts of Quality Management Systems, Environment and Safety, Integrated Management Systems, orientations, guidelines and

ISO standards as well as a group of other sources of knowledge, such as Integrated Management Systems QES.

Were identified the main benefits of implementing an EMS and it´s certification after receiving the QMS certification on Portuguese SMEs performance. In fact the main benefits that the Portuguese SMEs have gained from the referred certifications have been, among others, prevention of environmental risks, environment protection, improvement business image in the community, ensuring compliance with legislation and rational use of natural resources. In addition, the main reasons for non-certification were analyzed.

Those companies with non-certified EMS mentioned "lack of investment support" and "consider the certification as a form of marketing". Drawbacks that have been concluded were "overall costs increased on the early stages of certification", because there is a better control. The main difficulties uncovered in relation to EMS certification can be pinpointed to difficulties in changing company culture, high certification costs, and difficulties to motivate personal. With respect to environment, there is still a lot to do in Portugal. Several Portuguese SMEs have already implemented the EMS and others will follow, mainly, because money can't pay for an environmental disaster.

In terms of the potential benefits of the integration of the Environmental Management System (EMS) with the Quality Management System (QMS) and Occupational Health and Safety Management System OH&SMS and it´s certification, will be mostly a whole range of opportunities for performance improvements of the organization as a whole, and throughout it's supply chain such as: the elimination of conflicts between individual systems with resource optimization, creation of added value to the business by eliminating several types of wastes, reducing the number of internal and external audits, common policy management, greater valuation and motivation of Collaborators, among others.

The proposed model of IMS_QES has led to the simplification and consequent resolution of problems and gains in efficiency of existing management systems in the company (referred as Sub-systems), which along the years were adopted gradually, but individualized and often isolated between to each other.

All these benefits will enhance the competitiveness of the Companies and its differentiation by the positive in the face of competition, national and/or international.

The developed model of an Integrated Management Systems (IMS), generic, flexible, integrator, evolutionary and lean namely what concerns to Quality (ISO 9001), Environment (ISO 14001) and Health and Safety at work (OHSAS 18001/ NP 43397:2008), but too to others standards, such as, Risk Management (ISO 31000:2009), Social Accountability (SA 8000) and Information Security, among others, could be progressively more integrated and allow the Companies to even more capable, enhancing in this way too the development of the businesses and consequently their sustainable successes.

REFERENCES

1. T. Wright, 2000Certification and Integration of Environment with Quality and Safety – A Path to Sustained SuccessThe Quality Assurance Journal413742
2. A. Zorpas, 2010Certification and Integration of Environment with Quality and Safety – A Path to Sustained SuccessBioresource Technology10115441557
3. S. Burke, W. F. Gaughran, 2007Certification and Integration of Environment with Quality and Safety – A Path to Sustained SuccessRobotics and Computer-Integrated Manufacturing 23696703
4. Turk A M2009Certification and Integration of Environment with Quality and Safety – A Path to Sustained SuccessJournal of Cleaner Production172009559569
5. Kwon D M, Seo M S, Seo Y C2002A study of compliance with environmental regulations of ISO 14001 certified companies in Korea Journal of Environmental Management 65347353
6. D. Nawrocka, T. Brorson, T. Lindhqvist, 2009ISO 14001 in environmental supply chain practices Journal of Cleaner Production 171435
7. M. Casadesus, F. Marimon, Heras. H. Inaki, 2008Certification and Integration of Environment with Quality and Safety – A Path to Sustained SuccessJournal of Cleaner Production17411754
8. Zeng SX, Jonathan JS, Lou GX2007Certification and Integration of Environment with Quality and Safety – A Path to Sustained SuccessJournal of Cleaner Production1517601767
9. S. Karapetrovic, M. Casadesús, 2009Certification and Integration of Environment with Quality and Safety – A Path to Sustained SuccessJournal of Cleaner Production533540
10. G. E. Fryxell, A. Szeto, 2002The influence of motivations for seeking ISO 14001 certification: an empirical study of ISO 14001 certified facilities in Hong KongJournal of Environmental Management 65223238
11. Tarí J J, Molina-Azorín J F2010Certification and Integration of Environment with Quality and Safety – A Path to Sustained SuccessThe TQM Journal226687701
12. J. Fresner, G. Engelhardt, 2004Certification and Integration of Environment with Quality and Safety – A Path to Sustained SuccessJournal of Cleaner Production12623631
13. G. Santos, F. Mendes, J. Barbosa, 2011Certification and integration of management systems: the experience of Portuguese small and medium enterprises Journal of Cleaner Production 191965
14. B. Fernández-Muñiz, J. M. Montes-Peón, C. J. Vázquez-Ordás, 2009Certification and Integration of Environment with Quality and Safety – A Path to Sustained SuccessSafety Science47980991
15. L. S. Robson, J. A. Clarke, K. Cullen, A. Bielecky, C. Severin, P. L. Bigelow, E. Irvin, A. Culyer, Q. Mahood, 2007Certification and Integration of Environment with Quality and Safety – A Path to Sustained SuccessSafety Science45329353
16. M. F. Rebelo, G. Santos, 2012Integration of the Occupational Health and Safety Management System with the Quality Management System and Environmental Management System- from the Theory to the Action. International Symposium on Occupational Safety and

Hygiene SHO- 2012. Minho University 9, 10 March 2012. 978-9-72995-049-0

17. ISO2008Certification and Integration of Environment with Quality and Safety – A Path to Sustained SuccessSwitzerland.
18. F. Mendes, G. Santos, 2009Impacto de la certificacion de los sistemas integrados de gestion en las PMEs portuguesas. Forum Calidad nº 1984651
19. M. Mc Donald, T. A. Mors, A. Phillips, 2003Management system integration: can it be done? Quality Progress; 6774
20. K. Arifin, K. Aiyub, A. Awang, J. M. Jahi, R. Iten, 2009Implementation of Integrated Management System in Malaysia: The Level of Organization's Understanding and Awareness European Journal of Scientific Research 0145-0216X 312
21. M. Bernardo, M. Casadesus, S. Karapetrovic, I. Heras, 2009Certification and Integration of Environment with Quality and Safety – A Path to Sustained SuccessJournal of Cleaner Production1774250
22. A. Labodová, 2004Certification and Integration of Environment with Quality and Safety – A Path to Sustained SuccessJournal of Cleaner Production1257180
23. Guide ISO2001Guidelines for justification and development of management System standards.
24. ISO2011Guidelines for auditing management systems
25. G. Santos, et al.2008Implementação de Sistemas Integrados de Gestão (Qualidade, Ambiente e Segurança)- 978-9-72895-326-3Publindústria.
26. C. Suditu, 2007Positive and negative aspects regarding the implementation of an integrated Quality, Environment, health and Safety Management System. Annals of the Oradea University,- Fascicle of Management and Technological Engineering, Volume VI (XVI),
27. Jørgensen T H2008Certification and Integration of Environment with Quality and Safety – A Path to Sustained SuccessJournal of Cleaner Production1610711080
28. OHSAS2007Occupational Health and Safety Management Systems- Requirements- BSI, first published July.
29. M. R. Block, I. R. Marash, 2002Certification and Integration of Environment with Quality and Safety – A Path to Sustained SuccessASQ- Second edition. Milwaukee.
30. http://www.min-economia.pt/ 2007.
31. M. G. Santos, J. Barbosa, C. Pedro, 2004Integration of "QES" systems on the small and medium size foundry companies in Portugal. Communication presented at the 66th Would Foundry Congress. Istanbul, Turkey.
32. htpp://www.pme.online.pt/2007
33. F. Mendes, 2007O Impacto dos sistemas QAS nas PMEs portuguesas- Master Thesis- Univ. Minho.
34. Rebelo M F2011Contribuição para a estruturação de um modelo de sistema integrado de gestão QAS. Master Thesis. Polyt Inst Cavado Ave. Portugal.
35. A. Beckmerhageni, H. P. Berg, S. V. Karapetrovic, W. O. Willborn, 2003Integration of Standardized Management Systems: focus on safety in the nuclear industry. International Journal of Quality & Reliability Management, 20N ° 2, 210228
36. ISO2004Environmental management systems. Requirements with guidance for use.
37. ISO900420092009Managing for the sustained success of an organization- A quality management approach.
38. S. Curkovic, S. A. Melnyk, R. B. Handfield, R. Calantone, 2000Certification and Integration of Environment with Quality and Safety – A Path to Sustained SuccessIEEE Transactions on Engineering Management, 47Nº4, 444464

CHAPTER 10 QUALITY ASSURANCE IN HEALTHCARE ORGANIZATIONS

Víctor Reyes-Alcázar, Antonio Torres-Olivera, Diego Núñez-García, and Antonio Almuedo-Paz

INTRODUCTION

In recent years in the health services the need has been stressed to use management tools which highlight the central role of professionals and which support the implementation of a clinical leadership based on greater autonomy and decision-making in management. The purpose is to allow alignment with the ultimate goals of health systems, which are to strive for a service with a high degree of effectiveness, to respond to the needs and expectations of citizens, and to have medium and long term sustainability.

There are many conceptual approaches in the field of clinical management: its realization in defined organizational spaces (Clinical Units); synergy with other management tools such as the process or clinical pathway approach and the definition of competences; the use of clinical guidelines or the use of scientific evidence as guarantees of clinical effectiveness; the new relationship between professionals and patients where more proactive models promote the use of patient decision aids that encourage participation in shared decision-making, where core dimensions of healthcare quality such as continuity and safety are reasonably assured.

Clinical management could be defined as the ability of health professionals to manage the resources they use in their clinical practice efficiently and effectively (Torres-Olivera & Reyes-Alcázar, 2011). It establishes the effective involvement of professionals in achieving the objectives of the healthcare organization and is associated with greater decision-making capacity and autonomy. It also establishes greater commitment to the citizen (taking into account their needs and expectations) and to the healthcare organization by promoting sustainability in the short, medium and long term. There are many initiatives aimed at boosting clinical management in the public health sector as a strategy to ensure greater effectiveness and sustainability of the health services. This chapter seeks to analyze possible critical success factors to be considered when starting this type of project.

CRITICAL SUCCESS FACTORS

A Critical Success Factor (CSF) is a particular feature of the organization's internal or external environment that is important for it to achieve its objective. A factor is critical if its fulfilment is absolutely necessary to achieve these objectives, thus requiring action from the sectors involved. Critical success factors that can determine the proper development of clinical management can be summarized as follows:

Patient-centred care

From a public service perspective, the focus of healthcare is the citizen, so any approach to intervention should be based on their needs and expectations. To achieve this, these needs and expectations must be explored and understood. Their fulfilment must be seen as a fundamental dimension in the quality of service provided. In the last 40 years a large body of literature "has been advocating a patient-centred approach in healthcare" (Mead and Bower, 2000, 1087). Since then, different definitions of the concept have emerged. Byrne and Long (1976) proposed a definition that emphasized a style of medical consultation that uses the patient's knowledge and experience to guide the interaction between themselves and the healthcare professional. From a clinical management point of view rather than healthcare, Laine and Davidoff (1996) understood patient-centred care as more "congruent with, and responsive to patients' wants, needs and preferences." This entails: the inclusion of a biopsychosocial perspective

Citation: Víctor Reyes-Alcázar, Antonio Torres-Olivera, Diego Núñez-García and Antonio Almuedo-Paz (2012). Quality Assurance in Healthcare Organizations, Quality Assurance and Management, Prof. Mehmet Savsar (Ed.), InTech, DOI: 10.5772/33081.

in the treatment of disease; the patient being conceived as "a personal experience rather than an object" suffering from an illness (Mead & Bower, 2000: 1089); sharing decisions and responsibilities in a more cooperative manner; assuming an intersubjective character in the doctor-patient relationship, strengthening its human dimension. This way of approaching healthcare attempted to oppose the conventional "biomedical model" (Friedson, 1970) of doctor-patient relationship. In that conventional model the relationship is reduced to identifying the clinical signs and symptoms of a disease and the subsequent prescription of a standardized treatment.

At present the clinical setting is much more open. The traditional reliance of service organizations on changes in their environment was not applicable to health services imbued with technical self-importance, the guarding of information and one-sided communication processes with patients. The paradigm shift aimed at making the citizen the real objective of clinical practice, has opened a new scenario in which the units must build a new relationship with the patient in which new skills and abilities should form part of the action plans of professional teams.

From the clinical management standpoint, the model of patient-centred care carries certain elements of responsibility for the patient. In this sense, it is assumed that the information must be accurate and shared, rights respected and participation guaranteed. These elements define perfectly the changes of direction that a clinical unit or department must take in order to develop a clinical management plan, and which basically involve:

- Knowing the users and potential users of the health services. Knowing who they are and how many they may be, but above all, knowing their needs and expectations. A clinical unit or department must build its services on that foundation.
- Knowing the level of satisfaction among patients who have used a clinical unit or department and using this information to detect new areas for improvement and development.

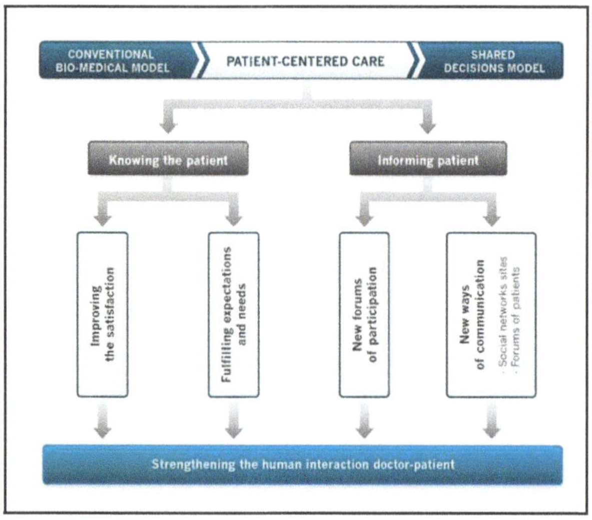

Figure 1: Patient-centered care

- Providing adequate and accurate information, promoting opportunities for participation and shared decision-making, properly handling procedures for informed consent and patient decision aids. To achieve this goal it is essential to improve the communication skills of the professionals in the clinical unit.
- Transparency, to bring the results of the clinical unit or department to the attention of society, opening channels of communication that support the transmission of information and knowledge, and encouraging participation through social networks, patient forums, etc.

Leadership

Clinical leadership is central to the strategy of clinical management. Studies, such as those of Cunningham and Kitson (2000) and West et al. (2004), have demonstrated the importance of clinical leadership in improving the quality of care and how the use of evidence-based medicine has resulted in a more patient-centred practice. The importance of the role played by the clinical leadership is acknowledged by the government agencies responsible for ensuring the quality of care, such as the National Health Service of Scotland being given responsibility for "driving service improvement and the effective management of teams to provide excellence in patient/client care" (NHS Scotland 2004: 4). Also, other organizations such as the Joint Commission speak of "effective leadership" that determines the strength and consistency of performance in areas such as planning, management, coordination, provision and improvement of health services (Joint Commission Resources, 2009).

However, this leadership is not an isolated factor and requires other support. As stated by West et al. (2004), other support mechanisms and staff must be deployed and promoted for clinical leadership to be successful in achieving greater quality of care. Among these mechanisms, those associated with the empowerment paradigm (Abdelrazek et al., 2010) are highlighted. There is broad academic consensus on the importance of empowerment in work environments. On the one hand, there is a macro perspective on the contextual agents and socio-structural conditions that facilitate empowerment. On the other, the micro perspective focuses on the feelings of employees about their role within the organization, and has been called "psychological empowerment" (Knol & van Linge 2009). Both aspects of empowerment, structural and psychological, provide clinical leadership with performance tools that improve both individual work and the work context in which they are located.

Therefore, professional leadership must be encouraged in all its aspects, making the stakeholders of the clinicians the objectives of the organization, striving for commitment to them and providing effective leadership tools from the management structures. This process necessarily involves the need to define the map of the competencies, attitudinal and/or knowledge and abilities, that healthcare professionals have to incorporate. In other words, it is a matter of cataloguing best practices to guide professionals to achieve their own development goals. It establishes a set of competencies that helps determine the gap between the actual competencies that a particular professional may have and those required by their competencies map. An appropriate training programmes can then be established to reduce any gap. Different international organizations, such as the International Union for Health Promotion and Education

(IUHPE), have encouraged and agreed standards for career development within the healthcare sphere, helping to establish a common international professional development framework (Shilton, 2009).

In this regard, the launch of an ambitious professional development project by the Andalusian Agency for Healthcare Quality (Spain) is highlighted. A tool for the Management of Individual Development Plans has been designed and implemented which allows the competence gaps to be identified among the professionals of the clinical units. This is achieved through a process of self-assessment based on identifying levels of achievement in relation to a catalogue of best practices for the job. Training or professional development programmes are established according to the identified gap. (http://www.juntadeandalucia.es/agenciadecalidadsanitaria/formacionsalud/)

It is also important to clearly define the figure of the manager or director of the clinical unit, establishing their competency map and their assigned functions. Interaction with the managers of other healthcare centres and political structures of the healthcare system is stressed as one of the core attributes that define clinical leadership, according to Christian and Norman (1998). They also play the role of manager of all the resources (human, financial, equipment and materials) that make up the Clinical Unit.

On this topic, it should be noted that the Observatory for Quality of Health Training-Spain, using the tool for the Management of Individual Development Plans, has defined the competency map of the managers or directors of the Clinical Units of the Andalusian Public Health System. This map consists of 26 specific practices and 106 requirements with different levels of achievement (from the essential to the strategic) in 12 key competencies: [1] Attitude of continuous learning and improvement [2], Scientific and technical capacity, [3] Capacity for decision-making, [4] Communication [5] Management and Planning, [6] Promotion of professional development, [7] Management of the quality of clinical safety, [8] Efficient management of resources, [9] Innovation and Leadership, [10] Promotion of research and teaching, [11] Guidance to citizens [12] Results-orientation.

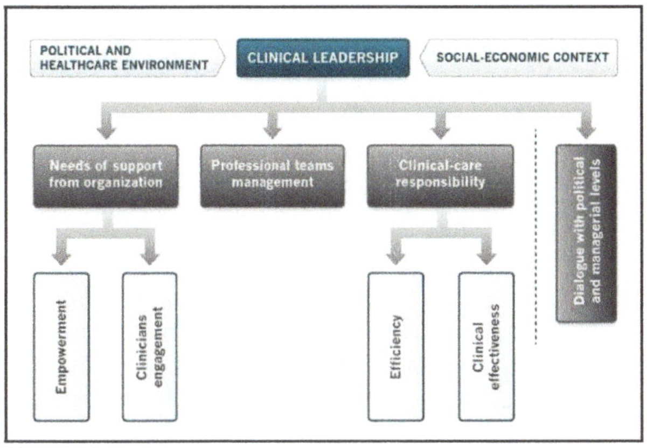

Figure 2: Leadership

Teamwork

A patient-centred approach to healthcare involves a multidisciplinary care process built around a team with common goals and developed in an integrated organizational model. The importance and effectiveness of teamwork in healthcare processes have been widely studied in recent decades. In fact, some studies have empirically validated their effectiveness through the study of their structures and dynamics (Mickan, 2005). Mickan (2005) indicates two large blocks of benefits of effective teamwork: collective and individual benefits. Among the collective benefits may be found those affecting the organization, such as reducing the time and costs of hospitalization and greater accessibility for patients, and those affecting the team such as a more efficient use of healthcare services or improved communications. The individual benefits affect the patients by improving satisfaction, greater acceptance of treatment and improved health outcomes, and the professionals, who experience improved satisfaction and well-being at work.

In the view of this chapter's authors, teamwork will play an important role in the effectiveness of the results obtained in clinical practice. In other words, the capacity of health professionals in a particular clinical unit to integrate will be directly related to their clinical effectiveness and their decision-making ability. This will therefore determine the final results of the unit. For example, the Strategic Plan 2010-2013 of the Hospital Clinic of Barcelona is based on teamwork as an essential element in the organization of healthcare units (Castells, 2011).

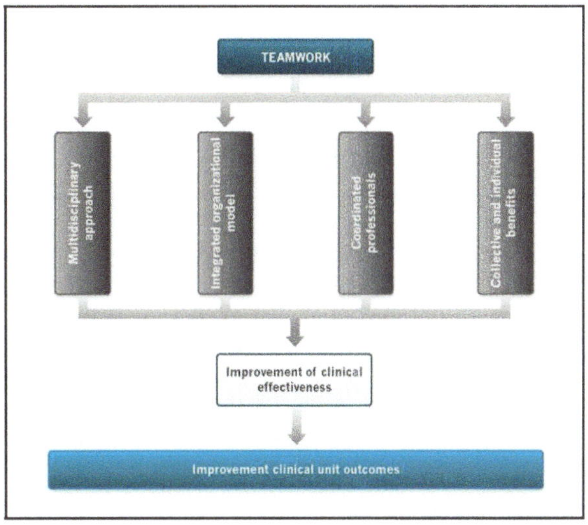

Figure 3: Teamwork

Teamwork encourages a sense of belonging and differentiation as a motivating element. The team must know what the objectives of the unit are, and what their individual contribution to them is, regardless of the professional group and level to which they belong. Similarly, they should know what their results are, both individually and collectively, and actively participate in the improvement processes that are instigated. The working model must transcend the limits of the clinical unit, with continuity of care being a dimension that the healthcare unit must take into account in order to improve clinical outcomes through consensus building between different levels of professionals involved in patient care.

Autonomy and responsibility

The ability to make decisions on resources in clinical practice is the core concept of clinical management. That capacity has to be based on the commitments established with the organization through procedural agreements that define the playing field between healthcare units (departments) and Corporate Management. This is probably one of the most difficult success factors to develop in practice because it incorporates a different culture, which clashes with the values, or rather with the roles traditionally assigned to the different actors in the system. There is widespread academic agreement on the need to maintain a certain degree of autonomy for healthcare professionals in order to improve not only their ability to cope with everyday challenges, but also as a fundamental aspect of their personal performance and motivation (Harrison and Dowswell, 2002). The demands of autonomy and responsibility for the clinical units stem from those benefits that have been empirically demonstrated in the professional field (Schulz et al. 1991, Akre et al. 1997, Kapur et al. 1999). The main focus of these analyses has been on the ability of professionals and clinical units to determine or establish their own clinical strategies and the assessment of their own performance. However, demands for autonomy and "decentralization" of decision-making in clinical practice have not been without developmental difficulties. As in any other field of work, autonomy in clinical practice has faced problems that derive from the ongoing "bureaucratization" of the processes and "mechanization" of the tasks of professionals, with their decisions subject to ever increasing controls. (McKinlay & Arches, 1985).

There is little tradition of managers delegating tasks and responsibilities to healthcare professionals, even though it is the clinical decisions that have a more direct impact on resource consumption. Furthermore, healthcare professionals are not inclined to take responsibilities which they believe are outside their healthcare role. To this can be added a traditional distrust between the two camps. The nature of this distrust is rooted in the culture clash between the medical corpus and those that Alford (1975) termed "corporate rationalists", these are managers and healthcare policy-makers that need not be medically qualified (Camprubí, 2011). For Alford, the corporate rationalists are confronted by structures that represent the interests of the "professional monopolists", i.e., the healthcare professionals, and they stress rational planning and efficiency over the decisions of healthcare experts (Alford, 1975, Lewis, 2006). Along the same line, Lewis states "...the power of the medical profession in the health policy arena, by analysing which actors are perceived as influential, and how influence is structured in health policy" (Lewis (2006). Despite the claims of other studies, Lewis empirically demonstrates the increasing capacity of healthcare professionals to influence health policy, and therefore they have greater responsibility in decision-making.

It is therefore essential to incorporate new management styles where the prime role of managers is to facilitate healthcare processes and to support the operation of clinical units. On the other hand, professionals must be introduced to, and trained in, the various competencies that encourage their participation and involvement in decision-making on the use of resources. Finally, all this must be articulated through management or grant agreements that clearly establish the commitments made by both sides, linking the achievement of individual objectives, and those of the clinical unit, to an incentives model. Although there is broad consensus on this, when it comes to it being put into practice, healthcare organizations face difficulties caused largely by the, not always peaceful, coexistence of strong, pre-existing corporate interests or divisional structures that detract from the patient-centred vision and which make decision-making difficult at the clinical unit level. At other times, it is the managers of the healthcare organizations themselves who are reluctant to redirect their own role to allow real decentralization of management processes, incorporating and engaging clinical decision makers. It is probably necessary to introduce different rules which enable some professional and management roles to be redefined, or to create less hierarchical structures that more obey effectiveness and efficiency criteria, that allow effective integration of resources to give a more cohesive response to the needs and expectations of the citizens.

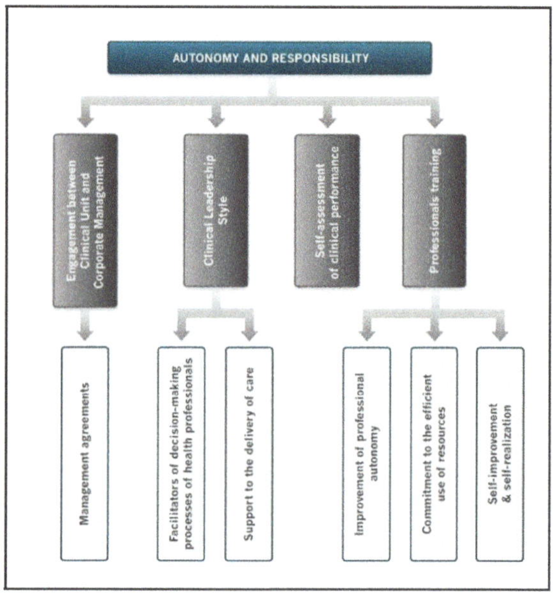

Figure 4: Autonomy and responsibility

Care organized from an integrated view of processes

In today's information society the citizen plays a major role, in such a way that their expectations have a direct impact on the modes of action of any service delivery organization. Factors such as user-perceived quality have become essential elements that bring legitimacy to any organization providing services, and thus become an important value to be analyzed by any healthcare organization (Torres Olivera, 2003).

This scenario requires an analysis of what healthcare organizations are doing, how they are doing it and what level of response is given to the needs and expectations of the user of healthcare services. However, this may not be sufficient unless it is done from a comprehensive view of healthcare processes. For instance, it is difficult to refer to concepts such as total quality, or a comprehensive view of quality, if some issues on continuity of care and appropriateness of healthcare processes have not been previously resolved.

The possibility of receiving comprehensive and continuous healthcare currently faces a number of difficulties, largely caused by how the health services are organized. Departmental segmentation is possibly due more to the interests of managers and professionals than the needs of users. Organizations can be unnecessarily complex, and often "super-specialization" does not properly address the diversity or multisystemic nature of the problems that health services face. If inadequate mechanisms for coordination between different levels of care and a poor patient-centred tradition are added, the idea of comprehensiveness that encompasses the concept of total quality may seem a little beyond reach (Torres Olivera, 2003 2004).

On the other hand, if the expectations of citizens regarding what they demand from healthcare organizations, especially if they are public, are explored in depth, it is seen that they express a desire for higher quality healthcare in terms of accessibility, effectiveness , safety and information. Satisfaction must be measured, but it is increasingly conditioned by elements of comprehensiveness. In fact, poor coordination between levels of care has a negative effect on accessibility to services, and the effectiveness and safety of clinical performance.

Evolving from "how much" is it done to "how" is it done, is undoubtedly an important qualitative step in healthcare organizations, and is related to a different vision of healthcare that assumes a commitment to quality and which requires a comprehensive view of the processes taking place in their services. The integrated approach to these care processes should pursue the following objectives: [1] Ensure continuity of care through a continuous and shared vision of healthcare [2] Adapt the functional structure of the services to the needs and demands of citizens, [3] Link professional effort to the final objective, the patient outcome, sharing responsibilities, [4] Put the resources (costs) in the right place (greater benefit).

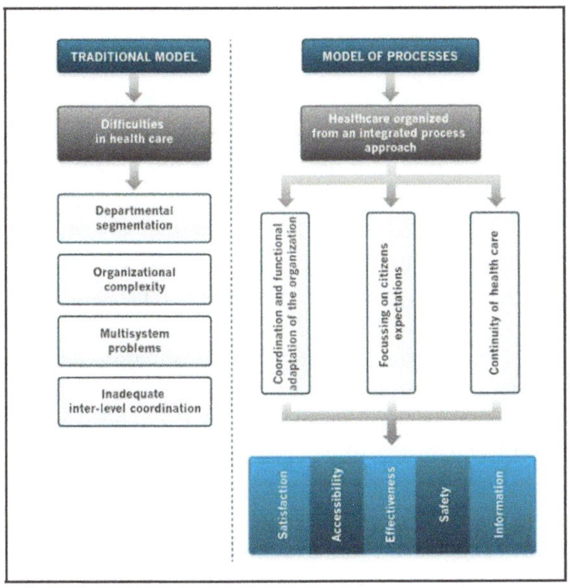

Figure 5: Care organized from an integrated view of processes

Process management is organized through a number of key elements such as: [1] usercentred approach, [2] greater involvement of healthcare professionals, [3] support from the best scientific evidence available, and [4] use of integrated information systems. Process management attempts to ensure continuity of care at all times, and is therefore intended to seek a unique and coordinated provision of services, avoiding fragmentation of care at multiple levels (Consejería de Salud - Regional Ministry of Health, 2001). Therefore, process management is understood as the set of elements that are linked sequentially to meet the health needs of citizens. It provides a vision that goes beyond inter-level coordination and attempts to delve into the meaning of "Care Continuity" (Torres Olivera, 2001). This approach requires healthcare organizations to order the actions that are performed in different areas, by different professionals at different times. The processes are thus approached horizontally, involving all levels of care and all the professionals involved in them.

Integrated process management is an approach to patient healthcare that seeks to coordinate resources across the health system (Fernández, 2003). This means an integrated approach to preventive actions and health promotion, the use of clinical practice guidelines, appropriate criteria in the management of resource and support to diagnosis, the appropriate use of drugs and the evaluation of results.

This means trying to analyze working methods in the light of the best available evidence, proposing elements for improvement so that added value is given to recipients of the healthcare process, i.e. the citizens and patients. Process mapping a clinical unit or department will determine its portfolio of services and its quality characteristics, as well as establish roadmaps for patients in the healthcare setting and establish the competencies that professionals have to develop (Mora Martínez, 2002). The approach to healthcare with a focus on processes and the definition of roadmaps for patients allows the identification of critical elements related to information or communication with the patient, or the introduction of important aspects related to healthcare quality such as patient safety.

Professional competencies

The term Competence in its current sense is due to David McClelland, a psychologist at Harvard University, an expert in motivation theory, who published an article in 1973 which caused a radical shift at the time. The article suggested going beyond the traditional evaluation methods in human resources management to focus on directly searching for those behaviours that were shared by those who were excellent at their job within a specific culture, and which differentiated them from the rest (McClelland, 1973).

From this perspective, the determination of professional competences, and the generation of tools that manage them, becomes a key to continuing professional development (ReyesAlcázar et al., 2011). Competence management not only encourages professional development but also innovation in learning models and processes of exchange and dissemination of knowledge. It also directs an organization towards professional excellence, cooperative work and the development of models of professional recognition and incentives.

The map of competencies of healthcare professionals should be set as a Gold Standard that contains the knowledge, skills and attitudes desirable for developing excellent clinical practice. A typical competency map consists of a set of key competencies for a specific job and the best practices that a professional should develop for optimum performance in that job. The map should be related to the desired results and the individual and organizational objectives. Consequently, competence refers to a person's ability to efficiently undertake a specific job. Thus, competence has to meet certain criteria: [1] Consider the context, i.e., the real world scenarios where these competencies have to be developed. [2] Identify the desired results in terms of level of development, achievement or mastery of tasks or functions. [3] Associate the level of development of each task or function with the performance, requirement or evidence criteria. [4] Involve the areas of responsibility of the professional.

By comparison with the competence map, the healthcare unit professionals can carry out a process of self-assessment to establish the competence gaps, and produce individual professional development plans that will determine the training and learning processes that are needed for their development. One of the most important projects currently under development in the field of competence management is that undertaken in Andalusia (Spain) by the Andalusian Agency for Healthcare Quality for the Public Health Service since 2006. This accreditation model is intended to recognize excellence of professionals through a self-assessment system that identifies the competences that a particular professional should have, the good practices that should be present in each job and the evidence that must be provided to demonstrate those competences.

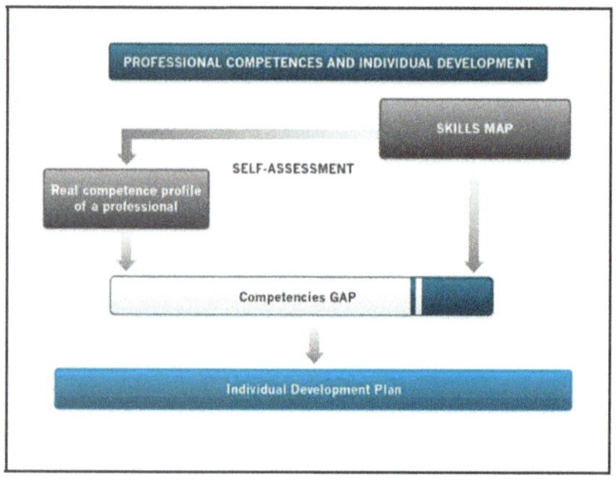

Figure 6: Professional competencies

In the Competence Management Model of the Andalusian Public Health System, the Accreditation is defined as a recognition, explicit and public, of meeting the necessary requirements for the provision of quality care, as well as the beginning of a line of continuous improvement by a professional. (Almuedo-Paz et al, 2011). The Competence Management Model of the Andalusian Public Health System has defined a total of 70 Competence Manuals, aimed at all professional healthcare groups. Specifically, 50 Competence Manuals have been published for the medical specialties, 9 for nursing specialties, 3 for the pharmacy disciplines and another 8 for healthcare specialties.

These Competence Manuals are structured into 5 blocks and 10 criteria, each of which contains a set of Competencies. In turn, each Competence is expressed through a set of observable and measurable behaviours called "Best Practices". The fulfilment of Best Practice is demonstrated through the contribution of Evidence by each professional, from their actual practice. This Evidence is an objective tool for assessing their competence.

Also in Spain, the Catalan Institute of Health (ICS) began Project COM-VA© in 2005, a healthcare and management competence assessment for hospital nursing professionals. (Juve-Udine, 2007). In this model, the competencies encompassed the individual qualities indicative of effective performance. These attributes include knowledge, abilities and attitudes that enable the professional to make the right decisions in each case. Moreover, the term competence also means the sphere of responsibility or professional area in which the law gives the professional the right to make autonomous decisions. The healthcare competencies of the COM-VA© model define 6 domains: 1) caring for the patient; 2) assessing, diagnosing and addressing changing clinical situations; 3) helping the patient to keep to their treatment; 4) helping to ensure safety and the healthcare process; 5) facilitating the process of adaptation and coping, 6) teamwork and adapting to a changing environment (Juve-Udine, 2009).

Results-orientation

Results-oriented concerns in clinical management are such that some authors have stated that "healthcare management is inconceivable without a measurement of results" (Marín-León, 2011: 90). Healthcare units have to establish mechanisms to measure their results, as much in terms of healthcare outcomes as in management and user satisfaction. An evaluation programme is defined as "the systematic collection of data related to a programmes activities and outcomes that results in decisions to improve efficiency, effectiveness, or adequacy" (Keller et al., 2002; Washington County Department of Health and Environment, 1999; Patton, 1997; Berkowitz, 1995). The evaluation process must be accompanied by a prior planning process that delineates the compliance objectives, both those that are strategic to the unit and those operational and care objectives of the processes. This will allow the objectives in the Procedural Agreements made with the Corporate Management to be assessed.

In this sense, healthcare units must have a Balanced Scorecard to collect information in summary form, identifying areas for improvement and allowing the unit to establish benchmarking processes. The information systems of the centre (hospital, primary care, etc.) must support the collection of information necessary to enable the unit to analyze its results and propose actions for improvement. According to Keller et al. (2002), an integrated evaluation programme and results-oriented planning consists of two fundamental elements in its design. First, it involves the selection of aims, which will clarify the objectives to be achieved. Generally, the objectives are difficult to measure and should be broken down into measurable indicators, according to criteria of continuity in time and external comparison. Second, it involves designing a specific strategy to enable the achievement of those aims and objectives identified. From the standpoint of healthcare units, the selection of an appropriate strategy will help improve quality in terms of efficiency and effectiveness, while the identification of aims will improve quality in terms of adaptation.

Indeed, the development of a Balanced Scorecard helps to translate the strategy of an organization into measurable objectives. In a sense, the healthcare unit is put to the test to see if it is capable of monitoring what it does. The Balanced Scorecard developed by Kaplan and Norton in 1992 has gained enormous popularity in recent times. It was the result of a year-long study that arose out of a general notion that as knowledge became a basis for competition, conventional financial measures were becoming obsolete (Kaplan and Norton, 1992 en Keller et al., 2010). The term balanced reflects the balanced consideration given to long- and short-term objectives, financial and nonfinancial measures, leading and lagging indicators, and external and internal performance perspectives (Keller et al., 2010). The BSC is a system of causal relationships among composite indicators (Key performance areas), that integrate large amounts of information (Key performance Indicators) into an easily understood single metric (Lovaglio, 2011). This basic outline of corporate and business management has also been exported to the healthcare setting. The work conducted by Baker and Pink (1995) is highlighted among the first in this field. In that study, the authors proposed a balanced scorecard model for hospitals with which they hoped to obtain a balanced view between the areas for improvement identified by the organization and those identified by patients. As Lovaglio (2011) confirms, the basic principles of a balanced scorecard model for the health sector have been adequately agreed in the scientific literature (Chow et al. 1998, Zelman et al. 1999), and have also been widely applied in public healthcare systems and organizations (Inamdar, Kaplan and Bower, 2002; Northcott and France, 2005). This reinforces the certainty of its feasibility and applicability for any healthcare unit. The indicators of a clinical unit must include those of an operational nature that assess processes and tasks from the standpoint of efficiency, and those of a comprehensive nature that allow the monitoring of fulfilment of the strategic goals previously agreed by the organization. Recently, studies have proliferated which investigate the factors affecting the variability of healthcare. Variability attributed to medical practice itself is, from the standpoint of clinical management, an inefficient use of resources because resources are allocated to services of dubious effectiveness (Bernal-Delgado, 2008; Peiró et al., 2009). In other words, setting strategic goals also means avoiding variability in clinical practice and moves the model closer to evidence-based practice.

The existence of both strategic and operational level indicators in clinical units facilitates designing a more accurate results orientation, and thus management structures can align the Mission, Vision and Values of the unit with the desired results. In general, it can be theorized that a Mission of a clinical unit or department would be to efficiently and effectively manage the resources used in its normal clinical practice. Its Vision would be to achieve a continuity of care model to meet the expectations of patients and professionals. Finally, the Values that underpin the daily work would be, at least, transparency, integrity, cooperation, and scientific rigor.

In short, promoting results orientation within healthcare units provides four basic results focused on quality improvement: 1) A set of healthcare indicators that can be subjected to longitudinal comparison over time; 2) Another set of indicators of the satisfaction with the care given to users/patients; 3) A map of areas that need improvement; 4) The possibility of establishing standardized processes of comparison with the best units, or in other words, monitoring performance using the benchmarking criteria.

Capacity of self-assessment and external assessment

The concept of Continuous Quality Improvement (CQI) should permeate the entire development of clinical management. Initially designed for the business sphere, the concept of CQI has been gradually incorporated into healthcare models (Chovil, 2010; Hyrkäs & Lehti, 2003; LeBrasseur, Whissell, & Ojha, 2002; Shortell, Bennett, & Byck, 1998). Its adoption by a healthcare unit "enables it to be proactive rather than reactive by relying on a continuous evaluation of processes and outcomes" (Chovil, 2010: 22).

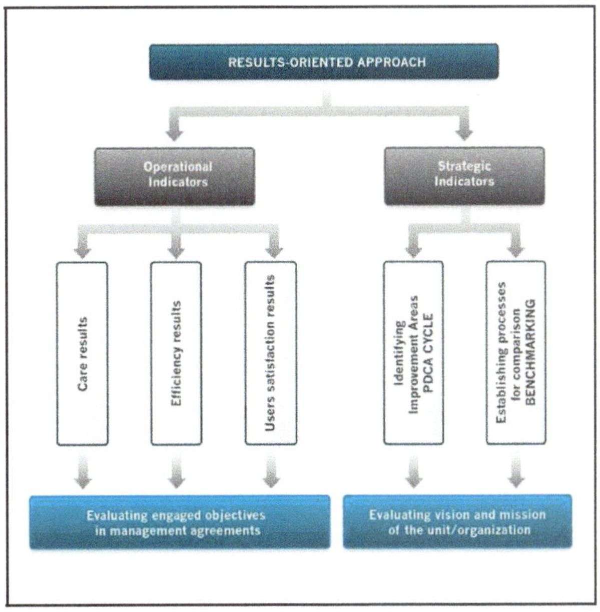

Figure 7: Results-orientation

One of the most widely used methods to achieve this has been the process of self-assessment by professionals and healthcare units. Studies such as that of Hyrkäs & Lehti (2003) have demonstrated the favourable impact of self-assessments in healthcare units on the satisfaction perceived by patients. However, self-assessment cannot be the only means of monitoring the performance of healthcare units. This self-assessment process must be endorsed on a regular basis through a process of external assessment to objectively establish achievements and examine the quality of healthcare provided by the healthcare unit. As noted above, the external assessment of performance of a healthcare unit can be given by indicators of satisfaction of the users/patients. In fact this is a process of external assessment of results focused on the evaluation by end users. However, external assessments do not address all aspects that must be evaluated to identify the greatest possible number of weaknesses, areas for improvement and subsequent corrective actions. All these dimensions, much more specific regarding the efficiency of processes and reflections on the potential of healthcare units, must be determined by agents specialized in the field of healthcare assessment. In recent years, the commitment to healthcare quality has encouraged the emergence of agencies, organizations and international agreements responsible for the assessment and accreditation of healthcare professionals, centres and units.

Some of the most important international, national and regional organizations and agencies dedicated to the accreditation of healthcare units and centres are the following. Firstly, The International Society for Quality in Health Care (ISQua) which is a not-for-profit organization that emerged in 1986. The International Journal for Quality in Health Care is published on behalf of ISQua. Also, ISQua organizes an international conference which provides a forum and meeting place for agencies specialized in accreditation and external assessment, organizations dedicated to healthcare and all types of stakeholders.

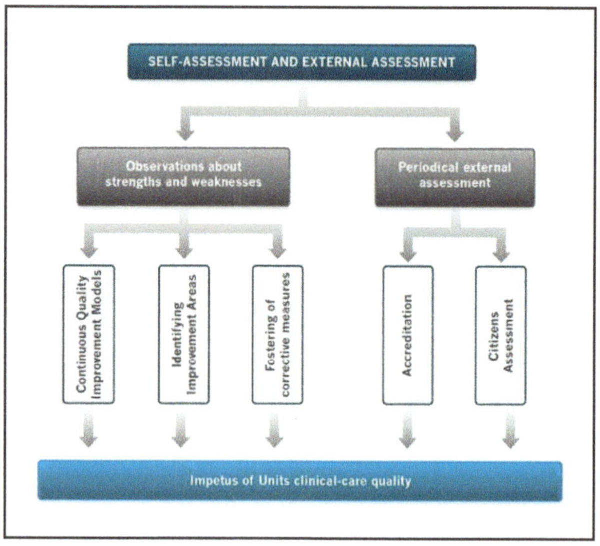

Figure 8: Capacity of self assessment and external assessment.

The Joint Commission of the USA is highlighted among the accreditation and external assessment organizations in the Anglo-Saxon sphere. This independent not-for-profit organization was originally founded in 1917 and re-founded in 1951 with the purpose of hospital accreditation. The stated mission of the organization is "To continuously improve health care for the public, in collaboration with other stakeholders, by evaluating health care organizations and inspiring them to excel in providing safe and effective care of the highest quality and value" (Joint Commission, 2011). The following are also highlighted in the Anglo-Saxon sphere: the Australian Council on Healthcare Standards (ACHS), Australian General Practice Accreditation Limited (AGPAL), Australian Quality Improvement Council (QIC), Accreditation Canada, Agency for Healthcare Research and Quality (AHRQ) of the USA, Institute for Healthcare Improvement (IHI) of the USA, National Committee for Quality Assurance (NCQA) of the USA and Quality Health New Zealand.

Among the accreditation and external assessment organizations in the European sphere are highlighted: the French National Authority for Health (HAS), Netherlands Institute for Accreditation in Healthcare (NIAZ), Health Information and Quality Authority (HIQA) of Ireland, Healthcare Accreditation and Quality Unit (CHKS-HAQU) of the United Kingdom, and the Andalusian Agency for Health Care Quality (ACSA) in Spain, among others.

In Latin America are highlighted: the Technical Institute for the Accreditation of Health Care Establishments (ITAES) of Argentina, Consortium for Brazilian Accreditation (CBA), Superintendence of Health of Chile, and the Colombian Institute for Technical Standards and Accreditation (ICONTEC). Finally, in Asia and Africa are highlighted:

Malaysian Society for Quality in Health (MSQH), Health Service Accreditation of Southern Africa (COHSASA) and the Taiwan Joint Commission on Hospital Accreditation (TJCHA). In short, the external assessment of healthcare units through accreditation means the certification of compliance with predetermined quality standards by an external organization. This accreditation ensures the commitment of the healthcare unit to the continuous quality improvement developed in its process of self-assessment.

As discussed above, there are a significant number of quality accrediting or certifying agencies or organizations in different countries, some public but most of them private entities. Their approaches are different even though their terms of reference (standards) are very similar. The differences lie primarily in the field of accreditation, [a] in how the selfassessment processes are managed, [b] in whether the assessment processes are systemic or fragmented [c] in the possibilities of exploiting the information that results from the certification process. In this sense a model focused on continuous improvement in the context of a clinical unit is a model best suited to promote cultural change in healthcare organizations. This is because they take a different approach to clinical practice compared with models oriented to the global accreditation of health centres -which may improve some aspects of management and organization of the centre but have little impact on actual clinical practice- (Cutler, 2000). The continual use of external assessment results to promote the identification of areas for improvement in ongoing self-assessment processes is an important way of promoting real changes in the way of doing things at the level of clinical units and departments (Schrijvers 2003).

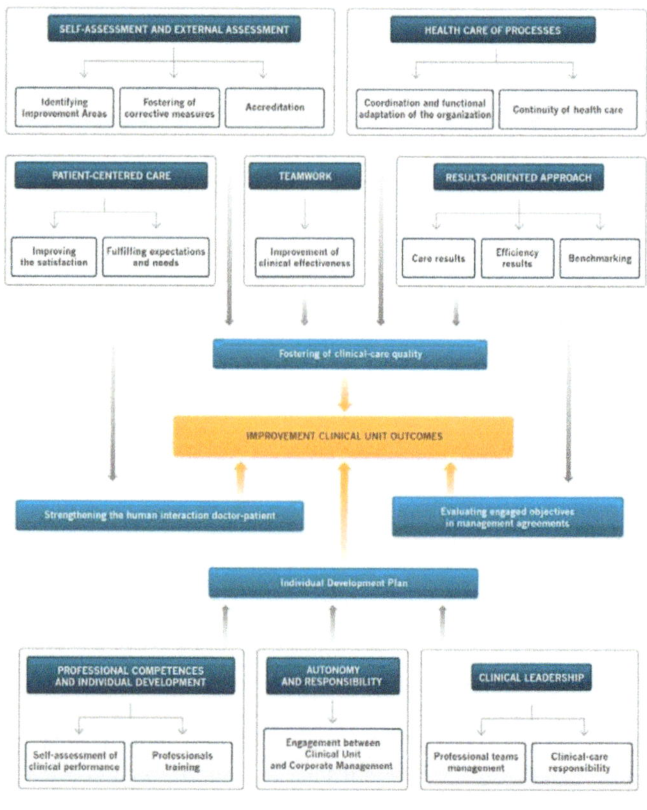

Figure 9: Critical Success Factors for quality assurance in healthcare organizations.

CONCLUSION

Clinical management encourages the capacity of self-organization and professional autonomy, it stimulates accountability in the management of the resources used in clinical practice, and it instils the culture of continuous improvement and results orientation. It thereby facilitates an organizational design which is more adaptable to the needs of professionals and citizens.

Critical success factors that can determine the proper development of clinical management can be summarized in the following key ideas:

- Orient health services to citizens and patients, exploring their needs and expectations, promoting their participation by providing accurate and quality information. To ensure the achievement of this critical success factor it is essential to measure patient satisfaction and use this information to improve healthcare.
- Form multidisciplinary teams which provide integrated responses and share common goals.
- Establish procedural agreements with corporate management which clearly set out the commitments of both parties, agreements that signify a greater capacity for decisionmaking and greater accountability on the part of the clinical units and departments.
- Define the set of healthcare processes of clinical units and departments that address their quality characteristics and critical safety points.
- Determine professional competence maps for members of healthcare units, departments and organizations, which allow individual development plans and specific training plans to be established.
- Set indicators so that healthcare outcomes, satisfaction, efficient resource management and benchmarking can be measured.
- Promote self-assessment and submit to periodic accreditation processes and/or external quality assessment.

By taking into account the critical success factors outlined above, a management plan for a clinical department or unit can be approached with a guarantee of success. Essentially it involves: Optimizing the existing knowledge in the organization and putting it at the service of citizens. Increasing the quality in healthcare processes through further development of competence of the professionals involved in them. And finally, using a different vision of the organization to orientate it to processes, by decentralizing decision-making and encouraging greater involvement of professionals in corporate objectives.

ACKNOWLEDGMENT

We would like to acknowledge the research's support team of the Andalusian Agency for Health Care Quality. This includes our research's technicians, Manuel Herrera-Usagre and Ángela Aguilar-de-Leyva, PhD, as well as the contributions Habibullah Rodríguez Contreras, graphic designer.

REFERENCES

1. Abdelrazek F., Skytt B., Aly M., El-sabour M.A., Ibrahim N. & Engstro¨ M. M.(2010). Leadership and management skills of first-line managers of elderly care and their work environment. Journal of Nursing Management, vol.18, pp.736–745
2. Akre, V., Falkum, E., Hoftvedt, B.O. and Aasland, O.G. (1997). The communication atmosphere between physician colleagues: competitive perfectionism or supportive dialogue? A Norwegian study. Social Science and Medicine, vol.44, no.4, pp.519–26
3. Alford, R.R. (1975). Health Care Politics, University of Chicago Press, Chicago
4. Almuedo-Paz A, Brea-Rivero P, Buiza-Camacho B, Rojas-De-Mora Figueroa A, TorresOlivera A. (2011). Skills Accreditation as an impetus for continuous professional development. Revista de Calidad Asistencial, Vol.26, no.4, (forthcoming)
5. Bernal-Delgado, E. (2008). How can we improve effectiveness (quality) by reducing the gap between research and action? 2008 SES-PAS Report. Gaceta Sanitaria. vol.22, no.1, (April 2008) pp.19-26
6. Byrne, P. & Long, B. (1976). Doctors Talking to Patients, HMSO, London:
7. Camprubí, J. (2011). Una nueva forma de trabajar que mejora las decisions: Gestión Clínica de la Efectividad, Una nueva forma de trabajar… mirando al futuro III Congreso de Gestión Clínica, pp. 79-85, ISBN 978-84-694-2735-4, Madrid, Spain, Oct 18-19, 2010.
8. Chovil, N. (2009). One Small Step at a Time: Implementing Continuous Quality Improvement in Child and Youth Mental Health Services. Child and Youth Services, vol.31, no.1, pp.21-34.
9. Chow, C.W., Ganulin, D., Teknika, O., Haddad, K., Williamson, J. (1998). The balanced scorecard: a potent tool for energizing and focusing healthcare organization management. Journal of Healthcare Management. Vol.43, no.3, pp.263–280
10. Christian, S.L., Norman, I.J. (1998). Clinical leadership in nursing development units. Journal of advanced nursing, vol.27, no.1, pp.108-116
11. Cunningham, G. & Kitson, A. (2000). An evaluation of the RCN Clinical Leadership Development Programme: Part 2. Nursing Standard, vol. 15, no. 13-15, pp. 34-40.
12. Cutler, D. McClellan, M. Newhouse, J. (2000). How does managed care do it? Rand Journal Economist vol.31, pp.526-48
13. Castells, A. (2011). Gestión Hospitales basada en resultados: Hospital Clinic de Barcelona, Una nueva forma de trabajar… mirando al futuro III Congreso de Gestión Clínica, pp. 105-109, ISBN 978-84-694-2735-4, Madrid, Spain, Oct 18-19, 2010
14. Deem, J.W., Barnes, B., Segal, S. & Preziosi, R. (2010). The Relationship of Organizational Culture to Balanced Scorecard Effectiveness. S.A.M.Advanced Management Journal, vol. 75, no. 4, pp. 31-39
15. Fernández Fernández, I., Fernández de la Mota, E., Sanz Amores, R. (2003). Gestión por procesos asistenciales: aplicación a un sistema sanitario público. Cuadernos de Gestión vol.9 pp.19-37
16. Friedson, E. (1960). Client control and medical practice. American Journal of Sociology, vol.65, pp.374-382.

17. Consejería de Salud (2001). Guía de diseño y mejora continua de procesos asistenciales: calidad por sistema. Available from: http://www.juntadeandalucia.es/salud ISBN 84-8486-024-8

18. Harrison, S. & Dowswell, G. (2002). «Autonomy and bureaucratic accountability in primary care: what English general practitioners say [Autonomie et responsabilité bureaucratique en soin primaire : ce que disent les praticiens généralistes Anglais]. Sociology of health & illness, vol. 24, no. 2, pp. 208-226

19. Hyrkas, K. & Lehti, K. (2003). Continuous quality improvement through team supervision supported by continuous self-monitoring of work and systematic patient feedback. Journal of nursing management vo.11, no.3, pp.177-88

20. Inamdar, N., Kaplan, R.S., Bower, M. (2002). Applying the balanced scorecard in healthcare provider organizations. Journal of Healthcare Management, vol.47, pp.179–195

21. Joint Commission Resources. (March 2009). The New Standards: Section 3. Leadership. 18.7.2011. available from http://www.jcrinc.com/The-New-Standards/The-NewStandards-Section-2-Improving-Organ/The-New-Standards-Section-3-Leadershi/

22. Joint Commission. Resources. (July 2011). 2011 Accreditation Process Guide for Hospitals. 18.7.2011. available from http://www.jcrinc.com. ISBN: 978-1-59940-400-4

23. Juvé-Udina ,M.E., Farrero, S., Matud, C., Monterde, D., Fierro, G., Marsal, R. (2007). ¿Cómo definen los profesionales de enfermería hospitalarios sus competencias asistenciales? Nursing vol.25 no.7 pp.50-61

24. Juvé-Udina, M.E., Farrero Muñoz, S., Matud Calvo, C., Rius Ferrus, L., Monterde Prat, D., Cruz Llauna, R., Artigas Lage, M. (2009). Pesos competenciales asociados a las diferentes áreas de cuidados en el ámbito hospitalario. Nursing vol. 27, no.7, pp.54-58

25. Kaplan, R. S., & Norton, D. P. (1992). The Balanced Scorecard: Measures that drive performance. The Harvard Business Review, vol.70, no.1, pp. 71-80

26. Kapur, N., Appleton, K. & Neal, R.D. (1999). Sources of job satisfaction and psychological distress in GPs and medical house officers. Family Practice, vol. 16, no. 6, pp. 600– 601

27. Knol, J. & van Linge, R. (2009). Innovative behaviour: the effect of structural and psychological empowerment on nurses. Journal of Advanced Nursing, vol. 65, no.2, pp.359–370

28. Laine, C. & Davidoff, F. (1996). Patient-centered medicine: a professional evolution. Journal of the American Medical Association, vol. 275, pp. 152-156.

29. LeBrasseur, R., Whissell, R. & Ojha, A. (2002). Organizational learning, transformational leadership and implementation of continuous quality improvement in Canadian hospitals. Australian Journal of Management, vol.27, no.2, pp.141–62

30. Lewis, J.M. (2006). Being Around and Knowing the Players: Networks of Influence in Health Policy. Social science & medicine, vol. 62, no. 9, pp. 2125-2136

31. Linda, O.K., Schaffer, M.A., Lia-Hoagberg, B. & Strohschein, S. (2002). Assessment, program planning, and evaluation in population-based public health practice. Journal of Public Health Management and Practice, vol. 8, no. 5, pp. 30-43

32. Lovaglio, P.G. (2011). Model building and estimation strategies for implementing the Balanced Scorecard in Health sector. Quality and Quantity, vol. 45, no. 1, pp. 199-212

33. Marín-León, I. (2011). Gestión de Hospitales basada en resultados, Una nueva forma de trabajar… mirando al futuro III Congreso de Gestión Clínica, pp. 89-94, ISBN 978-84- 694-2735-4, Madrid, Spain, Oct 18-19, 2010.

34. McClelland, D. (1973). Testing for Competence Rather Than for Intelligence. American Psychologist, vol.28, no.1, pp.1-14

35. McKinlay, J.B. & Arches, J. (1985). Towards the Proletarianization of Physicians. International Journal of Health Services, vol. 15, no. 2, pp. 161-195

36. Mead, N. & Bower, P. (2000). Patient-Centredness: A Conceptual Framework and Review of the Empirical Literature. Social Science and Medicine, vol. 51, no. 7, pp. 1087-1110 ISSN: 0277-9536

37. Mickan, S.M. (2005). Evaluating the effectiveness of health care teams. Australian Health Review, vol. 29, no. 2, pp. 211-217

38. Mickan, S.S. & Rodger, S.S. (2000). Characteristics of effective teams: a literature review. Australian Health Review, vol. 23, no. 3, pp. 201-208

39. Millward, L.J. & Bryan, K. (2005). Clinical leadership in health care: a position statement. International journal of health care quality assurance, vol. 18, no. 2, pp. R13-R13-R25. ISSN: 09526862

40. Mora Martínez, J.R., Ferrer Arnedo, C., Ramos Quirós, E. (2002). Gestión clínica de procesos: mapa de procesos de enfermería en centros de salud. Revista de Administración Sanitaria vol. 6, pp.135-59

41. National Health Service Scotland (2004) Leadership Development Framework for Discussion. NHS, Scotland.

42. Northcott, D. & France, N. (2005). The balanced scorecard in New Zealand health sector performance management: dissemination to diffusion. Australian Accounting Review, vol.15, no.37, pp.34–46

43. Patton, M.Q. (1997) Utilization-Focused Evaluation. Thousand Oaks, Sage Publications, California, USA

44. Peiró, S., Meneu, R., & Bernal-Delgado, E. (2009). Effectiveness, variation and inequalities. Hysterectomies and prostatectomies due to neoplasm in Spain (2002-2004). Revista Española de Salud Pública, vol. 83, no. 1, pp. 109-121

45. Reyes-Alcázar, V., Salvador-Sanz, A., & Segura, C. (2011). Mapa de competencias y buenas prácticas de los profesionales de una UGC del corazón. In: Gestión Clínica en Unidades del Corazón, Torres-Olivera, A. and V. Reyes-Alcázar, (Ed.), 93-118, Sociedad Española de

Calidad Asistencial, ISBN 978-84-615-0671-2, Madrid, Spain

46. Schrijvers, G., Oudendijk, N. & ,de Vries, P. (2003). In search of the quickest way to diseminate health care innovations. International Journal of Integrated Care, Vol. 3, pp.1-22, ISSN 1568-4156
47. Schulz, R.I., Girard, C., Harrison, S. & Sims, A.C.P. (1991). Perceived autonomy and work satisfaction amongst psychiatrists. Journal of Management in Medicine, Vol. 5, no. 2, pp. 54–65
48. Shilton, T. (2009). Health promotion competencies: providing a road map for health promotion to assume a prominent role in global health. Global Health Promotion, vol. 16, no. 2, pp. 42-46, 61, 75
49. Shortell, S. M., Bennett, C. L., & Byck, G. R. (1998). Assessing the impact of continuous quality improvement on clinical practice. The Millbank Quarterly vol. 76, 593–624
50. Torres Olivera, A., Fernández, E., Paneque, P., Carretero, R., & Garijo A. (2004). La Gestión de la calidad asistencial en Andalucía. Revista de Calidad Asistencial, vol.19, no.3, pp. 105-112
51. Torres Olivera, A., Lledó, R. (2001) La coordinación entre niveles asistenciales. Revista de Calidad Asistencial vol. 16, pp.232-234
52. Torres Olivera, A. (2003). Desarrollo de los Procesos Asistenciales Integrados en Andalucía. Cuadernos de Gestión, vol.9, pp.127-134
53. Torres Olivera, A. (2003). La gestión por Procesos Asistenciales Integrados: una estrategia necesaria. Atención Primaria, vol.31, pp.561-563
54. Torres Olivera, A., Reyes-Alcázar, V. (2011). Gestión Clínica en Unidades del Corazón, Sociedad Española de Calidad Asistencial, ISBN 978-84-615-0671-2, Madrid, Spain.
55. Washington County Department of Health and Environment. (1999). Community Health Service Plan, 1992–1996 and 1996– 2000. Department of Health and Environment. Stillwater, MN: Washington County, USA
56. West, B., Lyon, M.H., McBain, M. & Gass, J. (2004). Evaluation of a clinical leadership initiative. Nursing Standard, vol. 19, no. 5, pp. 33-41
57. Zelman, W.N., Blazer, D., Gower, J.M., Bumgarner, P.O., Cancilla, L.M. (1999). Issues for academic health centers to consider before implementing a balanced-scorecard effort. Academic Medicine, vol.74, no.12, pp.1269–1277

CHAPTER

11

INDUSTRIAL ENERGY AUDITING FOR INCREASED SUSTAINABILITY – METHODOLOGY AND MEASUREMENTS

Jakob Rosenqvist, Patrik Thollander, Patrik Rohdin, and Mats Söderström

INTRODUCTION

Industrial energy efficiency is a key component in the transition of the economy towards increased sustainability. For an industrial company, there are four means to reduce energy costs: implementing energy-efficient technologies, energy carrier conversion, load management, and more energy-efficient behaviour. The European end-use energy efficiency and energy services directive promotes, among other things, the removal of existing market barriers and imperfections that impede the efficient end use of energy [1]. Energy audits provide an important tool in reducing barriers to energy efficiency [2]. Furthermore, an initial, well-structured energy audit is the first important step in a successful in-house energy management program in industry [3].

From the global perspective, industrial energy efficiency is one of the most important means of reducing the threat of increased global warming [4] as the industry accounts for about 80 percent of the world's annual coal consumption, 40 percent of the world's electricity use, 35 percent of the world's natural gas consumption, and around 10 percent of global oil consumption [5]. Of great importance are thus different means which promote energy efficiency for the industrial sector. In Europe, growing concern for increased global warming has led to the implementation of a number of policy instruments such as the EU Emission Trading Scheme (ETS) and the European Energy End-Use Efficiency and Energy Services Directive (ESD). From the industry's perspective, supply side policy instruments like the EU ETS will most likely result in higher European energy prices which will stress the industry to take actions toward increased energy efficiency. On the other hand, this may lead to competitive disadvantages compared to industries outside the EU [6].

The role and importance of energy audits varies from country to country. In a comparing study of factors influencing energy efficiency in the German and Colombian manufacturing industries [7], firms and associations were asked about their view on energy audits. Among the German respondents 57 percent states that volontary audits is an important factor influencing the energy efficency in their country, while 61 percent of the Colmbian respondents states that volontary audits is an important or very important factor. When they were asked about their own measures and actions, 71 percent of the German respondents and 54 percent of the Colombian respondents stated that they would consider energy audits to increase energy efficiency performance.

This audit method was developed in Sweden, in the Swedish manufacturing industry context. Evaluations of conducted energy audits in small and medium-sized manufacturing companies shows that the calculated technical potential for increasing energy efficiency performance varies from 16-40% of the total energy use. For electricity the calculated potential is up to 60% [8]. If the suggested measures are implemented and if the potential is reached or not depends on the barriers and driving forces for energy efficiency. The energy price can play an important role. For Swedish industry, energy prices have risen significantly in recent years. Between 2000 and 2006 electricity prices in Swedish industry almost doubled and oil prices rose by about 70 percent [9,10]. This trend has not declined. In January, 2010, prices on the Nordic electricity spot market arose to some 130 Euro per MWh. The electricity price increases were partly due to the deregulation of the European electricity markets as the deregulation has caused the national markets to converge and Sweden has for a long time enjoyed one of the lowest electricity prices in Europe [11]. While the oil price increases may not create competitive disadvantages for Swedish industry, the electricity price increases most likely

Citation: Jakob Rosenqvist, Patrik Thollander, Patrik Rohdin and Mats Söderström (2012). Industrial Energy Auditing for Increased Sustainability – Methodology and Measurements, Sustainable Energy - Recent Studies, Dr. Alemayehu Gebremedhin (Ed.), InTech, DOI: 10.5772/51717.

will, as this is particularly related to the Swedish industry and the fact that the previously low electricity prices have resulted in a higher use of electricity in many Swedish industrial sectors compared to their European competitors.

The methodology described is primarily for a technical energy audit with the aim to make the energy use more efficient and sustainable. In the audit, organizational issues and the surrounding society are regarded mainly as means to reach the goal, and are important driving forces to implement changes.

Classification of Energy Audits

Energy audit models can be described in terms of the scope, thoroughness and aim of the audit [12]. The method presented in this chapter normally is used with a broad scope, covering the entire studied site. The thoroughness can vary from rough comb to fine comb and often the thoroughness varies between different unit processes in the same audit. As a top-down approach is used, the auditor always starts with a broad scope and a rough comb. As the audit progresses and the key areas are pointed out, the data collection and analysis become more detailed. Lytras [12] also describes the aim of an energy audit as either to point out general energy saving areas or to propose specific energy saving measures. With the method described in this chapter, pointing out the general energy saving areas is one way to identify specific measures and prioritize them.

Energy audits can also be described with the classification of energy audits from ASHRAE [13]. This classification involves three levels, defined in reference [14], and is similar to the audit procedure presented in reference [15]. The three levels presented in [13] are Level I (Walk-through assessment), Level II (Energy survey and analysis), and Level III (Detailed analysis of capital-intensive modifications).

The Level I walk-through assessment involves an assessment of the energy cost and efficiency by analyzing energy bills and a brief survey of the site. This first-level assessment targets low- or no-cost measures and presents a listing of capital improvements that need to be studied further. Level II, energy survey and analysis, includes a more detailed survey and analysis of the plant studied [13]. This is usually done by some form of detailed breakdown of energy use, either in activities and energy carriers or, as in this chapter, in unit processes. An energy audit with the method described in this chapter always involves the assessment at Level I and Level II.

Unit Processes

A unit process is defined by the energy service to be performed and industrial processes may thus be divided into two categories of unit processes:

- Production processes – the processes needed to manufacture the products.
- Support processes – the processes needed to support the production processes but not needed for production.

Unit processes are a way to divide the energy use of an industry or other businesses into smaller parts. The unit process perspective also enables one to question the methods used for different processes. Air flows in ventilation systems are sometimes high because the ventilation system may be dimensioned both for ventilation and cooling. If you see that the device is taking care of two different processes you also see that there is a point in adjusting the flow depending on the cooling demand.

Table 1: The unit processes used at Linköping University, divided into production and support processes

Production processes	Disintegrating	Support processes	Administration
	Disjointing		Cooling
	Mixing		Lighting
	Jointing		Compressed Air
	Coating		Ventilation
	Moulding		Pumping
	Heating		Tap water heating
	Melting		Internal Transport
	Drying		Space Heating
	Cooling/Freezing		Steam
	Packing		

The concept is based on the objective of the industrial process, the mixing of materials, cooling or drying a product, the production of compressed air or to carry goods, etc. Unit processes are considered to be the smallest components within an industrial energy system. Unit processes are general for all industries, thus providing opportunities for comparisons of a given unit process, such as forming, between different industries. Using the unit processes to represent the "building blocks" of energy use also enables modelling, e.g. simulation or optimization modelling of industrial energy use. For example, see [16].

METHODOLOGY

This section describes one method to survey and analyze the energy use of an industry. The industrial energy audit may be divided into three main parts: the survey, the analysis and the proposed measures. The expected result of the energy audit is a number of measures that will increase the energy efficiency, switch from non-renewable to renewable sources and decrease the energy use of the company or in the energy system as a whole. The result is normally presented in a report.

In the three parts of the audit you have different tasks:

Energy survey – What do we have?

- Define the system boundary.
- Identify unit processes.
- Quantify energy supply.
- Allocate energy use to different unit processes.

Energy analysis – How "bad" is the utilization of the supplied energy? Where does it go wrong? How far can we reach?

- Identify both system errors and detail problems.
- Identify idling power and energy.
- Identify technologies that are far from BAT (Best Available Technology).

- Identify mismatching energy quality, where high quality energy is used for non-demanding purposes, for example, electricity for low temperature heating.
- Identifying barriers and driving forces.
- Sum up the potential for energy efficiency and conversion for the system as a whole.

Suggested measures – What can we do about it?

- Identify possible solutions.
- Calculate the impact of the solutions and analyze them.
- Calculate the economic impact.

Top-Down Approach and Iterative Method

The energy audit is basically a project with the aim to suggest energy efficiency and conversion measures. The basic method is the project method, but the actual workflow does not follow the straight project line from survey to measures. In practice you will start analyzing problems and identifying solutions as soon as you start collecting information for the survey. The analysis and ideas for measures will also affect the need for data collection. Ideally, the method may be described as an iterative process, as shown in Figure 1, where the iterations stop when you have enough data to suggest relevant measures.

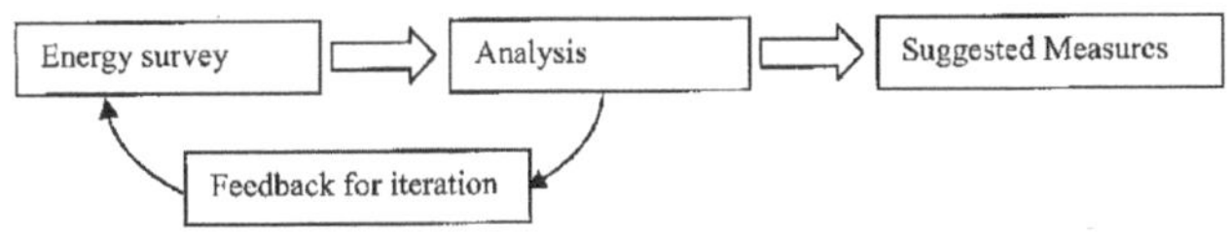

Figure 1: Schematic workflow for an industrial energy audit.

The iterative method is combined with a top-down approach. In this case, it means that the studied object (organisation, business or site) is initially considered as a unit, with its streams of energy and materials (Figure 2). The total use of different kinds of purchased energy is quantified. The material use and the products may be described but not necessarily quantified.

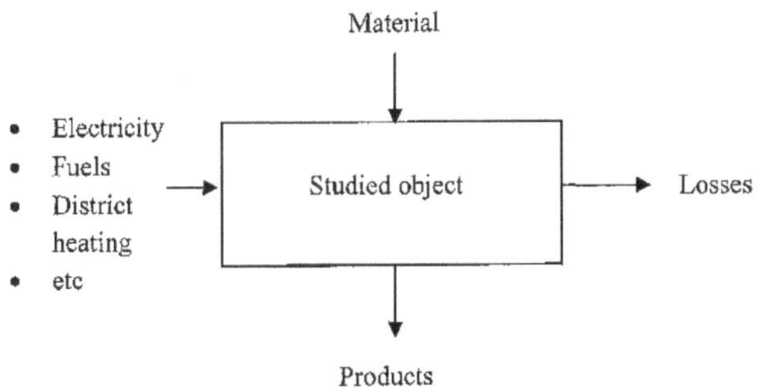

Figure 2: The top level of the top-down perspective for an energy audit.

The next step is to describe the unit processes and analyse them in terms of energy use (Figure 3). The first overview of the energy use makes it possible to relatively quickly identify key areas where additional resources are needed for measurements and analysis [17].

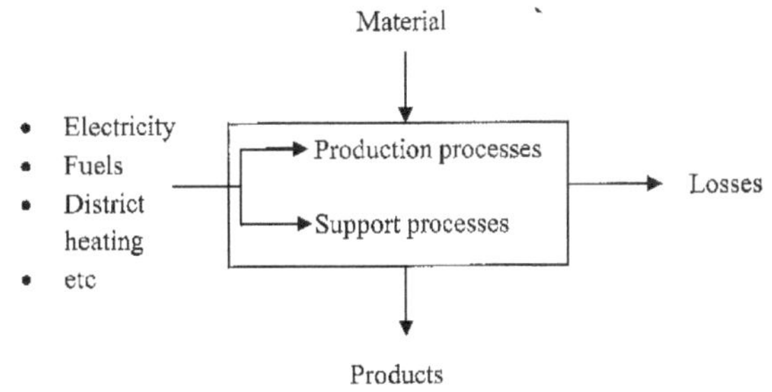

Figure 3: The second level of the top-down perspective for an energy audit means going into more detail concerning unit processes.

The next possible level is to find the data that enables you to allocate the energy use to the relevant unit processes. Which processes are relevant depends on the purpose of the audit. The top-down approach can continue further down, to individual components if necessary. How much detail the investigation will involve depends on the purpose of the audit, the possibility to acquire data, the complexity of the suggested measures, the timeframe for the audit, etc.

The point of starting from the top and working your way down is that the detailed information should be provided where the auditor thinks that it is needed, but not necessarily everywhere. The level of detail will vary between different unit processes. Sometimes the energy of all unit processes in a production line is summarized under the heading of Production Processes. It can be done for practical reasons, such as when a machine with only one energy supply handles multiple unit processes, or because the audit is delimited to focus only on support processes.

Typical Process for an Audit

In practice the activity schedule for a project can look like this:

Week 1: Start meeting with the company for project start and start collecting information. Wait for data from the company. Describe the unit processes. Collect basic data, like annual energy statistics (from energy supplier) and if available figures from sub-metering at the plant, as well as technical drawings. Finally, analyze the collected material. For example, where may the largest energy efficiency potentials be located? Where can we probably measure what we want?

Week 2: First visit on site – identify energy supply to different unit processes, collect data, measure, put loggers in place, count equipment.

Analyse data from visit. Detailed data is now available, but a top-down perspective is still applied, e.g. where may the largest energy efficiency potentials be located, which unit processes are most promising and in which areas do we need more data or knowledge?

Week 3: Second visit on site – remove loggers, additional instantaneous measurements. Analyse data from loggers. Completing the survey.

Week 4: Calculate the energy efficiency potential of the measures. Find suppliers of equipment needed for the measures, and wait for data from them. Complete the report.

Week 5: Third visit on site – present the results. Validate the proposed measures with the company staff. Some optimal (in terms of calculation) energy efficiency measures may be switched to second or even third-best choice after discussion with company staff.

Please note that this is a schematic example of how an energy audit could be carried out. The same method can be applied on different scales. A quick Level I audit at a small facility (i.e., five employees and 500 MWh electricity per year) can be finished in two weeks and less than 30 working hours. It would be fully possible to spend several months on a larger and more complex object (i.e., >5 buildings, many energy supplies, several production lines) which demands a more thorough audit and detailed measures.

Defining the Object and the System Boundaries

The object for the audit and its system boundaries have to be defined. As it is an energy audit, you will study energy flows, but the focus may be limited. The focus can be on decreasing a supply, e.g. electricity, fossil fuels or purchased energy, or on a part of the object, e.g. the building envelope or support processes only. The system boundaries can be an organisation or a part of an organisation, a building or a physical area with more than one organisation. The perspective can also be broader, for example, taking management or economic aspects or embedded energy into account.

As the method is iterative, you might have to narrow or widen the system boundary, depending on the limitations and possibilities you find on the way. One example is if the organisation you study owns the building where they work, but you discover that they also have a tenant working in a smaller part of the building. Instead of trying to calculate how much energy the tenant uses, the system border can be redefined to cover the tenant too.

Another example is when there is an existing or possible symbiosis between two neighbouring businesses. In this case the system is growing from one to two companies. A very common case is that the audited business is renting the building they work in. In this case you have the choice to exclude the building from the audit, but you will most probably find more and better efficiency measures by treating the building and the business as one system, with the business owner and the landlord as two participants.

Energy Survey and Analysis – Introduction

With the energy survey you will be able to create a power balance and an energy balance with the incoming energy allocated to different unit processes. To be able to suggest energy efficiency and conversion measures you also need to understand how the processes work, at least when it comes to energy use. The aim of the energy survey is not necessarily to create a very detailed map of the energy use, but to find the potential for energy efficiency measures and potential conversion to renewable energy sources.

By starting with an overview of the energy system and using a top-down approach it is possible to find the potential changes at the structural level, and avoid being limited to details. By combining the top-down approach with an iterative method for the data collection, it is possible to go further into details without getting overwhelmed with detailed data that is not really needed.

There are different ways to get the data you need. Provided that the top-down perspective is used, you don't have to collect all possible data about every device. The data collection begins with the most accessible data at the most general level which is considered useful by the auditor (using a top-down approach). The analysis starts with analyzing that initial data. The analysis will probably raise questions, which are used to guide the coming data collection procedures.

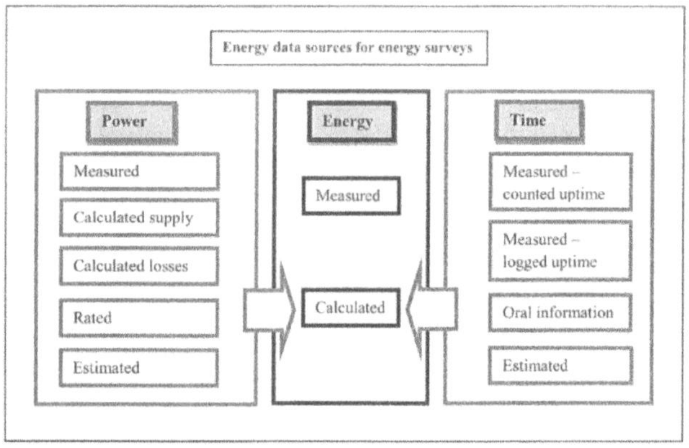

Figure 4: Some possible energy data sources for energy surveys.

At some level you have to stop the data collection despite not having all the answers. The limit is often the time reserved for the project, but it can also be the possibility to measure, practical obstacles to changing a process or the lack of historical data. It is often necessary (and possible) to use data from a more aggregated level, together with some analysis, calculations and assumptions. The data collection procedure could be carried out in the following way:

- Step 1: Gather statistics: electricity, district heating, fuel, water, production rate, etc. Gather drawings and plans.
- Step 2: Visit the company during operating hours.
- Step 3: Visit the company during non-operating hours.
- Step 4: Create a power balance, energy balance and allocate energy use.

To complete the audit you need to take two more steps:

- Step 5: Create an energy balance after adjustments (showing the impact of the suggested measures).
- Step 6: Confirmation of audit results.

The main purpose of the data collection is to give you basic data to identify relevant unit processes, to create a power balance and energy balance for these processes. Another purpose is to get enough data to be able to suggest adequate measures for energy efficiency and conversion. The origin and quality of information can vary greatly. Focusing solely on the energy data, the potential data sources can be categorized as shown in Figure 4.

Step 1: Gather Statistics, Drawing and Plans

Before you have even visited the object of your survey, you can review the statistics concerning the use of electricity, district heating, fuel and water. You might also have supply of other media, such as steam or compressed air. Also try to get statistics on (or estimate) the production rate during the same period. Production data will enable you to estimate the specific energy use, for example in terms of kWh per produced unit, per hours worked or per tonne of raw material used. This can be useful both for allocating the energy and for calculating the result of suggested measures.

You can also ask the staff what activities are going on at the studied site, to get a picture of the unit processes and energy flow you should look for when you get there.

Electricity Supply Data

The electricity sales company and the electric grid owner are sources for the electricity supply data you need. It is good to have as much detailed data as you can when it comes to electricity use. The grid owner can provide consumption data with hour by hour resolution to their customers (at least in Sweden). If the object of the survey is small or if it has small sub-meters, there might be a problem to get hour by hour data. Energy data for a whole year, regardless of the time resolution, is recommended for analyzing the dependence on outdoor temperature.

Detailed data on the total electricity use during the period for which you are mapping the unit processes is also important. Sometimes you can use the customer ID number and a PIN code to get the hour by hour use from the supplier via the Internet. In that case it is easy to also download data for the period when you make your own electrical measurements. Another option is to log the total incoming electricity during the same period.

From the invoices you can get information on prices, power use, reactive power, etc. The invoice from January typically contains a summary of the energy use for the last year.

To some extent it is possible to analyze the data before visiting the company. You can compare the energy use graphs for production hours during different seasons to find electrical heating and cooling loads. You can also compare idling energy losses in different seasons and analyze total energy use, power peaks, reactive power, etc.

District Heating Supply Data

Sometimes it is possible to get historical data on the energy used for district heating with hour by hour resolution, but often you have to be satisfied with the amount of heat used per month. Sometimes you can use the customer number and a PIN code to get data from the supplier via the Internet. If you ask for the service in advance, the supplier might be able to give you hour by hour resolution data for the time of the audit.

Fuel Supply Data

Fuels such as oil, wood pellets or wood chips are mostly bought in batches. To be able to calculate how much fuel was used in the past, you need to know how much fuel there was to start with, the purchased amount and how much is left. If the needed data is not available you might be able to estimate the fuel use by calculating the heat losses.

Other Energy Supplies

There are also other possible energy supplies, such as steam, compressed air, liquid nitrogen for cooling, welding gas, etc. As long as someone is charging for the supply you might be able to get some historical data, but it is not always the case. It is a good idea to look for informal energy flows: Two neighbouring companies can share the same district heating supply, air handling unit or air compressor, there might be solar heating for hot tap water or the company uses residues, such as wood chips, from the neighbour for heating. Energy supply not considered as energy can sometimes turn out to be important. Liquid nitrogen for cooling and welding gas for oxy-fuel welding are two examples.

Miscellaneous Background Data

Some other data that might be useful include:

- Water supply data, to be able to calculate the hot water use.
- Drawings of the building, floor plans.
- Drawing of the electricity supply systems.
- Drawing of other energy supply systems, for example hot water pipes, compressed air pipes
- Information on the ventilation: Drawings of ventilation ducts, number of air handling units and air flows.
- Information on time schedules for production processes, ventilation or lighting.
- Energy efficiency measures that are already taken.

Drawings can guide you to where in the system or in the building measurements can be made and what information to ask for. The drawings can also give you information that you can use directly. Air flows can be noted on ventilation drawings. Rated power for electric equipment, like motors and heaters, can be noted on detailed electrical drawings at the distribution board level. When data such as documentation from a drawing is used, it is a good idea to make sure the data is up to date, by asking the staff about changes or by using measurements to validate.

Step 2: Visiting the Company to Collect Data

By visiting the company during production hours, you can find out how the processes work, examine the design and function of systems and equipment, validate the descriptions, drawings and layouts you already have (for example of building and air handling units) and fill in the gaps where you have no data at all. When you visit the company you have the opportunity to:

- Speak to the key persons in different areas, operational and maintenance staff.
- Note the uptime and downtime for different devices, by registering how the processes work and by asking the staff.
- Inspect the building envelope and the space heating system.
- Review the procedures for service and maintenance.

- Go through all the unit processes systematically.
- Assess the function and condition of the equipment.
- Make an inventory of installed power, for example for motors, light sources and other devices.
- Measure the power used by a selection of important equipment. It might be the most energy demanding devices or any equipment you identify as critical to be able to divide the energy flow into different unit processes.
- Look for control systems (for the ventilation or for a production line). If there are any, you can try to find out if they are used and how they work. From the control systems for example you might get timetables with operation hours or logged data on production rate.
- Count the number of devices (for example light sources or computers) to make calculations later, using templates.

By speaking to key persons you can find out which unit processes are used at the company, uptime and downtime for different devices, operating hours for the factory and more. The key persons can be found among energy managers, production managers, caretakers, machine operators or others, depending on the organization. A caretaker or in-house electrician is a good guide when you want to find the devices you want to examine and the switchgear where to measure electricity. The production manager can inform you about the different production processes and their operating times.

Data on electricity use is mostly in focus. Data on airflows, water flows, pressure, temperature and size is often useful. Often you find set values and statistical data from sources like plans, technical documentation or monitoring systems. The main purpose of the survey is to get an overview - it is not necessary to measure all parameters during the survey to create the power and energy balance. Still, sometimes measuring is the easiest solution and more accurate and precise measurements might be necessary to be able to predict the results of proposed efficiency or conversion measures.

As the audit is a temporary project, the audit itself is not an incentive to install permanent meters. If sensors, for example, for power, current, air flow, pressure or temperature are already installed and relevant data already logged or is possible to log, of course they should be used for the audit.

Sometimes you can also log the output signal directly from the control system with a voltage or current logger, depending on the type of signal, mostly 0-10 V or 4-20 mA. The logged information can be used directly as indicator of the uptime of equipment, e.g., an air handling unit. For further calculations you also need to know what real condition the signal represents and adapt your logged values to that.

Electric Power Measurements

The data from the energy supply company is not sufficient for allocating energy use to all different unit processes. Internal energy measurements from the studied facility can sometimes be found, especially for well-monitored core production processes. Still you will probably have to measure the electric power used by a selection of important equipment to be able to allocate the energy use and construct the power and energy balance. To make electrical measurements is very often the main activity when the studied object is visited.

Apart from measuring the energy use directly with permanently installed meters, there are different ways to measure the power or current for electric equipment to help you calculate the energy use. To calculate the energy use from electrical measurements you will need the active power. When visiting the company, it is preferable to measure the active power directly with a wattmeter. Measuring the current and voltage separately will enable you to calculate the apparent power, which cannot be used directly for energy calculations. The apparent power is only useful when the power factor is known from previous measurements or from technical documentation. Rated power for different electric equipment can be used to some extent, but normally it should not be used for the calculations. Rather, it is more appropriate to obtain the power or current and power factor from measurements.

A short visit to the studied site will not provide sufficient information to allocate energy use. To see changes in power use, a combination of current transducers (AC current clamps) and digital recorders (data loggers) can be used. A useful method is to let the data loggers record the current for one week. This will give you information about changes in usage patterns during working hours as well as nights and weekends.

The use of electric energy is very often in focus in the energy audits conducted by Linköping University. Methods and material for electric measurements and evaluation of data are also developed for energy audit purposes. Examples are shown in section 3. Practical examples - Measurements and analysis.

Air Flow Measurements

Air flow measurements can be used to calculate the ventilation heat losses, and also to roughly estimate the electric power used for the fan motors. On the other hand, the electric power used for the fan motor can also give you an idea about the air flow, and the electricity is often easier to measure. Sometimes the optimal way to find out the operating time for a machine or the working hours in a building is to log the ventilation air flow or temperature or the electricity used by the fan motor.

Temperature Measurements

Temperature data are particularly useful for calculating the energy use of the unit processes Space Heating and Cooling and Ventilation. Temperature measurements can be used to calculate the efficiency of heat exchangers for AHUs. To calculate the heat losses, the exhaust air temperature is crucial, but seldom registered by the monitoring system and even more seldom logged. To use standard values for efficiency of the heat exchanger is a useful shortcut.

Temperature logging can be used to identify operating time for equipment. A temperature probe can be attached directly to the surface of a machine or in an air flow or other medium connected to the studied equipment.

Size Measurements

To analyze the heat losses from a building the size of the building and the properties of the building materials must be known. Measuring the size of windows and doorways, thickness of walls and height of ceilings is often part of the survey. For air flow measurements in ventilation ducts, the size of the duct must be known.

Make an Inventory of Installed Load and Operating Time

A fast and effective means is to count motors, light sources, computers and other devices and note their rated power. You find the rated power for motors and other devices on name plates or in technical documentation. Also note the rated cos φ for the motors, for future loggings of electricity - if you don't get the opportunity to measure the true power factor or cos φ, at least you have an idea of the figure. Even though the scientific literature provides examples of this approach, see e.g. [18], it is strongly recommended that the power factor is obtained by measurements. This is due to the wide variation of power factor which occurs from different applications.

To get the energy use for computers, copiers, servers and printers, you can get a good enough estimate by counting the number of devices and calculating the power and energy used. You probably have to use templates and estimates for these.

To get the power and energy for light sources, a good method is to count the number of different light sources and note the different rated power, printed on the light source, on the package or in technical documentation. This method works as long as the lighting is controlled by an on/off switch only. When you have discharge lamps, such as light strips, you have to add the power used by the ballast (control gear). Make sure to find out if it is a magnetic ballast (very common, always in older installations but still used today) or the more modern electronic ballast. Magnetic and electronic ballast differ in power use. For light strips with the common magnetic ballast it means multiplying the rated power by 1,2 and for the more modern electronic ballast it means multiplying by 1,1.

The uptime for the lighting might be hard to find out. You can simply ask the staff, log the light or temperature at selected light sources or log current used for lighting to be able to see the true uptime and downtime.

Step 3: Visit the Company during Non-Production Hours

This step is performed to find out what equipment is operating during non-production hours and find out if it must be operating. You might find support processes - lights, air handling units, compressors - being switched on though there is nothing to support, but also production processes in idle or stand-by mode.

Eyes and ears are useful to find equipment running during non-production hours. The measurement methods used are the same as during production hours, but the focus may be on other processes.

Step 4: Create a Power Balance, Energy Balance and Allocate Energy Use

When you start constructing the energy balance, you will have data with different quality – detailed production data, estimated operating time, rated data, etc. You will have data with different time spans and time resolutions - statistical data for a whole year, one week measurements, instantaneous measurements, etc. The data will also describe different parts of the energy flow - sometimes the energy supply, sometimes the usage and sometimes the energy loss. In Figure 5, an example of an energy balance is presented.

Below some different common cases related to allocating energy use are outlined.

Case 1 - All the supplied energy is allocated to one specific unit process. Sometimes you can find this phenomenon for support processes, such as fuels for internal transport or district heating for space heating. Some of the supplied energy can also be very specific for a certain production process, such as gas for welding or liquid nitrogen for cooling.

Case 2 - Almost all of the supplied energy is allocated to one specific unit process – all you have to do is to take something away. In Figure 5 this is the case for Space Heating and Hot Tap Water which are the only processes supplied by the oil boiler.

This can often be the case when you use a hot water system for both production and Space Heating and Cooling. One example is a district heating hot water supply used for both a washing machine for surface treatment and for the indoor climate and space heating system. The space heating is mostly weather dependent and varies with the seasons. The energy use of the washing machine totally depends on the rate of production. Given that you have at least monthly data from the district heating supplier and that you know the production rate during the summer, when the heating system is mostly turned off, you can estimate the energy use for the washing. Then you can compare the energy use during the summer and winter, subtract the energy use for washing and assume the rest to be heat for space heating and air handling.

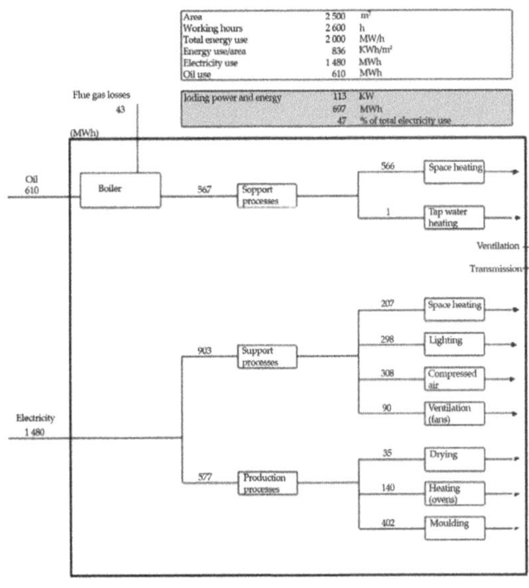

Figure 5: Energy balance for an audited plant [19].

Case 3 - Many different unit processes have the same supply, but at least some of them are running in a predictable way. This is often the case when it comes to electricity, as seen in Figure 7. From the switchgear or the distribution board, where you often have the practical possibility to measure, electricity is supplied to many different processes. Typically you find all the processes in one part of the building mixed. Even if the distribution board is totally dominated by one production process, like a laser cutter, you might also find support processes for that production process, like a compressor and a chiller, attached to the same board. The energy use for the laser cutter itself will vary a lot, but if the chiller works constantly as soon as the cutter is on and the uptime of the compressor already is measured for service reasons, you might be able to allocate the energy use by logging the total current to the distribution board.

If you have a common supply for even more processes, try to find the ones with constant power use, like light strips, or constant power use and programmed uptime, like air handling units with constant air volume and an autotimer.

Case 4 - A process has more than one energy supply. This is of course a common case. In a building with many air handling units, the units are all doing the same job – they are running the ventilation process. Even if there is a central remote control system for all air handling units, usually the energy use is not logged. The solution is to add up all the air handling units, accepting that your input data quality will range from rated power and estimated uptimes to detailed measurements.

You can also have one process with different energy carriers, e.g. a dryer consisting of an electric fan and a hot water heater. If you are not able to register everything, you might be able to use data from one of the carriers to calculate the uptime for the other. For example, the temperature of the heat exchanger can reveal if the fan is running or not.

You might also find two separate electricity supplies to the same unit process for safety reasons, i.e., two separate air compressors connected to two different switchgears to prevent stoppage. Of course you can have more than one supply to a single unit process for other reasons, for example if the electric distribution system has been supplemented because the process needs more electricity than the original switchgear was designed for.

Step 5: Creating an Energy Balance after Adjustments (Showing the Impact of the Suggested Measures)

Depending on what kind of problems the auditor has found, different solutions are proposed. There are four principal means of reducing industrial energy costs as shown in Table 2.

Table 2: Four principal means of reducing industrial energy costs

Principal means of reducing industrial energy costs	Comment
Energy-efficient technologies	Improved efficiency among technologies using energy is one of the foremost and most common means of increasing energy efficiency in industry.
Load management	Reducing power costs by aiming to minimize the power loads is a common means for industry
Change energy carriers	Changing energy carriers, e.g. switching from oil to district heating is a means for industry to cut costs
Energy-efficient behavior	Energy-efficient behavior is a simple measure involving more efficient behavior among staff at the industry

It should be noted that the above table concerns energy costs. As regards reduced energy use, load management is not an energy-saving measure as it solely shifts the use of energy to times where it is more appropriate. Moreover, change of energy carrier may be a splendid way to reduce the use of non-renewable resources or energy costs. However, it may not lead to reduced energy use.

When the impact of the proposed measures is calculated, a new balance is presented (Figure 6). The new balance can have two different purposes: It can show the potential for changes in the energy use or it can show the calculated impact of the measures. The potential for energy efficiency can be estimated with standard values for the best available technology. If the impact of the suggested measures is to be presented, more detailed technical and economical calculations are made.

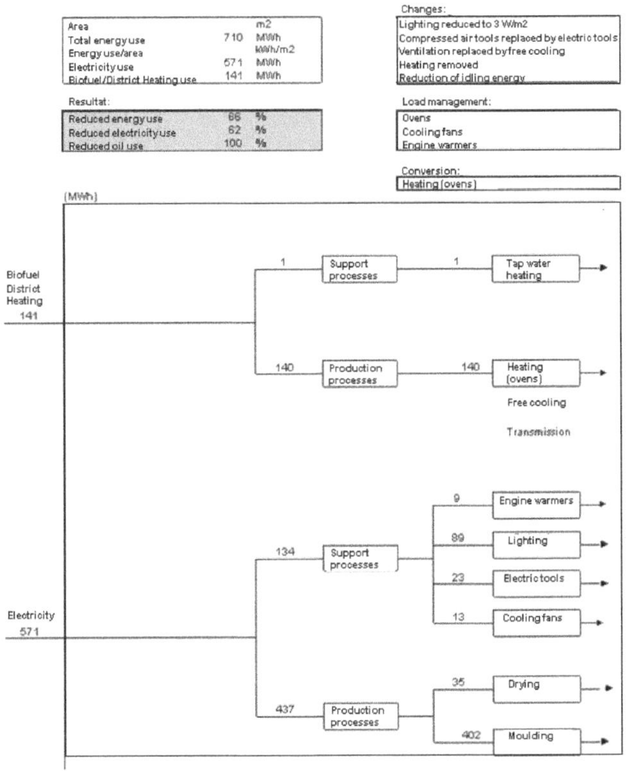

Figure 6: Energy balance after suggested adjustments [19].

Step 6: Confirmation of Audit Results

This part is of crucial importance, not least in regard to whether the energy audit results will, in fact, be accepted, and not discarded. Normally, a meeting is held with representatives from the industry concerned and the conductors of the audit about the proposed energy efficiency measures, and the analysis of the energy balance. In this step, the primary focus is on the proposed measures. For some processes, there are a number of different alternatives. This step enables the energy auditor and the industry representatives to discuss which measure is most suitable for the industry. Normally, this meeting is not with high level executives but is held with the maintenance manager or the energy controller.

PRACTICAL EXAMPLES – MEASUREMENTS AND ANALYSIS

This section shows a few practical examples of measurements and analysis for energy audit purposes, focused on electricity. The building properties and heating and cooling systems are often important to examine in an energy audit. Air flow and temperature measurements are often needed. As there are fairly standardized methods for these tasks, they will not be further discussed in this chapter.

Allocation of Electricity Use – Measurement Case Description

In a typical measurement case we want to separate the electricity use for the unit processes air handling, lighting, compressed air, internal transports and packing. Instantaneous power measurements, current logging and rated power for equipment are used to allocate the electricity use.

Based on information from the staff at the industry, we know that the distribution board in Central Picking Stock is used for ventilation, lighting and electric tools for packing. The Central Garage distribution board is used for ventilation, lighting and a forklift charger. From the board Central Large Hall electricity for lighting, ventilation and packing equipment is distributed. Based on that information, and the drawings of the electricity distribution system in Figure 7, the plan for measurements may look like in Table 3.

The logging period is the same for all the current clamp meters, in this case seven days, to cover the variations in energy use in production hours as well as during the weekend. The range setting of the current clamp meters is to be appropriate for the load, but also depends on the type of clamps and loggers available at the moment. In this case we have 500 A, 200 A and 20 A current clamp meters.

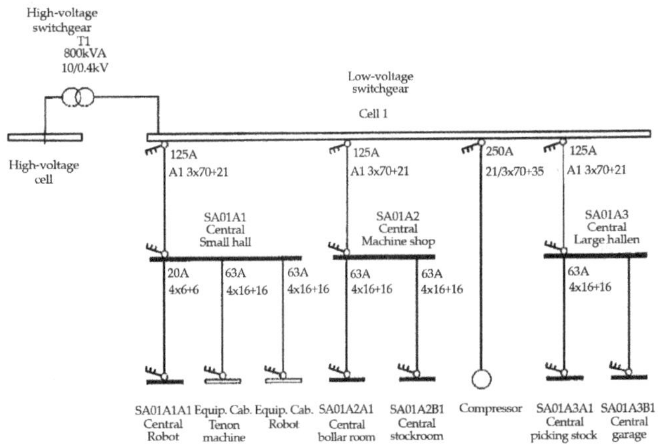

Figure 7: Example of a schematic drawing of an electricity distribution system.

The sampling interval for the current clamps can be changed depending on what we want to know. For the air compressor we may log more frequently, for example every five seconds, if we find that the compressor is switching mode very frequently, otherwise logging at 60-second intervals may be enough.

The purpose of the continuous measurement will also affect the logging interval. If the first visit gives us the impression that the compressed air system is an important part of the energy use, we may measure more carefully to have enough information to suggest detailed measures. The drawing of the electric distribution tells us that the fuse for the compressor is 250 A, but based on the information from the instantaneous measurements we plan to carry out, we might be able to replace the 500 A clamp with a 200 A clamp.

In this case we will have a measurement from a switchgear cabinet that covers several unit processes, for example lighting and forklift charging for a garage and picking stock, as shown in Figure 8. The data from clamp no. 1 in the switchgear must be complemented by simultaneous measurements from clamps 2 and 3 in the distribution board, where clamp 2 measures the total incoming current to the Central Garage board and clamp 3 measures the outgoing current to the forklift chargers.

Table 3: Example of plan for energy measurements to allocate electricity use to unit processes

Unit process	**Power data source**	**Time data source**	**Comments**
Compressed air	Instantaneous measurements.	Logged data from current clamp 4.	Clamp 4 settings: range 200 or 500 A, sampling interval 5 to 60 s.
Lighting	Rated power, verified by instantaneous measurements.	Oral info on working hours. Verify with data from current clamp 1 and 2.	Clamp 1 settings: range 200 A, sampling interval 60 s. Clamp 2 settings: range 200 A, sampling interval 60 s.
Ventilation	Instantaneous measurements.	Air handling unit control system. Verify with data from current clamp 1 and 2.	
Internal transport	Rated power for forklift chargers combined with logged data from current clamp 3.	Logged data from current clamp 3.	Clamp 3 settings: range 20 A, sampling interval 60 s.
Packing	Rated power, instantaneous measurements.	Logged data from current clamp 1.	The residual energy is logged data from current clamp 1, minus clamp 2 and the energy for lighting and ventilation. The residual is equal to the energy for Packing.

Later, the data from clamp 2 in the Central Garage distribution board can be subtracted from clamp 1 in the switchgear to get a picture of the energy use in Central Picking Stock and Central Large Hall.

At the same time you have parallel measurements of the air compressor from clamp no 4. The clamp meter is placed in the switchgear, where the compressor has directly connected conductors, or in the compressor, depending on where you have the best access.

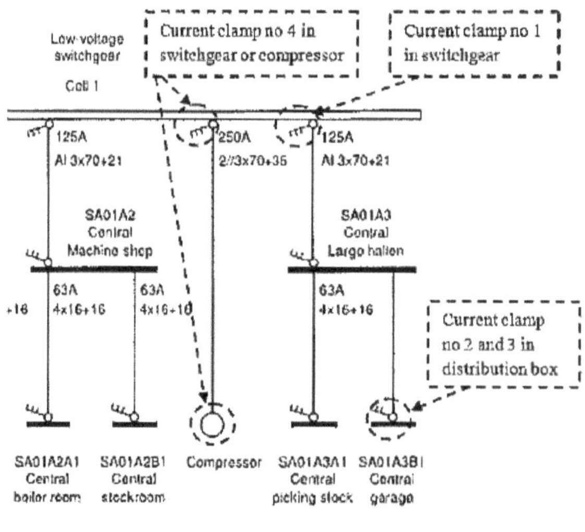

Figure 8: Part of a schematic drawing of an electricity distribution system, with locations for current clamps for simultaneous current measurement, to make it possible to subtract a part of the load from the total and separate electricity used for different unit processes.

Calculating the Electricity Use from Logged Data

Logged data can be used for calculating:

- Uptime.
- Average power for operating hours.
- Idling power.

In the example below the case is an hydraulic press, but the same procedure can be used for other equipment, for example to calculate the energy used to cover leakage in compressed air systems. With some more measurements and analysis, it can also be used for a complete building or workshop.

The idling energy, uptime and average power can be calculated in a few steps:

1. Measure the power factor at different loads.
2. Log the current.
3. Analyse the graph.

4. Convert the current to power.

5. Analyse the data again.

How to do this will be shown with measurements from a hydraulic machine for sheet metal processing.

Measure the Power Factor at Different Loads

The power factor is measured while the machine is running. The machine has two well-defined modes of operation – one when the metal sheets are actually shaped and one when the hydraulic motors are running without any load, i.e., idling.

Table 4: Measured power and power factor for a hydraulic press

Mode	Power (kW)	Power factor, λ
Active	<250	0,82
Idling	48	0,38

Log the Current

The current is logged for about a week, to cover working days as well as the weekend. The original current logging data is presented in a graph (Figure 9).

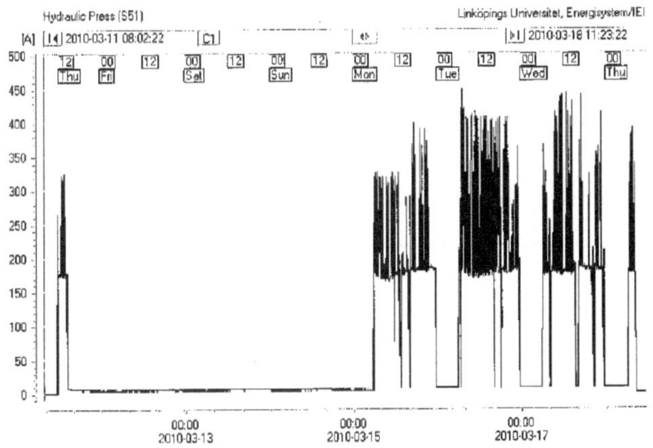

Figure 9: The current used by a hydraulic press during one week.

Analyse the Graph

From the graph (Figure 9), it is clear that the machine is not used Friday to Sunday and for some hours during the nights. The machine is turned off during non-production hours. Nonetheless it has some idling power during the weekend and nights. The conclusion is that there are in fact three different modes to consider: active, idling and standby. The periods with zero current in the beginning and the end of the graph is the time before the logger was connected to the machine and after it was disconnected.

One way to analyse the graph is to create a duration diagram with the logged data, as in Figure 10. The duration diagram can be used to distinguish between the modes and to estimate the energy use for the different modes.

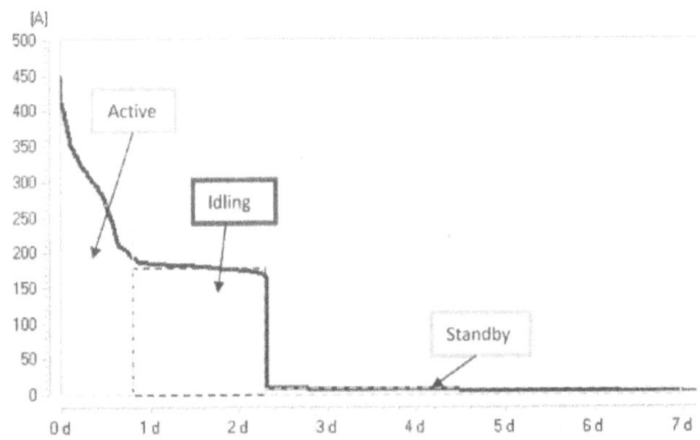

Figure 10: Duration diagram of the current used by a hydraulic press during almost one week (6,8 days). The active mode lasts for about 20 hours, the idling mode for about 1,5 day and the standby mode for about 4,5 days.

Convert the Current to Power

The power can roughly be estimated with the duration diagram together with the instantaneous measurements of the power factor.

Table 5: Power and energy use for a hydraulic press during one week.

Mode	Power factor, λ	Current (A)	Voltage (V)	Power (kW)	Duration (h)	Energy (kWh/week)
Active	0,82	270	230	150	20	3000
Idling	0,38	180	230	47	36	1700
Standby	?	5	230	3,5	108	400
SUM						5100

In this case a close calculation based on the raw data gave a similar result (5176 kWh) to the rough estimate, but that is mostly because the same assumptions were used. Changing the duration or average power just a little affects the result a lot. The power factor at partial load and at standby load is also unknown, which affects the accuracy of the calculations.

Analyse the Data Again

Together with information about the rate of production and the working hours, the annual energy use for this equipment can be calculated.

If this is a representative production week, the result can simply be multiplied by the number of working weeks per year. In this case it is not a typical week but information from the production manager tells us the working days are representative. The average power use during working hours can be calculated and multiplied by the number of working hours per year. In this case the rest of the year can be considered as standby time. In other cases equipment can be completely turned off during longer holidays.

Table 6: Calculated annual energy use for a hydraulic press

Mode	**Power, average (kW)**	**Duration (h/year)**	**Energy (MWh/year)**
Working hours (active and idling mode)	84	3456	290
Standby	3,5	5304	19
SUM		8760	309

We know from previous calculations that about 35 percent of the energy use during working hours is really idling energy. That information is not needed for the allocation of the energy use to the right unit process, but it is important information for further analysis and to suggest measures. A closer look at the graph of the current used during a week also reveals that the machine sometimes is idling for more than one hour without producing (see Figure 9). One example is Monday before midnight, when it is idling for about two hours before it is at last turned off for the day. An automatic control system or changed routines for the operator can be used to switch to standby mode faster. The aim of the analysis was to be able to calculate the energy use, but on the way some possible measures were also found.

CONCLUDING DISCUSSION

This chapter has presented the energy audit methodology being developed at the Division of Energy Systems at Linköping University for a period of more than 30 years. Despite extensive research and experience in the field – about 500 energy audits have been carried out based on this methodology - the energy audit methodology has not been explicitly outlined previously. This chapter may therefore still contain areas for improvements. This chapter has for example not covered in depth the obvious risk of errors when collecting and analyzing the data and results in an energy audit. For practical reasons, measurements are normally carried out for one or two weeks. When setting up an energy balance, this period of time is normally assumed to be a representation of a "normal" week, and thus multiplied by a factor in order to gain an annual balance.

Moreover, it must also be mentioned that this methodology covers a Swedish and Scandinavian context, for which reason some material might be difficult to adapt in countries outside of Scandinavia. Finally, this chapter has not explicitly covered the in-depth calculations needed for various parts of an energy audit as there is no room for that in this context. The chapter does not cover all the various aspects of the energy audit methodology but rather gives the reader a basic introduction to the subject. After all, becoming a good energy auditor is not about reading a book, but is rather a continuous learning process where experience, not theory, is the major part of increasing skills.

REFERENCES

1. European Commission2006Directive 2006/32/EC of the European Parliament and of the Council of 5 April 2006 on energy end-use efficiency and energy services and repealing Council Directive 93/76/EEC, Brussels.
2. J Schleich, 2004Do energy audits help reduce barriers to energy efficiency? An empirical analysis for Germany. International Journal of Energy Technology and Policy 2226239
3. C Caffal, 1996Energy management in industry. Centre for the Analysis and Dissemination of Demonstrated Energy Technologies (CADDET). Analysis Series 17. Sittard, The Netherlands.
4. IPCC2007Contribution of Working Group III to the Fourth Assessment Report of the Intergovernmental Panel on Climate Change. Summary for Policymakers. http://www.ipcc.ch/SPM0405pdf (accessed October 8, 2007).
5. IEA (International Energy Agency)2007Key world energy statistics 2007, Paris. from:http://195.200.115.136/textbase/nppdf/freekey_stats_2007.pdf (accessed January 8, 2008).
6. ECON2003ECON centre for economic analysis AB. Konsekvenser på elpriset av införandet av handel med utsläppsrätter [Impact on price of electricity of the introduction of trading with emission rights]. Ministry of Industry, Employment and Communications, Stockholm. [in Swedish]
7. Clara Pardo Martinez 2010Factors Influencing Energy Efficiency in the German and Colombian Manufacturing Industries, Energy Efficiency, Jenny Palm (Ed.), 978-9-53307-137-4InTech, Available from: http://www.intechopen.com/books/energy-efficiency/factors-influencing-energy-efficiency-in-the-german-and-colombian-manufacturing-industries
8. Patrik Thollander, Maria Danestig and Patrik Rohdin, Energy policies for increased industrial energy efficiency- Evaluation of a local energy programme for manufacturing SMEs, 2007Energy Policy, (35), 11, 5774-5783.
9. B Johansson, G Modig, L. J Nilsson, 2007Policy

instruments and industrial responses- experiences from Sweden. In: Proceedings of the 2007 ECEEE summer study "Saving energy- just do it", Panel 714131421

10. SEA (Swedish Energy Agency)2006aEnergy in Sweden 2006. Swedish Energy Agency Publication Department, Eskilstuna.
11. EEPO2003Year 2002 Results. European Electricity Prices Observatory (EEPO), Brussels.
12. K Lytras, C Caspar, 2005Energy Audit Models. SAVE-project AUDIT II, Topic Report.
13. ASHRAE 2003Application handbookAmerican Society of Heating, Refrigerating and Air-Conditioning Engineers, Atlanta.
14. R. P Mazzucchi, 1992A guide for analyzing and reporting building characteristics and energy use in commercial buildings, ASHRAE transactions 98110671080
15. P. E Nilsson, ed. 2003Achieving the desired indoor climate- Energy efficiency aspects of system design. Commtech group, Lund: Studentlitteratur.
16. P Thollander, M Mardan, M Karlsson, 2009Optimisation as investment decision support in a Swedish medium-sized iron foundry- a move beyond traditional energy auditing. Applied Energy864433440
17. T Franzén, 2005EnergiSystemAnalysMetod, EnSAM, för industriella energisystem [Energy System Analysis Method, EnSAM, for industrial energy systems]. 2005, Linköping Institute of Technology, Lin-köping. [in Swedish]
18. R Saidur, N. A Rahim, H. W Ping, M. I Jahirul, S Mekhilef, H. H Masjuki, 2009Energy and emission analysis for industrial motors in Malaysia. Energy Policy37936503658
19. L Trygg, B Karlsson, 2005Industrial DSM in a deregulated European electricity market- a case study of 11 plants in Sweden. Energy Policy331114451459

CHAPTER 12 PROCESSES MANAGEMENT FOR QUALITY OF THE MAINTENANCE SERVICE

Jarmo Heinonen, Mika Raassina, and Nick Moss

INTRODUCTION

The challenges when ensuring operational excellence in service business

There are many concerns when organizations strive to ensure quality and operational excellence in their operations and the challenge as organizations grow bigger more global is sustainable operations.

When we come to service organizations the challenge will have new dimensions. For a long time researchers have stated that service is intangible by nature and it is difficult to set consistent and accurate measures for quality assurance. External auditors often find difficulties when trying to assess the quality management system: whether the organization audited has a consistent and communicated quality plan; or that there is a traceable system in place to prove that key quality characteristics have been planned and further more they have also been followed and documented; or what the organizations own process is to ensure operational excellence.

The challenge above is due to certain characteristics that separate service from physical products. When new service development is concerned; the literature relates largely to traditional service products such as financial and hospitality services, not to a great extent to industrial services. Five key characteristics that distinguish service products from physical products have generally been identified as intangibility, perishability, non-ownership, inseparability of production and consumption, and variability (Kundu et al., 2007)

- *Intangibility*: Services are predominantly performances of actions rather than objects that can be perceived using any of the physical senses.
- *Perishability*: Services must be consumed as they are provided. In general, they cannot be saved, stored, returned or carried forward for later use or sale.
- *Non-ownership:* Largely as a result of their intangibility and perishability, customers do not obtain ownership of services; rather, they experience the delivery of the service.
- *Inseparability of production and consumption*: Service products are typically produced and consumed at the same time - consumption cannot be separated from the means of production.
- *Variability:* Service product quality is subject to variability because services are delivered by people to people.

Two dimensions of variability have been identified (Zeithaml & Britner, 2003)

- the extent to which delivery standards vary from a norm, and
- the extent to which a service can be deliberately varied to meet the specific needs of individual customers.

Productizing (or productification) of services is the key word that has been used in service management. It is a key approach that has given organizations the opportunity to standardize offerings, service delivery and also many related development activities. It has also enabled increased accuracy in service cost determination, as well as enabled improvements in competence management and thus reduced dependency on some key service specialists which is a typical concern especially in the maintenance services field. Well defined and managed service productizing has given international service companies a remarkable differentiator – global, standardized implementation of service management model. One key

Citation: Jarmo Heinonen, Mika Raassina and Nick Moss (2012). Processes Management for Quality of the Maintenance Service, Business Dynamics in the 21st Century, Dr. Chee-Heong Quah (Ed.), InTech, DOI: 10.5772/38590.

thing in productizing also is that it has given the marketers the opportunity to create sales collateral to create image and brand for the service organization. We can say that thanks to productizing we can now see well defined and well marketed service products available for both business and consumer customers. And information technology has enabled that even bigger part of the services are delivered by the customers of the organizations themselves. The public sector is following fluently the private one; just think how clarification of the state taxes in some countries has evolved during the last few years, making tax announcement handling easy both for the customer, the tax payer and the supplier, the taxman.

- But when we take steps beyond the service products we will face large variance. We find two big challenges concerning the service delivery.
- How the organizations ensure operational excellence of the whole service set-up over the lifetime of the entire product portfolio they have the obligation to serve?
- How the organization ensures constant high quality and meeting the customer requirements when its business is about delivering the s

Both of the research questions above have become vitally more important as the service models have been evolving from transactional contracts to KPI based service level agreements and further to long term performance based agreement where company is e.g. outsourcing its entire maintenance function to an external service provider.

The aim of the chapter

In this chapter the authors aim to provide an illustrative dialogue of the challenges that ensuring operational excellence includes and how a comprehensive processes management system can tackle the challenge over the life-cycle of the number of the agreements that the service provider has. The methodology is based on case presentation linked to background from literature and on the experience of the authors. The chapter gives input to further research as well as having a solid educational purpose.

Defining the business environment studied

The Authors have long experience in developing services and improving quality in a global industrial service business environment. Our recent work experience is with ABB, the leading, truly global and multinational power and automation Technology Company. Out of 135.000 people working at ABB more than 20.000 are working directly in service businesses, a fact that is not so well known in the market. Recently ABB has developed the ABB Group Service Strategy, aiming to triple the volume of the service business by the year 2015. ABB classifies its services into three very different main categories:

- Life-cycle services for ABB's own installed base
- Consulting services for reliability, safety, and energy efficiency
- ABB Full Service® for outsourced, performance-based maintenance of the entire production plant

As the business is a global one, productizing is essential in the ABB approach for standardizing and packaging service offerings. Service products are developed for the different phases of a product life cycle. The target is to offer customers service already before the introduction of the product up to the phase when product itself is obsolete but service is still required to lengthen the life cycle of the product or even to ensure the best result is achieved at the end of life and when a product is replaced/upgraded. The service development phase is very important when securing the successful launch and quality of ongoing activities. Thus the new service development is done in accordance with a specific service development process, the Stage-Gate Model. Service productizing itself does not guarantee the quality, thus the organization has developed a set of design, sell and deliver processes. The challenge is to agree and maintain a consistent approach across more than two dozen globally managed Business Units and in more than one hundred countries where local country service organizations are delivering the service.

ABB's maintenance outsourcing business differs strongly in nature from the product life cycle business. For the maintenance outsourcing business ABB has developed ABB Full Service® with the following definition:

"Globally supported long-term, performance-based agreements in which ABB commits to maintain and improve the production and equipment performance, energy efficiency and reliability for an entire facility with agreed cost base."

The definition above includes the following special characteristics when compared with life cycle service businesses or typical man-power related services:

- The service is performance based, the performance clause is linked directly to the customers production process outcome and customers financial results than just with the service providers own performance.
- The service agreement is long-term, typically a greater than five year evergreen agreement. Thus the quality must be defined for a long period into the future, the strategy, requirements and KPIs will probably change in the course of the time.
- The value proposition includes production performance improvement, energy cost saving and total maintenance cost optimization or saving, thus opening a very interesting but also a complex benefits definition.
- The provider will have a contractual commitment to some main customer KPIs. That commitment forces the provider to assume total management responsibility of the whole maintenance function, and the scope of the services is thus wide, typically covering maintenance management, development, engineering and execution. The typical pricing model is a fixed price covering labor, materials and sub-contracting.
- In outsourcing service the customer's related personnel is typically transferred to the provider, who in turn takes the responsibility for the safety, competence development, motivation and supervision of the people to be transferred. The service includes an enormous change management activity and potential as well.
- Also management of the maintenance materials and subcontracting are typically part of the agreement. The suppliers also need to be empowered, common targets created, and synergies plus economy of scale obtained. Suppliers will be used both for specialist services when suppliers are the technology owners and at the lower

end when they are expected to provide competitive man-power.

SERVICE MODELS EVOLVING TOWARDS PERFORMANCE PARTNERSHIPS

Nearly all industrial companies see production as a core competence, meaning that development of any production and product feature will directly connect the company into a position of competitive advantage. Production strategy is one of the core strategies of the company. To maintain the competitive position companies have started to ensure they are keeping focus in core competence by outsourcing non-core activities. In western countries support functions such as IT, payroll, cleaning, canteen, health care, security and facility management have been outsourced to external companies, rates usually being connected to the volume of labor consumed. These outsourcing projects are usually easy to do and argue – the function is outsourced to a provider who can give the most attractive, often man-hour based offering with low risk. These functions are not life important to the customers which is often demonstrated to the service provider as one inconvenient fact – very seldom does the facility management company get the chance to present and review the business case to a customer's CEO or COO.

In above cases the quality can be defined relatively easily. There exists a requirement for the service quality; service is usually seen in a transactional way where a key feature is to do the required amount of service correctly the first time. The customer controls the key service characteristic, (cost) by controlling the unit price and amount of the work done based on a clear contract and a bill of quantity based service contract. As we are in service, however the most relevant measure in transactional service is customer satisfaction, as the service outputs review will be basing on reporting certain jobs done.

Figure 1 illustrates how the transactional service is evolving to being KPI based and then further to performance based agreements. We can see that as the business model develops also the strategic nature of the agreement increases.

Table 1: Comparison of different business types regarding quality planning

Characteristic / OPEX topic	Business type		
	Product Supply	Product Based Services	Performance Based Services
Product Development	At Supplier	Mainly at Supplier	Close to customer Mainly with customer
Production	At Supplier	Visiting customer	Permanently at customer
Follow-up, KPI	On-time delivery	Response time	Customer output KPI
Reporting Analysis	Internal	Mainly internal	Mainly to customer
Review	At Supplier	Mainly at Supplier	Mainly at customer

We would want to add a quality angle in the figure as well. In a transactional relationship the service product is a commodity and the quality measurement is tied solely with the supplier's delivery. When we reach the "Performance Partnership" stage the service product is based on strategy and risk sharing and the quality measurement is clearly linked with the customer's outcomes, outcomes that will be obtained together, under a partnership relationship. We have here many angles and very seldom companies have clearly been able to specify the quality responsibility being of either partner's sole responsibility. Quality measurement and operational excellence become both more important and difficult.

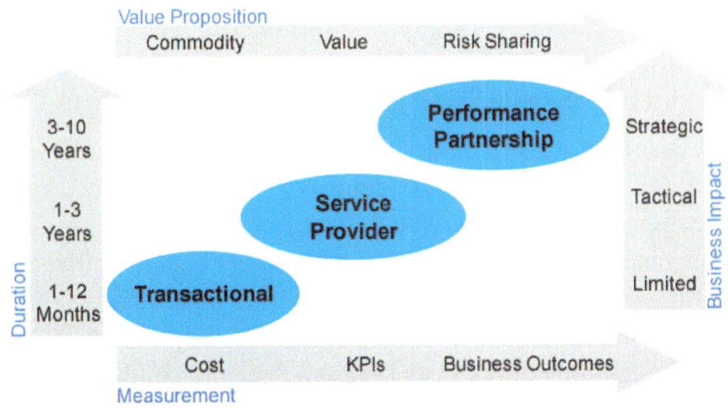

Figure 1: Evolution of service models (ABB, 2006).

When comparing characteristics of product based businesses, transactional based service businesses and performance based service businesses, the following characteristics can be found.

CUSTOMER'S PAINS REGARDING MAINTENANCE AND THE STRATEGIC OUTSOURCING DECISION

Asset performance management constraints

During the downturn many companies have significantly reduced maintenance costs, either by themselves or by reducing external services to a minimum and without proper management and a systematic approach. This approach has introduced significant risks for the future by generating remarkable levels of maintenance debt. Too often important reliability programs have been stopped and even banned, CMMS usage is often reduced and, too often, there is a clear drop in investments for asset health, maintenance management and competence development. Many maintenance managers are now struggling to convince higher management of the need to increase the maintenance to more sustainable levels.

The key element in industrial maintenance service is still cost. However when industries are expecting the market to recover, the focus on costs becomes focus on the costs of each produced unit and into increased manufacturing flexibility. Certainly, availability and total output (e.g. measured in terms of Overall Equipment Effectiveness, OEE) will be of greater importance as we are beginning to see a new born market for the increased output requirement. The key factor in requirements is the commodity price development. It has been favorable for most raw materials within the last year. But the expectation has been shaken more and more often with every new crisis somewhere in the world. Locally it can be the problems of a single industrial company, and also globally it is affected by, for example, the sudden political unrest in a number of Middle East countries in 2011.

Operations and maintenance are the key contributors to the operational profit of a company. The main pressures are in reducing costs and increasing efficiency. This includes efficiency in the use of raw materials e.g. Energy.

This is of particular relevance since maintenance has at least as high an impact on energy consumption as on plant availability itself. A good maintenance operator does not only contribute strongly in shutdowns, ramp-ups, and ramp-downs but also is key to considering how much energy is wasted during any phase of instability in production. We see a clear trend that a traditional maintenance outsourcing company will soon become a maintenance and energy stability company.

But there are also other challenges. Operational constraints need to be managed while improving sustainability. Asset Management has to be kept in balance over the long term. The main responsibility of operations is the maximum utilization of the assets and the main responsibility of maintenance is asset availability while managing the critical issues and operational constraints of the plant, especially in the areas of EHS. This means excellent cooperation between operations and maintenance while both need to be specialists in their own areas.

Figure 2 illustrates the challenges production and maintenance have. Without a good business plan, clear agreement between the two players and a consistent well defined process organization cannot take the best out of the two contributors. There must be a process management system in place and good comprehensive KPI's, i.e. we need Operational Excellence.

As the challenge is cost and the need for increased technological, automation and software know-how at the same time when the real specialists and performers are ageing, companies use more and more external services to solve bottlenecks and to balance consumption peaks, it is a strong trend and seldom is there a way back. Six clear arguments for maintenance outsourcing are listed below.

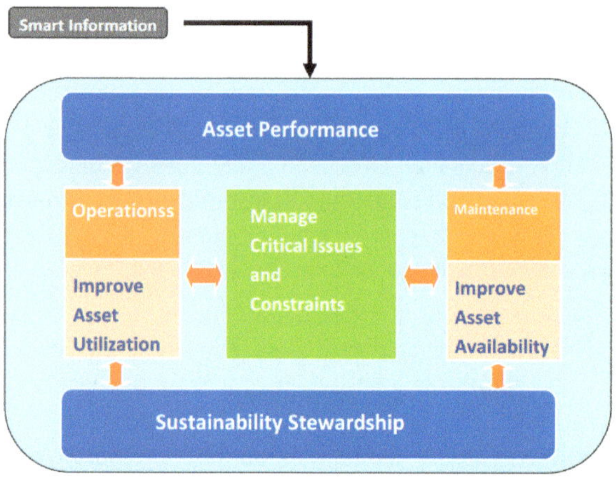

Figure 2: Asset performance management for process industries (ARC Strategies, 2010)

- Outsourcing companies are continuously developing their own core business, operational personnel and key management employees
- Allows company to concentrate its attention, efforts, and investments on core business and reallocate key resources and focus to strategically important issues
- Makes company lighter, more agile and able to react to the market with increased flexibility
- Improves access to knowledge not available internally to help address key problems
- Brings in world class resources, processes & best practices to;
  a. Reduce operating and ownership costs
  b. Make budgeting simpler and obtain predictable cash flow
  c. Speed up changes and improvements
  d. Reduce the dependency on individuals' skills
  e. Improve the utilization of resources
- Outsourced scope is clearly defined and measured to introduce disciplined execution and better management of risks

However there are also large concerns related with the outsourcing business case, labor issues, confidentiality, high dependency, staff moral, the binding nature of service agreements etc. Loss of control is also a concern, and for some individuals the concern is also around the perceived loss of power. In many instances the solution is to use strong purchasing tactics and to outsource to several service providers. The effect of this tactic is to keep the power status clear, however in everyday life there will be constraints when trying to enhance seamless co-operation, innovation and responsibility to solving the main production constraints (Figure 2).

Maintenance outsourcing to one single provider is a successful model when searching for better asset performance and short & long term nurture of the equipment. With good agreements the focus can be turned from constant control to collaboratively solving the production challenges and constraints and hence there is a solid opportunity for a win-winwin performance based approach and set of KPIs. But a lot is required when targeting to reach a performance based partnership (Figure 1). There needs to be a clear strategy and decision, the partners' cultures, business ethics and principles need to match at a company and also at a personal level, and a good business case must be on table before the customers' management, usually the board will make the decision.

The challenge for the service provider is to prove that a) total outsourcing is the solution and b) they are the right choice. Thus maintenance outsourcing companies need to show a good business case, solid references and evidence of solid approach, i.e. Operational Excellence in their own operations is a must. Both CAPEX and OPEX expenditure needs to be addressed in the business case, the decision maker must also look at both.

Service providers' challenge to respond

The adoption of strategic, performance based outsourcing has not been extremely fast. That is primarily due to the fact that at the end of the day proving the benefits of the agreement have not always been easy. In this area the following topics must be addressed:

- The benefits and targets must be agreed and communicated. Even if there is a study and a business case as a basis of the agreement the parties may not have made the contract review as defined e.g. in ISO 9000. The parties responsible for the delivery of the agreement are not always aware of the targets and KPIs. That can be the case on at the customer's side, on the provider's side or also on both sides.

- There must be a governance model and sponsors in place. As the key nature of performance based outsourcing is strategic, there needs to be top management support and understanding that the targets will be reached only by working together. That fundamental cannot be maintained in an everyday operational business environment without having champions that can review and solve any issues with objectivity and a view that is from external to the plant.
- Partners need to understand that moving to performance based partnership is a process of change. The change is deeply touching the existing maintenance team at a personal and identity level but it is also a remarkable opportunity to shake up the customer's organization. Colleagues become business partners and operators become real customers. That change is a remarkable resource which must also be understood. The service provider must have delicacy, experience and skills to run a professional change program and the customer must commit to be part of that program, standing as partner not as a master.
- The economical changes and multiple financial crises' one after another have changed the business case dramatically, huge flexibility has been required and the fundamentals of the clear, compelling business case have sometimes been crushed permanently. The performance based business case may have changed purely into a series of cost cutting requirements. Whatever investment that would have needed to guarantee successful and renewing implementation has often been taken away.
- The service provider must be extremely capable, must manage maintenance as a process and must be able to implement generic, industry and customer specific leading practices. That calls for a strong methodology, implementation skills generally and in the country or business in question, as well as a well prepared, experienced and motivated team. The site team must get coordinated support from service organizations, country organizations but importantly from the international specialists. We see too often cases where the service provider is not mature enough and has failed on the topics above, company has seen this as field service and the site team has been parachuted into the "jungle" without support, tools and processes.

We can conclude from above that successful performance based outsourcing requires a longterm view, a long and dedicated business development as well as execution process; agreement development skills and good sensitivity in identifying the motives of different levels of the organizations. Several workshops are needed to reach a good mental connection. The risks have to be identified and a mitigation plan must be developed. We must stress that to be successful, the mitigation plan is to be common, not just the providers' one.

MULTIPLE CUSTOMERS AND MULTIPLE INDUSTRIES – WHY A PROCESS IS NEEDED

The disciplined approach to respond to challenges that we analyzed in chapter two requires the service provider to have a clear strategy and a strong business model. Those need to be deployed efficiently across customer types and regions. Good way to deploy is to have a process management in place. Customers do want to see that the service provider can implement maintenance solution that supports customer's ever more changing strategy, is transparent and after all turns previous reactive maintenance strategy into more preventive and predictive mode, they key words in modern maintenance. In other words industrial customers want to see a process approach instead of fire fighting.

As most providers offering industrial maintenance are specialized not just one but various industries we have to discuss the nature of process model; is it general, do we need a specific process for each industry or shall the maintenance process model be customer specific? We analyze the topic here starting by understanding first what industrial maintenance is.

What is an industrial maintenance service?

Industrial maintenance usually refers to the repair and upkeep of the different types of equipment and machines used in an industrial setting. The basics of industrial maintenance know-how can be broken down into the following five categories:

- General knowledge,
- Mechanical knowledge,
- Electrical knowledge,
- Welding knowledge, and
- Preventative maintenance (Sasser).

According to this wide variety of areas of expertise, industrial maintenance technicians are usually multi-skilled individuals who are proficient in many tasks.

Industrial maintenance also involves a great degree of problem-solving skill. Identifying the problem along with the best and safest means of resolving the difficulty are typically integral parts of the industrial maintenance process. The general knowledge usually required in industrial maintenance is an understanding of tools, blueprint reading, and safety. The correct tools and the comprehension of how to use them can be crucial for fixing potential machinery problems. Blueprint reading enables the industrial maintenance technician to understand how a particular machine works. Safety is also a pivotal aspect of maintenance, as most industrial machines can be considered dangerous. Usually it is important for the technician to maintain his or her own safety, as well as that of other workers using the machinery.

The Industrial Services market may be defined by the level of added value provided by the services offering. The outsourcing task can be divided on the basis of value or coverage of the service into following four categories (AlixPartners):

- Outsourcing with low added value (Cleaning / Catering / Trade Fair Service / Security Service)
- Outsourcing with medium added value (Facility Management / Maintenance / Scaffolding / Installation)
- Outsourcing with high added value and/or project business (Planning of Facilities / High Value Services (IT, ...) / Maintenance of complex facilities)
- Industrial / Chemical park service (Utilities / Technical Service / Waste Management / Safety & Administration / Security)

Business models for industrial service

The maintenance provider's most critical task is to select the business model that enables sustainable business and satisfies the industry customer's present and anticipated needs. The strategy of an industrial maintenance provider needs to balance two main aspects:

- Customers' maintenance strategy. What will be customers' present and future decisions towards the needs of the external services; what do customers see as core competence; will the solutions be centralized/decentralized; which part of the maintenance management value chain will customers manage and provide themselves and which will they outsource; which kind of agreement models are preferable; what are customers' attitudes towards networking and partnership models; where will the pain points be; where are the competence and technology requirements; which are the internal factors that affect decision making; and, interestingly, how does time and new generations affect choices.
- Maintenance provider's own strategy. Where in the customers' value chain do we want to operate; where is the basis of our own competence and competitiveness; how do we differentiate; are we operating centralized/decentralized, locally/globally; what are our resources to develop competencies, maintenance solutions and technologies; how much can we add value; what is our readiness and capability to take risks and go for benefit sharing models; do we offer performance based models, know-how, resources; are we working in networks and for partnership; and do we see how time and selected industries to be served will affect our strategy.

As a result, the selected business model affects the market the industrial service provider is operating in. It is not just in which category but it is also which kind of service the provider offers. A maintenance provider with lower technology and industrial know-how usually focuses on offering workforce, managing capacity peaks, shorter term service or service level agreements, short response time, limited responsibility and risk taking. The maintenance provider that has industrial background and is a provider of some key equipment usually provides more technological services, spare parts, upgrades, training, etc. The maintenance provider who has experience in both maintenance management and has an industrial/equipment background can split the offering according to which customer strategy and needs as well as according to which markets are selected. For example, our company, ABB, has several categories in the service tree which can all be developed and differentiated in the industrial maintenance marketplace, see section 1.3.

Each business model has its own value proposition, commitment level, and agreement structure. Each business model's characteristics differ from the other models so that the business management structure and core processes to provide value to customers are also different to a certain extent.

What is general and what is industry specific?

However, 70–80% of maintenance can be claimed to be general, and the rest is industry- and customer-specific. We do not consider fire fighting and issue solving heroes as general maintenance but systematic maintenance core processes, including the management of partnership, designing for reliability and life-cycle, planning and scheduling, the management of the supplier network, re-engineering maintenance work-flows and integrating safety practices with work instructions and work orders, systematic root cause analysis, etc.

What can be seen as industry-specific are the specific safety procedures, equipment condition upgrades, process specific know-how, automation solutions, OEE measurement definitions, process optimization activities, and, naturally, industry-specific technologies.

Taking the Pulp and Paper Industry as an example, the following are considered as industry-specific issues within maintenance (Weissenfelt, 2011):

- Pulp and paper producing equipment knowledge. Knowledge of all the equipment needed from the wood yard to the end of the last conveyor before the forklift takes the paper roll or the pulp bale to the ship.
- Safety at work
- Troubleshooting
- Knowledge about chemicals used in the process and proper equipment materials to be used with special conditions
- Roll Service
- Quality Control System Service
- Drives Service and Optimization
- Profiling management
- Web Inspection System Service
- Quality requirements for the final product for customers
- Hydraulics
- Condition monitoring
- Lubrication

As the professional maintenance provider must focus on industry and understand industry requirements, a very specific advantage is the ability to learn from others. Maintenance related methodologies have been developing in different ways and been implemented at different levels in industries. As maintenance specialists we know a variety of good approaches but struggle with implementation. That is often because each industry has its own tradition and there are walls between the outside world and the plant; the "outside world" here means other industries. Learning from another industry is an extremely valuable source of continuous improvement when it comes to performance-based maintenance practices.

From the discussion above we can conclude the rationale that in an industrial maintenance outsourcing business environment the following process management characteristics are a good basis for a successful process management model:

- The maintenance management processes, core functional processes to deliver the maintenance and the required support processes are generic by nature. Greater value is created if the service provider has a learning environment where the leading practices as well as past mistakes are identified, reviewed and utilized in continuous improvement of the process than tailoring this level processes to specific industry or customer.

- The industry specific processes will become very valid when we are looking at maintenance at a task level. Job instructions, preventative maintenance plans, special tools and skills must be looked at with regard to industry competence level – as defined e.g. for the Pulp and Paper industry as addressed above. For example the root cause analysis methodology is standardized but the cause and solution is often industry specific.
- Customer customization will be seen in a very specific, exceptional equipment level where the technical solution is really tailored for that customer only. Key customer specific nominator is the customer's production and maintenance strategy. That does not specify the maintenance process itself but feeds the essential criticality and focus into the process. Well understood strategy will lead to update of plant, line or equipment level (technical) maintenance strategy, criticality classification, scheduling of maintenance tasks and to addressing relevant KPI's and reporting guidelines. As such it does not change the process.

THE SERVICE DELIVERY PROCESS – FROM SINGLE ACTIVITY TO DELIVERING MULTI-YEAR AGREEMENTS

Here we present ABB Full Service® approach to develop a processes management system. We will introduce the ABB model; determine the specific elements and the link between the approach and the results. We also give a general process description and a more detailed definition of each process.

After analysis conducted in ABB we have decided that the process management model is a good approach for managing operational excellence in a long-term outsourced maintenance business. The model needs to cover the whole business to ensure consistency, discipline and learning. Thus a good process management model needs to cover:

- The whole life-cycle of the maintenance outsourcing agreement. There shall be a process for service design and development, sales and business development, delivery of the multidimensional service tasks and finally the review and assessment cycle.
- The different types of processes. We can use general definitions of different process types, e.g. EFQM (European Foundation for Quality Management) categorizes processes into management processes, support processes and core processes.
- Processes for the life-cycle of a customers' plant. There is a slightly different need for existing plant (Brownfield), newly built pant (Green field) and also for demobilizing of the plant.
- The industry applications. As mentioned above each industry needs adaptation of the process to cover specific technically detailed areas.

Tools to define a process

To define a good process is a piece of art itself. Key attributes of a process are that the process is crossing several organizational boundaries, it is directed to meet the external or internal customer requirement, it can and will be repeated again and again and it needs to be measured and monitored. A good process is robust; it is designed to be in use for long periods, even if continuously reviewed for improvements. We say that organizational structures come and go, processes will remain.

A very important feature of the process is that it needs to be understandable and logical. People should understand why we do this, what is the purpose of the process and what is going on in the chain of activities, how information is shared. Processes cannot just be huge, room-size flow-charts or to be hidden into fancy process management IT system. Process must be visual.

The cross-boundary nature of the process gives a challenge for leadership and management. Executives need to show the commitment to the process, participate in process definition and meaningful process KPI set-up, they need to empower teams to work across the process, define clear ownership with mandate, and they need to demonstrate the process and results-finally presenting the process rather than the organizational chart. Process KPIs should be the key KPIs and process champions making the process successful shall be recognized. Companies should also be proud of their processes, present to customers and make sure that customers and suppliers are part of the process also giving valuable input for the improvement.

There are plenty of excellent tools to define and manage a process, as process management is definitely one of the key approaches in any Quality Management program or Six Sigma approach. We address here some central approaches ABB has used in maintenance outsourcing services.

SIPOC

As learned from above, good process definition is the key. There is not such a thing as "the right process", we can only talk about process in terms of excellence – more or less excellent.

That is why there must be a cross-function and or cross-border team to define the process together, involvement means commitment. The purpose of the process is necessarily not at all clear when the definition works starts, each participant views the purpose, inputs and out puts from his/her own point of view. The SIPOC tool is particularly useful when it is not clear (Simon, 2011):

- Who supplies Inputs to the process?
- What specifications are placed on the Inputs?
- Who are the true Customers of the process?
- What are the Requirements of the customers?

The SIPOC comes from the key words of process principle definition: Suppliers, Input, Purpose, Outcomes, and Customers. We have learned that any process has more than one customers, or stakeholders. So there will b a variety of other factors as well. SIPOC can be used for defining the purpose of one single process as well ad the whole business system. Figure 3 gives a visual template used in process definition.

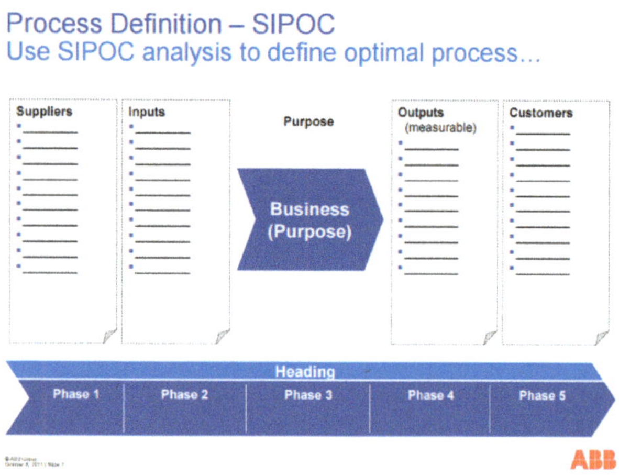

Figure 3: SIPOC template used as business and process purpose definition

RACI

Another key issue on top of purpose is the ownership of the process. As process nature is most often cross organizational clear roles and information principles are needed. If these are not in place the process gets stuck, becomes meaningless or causes more problems than brings benefits. When talking about responsibility we find that that different kind of roles are needed to make a process successful. The approach widely adapted is RACImatrix.

The RACI model is a straightforward tool used for identifying roles and responsibilities and avoiding confusion over those roles and responsibilities during a project. The acronym RACI stands for (Haughey, 2011):

- *Responsible*: The person who does the work to achieve the task. They have responsibility for getting the work done or decision made. As a rule this is one person; examples might be a business analyst, application developer or technical architect.
- *Accountable*: The person who is accountable for the correct and thorough completion of the task. This must be one person and is often the project executive or project sponsor. This is the role that responsible is accountable to and approves their work.
- *Consulted*: The people who provide information for the project and with whom there is two-way communication. This is usually several people, often subject matter experts.
- *Informed*: The people who are kept informed about progress and with whom there is one-way communication. These are people that are affected by the outcome of the tasks so need to be kept up-to-date.

Without clearly defined roles and responsibilities it is easy for projects to run into trouble. When people know exactly what is expected of them, it is easier for them to complete their work on time, within budget and to the right level of quality.

A RACI matrix supports the model and is used to discuss, agree and communicate roles and responsibilities.

Process visualization

There are several ways to visualize how the process flows on. Selection of the visualization depends on the purpose and on the amount of information that is intended to show. Typically organizations want to show task, responsibilities and time in the process description. Then the model is flow-chart. Flow-chart is the most popular process definition format as it brings in time well. Strength is that each unit or department can easily see and understand in which tasks own and other's responsibilities are. There are also many IS solutions for process mapping that support flow-chart appearance, so the visualization can be linked with some real data.

A flowchart is a diagrammatic representation that illustrates the sequence of operations to be performed to get the solution of a problem. Flowcharts are generally drawn in the early stages of formulating computer solutions. Flowcharts facilitate communication between programmers and business people. These flowcharts play a vital role in the programming of a problem and are quite helpful in understanding the logic of complicated and lengthy problems. Once the flowchart is drawn, it becomes easy to write the program in any high level language. Often we see how flowcharts are helpful in explaining the program to others. Hence, it is correct to say that a flowchart is a must for the better documentation of a complex program (WebZip News, 2011).

The negative side of flow-chart is that it easily gets very extensive and complicated, and the purpose may remain unclear. The font in the print is either too small to see or the print becomes so big that printing is troublesome and expensive. On computer screen flow-chart is seldom visible at one glance.

Process arrow is very practical when organization wants to address the purpose and overall understanding. The important phases and activities can easily be listed and agreed, and the print and screenshot can be visual and even attractive. Process arrow can be broken down into sub-arrows when a good structure from high level to detail can be built, organization is forced to build structured model which e.g. is typical way of thinking in maintenance people who are used to build equipment hierarchies and criticality and root cause analysis.

Downside in process arrow is that phases and tasks are by assumption sequential by time and that is not the case in all cases. Also detailed responsibilities cannot be shown easily in the arrows. Well managed process arrow needs either flow-chart or instruction to be more specific.

Closed loop is typical way of process visualization when there is the need to show loops. Annual planning and reporting cycles are typical closed circle visualizations, in these is easy to show moving to next quarter or next phase. However circle can include limited amount of information and making good visualization is bigger job and needs specialist support for tools to be used.

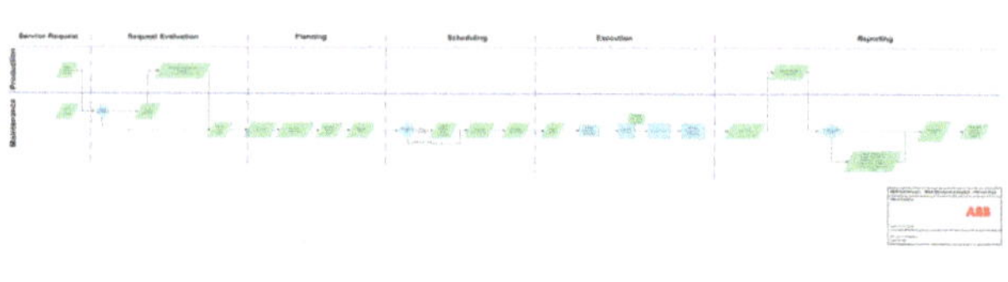

Figure 4: Example of a simplified flow-chart, Maintenance work-order flow

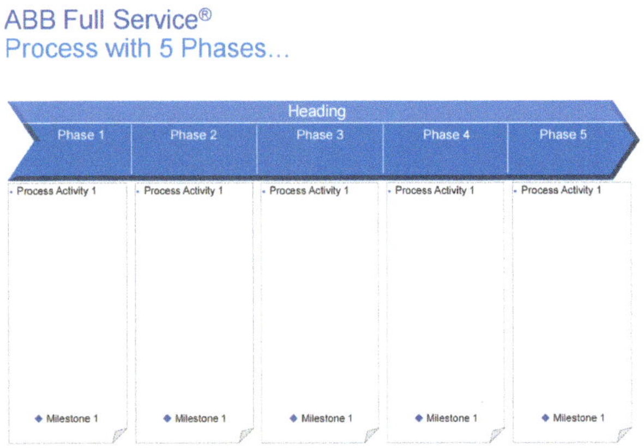

Figure 5: Process arrow, ABB process arrow template, 5 phases

In ABB Full Service® Concept they key process definition approaches are to create first an overall process model, the big picture where all the management, support and core processes needed to bring the results are visualized, including the results area. Then the main process description level is process arrow, as it is highly visual, all the different processes can be shown with standardized format, and needed tools can be "hung" on the process. For many design and sales related processes the arrow model is sufficient and much more detail is not needed. When we speak about very operational processes like doing preventative maintenance task or managing a shutdown the applied model is flowchart. In many instances the flow-chart supports the process arrow, and is also furnished with IT solution such as CMMS system work flow.

Case: The ABB Full Service® process model

The ABB Full Service® business excellence model is the comprehensive management model of the outsourced maintenance business, presented in figure 6. The model is designed to cover the overall life cycle of the maintenance outsourcing business.

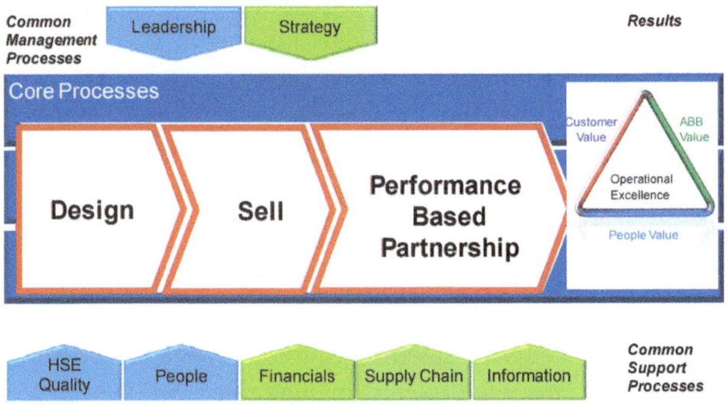

Figure 6: ABB Full Service® Business Excellence model

The main process types are common management processes, core processes and common support processes. The core processes main focus is to deliver the results for the maintenance outsourcing agreement. Common management processes give the framework for the important management processes Leadership and Strategy. The common support processes are vital to support core processes in the creation of value. This model is based on the experience of managing a 1 BUSD global maintenance outsourcing business and in the structure we have adapted the global business excellence models, i.e. EFQM Excellence Model (EFQM, 2011). When considering the definition of the processes the level and phase of the operation must be considered. In the business management model we need to identify how the service product and business model is designed, how the business development or sales is conducted and how the service itself is delivered. In the chain of core processes we have identified processes designing and delivering client value as core processes. Others then are considered as management or support processes. We have to remember also that these definitions can be considered as an agreement within the organization. The definition of what is core is dependent on the strategy and interpretation of customer needs, and the result is an agreement and most often a consensus.

In the ABB Full Service® model the first core process is "Design". That process covers the sub processes that help to identify the market evolution, select the service product strategy with related business models, the development process of those models and finally the exposure, all related marketing activities. That process is globally led and coordinated, to ensure that we have a unified service product and offering in each target market. The Design process can be seen as global process even if the delicacy or specialization comes from the regional and local distribution of the responsibilities.

The second core process is "Sell". In the performance partner model maintenance outsourcing business a more descriptive name could be "Business Development". Each pursuit goes through a long sequence before the business case and value proposition is possible to be developed, identified and presented to the customer. The Sell process can be globally or locally executed but we see that the sales management is best to be global to ensure correct customer selection and focus, professionalism in pursuit development, value proposition creation and agreement development. Most often the maintenance outsourcing pursuits are also big and developing the value proposition requires special skills and knowhow, i.e. teaming cross borders and industries. The sales is performed by a capture team and the phases from "Screening" all the way to executing the "Performance Based Partnership" is visualized in Figure 7.

The third core processes model is "Performance based Partnership". Here the globally developed maintenance alliance agreement will be executed under a long term agreement. Differently from the former processes which have been clearly globally managed this set of processes needs to be managed at site level. Site level capability to manage the core processes in value adding way always requires utilization of external support and tools. A consistent process model is necessary to enable efficient external support for site operations; it is also the key to operational excellence as the performance partnership model calls for implementing world-class approaches.

The core execution processes in ABB Full Service® concept are based on the strategic targets of the value proposition.

Partnership Fulfillment is the customer relationship focused process that is vital to ensure that the agreement targets will be turned into strategy based operational targets, customers are listened too at any moment as well as value is created and benefits validated.

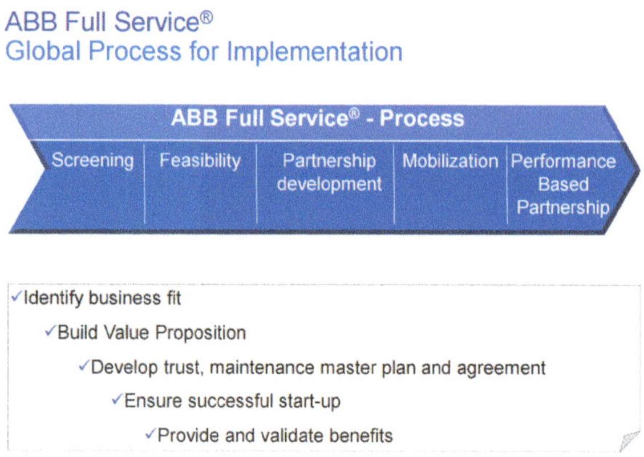

Figure 7: ABB Full Service® business development process from screening to execution

Reliability Maintenance is the backbone process of the model, ensuring that customer's asset value is maintained properly, reliability is improved based on critical issues from the customer's production strategy, and the life-cycle of assets is managed with systematic approach.

Maintenance Operations is a process to ensure that the work-flow for different maintenance technical strategies is optimized, the customer's short and long term requirements are fulfilled at shop floor level; and that systematic planning leads to reducing total maintenance hours used at the same time than reliability is improved. A very essential component is the smart and disciplined utilization of the CMMS.

Energy Efficiency Improvement is the process where professional maintenance can deliver a large amount of value. It is about everyday awareness and focus to manage maintenance, shut-downs, ramp-ups and ramp-downs in a smart, energy efficient way. It is also monitoring energy waste, planning, implementing and financing investments that are proposed based on monitoring and identifying waste.

Plant Performance Improvement is the process that has the most impact on the performance based maintenance agreement. Here the service provider has the strong motive to capture plant performance and other relevant KPI's, drive with passion the root cause analysis and continuous improvement activities, provide technological and soft solutions to improve the production and maintenance processes and to bring in global resources to support the customer to gain a competitive edge in terms of plant performance and operations.

As the site can and must focus on agreement fulfillment it needs a guideline and support from a combination of management and support processes. Leadership is to be seen mostly at a site level process where the leader demonstrates target orientation, partnership. Strategy sets up the strategy process, ensures that maintenance outsourcing agreement brings benefits to all stakeholders, customer, ABB and employees. The support processes take care of the essential support activities around HSE, people management, financial management, supply chain and welding business supporting IS systems of the partners together.

Results is the area that proves that the outsourcing agreement has been the right choice. In ABB Full Service® this essential part of the business model is visualized by a balanced score card model. The model is visually stronger and more attractive by using a triangle to addresses the key essential values, client, ABB and people.

The process models described above are the standard "Boilerplate" model, however variations need to be considered depending on the scope of the agreement, whether the customer's business type is an existing plant (Brownfield) or where we would work with a cradle to grave approach (Greenfield) Also considered but of less importance is the variations between customer industries where a more specific or detailed process is required.

EXAMPLE OF A SPECIFIC PROCESS – RELIABILITY MAINTENANCE

In this chapter we dive deeper into the detail of the most essential service process in maintenance; Reliability Maintenance, which is ABB's approach for implementing worldclass reliability engineering. Introduced in this section will be how ABB's reliability maintenance process contributes to operational excellence.

What then is reliability? The US military standard defines it as follows: "Reliability is the probability that an item will perform its intended function for a specific interval under stated conditions"(DOD, 1981). Reliability is a broad term that focuses on the ability of a product to perform its intended function. Mathematically speaking, assuming that an item is performing its intended function at time equals zero, reliability can be defined as the probability that an item will continue to perform its intended function without failure for a specified period of time under stated conditions. Please note that the product defined here could be an electric, electronic, mechanical hardware product, a software product, a manufacturing process or even a service.

When looking back to not so long ago, we find that the designers of new production equipment were also the builders, operators and maintainers of their equipment. They had a close relationship in all aspects with their hardware and they, for a fact did "know" their equipment; what worked, how well, and for how long, what broke, how to fix it, and how to take reasonable (but not too expensive) preventive actions to avoid future failures (Smith 2003). In this environment there also developed exceptionally good senses based condition monitoring routines and experience was the major source to define preventive maintenance programs.

As later there emerged a requirement for higher production capacity and increased efficiency, technology developed to be more and more sophisticated and more complicated, leading companies to specialize solely in manufacturing production equipment or operating those equipment to manufacture end products for their clients. This was a necessary development to enable economical growth throughout the world, but it came also with down sides, one was the increasing challenge to design effective preventive maintenance plans since experience over total life cycle of equipment was scattered between several companies making feedback from operators and maintainers to the designers difficult.

Presently when end users take over their operations they have limited knowledge about the reliability of the equipment, in parallel, the manufacturers try to design the most reliable products and systems but have limited information about the actual operating conditions. It is clear that the combined experience of both these parties will lead to the improvement in overall availability and reliability of the production equipment. Another factor greatly affecting equipment reliability is how limited resources, both financial and physical are utilized to maintain or improve reliability. Today too often we can see that preventive and predictive maintenance plans are inadequately designed or if those are well designed the execution of tasks are neglected. On the other hand there is constantly increasing demand for improved equipment reliability, demand coming from our society to conserve natural recourses and energy, protect our environment and to improve safety.

One of the ABB Full Service® core processes is Reliability Maintenance, which is presented in figure 8 under. In that picture it is also shown how the reliability maintenance process is embedded into the whole operational excellence model. In the next section ABB's reliability process will be discussed in more detail.

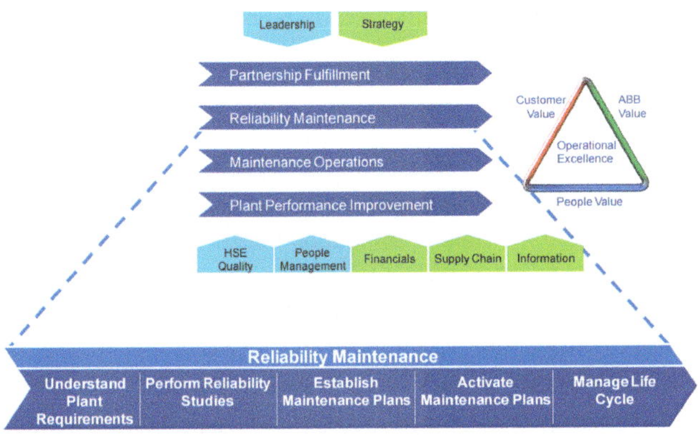

Figure 8: ABB Full Service® Reliability Maintenance process

The Reliability Maintenance process aims to maximize the life of equipment and minimize consequence of failures. It sets a consistent standard for processes and tools for all activities across the plant to assist the organization with the maintenance plan reviews and the asset life cycle management. In the next sections each phase of the process is discussed in more detail.

Understanding plant requirements

In this first phase of the Reliability Maintenance Process implementation, the main idea is to obtain a snap shot of the production facility and equipment with respect to reliability issues. There are several methods to assess the current state of reliability at the production plant. ABB has developed its own tool for this assessment, the Reliability Audit. Engineers at site assess four important aspects within reliability engineering, those are:

- Reliability Planning
- Maintenance plans
- Root Cause Analysis (RCA)
- Precision Maintenance

In each area there are predefined multiple choice questions. This enables ABB to compare, notify gaps and set targets for the reliability implementation (Vicente, 2011). Figure 9 displays an example of the reliability audit tool.

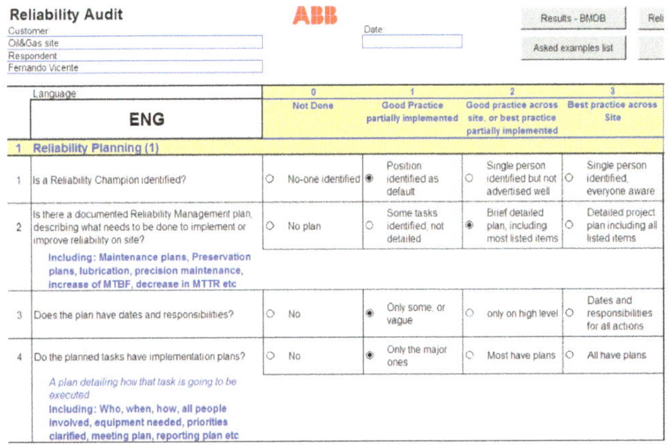

Figure 9: Example of Reliability Audit tool

Perform reliability studies

Once key reliability challenges have been identified, a complete equipment classification analysis will be completed to give an equipment maintenance prioritization. The purpose of equipment classification is to give each piece of equipment or in some cases subcomponent a single classification, A, B or C, considering all factors related to the impact of failure to the manufacturing process. The classification project highlights which equipment needs to be addressed first to ensure reliability; this type of analysis is performed together by engineering, maintenance and operational (production) personnel. An example of classification factors and equipment criticality are described in Figure 10 below. Before starting a new equipment classification project the description of classification levels will be thoroughly checked and agreed in advance between maintenance and production personnel. For example a paper mill will defined Frequency Factor totally differently to the electronics manufacturing plant. In a logical selection tree is prepared to assist personnel in coming to a conclusion of the classification of each equipment; an example of the logic selection tree is presented in Figure 11.

EVALUATION FACTOR	LEVEL 1	LEVEL 2	LEVEL 3
Safety Risks for people	Equipment failure affects seriously people	Equipment failure causes risks to people	No consequence
Environment Risks for the environment	Equipment failure affects seriously environment	Equipment failure causes risks to the environment	No consequence
Quality Effect of failure on product quality	Failure affects quality, generating out-of-specification products or affecting seriously the revenue	Equipment failure makes product quality variable and affects revenue	No effect on the product or revenue
Working Shift Working shift of the equipment	Equipment is required 24 hours per day	Equipment is used more than half of a day	Occasional use
Production Effect of equipment failure on production	Equipment failure causes total interruption of production	Failure causes interruption of an important system or unit, or reduces production	There is spare equipment or it is cheaper to repair the equipment after failure
Frequency Number of failures in determined period	Many shutdowns due to failures (more than once per 6 months)	Occasional shutdowns (once per 6 months)	Not frequent (less than once a year)
Cost Amount of money involved in the failure	Repairing time and costs are very high	Repairing time and costs are high	Repairing time and costs are not significant

Figure 10: Criticality classification table

All details of how class (A, B, C) has been assigned to equipment are documented. If modifications or investments are subsequently made to these equipment, it is easy to check from a well documented criticality analysis if the classification needs to be changed. The ABB logic tree is also translated into algorithms so that when equipment data is downloaded from the

Computerized Maintenance Management System (CMMS) there are ready made dropdown lists and formulas creating ease of use, documented traceability and efficient time utilization in the criticality analysis meetings.

Another important task inside this phase is to understand the operational context and failure behaviour based on equipment history and experience that can sometimes be very different to those failure modes considered by the OEM during the design phase.

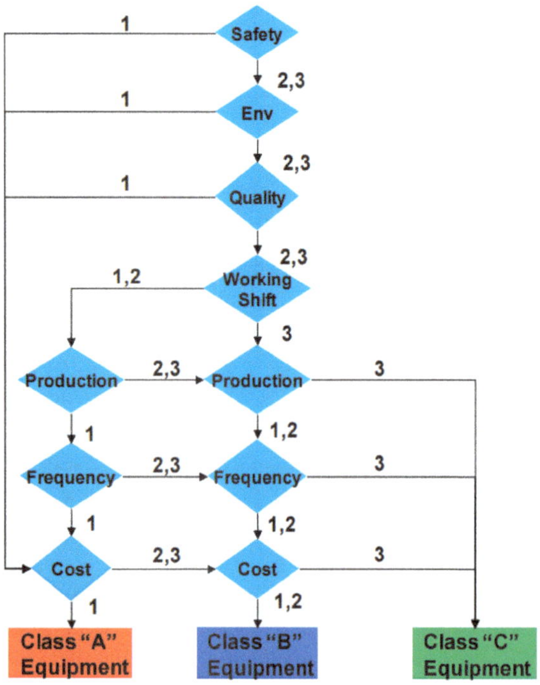

Figure 11: Decision logic diagram

As an end result of this phase there will be a criticality analysis completed and a classification assigned to each piece of equipment.

Establish maintenance plans

After equipment classification, failure and operational context are studied, reliability analysis developed and then preventative maintenance plans (PM's) will be uploaded or updated in the CMMS. For A-class (the most critical) equipment, common RCM principles like FMEA can be used to identify functional failures and then logical thinking used to define how each functional failure can be avoided. There is often temptation to utilize only existing experience to define preventive maintenance plans in this phase, without any documentation as to why those PM's were chosen. Again thorough documentation would support more effective future development.

There are numerous pieces of commercial software available for reliability analysis. It has to be noted that software itself does not create preventive maintenance plans, although in skilled hands they are powerful tools to assist in analysis, decision support and documenting arguments for preventive maintenance plans. Not having dedicated software is no reason to avoid running the reliability maintenance process; all phases of the process can be completed successfully without reliability software.

In figure XX there is one simple template presented to support documented failure prevention planning. This template is utilizing commonly available RCM methodology. After identifying functional failures the significance of each functional failure will be defined in the upper left part, questions 1 to 4 in Figure 12 under. For each question a yes or no answer is given and some documentation as to why each answer was given. When the significance of the failure is defined there will be questions (from A to F) to assist on formulating the functional failure preventive actions. The principle should be that actions to define equipment condition while it is left running are preferred to obtain an early indication of possible maintenance needs without disrupting the manufacturing process.

As a result of this phase there will be actions to prevent functional failures defined for the most critical equipment.

Activate maintenance plans

When the required preventive actions are defined, those actions must be planned and scheduled which means that each task will have resources assigned, possible materials to be identified and then the execution interval is to be defined.

In operational excellence it is important to recognize that it is not enough to define correct failure prevention actions, but those actions must be uploaded into the CMMS and most importantly for the execution of those important actions is the proper training and instruction for technicians. Getting feedback from the technicians to improve the preventive maintenance plans further is closing the loop of continuous reliability improvement on site.

Results of this phase of the process are detailed maintenance plans which are executed on time by trained and well instructed personnel.

Manage life cycle

After preventive maintenance routines have shown their value by reducing failure rates, there is then organisational capacity freed up for longer term planning of equipment strategies. Long term life cycle plans will be prepared for the critical or expensive equipment to determine when major repairs or replacement investments are most favourable to be undertaken. For this phase ABB reliability engineers also selectively connect equipment OEM's. From the OEM's there is often information of their equipment life cycle available, under (figure 13) is example from ABB's drives life cycle classification, which supports decision making on modernization of equipment if equipment are in obsolete or limited phase.

When considering capital investments life cycle costing (LCC) is one way of analysing equipment purchase choices. If the analysis is completed correctly, all factors are addressed, and the quality of information is good, the item that costs the least amount to own (buy and use) over its working life would be selected. When compared to other suitable items this piece of equipment would perform its lifetime service with the least total cost to the organization.

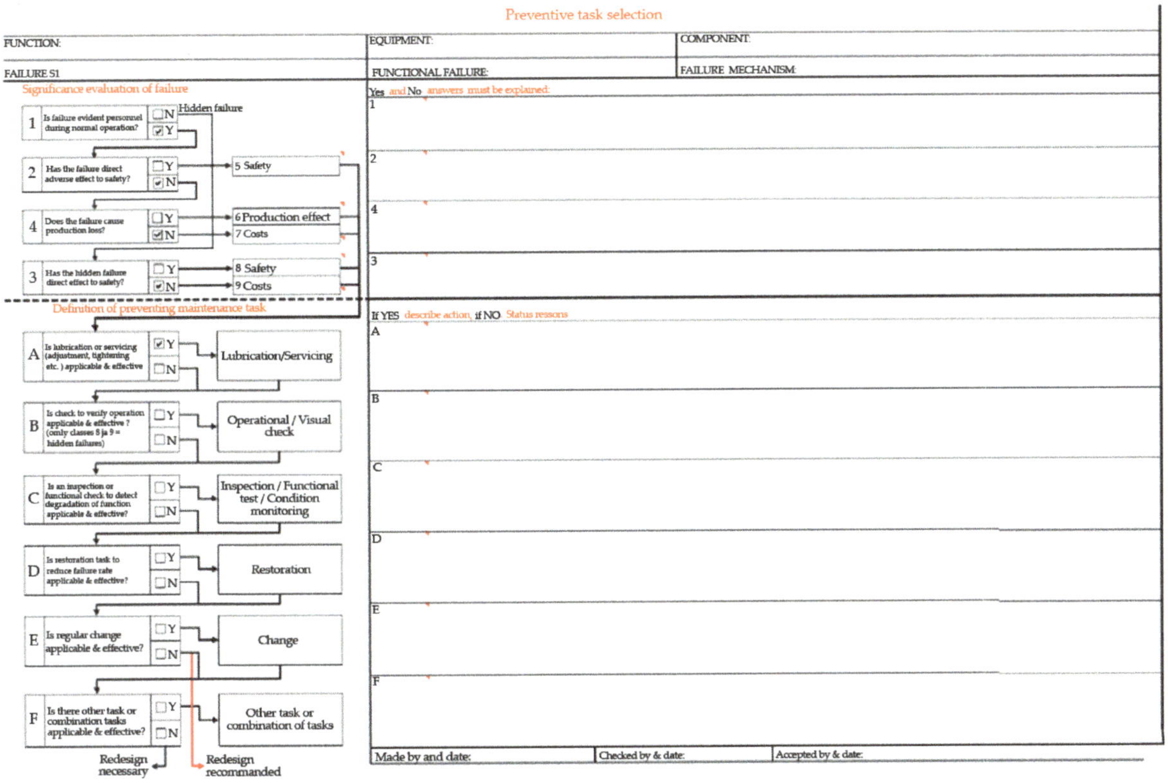

Figure 12: Preventive action planning support tool (adapted from Moubrey, 1997)

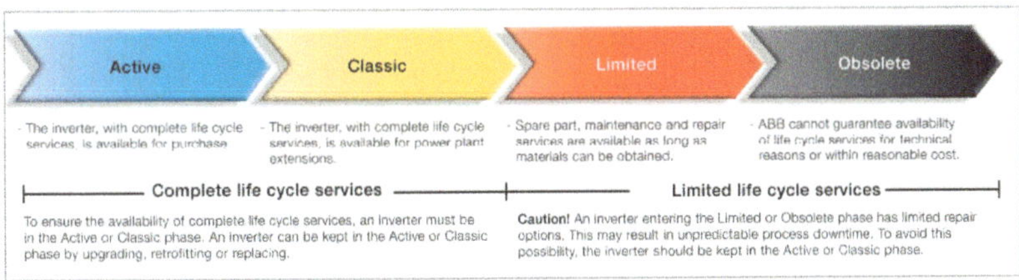

Figure 13: Example of solar drives life cycle classification (ABB, 2011)

When buying equipment there are three things to know - purchase cost, running cost and maintenance cost. The combination of these over the equipment's life is its LCC. A low LCC means the least amount of money necessary was spent on it, while a high LCC means extra money was spent and that money was then not available for other things. From a purely financial viewpoint it is sensible to go for equipment with the lowest LCC possible. But it is not only the cost of equipment that needs to be considered when purchasing it.

As a simple example of the process we will choose a lawn mower. The options are a reel mower or a rotary mower. First is started by developing a simple table like the one below listing the frequency and costs of the activities expected to occur throughout its working life. The costs and frequency are the standard ones from the manufacturers and the parts and service people. Then we take the recommendations of the manufacturers and service specialist so that the comparisons are based on facts and opinion of knowledgeable persons.

Above calculation shows that rotary mower has the best LCC being the cheapest to own. Does that mean people will not buy a reel mower? Off course not. People buy reel mowers because they leave a better quality of cut on the lawn and are self-propelled. It is not always the cost that determines the selection, at times the functionality of the equipment is also important. Putting a value on functionality is difficult when compared to putting a value on a piece of machinery. Functionality is measured in job time savings, accidents not incurred, overtime not worked, people not having to be employed, etc. LCC falls short in that aspect of justifying equipment.

Table 2: LCC calculation sheet

	Reel Mower	10 Year Cost	Rotary Mower	10 Year Cost
Purchase Price	1 off	$900	1 off	$700
Fuel for 10 Years	120lt.	$120	120lt.	$120
Service Every	5 year	$240	3 year	$240
Replace Blades Every	3 year	$600	1 Year	$500
Total Cost for 10 Years		$1860		$1560

Outcomes of this process phase are investment and major repair plans for the equipment owner. These long term plans are extremely important to give the owner the chance to plan future expendature and also to evaluate risks related with delaying investments.

Summary

The Reliability Maintenance Process is a good example of how operational excellence is implemented in practice; there is well defined standard process to be followed and all actions are carefully documented. As a result of successful work significantly reduced failure rates, reduced maintenance cost and improved reliability of machinery can be achieved. Also maintenance work is more motivating for the employees due to fact that only meaningful maintenance actions are kept and executed.

SUPPORTING THE PROCESS MANAGEMENT – KEY INFORMATION SYSTEMS CONSIDERATIONS

There are huge volumes of various information to be managed related to the maintenance of production equipment e.g. equipment technical data, warranty information, all planned work details, various reports and test results, monthly KPI information, personnel information and drawings. Commonly this data is scattered around the organization into different systems or archives, some data is in electronic format and some only exists on paper. On top of data management there is the challenge to make relevant data available for all personnel requiring access to it. An extra challenge comes when a service provider works for a different company than that of the machinery owner. These two companies will most probably have different IT/IS policies which can create obstacles for effective data sharing and access. And adding to this challenge, existing systems are not often capable of providing information easily and with user friendly interfaces.

When finding solutions for the above mentioned challenges there is often a lot of design work done before setting up any IS solution. The IS team who will be responsible for configuring the new system (CMMS or other knowledge sharing system) will be first updated with maintenance and production strategies so that they fully understand what the priorities are. Then that team will gather the reporting needs from maintenance, e.g. what KPI's are needed to be available from the system and what other standard reports are needed. When understanding needs it is easier to create standard workflows for maintenance (see figure 4 In section 5.1.3 as example of the workflow). Then all of this information is translated into configurations in the CMMS and other information systems. ABB has traditionally selected IBM Maximo to be utilized as a global standard solution for maintenance management. Into that global system standard workflows have been created for maintenance activities. This standardization brings benefits in faster start-ups of new installations and also when personnel move between sites it is easier to adapt into new working environment when there are familiar functions in the system, this also reduces training requirements.

The basic principle in ABB has been that the CMMS is the heart of knowledge, all maintenance related information should end up in that system. Unfortunately not 100% of information is economically viable to keep in that system, e.g. consider the cost of digitizing 100.000 paper format drawings only to have them in CMMS for an uncertain future need. But still, when ever new projects is executed and above mentioned principle kept in mind it steers the companies into requiring new documentation from supplier in such a format that it can be electronically linked to equipment in the CMMS. The same principle applies to reports created by maintenance or their subcontractors, e.g. thermography, oil analysis and vibration measurement reports should be also linked to the relevant equipment. Collecting comprehensive information can greatly help future planning, failure prevention and troubleshooting.

There is also information needed to be shared which is not necessarily so relevant to be kept in CMMS. Let's say for example the monthly performance reports generated for the customer need to available easily and to a large audience in two different companies. The newly developed SharePoint solutions bring a good platform for sharing various kind of information not shared through the CMMS.

IS solutions are one of the most challenging areas to be well managed when creating a partnership with two companies, these systems need to be in place to ensure a high quality service, open communication and development based on facts. Modern IS solutions offer all the needed functionality, although the cost to fully implement those is usually high, so to guarantee value on money spent advance planning is essential and must be completed with care.

CLOSING THE LOOP – MEASURES AND ASSESSMENT OF THE SERVICE DELIVERY

Measuring service delivery

Performance of the service delivery is measured with a predefined set of Key Performance Indicators (KPI). A Key Performance Indicator is an common word for identifying the most important measures of the performance. KPI's are usually supported with a set of Performance Indicators (PI's). KPIs are commonly used by an organization to assess its success or the success of a specific activity in which it is engaged. A Key Performance Indicator is a measurement used to quantify advancement towards strategic objectives set as elements of a strategy. These indicators will differ depending upon the nature of the business and its strategic objectives. KPIs differ per business areas where companies are functioning, although there are some common KPI's that can be used in any business the KPIs that maintenance a service company might use are: safety indicators (e.g. Lost Time Incidents, near misses) customer satisfaction, revenue, profitability, maintenance cost/produced unit, spare parts consumption cost, spare parts stock value, employee satisfaction, personnel utilization rate, portion of preventive and predictive maintenance out of total maintenance hours.

Service providers should invest a considerable amount of time and resources in understanding what is really the most significant performance information that describes success and indicates if the service unit is on track in executing its strategy. It is also significant to notice what KPI's are most suited to different level of the organization – not all KPI's that are critically important to maintenance team are so important for the finance team for example.

Then after KPI's have been agreed, those should be kept in force long enough to be able to show the development of the KPI result. It is vitally important to follow long term trends together with short term ones. For its service delivery ABB has developed a follow-up tool that fulfills the reporting needs of service delivery. An example of the output of one KPI is presented in Figure 14. Naturally all KPI's should be available in the same format. It is important to record why results have been reached, since KPI's must be later on analyzed.

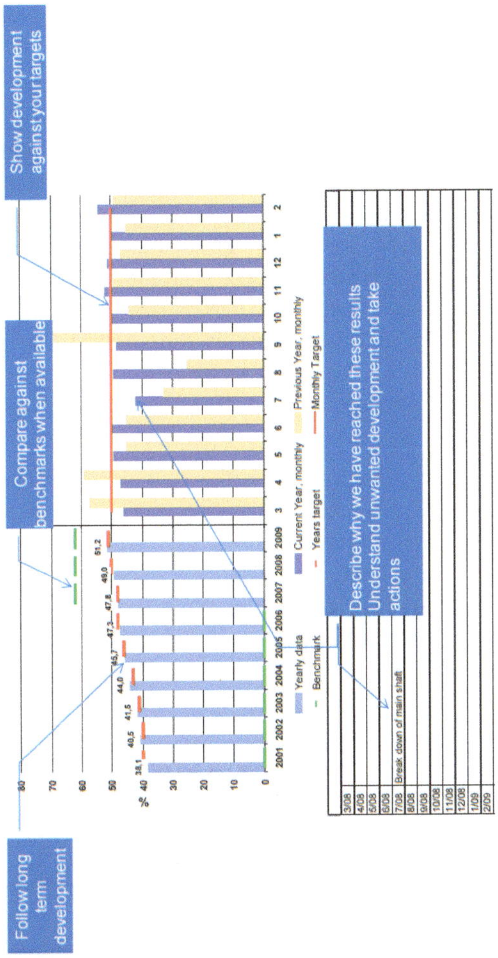

Figure 14: Example of Key Performance Indicator follow-up (ABB, 2006)

If benchmarks are available for the measured KPI's (either internally from the corporation or even external) those should be used to gain wider understanding of how much more room for improvement there is before becoming best in class. Most importantly there must be targets set for each KPI, otherwise less effective to measure.

Due to the need for understanding of what is significant the choice of KPI's is often associated with the use of various techniques to assess the current state of the service delivery, and its key activities. These assessments can be internal development meetings or external assessments of the service unit's performance. These assessments often lead into the identification of improvement potential and as a result, realization of the performance indicators normally initiates improvement projects. In the next sub-section the method ABB uses to assess its service delivery performance is described.

Assessment of service delivery

Full Service Assessment closes the loop for ABB Full Service® operational excellence. Assessment is the tool to verify how efficient the service unit is in the implementation of the Full Service model and how well it is fulfilling the value proposition previously supplied to the customer. The assessment model is an adaptation of a common quality and business excellence model for the maintenance outsourcing business.

Utilizing global and regional teams ABB performs assessments for every large contract biannually or more often if needed. The assessment is a major approach to educate, support and share leading practices as well as to strengthen the partnership with the customer.

After an assessment, the service unit and upper management will have a clear picture where the service unit stands compared to other ABB Full Service® units. Scoring identifies where the site is good and where major areas for improvement exist. By way of simple recognition the higher performing service units are rewarded with bronze, silver or gold certificates.

The goal of the assessment process is to ensure that the service unit has a sustainable business providing Client Value, ABB Value and People Value. The main objectives are:

1. To ensure contract renewal and to guarantee results according to the business objectives
2. To ensure the ABB Full Service® concept is implemented as proposed

Other objectives are:

1. To identify and share Leading Practices
2. To support implementation of standard ABB Full Service® processes and tools
3. To provide analyses of assessed sites in terms of scoring, Client, ABB and People Value
4. To support gathering and harmonizing the main KPIs for benchmark purposes

Assessment methodology

The results criteria of the assessment cover Client Value, ABB Value and People Value. The assessor needs to get an understanding of the KPIs utilized and other measures under these areas. The important topics are to have good coverage on KPIs, positive trends to reach the targets and comparisons or benchmarks.

The enablers are the important approaches with which the service unit reaches its results. ABB Full Service® can be defined as a set of core management and support processes with relevant phases, activities and tools which are made available commonly for all service units. In the enablers' criteria consist of an assessment of approaches, their implementation level and the way approaches are reviewed.

The Full Service® Site assessment is not a desktop study. That is why the program includes visits to the main production facilities as well as to the maintenance workshops. During those visits assessors will have the opportunity to get a good general view of the processes and can in turn relate interviews with the real situation. Before finalizing the site visit, it is a standard way to have a formal wrap-up meeting with the site management. Assessors provide feedback immediately with key findings prior to the supply of a written assessment report.

Assessment reporting and learning

Delivering the high level report from the assessment is the main learning part, both for the site itself and for the service community. The Assessors will typically divide the responsibility for different criteria assessed. However in reporting the goal is to finding consensus, not compromise. Assessors will agree on the main messages as well as on the detailed report and scoring:

- The Site Assessment Report is the document where the main observations and recommendations are detailed by each assessment criteria. The document is drafted so that it can be shared with ABB site personnel and customer personnel. The Maintenance Management Master Plan (MMMP) is the document where the improvement actions developed from the findings are captured and tracked.
- Scoring is the consensus by assessors on which level of maintenance is in place at the site. Scoring is affected by results and enablers but also by financial results. The scoring is then categorized to form the basis for the formal Site Certification. Based on assessment scoring and the financial results from the site, the ABB Full Service® Product Manager agrees on the Certification level with the main assessor. The Certification is to prove at which level the site is in terms of Full Service implementation thus giving tangible target setting for the continuous improvement.

Part of the learning process is to share the findings with other service units. Reports are stored in a common database where other service units have controlled access. Another important topic is Leading Practices. Assessors identify any leading practices and share them in the company's intranet based database.

Global assessors make analyses between results and enablers as well as between the individual scores, Customer Satisfaction/loyalty, People Satisfaction and EBIT. With the analyses complete ABB will understand better the relationship between the different aspects of the business.

The most important thing is to close the loop of continuous improvement. The assessor makes it clear that the reports, findings and recommendations are understood by the site. The ABB Site Manager's task is to review the recommendations with site personnel and with the customer as applicable and to integrate them into the service unit's strategy (MMMP).

Business excellence in the assessment process is not just writing the report but also supporting and helping the site to move forward. On a regular basis after the assessment the assessor and company management should review the action planning and accomplishments of the recommendations. The assessor should give guidance to the site on how to continue improvement based on and beyond the recommendations.

SUMMARY AND FUTURE CHALLENGE

In this chapter the authors have explained the business rationale behind modern performance based maintenance outsourcing, and also presented a validated approach for managing operational excellence. More detail has been given about one core process, called here Reliability Maintenance. The intent is to identify the nature of outsourced maintenance service, delivered at a customer's premises and repeated hundreds of times at global environment.

It is about changing service intangibility into tangible.

The challenge of successful and repeatable maintenance outsourcing activities accross multiple regions nd countries is to change

The success in running this business is heavily about managing the customer relationship extremely closely during the whole life-cycle, identifying a compelling business case and having the capability to design and implement a business model and set of processes that continuously address the strategy and requirements of the customer – with which the organization runs a long term, performance based agreement. Successful deployment is highly important; professionals having high level technical skills as well as strong leadership and change management are the vital success factors to implement the processes in consistent way.

The future challenge for the outsourced maintenance business model is to further add technology and automation into the solution to strengthen the maintenance role in asset performance management and data analysis. The market needs also more consistent, capable partners to utilize the benefits of long term performance based agreements and to jointly innovate new solutions to increase the competitiveness of the partners.

However the model will be seen successful only when good results have been proven. To demonstrate this by example ABB Full Service® pursuits have delivered the following typical results over the course of the last 10 years:

- Plant Overall Equipment Effectiveness increased 17 percent points in 4 years.
- Total maintenance cost decreased 20% while production was increased by 20% over three years.
- Exceeded 14 production records out of 15 measures over three years.
- Unplanned breakdowns due to maintenance reduced by 90% in four years.
- Achieved 105% of rated capacity in Greenfield plant just in three months.
- Achieved 1000 days with no lost time due to injury from the beginning of the agreement.
- In 5 months ABB have made significant changes to our plant. The same would have taken us 5 years.
- ABB Full Service site was selected the organization of the year 2006 by New Zealand's government.

REFERENCES

1. ABB, solar drives life cycle management, 2011, http://www.abb.com/solar
2. ABB, Ruutu Pekka, Raassina Mika, Client Value Reporting Tool, 2006
3. AlixPartners, 2010
4. ARC Strategies, August 2006
5. DOD, 1981, MIL-STD-721 C: "DEFINITIONS OF TERMS FOR RELIABILITY AND

MAINTAINABILITY" (Superseding 721B)

6. EFQM Excellence Model, European Foundation for Quality Management, 2011, http://www.efqm.org/en/

7. Haughey, D., RACI Matrix, Project Smart, 2000-2010, http://www.projectsmart.co.uk/racimatrix.html

8. WebZip News, 2011, http://www.nos.org/htm/basic2.htm

9. Kerry, S.,2011, SIPOC Diagram, iSixSigma® Newsletter, October 3 2011, http://www.isixsigma.com/index.php?option=com_k2&view=item&id=1013:sipoc-diagram&Itemid=219

10. Kundu, S; McKay, A; de Pennington, A; Moss, N; Chapman, N Implications for engineering information systems design in the product service Paradigm in: 14th CIRP Conference on Life Cycle Engineering, pp.165-170. 2007.asser K, wiseGEEK, 2011

11. Smith Anthony M., Hinchcliffe Glenn R. , RCM: gateway to world class maintenance, Butterworth-Heinemann, 2003

12. Moubrey John, Reliability-centered maintenance, Industrial Press Inc., 1997

13. Zeithaml, V, Britner M J, Services Marketing, 2005

14. Vicente Fernando., Using modern reliability tools to improve the availability of the installations and extend the lifetime of key electrical equipment, 8th Petroleum and Chemical Industry Conference Europe Electrical and Instrumentation, June 7 - 9, 2011 Rome, Italy

15. Weissenfelt P., Maintenance as a service business – industrial viewpoint, Maintworld 3, 2011

CHAPTER 13

QUALITY ASSURANCE IN DIAGNOSTICS

Stephen Inkoom

INTRODUCTION

It is well known that medical expsoure procedures such as diagnostic radiology, nuclear medicine and radiotherapy remains the largest source of manmade exposure to ionising radiation and continues to grow substantially. This makes the role of quality assurance (QA), an important tool in medical exposure procedures. This paper reviews the future of quality assurance in diagnostic medical exposures in Ghana from the perspective of a Medical Physicist, since a viable QA programme must be developed under the guidance and supervision of a medical physicist who is qualified in this area of expertise by education, training and experience. The Medical Physicist is expected to give guidance and supervision to the Technologists and other staff to execute the programme but should be prepared to perform higher level QA procedures as required. The focus of this review is on diagnostic radiology since it is the dominant mode of medical exposure as compared to nuclear medicine and radiotherapy procedures in Ghana as per the database of the Regulatory Authority Information System "(RAIS)" of the Radiation Protection Institute. It is also worth noting that most of the issues under consideration for discussion mirrors similar conditions in many developing countries. The main goal of a diagnostic quality assurance programme is to make sure that radiation doses to patients, staff and public are as low as reasonable achievable (ALARA) consistent with high quality diagnostic images of patients. An adequate diagnostic QA program involves periodic checks of all major components in the respective diagnostic imaging modalities. On the other hand, an optimum QA programme for any individual diagnostic facility will depend on some items such as the type of procedures performed, type of equipment utilized, patient workload, etc. The current scope of diagnostic imaging procedures in Ghana covers conventional, fluoroscopy, dental, computed tomography, interventional procedures and nuclear medicine scans. Interventional radiology procedures performed are quite few but the future looks promising in this field. The performance of QA practices are done on three fronts; namely at the hospital, equipment engineers and the Regulatory Authority (RA). The hospital based QA are done mainly by the Radiographic Technologist through their routine equipment warm ups and minor quality checks. Equipment Engineers perform engineer related QA checks through installation and acceptance testing, performance tests and periodic preventative maintenance procedures. On the other hand, the RA is largely in charge of major QA procedures through it's on site safety assessment inspections by assessing the compliance of the equipment within regulatory requirements. This is largely so because the RA has the technical expertise and equipment. Due to the expansion of diagnostic imaging procedures in medicine coupled with rapid technological advances, the availability of qualified and trained personnel is crucial if the desired quality is to be achieved. Some measures have been put in place for human resource development, but there is room for improvement. On the way forward, there is a strong need for the establishment of National Quality Control Centre for Diagnostic Radiology. This body must be equipped with the requisite state of the art equipment, highly qualified and trained personnel in order to coordinate all QA activities in the country. Such a body can initiate some guidelines on the minimum instrumentation requirements for all imaging modalities. Nevertheless, a good QA programmme is not a guarantee for the assurance of the radiation safety of patients, staff and public. What is also needed is a separate radiation safety programme, which is very essential in every diagnostic imaging facility and must also be under the direction of a qualified expert in radiation protection.

Citation: Stephen Inkoom (2012). Quality Assurance in Diagnostics, Latest Research into Quality Control, DOI: 10.5772/51445.

OVERVIEW OF QUALITY ASSURANCE

The 2008 United Nations Scientific Committee on the Effects of Atomic Radiation (UNSCEAR) report on medical exposures from the assessment of the global population dose from medical exposures for the period 1997-2007 indicates that medical exposure remains the largest source of man made exposure to ionizing radiation and continues to grow substantially. (UNSCEAR, 2008). A summary of the annual per caput effective dose to the global population due to all sources of ionizing radiation is illustrated in Table 1.

It is evident that diagnostic examinations result in a per caput effective dose of 0.66 mSv, while medical exposures now contribute around 20% of the average annual per caput dose to the global population. Medical exposures are defined as; (i) exposure of patients as part of their medical diagnosis or treatment; (ii) exposure of individuals as part of health screening programmes; and (iii) exposure of healthy individuals or patients voluntarily participating in medical, biomedical, diagnostic or therapeutic research programmes. These exposures include diagnostic radiology, nuclear medicine and radiation therapy (Fig. 1), out of which diagnostic radiology accounts for the largest contribution. Diagnostic radiology generally refers to the analysis of images obtained using x-rays. In nuclear medicine, a radiopharmaceutical is administered to the patient and concentrates primarily in a specific region of the body which allows: (i) external imaging of the body to evaluate structure and/or function, and (ii) or delivery of a large radiation dose to control a specific disease. Radiation therapy involves the use of intense radiation beams and high-activity sources for the treatment of many types of cancer.

This makes the role of (QA), an important tool in medical exposure procedures. Quality assurance procedures must aim at to produce images of optimal diagnostic quality while ensuring that the radiation exposures to patients, staff and the public are kept as low as practicable. In achieving this goal, QA procedures if well implemented would ensure that any problem in the imaging chain will be dealt without a compromise in the diagnostic quality of the images. The World Health Organization (WHO), (WHO, 1982), indicates that achieving adequate diagnostic information and least possible exposure of the patient to radiation should be done at the lowest possible cost. An adequate diagnostic QA program involves periodic checks of all major components in the respective diagnostic imaging modalities. On the other hand, an optimum QA programme for any individual diagnostic facility will depend on some items such as the type of procedures performed, type of equipment utilized, patient workload, etc. Any QA procedure must be in agreement with the relevant national and international legislation or regulations on the protection and safe uses of ionising radiation. Another form of QA is to establish clinical audit, which is an essential tool for quality improvement in any diagnostic centre. For instance, the European Council directive (Commission of the European Communities. 1997) defines clinical audit as: "a systematic examination or review of medical radiological procedures which seeks to improve the quality and the outcome of patient care, through structured review whereby radiological practices, procedures, and results are examined against agreed standards for good medical radiological procedures, with modifications of the practices where indicated and the application of new standards if necessary."

Table 1: Sources of ionizing radiation and the annual per caput effective dose to the global population

Source	Annual per caput effective dose (mSv)	Contribution (%)
Natural background	2.4	79
Diagnostic medical radiology	0.62	20
Diagnostic dental radiology	0.0018	<0.1
Nuclear medicine	0.031	1.1
Fallout	0.005	<0.2
Total	3.1	100

Source: UNSCEAR 2008 report on medical radiation exposures. (UNSCEAR, 2008).

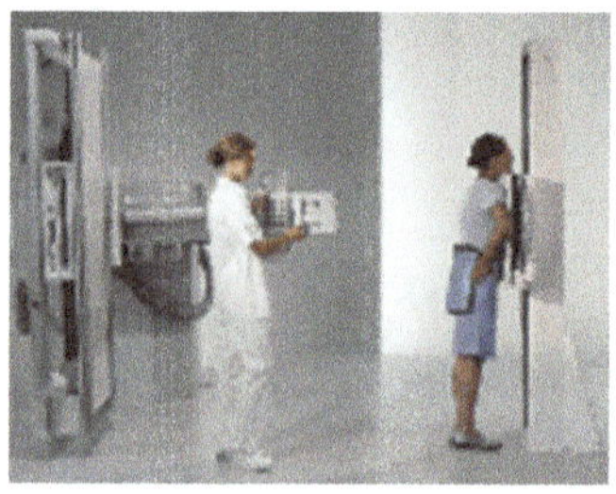

a

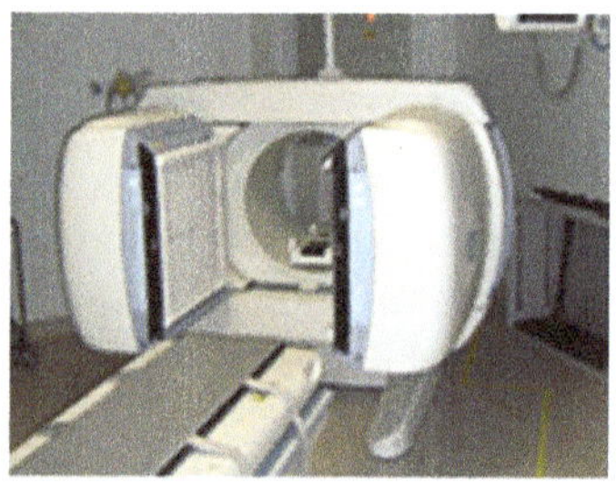

b

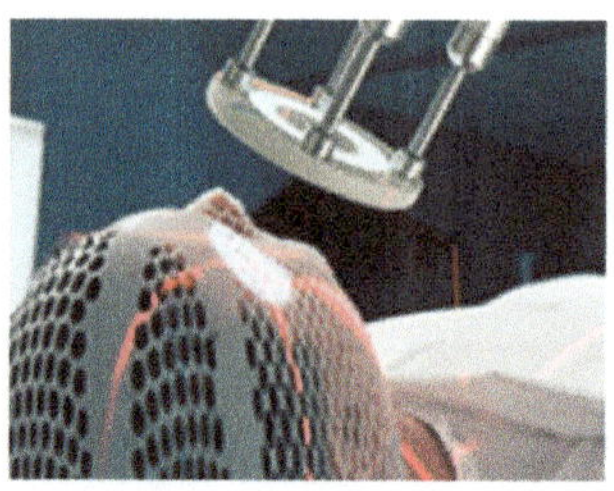

c

Figure 1: An illustration of (a) diagnostic radiology, (b) nuclear medicine and (c) radiation therapy procedures.

This paper reviews the future of quality assurance in diagnostic medical exposures in Ghana from the perspective of a Medical Physicist, since a viable QA programme must be developed under the guidance and supervision of a medical physicist who is qualified in this area of expertise by education, training and experience. The Medical Physicist is expected to give guidance and supervision to the Technologists and other staff to executive the programme but should be prepared to perform higher level QA procedures as required.

CURRENT STATUS OF QUALITY ASSURANCE IN DIAGNOSTIC MEDICAL EXPOSURES

The types of diagnostic medical exposure procedures in Ghana are;

- Plain radiography
- Mammography
- Fluoroscopy
- Computed Tomography
- Dental

In addition to the above procedures for diagnosis, some hospitals perform interventional or invasive procedures on a limited scale. On the other hand, the types of medical exposure in nuclear medicine procedures are the use of gamma camera and single photon emission computed tomography (SPECT/CT) for imaging various organs. Plain radiography (screen-film and digital systems) is the dominant mode of all the diagnostic medical procedures, accounting for more than 80% of the total contribution of all the imaging modalities. (RAIS, 2011).

The performance of QA practices are done on three fronts; namely at the hospital, equipment/service engineers and the (RA). The hospital based QA are done mainly by the Radiographers/Radiologic Technologist through their routine equipment warm ups and minor quality checks. In this scenario, a qualified Medical Physicist with the requisite expertise must supervise such QA procedures. Unfortunately, there are not many Medical Physicists in diagnostic departments as compared to radiation therapy centres. Equipment/service engineers perform engineer related QA checks through installation and acceptance testing, performance tests and periodic preventative maintenance procedures as well as when there is equipment down time. On the other hand, the RA is largely in charge of major QA procedures through it's on site safety assessment inspections by assessing the compliance of the equipment within regulatory requirements. This is largely so because the RA has the requisite technical expertise and equipment. In Ghana, Medical Physicists are engaged in service, teaching, research and administration activities. They perform some of the tasks outlined by the International Organisation for Medical Physics (IOMP) in its definition of who a Medical Physicist is and the roles and responsibilities (International Organisation for Medical Physics, 2010) such as:

- teaching principles of medical physics to physicians, residents, graduate students, medical students, technologists, and other health care professionals by means of lectures, problem solving, and laboratory sessions.
- conducting research into various human disorders, illnesses and disabilities, develop instrumentation, mathematical analysis and applications of computers in medicine; investigating biophysical techniques associated with any branch of medicine. Research is very important for advancement of medical physics as a profession and science.
- responsible for ensuring the quality, safety testing and correct maintenance of all radiation emitting devices in order to get an accurate diagnosis of illnesses. Medical Physicists also involved in the formulation of radiation protection guides and procedures specific to clinical environment and producing protocols to minimize radiation exposure of patients, staff and the general public.
- in administration, they supervise and manage radiation workers and other health professional workers.
- participating in and contributing to the development and implementation of national and
- prepares guidance on education and training drawing-up standards and guidance relating to medical devices.
- preparing, publishing and presenting scientific papers and reports

Ghana is involved in several International Atomic Energy Agency (IAEA) Technical and Research Projects. Some of the Projects in which Medical Physicists are involved are:

- RAF/9/033 - Strengthening Radiological Protection of Patients and Medical Exposure Control.
- RAF/9/034 - Establishment of National Capabilities for Response to a Radiological and Nuclear Emergency.
- RAF/9/035 - Education and Training in Support of Radiation Protection Infrastructure.
- RAF/9/032 - Development of Technical Capabilities for the Protection of Health and Safety of Workers Exposed to Ionizing Radiation.
- RAF/9/027 - National Regulatory Control and Occupational Radiation Protection Programmes.
- RAF/9/031 - Strengthening National Regulatory Infrastructure for the Control of Radiation Sources.
- GHA/6/015 - Upgrading and Expansion of Radiotherapy and Nuclear Medicine Services
- INT/6/054 - Strengthening Medical Physics in Radiation Medicine
- RAF/2/008 - Strengthening and Expanding Radiopharmacy Services in Africa (AFRA)
- RAF/6/032 - Promoting Regional and National Quality Assurance Programmes for Medical Physics in Nuclear Medicine (AFRA II-7)
- RAF/6/041 - Supporting the Development of Comprehensive National Cancer Control Programmes
- RAF/6/044 - Medical Physics in Support of Cancer Management (AFRA II-8)

- RAF/6/045 - Enhancing Accessibility and Quality in the Care of Cancer Patients (AFRA II-10)

The main objectives of some of the projects are discussed. For instance in RAF/9/033, the objectives are to upgrade / strengthen radiological protection of the patient in medical exposures due to:

i. Diagnostic Radiology and Interventional Radiological procedures

ii. Nuclear Medicine procedures

iii. Radiotherapy practice

The objectives of other projects are as follows:

- GHA/6/015 - To consolidate existing radiotherapy and nuclear medicine facilities at two leading Teaching Hospitals located in the southern part of the country, and establish a third one in the northern part to cater for the diagnosis, curative and palliative treatment of cancer patients and the efficient diagnosis and management of other diseases.
- INT/6/054 - To promote the recognition of medical physics in radiation medicine and to harmonize educational material in order to ensure safe and effective diagnosis and treatment of patients.
- RAF/2/008 - To strengthen radiopharmacy in support of in vivo and in vitro nuclear medicine in Africa.
- RAF/6/032 - To improve the effectiveness and safety of nuclear medicine procedures by providing support for design and implementation of quality assurance (QA) programmes and by establishing training and education programmes in medical radiation physics, focusing on aspects related to the application of nuclear medicine techniques.
- RAF/6/041 - To assist Member States in performing comprehensive cancer capacity need assessments and national cancer strategic planning via collaboration with IAEA, WHO, and other partners under the Programme of Action for Cancer Therapy (PACT) umbrella.
- RAF/6/044 - To strengthen national and regional medical physics capabilities to ensure efficient support of cancer management in AFRA Member States and to sustain quality assurance/quality control (QA/QC) programmes, including the promotion of safety culture and innovative practices in dosimetry.
- RAF/6/045 - To establish national and regional networks in clinical radiation oncology. To interact with National Organizations with the aim to promote the comprehensive management of commonest cancers. Support academic education, training and accreditation, patients and personnel safety in radiotherapy improvement of documentation of clinical outcomes through regular patient assessment.

REGULATORY GUIDELINES FOR QUALITY ASSURANCE PROCEDURES

The National Competent/Regulatory Authority in Ghana charged with the responsibility for authorization and inspection of practices using ionizing radiation sources and radioactive materials is the Radiation Protection Board (RPB) (Radiation Protection Instrument LI 1559, 1993). However, the operational functions of the RPB are carried out by RPI, which was established in 2000 to provide scientific and technical support for the enforcement of the provisions in LI 1559. Details about how the RA was established and the main activities have been described elsewhere (Inkoom et al, 2011). There are plans to establish a new Regulatory Body to regulate the peaceful uses of nuclear energy and technology which will be independent of any governmental agency. Currently, the RA is answerable to the Ghana Atomic Energy Commission (GAEC) which is a promoter for the peaceful uses of nuclear energy and technology and also plays the role of a regulator. However, the new RA is expected to be only a regulator and not a promoter of the application of nuclear technology.

HUMAN RESOURCE DEVELOPMENT

The categories of Radiographic Staff available in Ghana are Radiologists, Medical Physicists, Biomedical Engineers and Radiographers/X-ray Technicians. Most of our Radiologists were trained overseas until the last few years when local training of Radiologists started and the accreditation is given by either the Ghana College of Surgeons or the West African College of Physicians and Surgeons. Similarly, the other professionals were also trained overseas. Currently, the School of Allied Health Sciences (SAHS), College of Health Sciences (CHS) of the University of Ghana (UG) is responsible for churning out medical and dental technical graduates in physiotherapy, medical laboratory science and radiography. There are plans to establish another Allied Health University and some private institutions are also running some of the programmes. A Post-Graduate School of Nuclear and Allied Sciences which was established jointly by the GAEC and UG, in co-operation with the IAEA is training the Medical Physicists, Radiation Protection Professionals, Nuclear Engineers, etc. at the National and Sub-Regional levels.

RECENT TRENDS IN QUALITY ASSURANCE

The increasing expansion of diagnostic imaging procedures in medicine coupled with rapid technological advances makes the availability of qualified and trained personnel to be very crucial if the desired quality is to be achieved. This come with a lot challenges to the medical imaging community. This offers practitioners the opportunity to continually undergo retraining and other continuous professional development programmes in their respective fields. Also with the emergence of picture archiving and communication system (PACS) in many hospitals, there is the need for the development of appropriate on line QA procedures and in corporating them into hospital PACS systems. Special attention must also be given to the emergence of digital technology over the last decade as one of the greatest technological advances in medical imaging. This new technolgy poses a great challenge in medical imaging, requiring re-training of staff on the safe use of equipment and radiation protection issues. In Ghana for instance, the RPI of

GAEC, in collaboration with the IAEA, has in the previous years developed a lot of expertise in the training of occupationally exposed workers in Ghana and the rest of Africa, spanning a period of almost two decades (Boadu et al. 2011). This local expertise in training can be tapped. In this regard, a critical review of all QA procedures that were developed for screen-film systems needs special attention.

THE WAY FORWARD

Various practitioners in the medical imaging community must brace themselves in order to face challenges of technological developments. With the advent of digital radiography: advances in computed radiography, direct digital radiography, digital subtraction angiography, new digital receivers, image processing techniques, computer applications in radiology and PACS offers enormous challenges. The advantages of digital technology:post-processing capabilities, decreased costs, multiple viewing options, electronic transfer, possibilities of archiving, wide dynamic range of flat panel detectors and increased detection quantum efficiency has led to a high demand of this technology by the medical imaging community. Therefore, the development of the requisite human resource must be continued and sustained in order to deal with the challenges.

There is a strong need for the establishment of National Quality Control Centre for Diagnostic Radiology. This body must be equipped with the requisite state of the art equipment, highly qualified and trained personnel in order to coordinate all QA activities in the country. Such a body can initiate some guidelines on the minimum instrumentation requirements for all imaging modalities. With the training of more Medical Physicists sand Radiation Protection Professionals, it is expected that they would take up positions in all major hospitals which have a myriad of imaging modalities. The Ghana Society of Medical Physics, RA, Ministry of Health and other stakeholders must initiate procedures for the establishment of Medical Physics Departments in such hospitals. This would give the necessary recognition to the profession of Medical Physics in Ghana, which has been given recognition by the International Labour Organization (ILO) in its International Standard Classification of Occupations (ISCO) (ILO, 2008). With this recognition, Medical Physics has been accepted as modern applied branch of physics. Clinical audit should also be incorporated in the overall QA procedures in the country.

As the uses of ionizing radiation continue to increase in medicine, it is also expected that the services of Medical Physicist would increase. As such, more physicists would be required to be trained in subsequent years. Appropriate accreditation bodies charged with issuing accreditation certificates, for a period of years must be put in place to regulate the profession of Medical Physics and maintain international standards of practice.

CONCLUSION

The role of an effective QA programme in any diagnostic department cannot be overemphasized especially if the desired quality of producing good diagnostic images and the least radiation exposure are to be achieved. Nevertheless, a good QA programmme is not a guarantee for the assurance of the radiation safety of patients, staff and public. What is also needed is a separate radiation safety programme, which is very essential in every diagnostic imaging facility and must also be under the direction of a qualified expert in radiation protection or a Medical Physicist expert. With significant contributions in clinical service, education, and research, Medical Physics continues to grow in importance both as a profession and as science, driven by the technological developments of societies in general and medicine in particular.

ACKNOWLEDGEMENTS

The support received from the Radiation Protection Institute of Ghana Atomic Energy Commission is appreciated.

REFERENCES

1. M. Boadu, C. Schandorf, G. Emi-Reynolds, A. Faanu, S. Inkoom, Gyekye. P. Kwabena, M.C. Kaikor, Systematic approach to training of occupationally exposed workers in Ghana andthe rest of Africa. Health Phys 101 2: S116YS120 2011
2. Commission of the European Communities Council Directive 97/43/ Euratom of 30 Juneon health protection of individuals against the dangers of ionizing radiation in relation to medical exposure, and repealing Directive 84/466 Euratom Off. J. Eur. Commun. Rep. L. 180 1997 1997 22 27
3. International Labour Organization (ILO) International Standard Classification of Occupations (ISCO), Geneva, Switzerland, (ISCO-08), 2008.
4. International Organisation for Medical Physics (IOMP) IOMP Policy Statement No.1. The Medical Physicist: Role and Responsibilities, IOMP Working Group on Policy Statement 1 2010
5. Radiation Protection Instrument LI 1559 1993 Provisional National Defence Council Law 308, Accra, Ghana. Date of Gazette Notification: 2nd April, 1993.
6. Regulatory Authority Information System [RAIS] 2011 Radiation Protection Institute, Ghana Atomic Energy Commission, Accra, Ghana.
7. S. Inkoom, C. Schandorf, G. E. Reynolds, J. J. Fletcher, Quality Assurance and Quality Control of Equipment in Diagnostic Radiology Practice-The Ghanaian Experience Wide Spectra of Quality Control, Isin Akyar (Ed.) 2011 291 308 978-9-53307-683-6 InTechhttp://www.intechopen.com/articles/show/title/quality-assurance-and-quality-control-of-equipment-in-diagnostic-radiology-practice-the-ghanaian-exp
8. United Nations Scientific Committee on the Effects of Atomic Radiation. Sources and effects of ionizing radiation. Report to the General Assembly with scientific annexes (UNSCEAR) 2008
9. World Health Organization 1982 Quality Assurance in Diagnostic Radiology, Macmillan Procrom,9-24154-164-4

CHAPTER 14

FEASIBILITY OF TOTAL MANAGEMENT MODEL AND THE AWARENESS AND ATTITUDE OF THE MANAGERS OF HEALTH CARE

Fereshteh Farzianpour, Kazem Mohammad, Abbas Rahimi Foroushani, Samira Alirezaei, and Fatemeh Manafi

Keywords: Feasibility, Total Quality Management Model, Awareness, Attitude, Managers of Health Field

INTRODUCTION

Total quality management (TQM) has a great potential to address quality Problems in a wide range of industries and improve the organizational Performance [1] .

Concerning health services, quality has a special place since the great mission of maintaining and taking care of community health is undertaken by this system [2] . In addition, hospitals which offer health and care services are the inseparable part of the health system. Hospitals, although constituting a small part of the health system, considering their number, are viewed as its most important part/element, as a significant part of expenditure on health is related to them [3] .

TQM is a suitable way to relatively achieve efficiency and effectiveness which in turn leads to achievements such as success in long term, meeting the workers', customers' and other interested parties' needs in the society [3] . It is what can, as a key and efficient means, give a practical aspect to the total quality management and change it from being merely theoretical [2] [4] .

The role of the managers in quality is so essential. They should be the first ones who try to improve quality, recognizing both the usual and special causes and distinguishing them from each other [3] .

Citation: Farzianpour, F. , Mohammad, K. , Foroushani, A. , Alirezaei, S. and Manafi, F. (2015), Feasibility of Total Management Model and the Awareness and Attitude of the Managers of Health Care.Health, 7, 231-237. doi: 10.4236/health.2015.72027.

The quality management involves 8 principles which the executive manager of any organization can use to direct his organization in order to improve the performances. The principles are as follows: focusing on clients, leadership in management, workers' contribution, procedural approaches, systematic approach to management, continuous improvement, decision making based on facts and beneficial and mutual relationship to the providers [4] [5] .

TQM is one of the most important changes which have taken place in the field of health care management. After fields such as industry and business, it is now the turn of health field to benefit from TQM in principle. The ministry of health, treatment and medical education has chosen TQM as a comprehensive and applied strategy since 1998 to achieve administrative development and improve the quality of services in order to respond to the needs and expectations of the society. It is worth mentioning that the national committee of improving quality known as an educational-consultative committee to educate, direct and support the programs concerning quality improvement has started its work [6] .

In fact, the purpose of TQM is optimizing human powers and improving the quality of patient care through establishing the system in the wards [7] . TQM is not regarded as the final process of improvement, but everyone should try to achieve it and view improvement as a continuous process [8] [9] .

Despite the undeniable advantages of TQM for an organization, there is no consensus about its framework, but there is a general consensus about the need for a systematic method or framework in order to make TQM feasible [10] .

Concerning this matter, it can be said that patterns excellence such as the European-base pattern of TQM and Baldridge organizational improvement pattern and the operational patterns derived from them involve the presuppositions of TQM and the results of various studies indicate that they are a suitable framework to direct the systematic establishment of TQM as well as its evaluation in the organization [10] -[12] .

In this study, we decided to examine the feasibility of TQM and the attitude of the health managers of Yazd medical sciences university towards it.

METHODS

The present study is a descriptive-analytic one which was carried out cross-section ally in order to examine the attitude of the health general staff managers of Yazd medical sciences university, including those of the health nets and centers and also managers of hospitals of 10 health nets as well as the managers of health vice-chan- cellor of University.

The study was approved by the Ethics Committee of Tehran University of Medical Sciences (TUMS) IRB No. 88197-19/7/2011 and by the Ethics Committee of the Management College, Yazd University of Medical Sci- ences, Iran. The researchers described the purpose of the study and Potential risks/benefits to the health centers' managers and all the prospective participants. All subjects were required to sign consent form.

The tool used to gather data was a questionnaire consisting of 48 questions. Its validity has been proved by university professors and its reliability based on the method of calculating and Cronbach coefficient is 87%. The way used to score the questions was based on Likert scale. Awareness level of the participants in the study was divided into 5 levels: excellent, good, average, weak and very weak. Based on the scores acquired by each participant in the study, they were categorized to 5 levels (from 0 to 100). The attitude was examined in the same way and all the data were analyzed using the software SPSS V.18. The study population included 64 individuals. Finally, the information pertaining to 58 managers was gathered.

FINDINGS

Descriptive Findings

The area of activity of the managers was as follows. From health field 42 (71.4%) and 16 (28.6%) from treatment field. Concerning education, 29 (50%) had B.S., 4 (6.9%) M.S. and 25 (43.1%) PhD. The youngest was 30 years old and the oldest 49 years (Table 1).

Table 1: Frequency distribution of awareness level, mangers' attitude towards TQM and feasibility of TQM, considering area of activity, age, education of the mangers of the health field of Yazd Medical Sciences University

1. Level of awareness		Good awareness		Average awareness		Test	P-value
	Variable	N	%	N	%		
Area of activity	Health	30	71.4	12	28.6	Fisher careful test	0.343
	Treatment	13	81.3	3	18.8		
Age	Below 40	14	66.7	7	3	Chi-square test	0.328
	Above 41	29	78.4	8	21.6		
Level of education	B.S.	22	75.9	7	24.1	Chi-square test	0.764
	M.S. and PhD	21	72.4	8	27.6		
2. Level of attitude		Good attitude		Average attitude		Test	P-value
	Variable	N	%	N	%		
Area of activity	Health	35	83.3	7	16.7	Fisher careful test	0.523
	Treatment	14	87.5	2	12.5		
Age	Below 40	18	85.7	3	14.3	Fisher careful test	0.581
	Above 41	31	83.8	6	16.2		
Level of education	B.S.	24	82.8	5	17.2	Fisher careful test	0.500
	M.S. and PhD	25	86.2	4	13.8		
3. Level of feasibility		Feasible		Infeasible		Test	P-value
	variable	N	%	N	%		
Area of activity	Health	31	73.8	11	26.2	Fisher careful test	0.089
	Treatment	15	93.8	1	6.3		
Age	Below 40	16	76.2	5	23.8	Fisher careful test	0.451
	Above 41	30	81.1	7	18.9		
Level of education	B.S.	23	79.3	6	20.7	Chi-square test	1
	M.S. and PhD	23	79.3	6	20.7		

Analytical Findings

The mean percentage of the managers' scores concerning the questions on awareness' of TQM was 71.9 ± 8.7. Based on the scores acquired, the managers were divided into three groups, i.e. weak, average and good.

The weak ones included those whose score was less than 33.3%, the average between 33.4% and 66.6% and the good ones above 66.7%. The results indicated that nine of the managers (15.5%) had an average attitude and 49 (84.5%) a good attitude towards TQM. There was no manager with a weak attitude (Table 2). In total, 12 of the managers (20.7%) believed that TQM was not feasible in their organization and 46 (79.3%) considered it feasible (Table 3). Considering the feasibility of TQM, in order to examine the relationship between variables, Binary Logistic Regression was used. The results are shown in the form of Inter and Backward stepwise in Table 4 and Table 5. In view of this model, there is no relationship between the feasibility of TQM and the level of managers' education and age. So these variables are omitted from the model. Variables related to the level of awareness, attitude and field of study in logistic Regression model are shown in Table 5 in the form of Backward stepwise. The accuracy of prediction of this model is 79.3%.

Also in order to examine the relationship between the variables and the manager's attitude towards TQM, Binary logistic Regression was used. The results are shown in the form of Inter and Backward stepwise.

The results indicate that there is no relationship between the managers' attitude towards TQM and level of their education, age and their field of activity/study, so these variables are omitted from the model. The variables, the managers' level of awareness and the feasibility of TQM are present in Logistic Regression in the form of Backward stepwise. The prediction accuracy of the model is 87.9%.

Table 2: Frequency distribution of managers' attitudes towards TQM considering their level of their awareness

Level of awareness / Level of attitude	Average awareness		Good awareness		P-value
	N	%	N	%	
Average attitude	7	46.7	2	4.7	0.001
Good attitude	8	53.3	41	95.3	

Table 3: Frequency distribution of TQM feasibility from the point of view of the managers considering their level of awareness and their attitude towards TQM

Level of awareness / Level of feasible	Average awareness		Good awareness		P-value
	N	%	N	%	
Feasible	10	66.7	36	83.7	0.151
Infeasible	5	33.3	7	16.3	
Level of attitude / Variable	**Average attitude**		**Good attitude**		**P-value**
	N	%	N	%	
Feasible	8	88.9	38	76.6	0.397
Infeasible	1	11.1	11	22.4	

Table 4: The relationship between variables of the study and feasibility of TQM using logistic regression in the form of inter and backward stepwise

Variable	Variable coefficient (B)	Standard error (S.E.)	Wald	Degree of freedom (df)	P. value	Odds	Odds 95%	
							Limits below odds	Limits above odds
Level of awareness	1.49	0.893	2.77	1	0.095	4.43	0.77	25.55
Level of attitude	2.44	1.481	2.72	1	0.099	11.52	0.63	2.0
Level of education	1.04	0.847	1.53	1	0.216	2.82	0.54	15.02
Age	0.152	0.086	3.07	1	0.08	1.16	0.98	1.37
Field of study	2.57	1.290	3.97	1	0.046	13.1	1.04	164.1

Table 5: The relationship between the study variables and the feasibility of TQM using backward stepwise logistic regression

Variable	Variable coefficient (B)	Standard error (S.E.)	Wald	Degree of freedom (df)	P. value	Odds	Odds 95%	
							Limits below odds	Limits above odds
Level of awareness	1.689	0.859	3.839	1	0.05	5.385	0.999	29.019
Level of attitude	2.119	1.306	2.633	1	0.105	8.319	0.644	107.51
Field of study	1.773	1.134	2.442	1	0.118	5.886	0.637	54.36

Discussion and Data Analysis

In examining the feasibility of TQM and its relation with level of education, 23 of the managers with B.S. degree and 23 of those with M.S. degree or PhD consider TQM feasible. So there is no significant relation between different levels of education and feasibility of TQM.

Considering the results of the study, there is no significant relation between the levels of education of those who work in staff section and their awareness of and attitude towards the feasibility of T.Q.M.

In a study conducted to analytically examine the extent to which the faculty board (professors and managers) are ready to accept TQM, none of the participants (220 professors and managers) had negative attitude. 14.54% of them had positive attitude and 84.46% rather positive.

Also, there was no significant difference between the three faculty departments concerning TQM acceptance, but there was a significant difference between professors and managers concerning TQM acceptance [16] . In another study concerning awareness of and applying TQM principles by managers of area 2 of Ministry of education .The results indicated that there was a significant difference between the managers and teachers; the managers had a positive attitude towards TQM model [17] .

In a study conducted to find the relation between educational level of managers of Kohkiolyeh's high schools and acceptance of TQM model, the results showed that there was no significant relation between the two [18] [19] .

A study was conducted to examine the attitude of the managers and faculty board of Oromiyeh University towards TQM model and its relationship to demographic characteristics [3] [6] .

CONCLUSION

Considering the results of the study, there is no significant relation between the levels of education and age of those who work in staff section and their awareness of and attitude towards the feasibility of TQM. The result of the study showed that there was a significant difference between the managers' attitude and that of the faculty board. There was also a significant relation between the faculty boards' major and indices of management com- mitment, client-orientated attitude, using information and education.

AUTHORS' CONTRIBUTIONS

FF selected the topic and designed the study, analyzed the data, interpreted the findings, wrote the first draft of the manuscript and revised the manuscript; KM & ARF selected the topic and designed the study, analyzed the data, interpreted the findings, commented on the first draft of the manuscript and revised the manuscript; KM & ARF designed the study, analyzed the data, interpreted the findings and commented on the first draft of the manuscript; SH designed the study, analyzed the data, interpreted the findings and commented on the first draft of the manuscript; SA & FM & SHH designed the study, analyzed the data, interpreted the findings and commented on the first draft of the manuscript. All authors read and approved the final manuscript.

ACKNOWLEDGEMENTS

Fereshteh Farzianpour, Kazem Mohammad, Abbas Rahimi Foroushani*, Samira Alirezaei, Fatemeh Manafi This study was a part of a MPH thesis supported financially by Tehran University of Medical Sciences; according to contract number 10,495 dated May 23, 2010. We appreciate the efforts by the personnel of healthcare centers in the city of Yazd who play a key role in controlling health care management and in improving health standards in the society.

REFERENCES

1. Jackson, S. (2000) Successfully Implementing TQM within Health Care. International Journal of Health Care Quality Assurance (IJHQA), 14, 157-163.http://dx.doi.org/10.1108/09526860110392431
2. Hasan Zade, M. and Najafgholi Nezhad, A. (2008) Assessment and Evaluation of Libraries and Information Centers: Theories and Methods and Tools. Information Science & Technology, 25, 131-152. [In Persian]
3. Hashemi, A. (2003) Changing Key in Management and Leadership. Nazir, Iran. [Book in Persian]
4. International Organization for Standardization, Editors (2009) Quality Management Principles [Monograph on the Internet]. Geneva. http://www.iso.org/
5. Farzianpour, F., Rahimi Fouroshani, A., Kamjoo, H. and Hosseini, S.S.H. (2011) Organizational Citizenship Behavior (OCB) among the Managers of Teaching Hospitals. American Journal of Economics and Business Administration, 3, 534-542.http://dx.doi.org/10.3844/ajebasp.2011.534.542
6. Farzianpour, F., Rahimi Fouroshani, A., Beyzaiee, S. and Hosseini, S. (2012) Evaluation of the Selfesteem Managers in Clinical Wards of Hospitals Affiliated to Tehran University of Medical Sciences. World Applied Sciences Journal, 16, 686-692.
7. Bruner, L.S. and Sudarth, D.E. (2004) Internal-Surgery Nursing. Moradi, A., Translator. Afrang, Tehran. [Persian]
8. Farzianpour, F., Roholah Askari, R., Torabipoor Hamedani, A., Khorshidi, G.H. and Amirifar, S. (2011) Accreditation of Emergency Department at a Teaching Hospital in Tehran University of Medical Sciences in 2010. American Journal of Economics and Business Administration, 3, 498-505. http://dx.doi.org/10.3844/ajebasp.2011.498.505
9. Farzianpour, F., Hosseini, S., Mirsepasi, A., Honary, H., Hosseini, S.S. and Hosseini, S. (2013) Internal Evaluation of the Department of Environmental Health Science and Engineering. American Journal of Applied Sciences, 10, 58-63.http://dx.doi.org/10.3844/ajassp.2013.58.63
10. Bou-Llusar, J.C., Escrig-Tena, A.B., Roca-Puig, V. and Beltrán Martín, I. (2009) An Empirical Assessment of the EFQM Excellence Model: Evaluation as a TQM Framework Relative to the MBNQA Model. Journal of Operations Management, 27, 1-22.http://dx.doi.org/10.1016/j.jom.2008.04.001
11. Farzianpour, F., Geray, S., Rahimi Foroushan, A., Arab, M. and Hosseini, S.H. (2013) Evaluating the Average

Access to Care and Continuity of Care Patients in Tehran Teaching Hospitals. Health, 5, 2110-2115. http://dx.doi.org/10.4236/health.2013.512288

12. van der Wiele, A., Williams, A.R.T. and Dale, B.G. (2000) ISO 9000 Series Registration to Business Excellence: The Migratory Path. Business Process Management Journal, 6, 417-427. http://dx.doi.org/10.1108/14637150010353911

13. Westlund, A.H. (2001) Measuring Environmental Impact on Society in the EFQM System. Total Quality Management, 12, 125-135. http://dx.doi.org/10.1080/09544120020010147

14. Eskildsen, J.K. and Dahlgaard, J.J. (2000) A Causal Model for Employee Satisfaction. Total Quality Management, 11, 1081-1094. http://dx.doi.org/10.1080/095441200440340

15. Prabhu, V., Appleby, A., Yarrow, D. and Mitchell, E. (2000) The Impact of ISO 9000 and TQM on Best Practice/Per- formance. The TQM Magazine, 12, 84-92. http://dx.doi.org/10.1108/09544780010318334

16. Heidari Gorji, A.M. and Farooquie, J.A. (2011) A Comparative Study of Total Quality Management of Health Care System in India and Iran. BMC Research Notes, 4, 566. The Electronic Version of This Article Is the Complete One and Can Be Found Online.http://www.biomedcentral.com/1756-0500/4/566

17. Farzianpour, F, Emami, A.H., Davari-Tanha, F., Hosseini, S. and Farzanehnejad, A.R. (2010) Educational Programs' Quality Assessment Based on Graduates' Comments. IRCMJ, 12, 302-307.

18. Farzianpour, F., Dargahi, H., Hosseini, S., Hosseini, S.S. and Hosseini, S. (2011) Program Evaluation of Health Care Management: Is It Adjusted for Students Needs? American Journal of Economics and Business Administration, 3, 420- 424.http://dx.doi.org/10.3844/ajebasp.2011.420.424

19. Farzianpour, F., Dargahi, H., Eynolahi, N. and Aghababa, S. (2010) Evaluation in Department of Health Care Management in Faculty of Allied Medical Sciences Tehran University of Medical Sciences. Health Information Manage- ment, 7, 353-360.www.jhim.ir

20. Farzianpour, F., Aghababa, S., Delgoshaei, B. and Haghgoo, M. (2011) Performance Evaluation a Teaching Hospital Affiliated to Tehran University of Medical Sciences Based on Baldrige Excellence Model. American Journal of Eco- nomics and Business Administration, 3, 272-276.

21. Farzianpour, F., Mhammad, K., Malekafzali, H. and Nedjat, S. (2014) Determining the Quality of Management and Structural Elements of the Epidemiology and Biostatistics Department in Tehran University of Medical Sciences. Jour- nal of Service Science and Management, 7, 430-439. http://dx.doi.org/10.4236/jssm.2014.76040

CHAPTER 15 INTERNAL CONTROL AUDITING

Jianfei Leng and Lingfen Zhang

Keywords: Internal Control, Financial Statements, Auditing

INTRODUCTION

The internal control system is an important activity of enterprises operating smoothly, which is the important measure to achieve the long-term strategic development of the enterprise and which aims to improve the operating efficiency of the effect. The external audit of Internal Control over Financial Reporting (ICFR) is a very expensive and contentious aspect of the Sarbanes-Oxley Act (SOX). Wang Qin, Huang Dan, Ellen Young found that the disclosure of internal control self-assessment report is better; internal control audit report issued by the numbers is increasing year by year, but the accounting firm's internal control audit report's credibility has yet to be verified [1] . The current enterprise faces the problems which come from the aspects such as society, economy, law, foreign culture changes in the environment, which has prompted the development of internal control theory; furthermore, the internal control system mainly experiences five development stages. They include the internal check, internal control, internal control structure, internal control-integrated framework, enterprise risk management-integrated framework. Firms are more likely to be identified with an internal control weakness, if their audit committees have less financial expertise or, more specifically, have less accounting financial expertise and non-accounting financial expertise [2] . The first line of the enterprise internal control defense is to prevent financial reporting errors and frauds, which make sure that the internal mechanism of enterprises is a complete financial report. The second line of defense is against the enterprise financial report errors and frauds. The certified public accountants namely put forward the financial statements and express the opinion of the enterprise accounting information quality.

Citation: Leng, J. and Zhang, L. (2014) Internal Control Auditing. Modern Economy, 5, 785-790. doi: 10.4236/me.2014.57072.

Firms are more likely to be identified with an internal control weakness, if their audit committees have less financial expertise or, more specifically, have less accounting financial expertise and non-accounting financial expertise [3] . In recent years, auditing in China has made remarkable development; in June 2008 and April 2010, the ministry of finance, securities and futures commission, the national audit office, the China banking regulatory commission, insurance regulatory commission has jointly issued the enterprise internal control basic norms and three facilities, such as enterprise internal control audit guidelines, which are mainly aiming at the existing problem of Chinese enterprises and establishing internal control system, and for Chinese companies, a sound system of internal control is established which provides the basic framework, namely "to establish internal control system is the Chinese enterprises to participate in international competition, gradually accepted and conscientiously abided by rules of the market economy, perfecting enterprise system and the inherent requirement of fine management". Based on resource dependency theory that stresses entity's economic needs for internal control over administering federal funding, they select a sample of nonprofit hospitals subject to the Single Audit Act in the United States, from 2001 to 2008. Their results show that hospitals that had audit committees and also employed Big 4 auditors were associated with better internal control quality [4] .

The internal control goal guarantees enterprise operation and management in accordance with the provisions of the laws and regulations, the safety of the assets, and financial reports and related information and true, and improves the management efficiency and effectiveness, promotes enterprise development strategy—"internal control audit is a control behavior which can understand internal control whether the establishment is effective, can prevent the fraud, at last to provide reasonable assurance for the realization of the internal control goals" [5] . In Chinese state-owned enterprises occupying the dominant position in the national economy, the number is larger, and the relationship in the state-owned enterprise internal control audit has very important practical significance. It is beneficial to the state-owned enterprises to speed up the perfect internal control system, which is more advantageous to enhance the enterprise competition. The remaining part is organized as follows:

The second part mainly analyses the internal audit and explains its relationship with the audit of financial statements from the company's management aspect; the third part describes the main elements of the internal control; the fourth part is about the case description and analysis; the fifth part is the conclusions and recommendations.

From the Company's Management Aspect, It Mainly Analyses the Internal Audit and Explains Its Relationship with the Audit of Financial Statements

In the past, people used to focus on whether the management has the behavior beyond the control. Though we can't deny that this is still a part of the modern internal control auditing important content, under modern corporate environment, for the audit, the process of management aims to achieve effective utilization of resources. "On the one hand, the management is the vital position in the control environment."

As an example, Shanghai Stock Exchange main board listed companies to disclose Internal 2012 control selfassessment report and the audit report as a sample, follow the COSO internal control report, the five elements of internal control of 650 Shanghai-listed companies drawn from the analysis of defect types: Shanghai-listed companies to disclose Internal control deficiencies small percentage of the company; [6] management ideology, directly affect the whole process of, only we fully understand the intention of the authorities, we can do better to improve the internal control by the audit company, and perfect the process, so as to improve the company's operating purposes. This article combines internal control and information technology, suggesting how internal control plays a positive role in achieving company's goal and improving enterprise value [7] .

The process audit is a kind of more operational audit. "In Wang Haibin's paper, internal control self-assessment report is not only a reflection of the effectiveness of corporate financial reporting, it is the business of the whole process of implementation of internal control evaluation, development and implementation of the internal control system has a decisive role [8] ." The concept itself also has to ensure the efficiency of the internal control process and to determine the reasonable goal, evaluation of project risk, implementation of control behavior, guarantee the realization of the goal, and then make sure the new goal to adapt to the development of enterprise. "Internal control is a continuous cycle repeat steps, so for the evaluation of internal control and audit, it also should be to this process audit. So the audit of internal control should be a circulation of the audit process [9] ."

Enterprise internal control operates smoothly and that has important influence on enterprises to prepare financial statements. The following briefly introduces the relation and the distinction between the financial statements and the internal control.

The relationship between the internal control and the company's financial statements:

1) The audit in the same way.

Both took risk oriented audit mode. Audit procedures are same. Financial statements audit must understand the internal control environment of the enterprises, and even take control of the test; the internal control auditing must understand and test the internal control; at the same time the definition of the effectiveness of the internal control and evaluation method, they can be used to ask, examination, observation, through the test, to implement methods and procedures.

2) Focus on the same object.

Both of them need to identify key account, important deal category and so on. In the financial statements audit certified public accountant needs to evaluate these key accounts and key to make sure that whether they are the material misstatement category; in the internal control audit, they need to evaluate whether these accounts and transaction are covered by the internal control.

3) Determine the importance of the same level.

They need to check whether there is a material misstatement in the financial report; to determine the level of importance in the internal control audit, they also need to check whether there is a significant internal control defects.

Therefore, only internal control get to formulate and effective implementation, can they guarantee the audit report is issued by officially. But the specific part of the internal control and those content will be namely introduced in the next section.

MAIN COMPONENTS OF THE INTERNAL CONTROL

First of all, the control environment is the first part of the internal control framework. It sets the tone for the company as a whole and it also affects the execution of its staff awareness. This is an integral part of the internal control components and the basis of internal control procedures provides the tone and organizational structure. In this phase, the company determines the business goals and the overall business philosophy. It is used to identify and analyze and realize the risks associated with the company's objectives. Every company is faced with various risks from internal and external, therefore, to maintain the continuing operations of the enterprise, they must assess the risk. At this stage, the company should find out all kinds of risks and determine the basic measures of risk management; control activities is the third part of the internal control framework, it helps to reduce the risk of company objectives, control activities including account reconciliation, separation of duties, decentralization, and uses the serial number of the documents in advance to aim to overcome these activities, such as the company may face the potential risks, and help the company achieve its business goals [10] . So the company must be in the form of appropriate and at the appropriate time determine and communicate relevant information about the internal control so that in the fourth part of the internal control people can perform their duties of communication and information.

It must be communicated with the company's business objectives, and control activities should control activities so that the staff can find the management information and also need to monitor by monitoring, and control activities over a period of time can be evaluated, as well as the whole internal control, you can determine the effectiveness of the control activities to make sure whether the control activities need to be scaled, or whether it is no longer needed to perform. They also should be evaluated at this stage of the company's business objectives.

The above five aspects is necessary for the enterprise to develop sustainable and healthy which include the control environment, risk assessment and supervision process, and the business process level control include the control activities, further, only will do the business flow, daily life and from the overall level, enterprise's control can continue to operate normally [11] . Today's enterprise internal control audits are almost large enterprise internal. And big enterprise is mainly state-owned enterprises. They can be stated through the specific case below.

CASE IS INTRODUCED AND ANALYZED

The company is listed in 1986. In the same year, in February's it issues 270 million new shares to the China international trust and investment group (Hong Kong) co. LTD. This make the CITIC group (Hong Kong) hold company's 64.7% [12] stake. Since then, it had become a subsidiary of CITIC. In Western Australia CITIC Pacific's operated iron ore, in order to reduce the currency risk of the company, since 2007, CITIC Pacific began to buy foreign currency options contracts to hedge. On December 5, 2008, CITIC Pacific's shares closed at 5.80 Hong Kong dollars and declined more than HK $21 billion in more than a month's. On November 12, 2008, CITIC Pacific's made an announcement again, with the parent company of CITIC group restructuring reaching a preliminary agreement, one of them was to convert the bond manner and to CITIC capital injection of $1.5 billion. At the general meeting, according to leaked CITIC Pacific on December 19, shareholders got 99.94% of the vote. Second is the "surgical" way of the partial derivatives contracts from the listed company, CITIC group will assist in CITIC Pacific two-step restructuring the existing a $8.7 billion contract. According to the announcement, CITIC group hopes to complete restructuring in December 30. The derivatives losses are over periodically.

In the second part we introduced the five elements of internal control, now we will explain the cause of the problem from the aspect of the business flow and the overall level in this paper.

The Business Flow

It mainly includes two parts: control activities and information systems. In CITIC Pacific's case, its defects embodied in investing heavily, within the scope of a certain amount, there are corresponding level for examination and approval of personnel, but in the actual execution process, because of the amounts involved, numerous and complicated formalities, it finally results in the defect of the control activities; in information systems, because there are specific legal provisions of the state-owned enterprises overseas futures hedging business management method, it clear stipulates the total trading spot trading volume shall be a limited amount, while CITIC Fu Tai chairman Larry Yung and managing director Henry Fan has been aware of this situation. But he did not communicate timely; finally, the circumstance led to the delay of information, as a result, the amount made losses increase greatly.

The Overall Level

It mainly includes three parts: control environment, risk assessment and supervision. In this case, they don't have a design about the necessary risk assessment process; they also don't make the overall understanding of the overall control environment. Without the approval of the board of directors the company executives make a major strategic decision which makes the CITIC Pacific exists a huge hole in corporate governance. Standard & poor's, a rating agency, at the same time according to the report, CITIC Pacific's huge foreign exchange trading losses reflect that the company lacks proper internal regulation and transparency insufficient which cause huge losses of CITIC Pacific.

For any management decision-making activities of the enterprise, they must consider the basis of the above five aspects, then the company could have much better development.

THE CONCLUSIONS AND RECOMMENDATIONS

To Ensure Effective Implementation of Internal Control

Since 2002 the United States has gradually strengthened the construction of enterprise internal control and supervision, and the most representative is issued by the US President George Bush in 2002 Sarbanes Oxley Act which puts forward the effectiveness of internal control self-assessment, hires a certified public accountant audit self-assessment report required and classified according to the type and size of listed companies gradually, and strengthens the supervision of the internal control of listed companies. The enterprise that has investment value needs not only to have a good business performance and developing prospect, but also to have a perfect internal control system; to some extent, the internal control failure faced a greater risk of decline in operating performance. This may bring fatal harm to the significant internal control defects.

In our country, commodity business has entered the era of meager profit. As an example of the steel industry, according to the survey, in 2009 profit margin of annual sales of large and medium-sized steel mills is only 2.5%, however, capital operation is more risky than the traditional commodity business. Deron, Gelinkeer events and a series of failure cases are being exposure, which show the significance and urgency of the internal control and economic globalization. Enterprises are facing the risk of more complex control and the most important way of avoiding these risks is to establish and implement internal control system, and make the effect about the internal control audit.

The development of our country enterprises is more and more restricted by market and a buyer's market has initially formed. The increasingly competitive market focuses more on high quality, many varieties, famous brand, low cost, economies of scale of enterprises and products; this has forced companies to enhance their own brand strength by controlling the cost, improving the management level and finally to ensure the realization of business objectives.

The Establishment of Independent Internal Control Audit Institutions

"In view of the state-owned enterprise, internal audit independence is not recognized by the public of the status, I think they should set up internal audit institutions under the highest decision-making and enforcement agencies, and they also should appoint the nomination or specific head to ensure the independence and authority of internal audit institutions; at the same time, we should follow our country enterprise internal control basic norms and the enterprise internal control audit guide specification requirements to make sure that audit content and audit procedures are reasonable and find weak link of enterprise internal control and internal management and at the same time we should put forward opinion to improve the enterprise internal control."

In our country, enterprise internal control supporting guidance of certified public accountants audit guidelines demands that the CPA should implement the audit work in accordance with the method of top-down which requires the auditor to focus on the level control first, then the big account, and the final focusing on trading or application level in the process of the specific control in the state-owned enterprise internal control audit work; commonly used methods are mainly about the appropriate personnel, observing activities, checking the related documents through testing, and the methods of execution, but the question itself is not enough to obtain sufficient and appropriate evidence, and it should be combined with other internal control auditing method together.

Improve the Quality of the Internal Auditors

Perfecting the internal audit work—"the internal control auditing practice standard is the internal control audit personnel's professional standard; they need to have a number of highly qualified internal control auditing professionals", it is important to strengthen audit professionals follow-up education. "Through enhancing the auditor's professional ethics consciousness, strengthening audit professional training, strengthening the internal auditors of the certification exam and continuing education training, they aim to improve risk analysis of the internal audit staff proactive; they need to meet the requirements of the development of state-owned enterprise internal audit in the aspects such as personnel structure and quality."

Strengthening the Internal Control Auditing Supervision

At the end of each year, according to the principle of cost and the importance, SASAC available should make spot check about whether the state-owned enterprise internal control is effective; the internal control evaluation report is a true reflection of enterprise internal control; internal control of the auditing reports issued by certified public accountants is real fair. Only when they strengthen the regulation, the state-owned enterprise internal control construction and the effect of the internal control auditing will be strengthened.

REFERENCES

1. Wang, Q., Huang, D. and Young, E. (2014) Internal Control Information Disclosure Situation Analysis—Based on Studies of the Shenzhen Stock Exchange from 2008 to 2012. Taxation and Economy, 1, 57-62. (in Chinese)http://mall.cnki.net/magazine/Article/SWYJ201401010.htm
2. Herda, D.N., Notbohm, M.A. and Dowdell, T.D. (2014) The Effect of External Audits of Internal Control over Financial Reporting on Financial Reporting for Clients of Big 4, Second-Tier, and Small Audit Firms. Research in Accounting Regulation, 26, 98-103. http://dx.doi.org/10.1016/j.racreg.2014.02.010
3. Dey, R.M. and Sullivan, M.W. (2012) Was Dodd-Frank Justified in Granting Internal Control Audit Exemption to Small Firms? Managerial Auditing Journal, 27, 666-692. http://dx.doi.org/10.1108/02686901211246804
4. Keane, M.J., Elder, R.J. and Albring, S.M. (2012) The Effect of the Type and Number of Internal Control Weaknesses and Their Remediation on Audit Fees. Review of Accounting and Finance, 11, 377-399. http://dx.doi.org/10.1108/14757701211279178
5. Pridgen, A. and Wang, K.J. (2012) Audit Committees and Internal Control Quality: Evidence from Nonprofit Hospitals Subject to the Single Audit Act. International Journal of Auditing, 16, 165-183. (in Chinese) http://onlinelibrary.wiley.com/doi/10.1111/j.1099-1123.2012.00448.x/abstract
6. Wang, T. (2013) Shanghai Stock Exchange Main Board Listed Companies to Disclose Control Deficiencies. Analysis Foreign Trade, 12, 105-107. (in Chinese) http://d.wanfangdata.com.cn/periodical_hljdwjm201312035.aspx
7. Li, R.M. and Zhang, S.Q. (2013) Empirical Study on the Correlation between the Internal Control and Enterprise Value—Based on the Information System. Journal of Computers, 6, 126-129. (in Chinese) http://www.nssd.org/articles/article_detail.aspx?id=48121100
8. Wang, H.B. (2014) Internal Control Self-Assessment Report Literature Review Study. Disclosure of Beijing Technology and Business University (Social Science Edition), 1, 89-95. (in Chinese) http://d.g.wanfangdata.com.cn/Periodical_bjgsdxxb-sh201401013.aspx
9. Chen, L.R. and Huang, Y. (2013) Management Residual Control Rights, Residual Claim and Internal Control Audits Correlation. Chinese CPA, 7, 88-94. (in Chinese) http://cdmd.cnki.com.cn/Article/CDMD-11660-1013358970.htm
10. Wang, H.C. and Kim, J.J. (2013) Internal Control over Financial Reporting of Listed Companies Audited Problems. Green Accounting, 7, 18-20. (in Chinese) http://mall.cnki.net/magazine/Article/LCWJ201307007.htm

11. Zhu, C.J. and Han, X.W. (2013) Audit of Internal Control over Financial Reporting Audit Opinions Impact Study—Evidence from China's A-Share Listed Companies in 2011. Beijing Technology and Business University (Social Science Edition), 5, 77-82. (in Chinese) http://www.cnki.com.cn/Article/CJFDTotal-BJSB201305012.htm

12. Ding, H. (2009) CITIC Pacific for ex Derivatives Investment Losses Case Studies and Inspiration. Southern Finance, Section 3. (in Chinese)http://www.citicpacific.com/upload/b5/20081020-2c.pdf

CHAPTER 16

CORPORATE ACCOUNT FRAUD

Madan Lal Bhasin

Keywords: Corporate Accounting Frauds; Satyam Computers; Case Study; India; Corporate Governance; Accounting and Auditing Standards

INTRODUCTION

What Is Fraud?

Fraud is a worldwide phenomenon that affects all continents and all sectors of the economy. Fraud encompasses a wide-range of illicit practices and illegal acts involving intentional deception, or misrepresentation. According to the Association of Certified Fraud Examiners (ACFE), fraud is "a deception or misrepresentation that an individual or entity makes knowing that misrepresentation could result in some unauthorized benefit to the individual or to the entity or some other party" [1]. In other words, mistakes are not fraud. Indeed, in fraud, groups of unscrupulous individuals manipulate, or influence the activities of a target business with the intention of making money, or obtaining goods through illegal or unfair means. Fraud cheats the target organization of its legitimate income and results in a loss of goods, money, and even goodwill and reputation. Fraud often employs illegal and immoral, or unfair means. It is essential that organizations build processes, procedures and controls that do not needlessly put employees in a position to commit fraud and that effectively detect fraudulent activity if it occurs. The fraud involving persons from the leadership level is known under the name "managerial fraud" and the one involving only entity's employees is named "fraud by employees' association".

Magnitude of Fraud Losses: A Glimpse

Organizations of all types and sizes are subject to fraud. On a number of occasions over the past few decades, major public companies have experienced financial reporting fraud, resulting in turmoil in the capital markets, a loss of shareholder value, and, in some cases, the bankruptcy of the company itself. Although, it is generally accepted that the Sarbanes-Oxley Act has improved corporate governance and decreased the incidence of fraud, recent studies and surveys indicate that investors and management continue to have concerns about financial statement fraud. For example:

- The ACFE's "2010 Report to the Nations on Occupational Fraud and Abuse" [1] found that financial statement fraud, while representing less than five percent of the cases of fraud in its report, was by far the most costly, with a median loss of $1.7 million per incident. Survey participants estimated that the typical organization loses 5% of its revenues to fraud each year. Applied to the 2011 Gross World Product, this figure translates to a potential projected annual fraud loss of more than $3.5 trillion. The median loss caused by the occupational fraud cases in our study was $140,000. More than one-fifth of these cases caused losses of at least $1 million. The frauds reported to us lasted a median of 18 months before being detected.
- "Fraudulent Financial Reporting: 1998-2007", from the Committee of Sponsoring Organizations of the Treadway Commission (the 2010 COSO Fraud Report) [2], analyzed 347 frauds investigated by the US Securities and Exchange Commission (SEC) from 1998 to 2007 and found that the median dollar amount of each instance of fraud had increased three times from the level in a similar 1999 study, from a median of $4.1 million in the 1999 study to $12 million. In addition, the median size of the company involved in fraudulent financial reporting increased approximately six-fold, from $16 million to $93 million in total assets and from $13 million to $72 million in revenues.
- A "2009 KPMG Survey" [3] of 204 executives of US companies with annual revenues of $250 million or more found that 65 percent of the respondents considered fraud to be a significant risk to their organizations in the

Citation: M. Lal Bhasin, "Corporate Account Fraud," Open Journal of Accounting, Vol. 2 No. 2, 2013, pp. 26-38. doi: 10.4236/ojacct.2013.22006.

next year, and more than one-third of those identified financial reporting fraud as one of the highest risks.

- Fifty-six percent of the approximately 2100 business professionals surveyed during a "Deloitte Forensic Center" [4] webcast about reducing fraud risk predicted that more financial statement fraud would be uncovered in 2010 and 2011 as compared to the previous three years. Almost half of those surveyed (46 percent) pointed to the recession as the reason for this increase.
- According to "Annual Fraud Indicator 2012" conducted by the National Fraud Authority (UK) [5], "The scale of fraud losses in 2012, against all victims in the UK, is in the region of £73 billion per annum. In 2006, 2010 and 2011, it was £13, £30 and £38 billions, respectively. The 2012 estimate is significantly greater than the previous figures because it includes new and improved estimates in a number of areas, in particular against the private sector. Fraud harms all areas of the UK economy".

Moreover, financial statement fraud was a contributing factor to the recent financial crisis and it threatened the efficiency, liquidity and safety of both debt and capital markets [6]. Furthermore, it has significantly increased uncertainty and volatility in financial markets, shaking investor confidence worldwide. It also reduces the creditability of financial information that investors use in investment decisions. When taking into account the loss of investor confidence, as well as, reputational damage and potential fines and criminal actions, it is clear why financial misstatements should be every manager's worst fraud-related nightmare [7].

Who Commits Frauds?

veryday, there are revelations of organizations behaving in discreditable ways [8]. Generally, there are three groups of business people who commit financial statement frauds. They range from senior management (CEO and CFO); midand lower-level management and organizational criminals [9]. CEOs and CFOs commit accounting frauds to conceal true business performance, to preserve personal status and control and to maintain personal income and wealth. Midand lower-level employyees falsify financial statements related to their area of responsibility (subsidiary, division or other unit) to conceal poor performance and/or to earn performance-based bonuses. Organizational criminals falsify financial statements to obtain loans, or to inflate a stock they plan to sell in a "pump-and-dump" scheme. While many changes in financial audit processes have stemmed from financial fraud, or manipulations, history and related research repeatedly demonstrates that a financial audit simply cannot be relied upon to detect fraud at any significant level.

Consequences of Fraudulent Reporting

Fraudulent financial reporting can have significant consequences for the organization and its stakeholders, as well as for public confidence in the capital markets. Periodic high-profile cases of fraudulent financial reporting also raise concerns about the credibility of the US financial reporting process and call into question the roles of management, auditors, regulators, and analysts, among others. Moreover, corporate fraud impacts organizations in several areas: financial, operational and psychological [10]. While the monetary loss owing to fraud is significant, the full impact of fraud on an organization can be staggering. In fact, the losses to reputation, goodwill, and customer relations can be devastating. When fraudulent financial reporting occurs, serious consequences ensue. The damage that result is also widespread, with a sometimes devastating "ripple" effect [6]. Those affected may range from the "immediate" victims (the company's stockholders and creditors) to the more "remote" (those harmed when investor confidence in the stock market is shaken). Between these two extremes, many others may be affected: "employees" who suffer job loss or diminished pension fund value; "depositors" in financial institutions; the company's "underwriters, auditors, attorneys, and insurers"; and even honest "competitors" whose reputations suffer by association.

As fraud can be perpetrated by any employee within an organization or by those from the outside, therefore, it is important to have an effective "fraud management" program in place to safeguard your organization's assets and reputation. Thus, prevention and earlier detection of fraudulent financial reporting must start with the entity that prepares financial reports. Given the current state of the economy and recent corporate scandals, fraud is still a top concern for corporate executives. In fact, the sweeping regulations of Sarbanes-Oxley, designed to help prevent and detect corporate fraud, have exposed fraudulent practices that previously may have gone undetected. Additionally, more corporate executives are paying fines and serving prison time than ever before. No industry is immune to fraudulent situations and the negative publicity that swirls around them. The implications for management are clear: every organization is vulnerable to fraud, and managers must know how to detect it, or at least, when to suspect it.

REVIEW OF LITERATURE

Starting in the late 1990s, a wave of corporate frauds in the United States occurred with Enron's failure perhaps being the emblematic example. Jeffords [11] examined 910 cases of frauds submitted to the "Internal Auditor" during the nine-year period from 1981 to 1989 to assess the specific risk factors cited in the Treadway Commission Report. He concluded that "approximately 63 percent of the 910 fraud cases are classified under the internal control risks". In addition, Smith [12] offered a "typology" of individuals who embezzle. He indicated that embezzlers are "opportunist's type", who quickly detects the lack of weakness in internal control and seizes the opportunity to use the deficiency to his benefit. Similarly, Ziegenfuss [13] performed a study to determine the amount and type of fraud occurring in "state and local" governments. His study revealed that the most frequently occurring types of fraud are misappropriation of assets, theft, false representation; and false invoice.

On the other hand, Haugen and Selin [14] in their study discussed the value of "internal" controls, which depends largely on management's integrity and the ready availability of computer technology, which assisted in the commitment of crime. Sharma and Brahma [15] emphasized on "bankers" responsibility on frauds; bank frauds could crop-up in all spheres of bank's dealing. Major cause for perpetration of fraud is laxity in observance in laid-down system and procedures by supervising staff. Harris and William [16], however, examined the reasons for "loan" frauds in banks and emphasized on due diligence program. Beirstaker, Brody, Pacini [17] in their study proposed numerous fraud protection and detection techniques. Moreover, Willison [18] examined the causes that led to the breakdown of "Barring" Bank. The collapse resulted due to the failures in management, financial and operational controls of Baring Banks.

Choo and Tan [19] explained corporate fraud by relating the "fraud-triangle" to the "broken trust theory" and to an "American Dream" theory, which originates from the sociological literature, while Schrand and Zechman [20] relate executive over-confidence to the commitment of fraud. Moreover, Bhasin [21] examined the reasons for "check" frauds, the magnitude of frauds in Indian banks, and the manner, in which the expertise of internal auditors can be integrated, in order to detect and prevent frauds in banks by taking "proactive" steps to combat frauds. Chen [22] in his study examined "unethical" leadership in the companies and compares the role of unethical leaders in a variety of scenarios. Through the use of computer simulation models, he shows how a combination of CEO's narcissism, financial incentive, shareholders' expectations and subordinate silence as well as CEO's dishonesty can do much to explain some of the findings highlighted in recent high-profile financial accounting scandals. According to a research study performed by Cecchini et al. [23], the authors provided a methodology for detecting "management" fraud using basic financial data based on "support vector machines".

From the above, it is evident that majority of studies were performed in developed, Western countries. However, the manager's behavior in fraud commitment has been relatively unexplored so far. Accordingly, the objective of this paper is to examine managers' unethical behaviors in Satyam Computer Limited, which constitute an ex-post evaluation of alleged or acknowledged fraud case. Unfortunately, no study has been conducted to examine behavioral aspects of manager's in the perpetuation of corporate frauds in the context of a developing economy, like India. Hence, the present study seeks to fill this gap and contributes to the literature.

RESEARCH METHODOLOGY, OBJECTIVES AND SOURCES OF INFORMATION

Financial reporting practice can be developed by reference to a particular setting in which it is embedded. Therefore, "qualitative" research could be seen useful to explore and describe fraudulent financial reporting practice. Here, two issues are crucial. First, to understand why and how a "specific" company is committed to fraudulent financial reporting practice an appropriate "interpretive" research approach is needed. Second, case study conducted as part of this study, looked specifically at the largest fraud case in India, involving Satyam Computer Services (Satyam). Labelled as "India's Enron" by the Indian media, the Satyam accounting fraud has comprehensively exposed the failure of the regulatory oversight mechanism in India. No doubt, to design better accounting systems, we need to understand how accounting systems operate in their social, political and economic contexts. The main objectives of this study are to: 1) highlight the Satyam Computers Limited's accounting scandal by portraying the sequence of events, the aftermath of events, the key parties involved, and major follow-up actions undertaken in India; and 2) what lesions can be learned from Satyam scam?

To complement prior literature, we examined documented behaviors in cases of Satyam corporate scandal, using the evidence taken from press articles, and also applied a "content" analysis to them. In terms of information collection "methodology", we searched for evidence from the press coverage contained in the "Factiva" database. Thus, present study is primarily based on "secondary" sources of data (EBSCO host database) gathered from the related literature published in the journals, newspaper, books, statements, reports. However, as stated earlier, the nature of study is "primarily qualitative, descriptive and analytical".

CORPORATE ACCOUNTING SCANDAL AT SATYAM COMPUTER SERVICES LIMITED: A CASE STUDY OF INDIA'S ENRON

Ironically, Satyam means "truth" in the ancient Indian language "Sanskrit" [24]. Satyam won the "Golden Peacock Award" for the best governed company in 2007 and in 2009. From being India's IT "crown jewel" and the country's "fourth largest" company with high-profile customers, the outsourcing firm Satyam Computers has become embroiled in the nation's biggest corporate scam in living memory [25]. Mr. Ramalinga Raju (Chairman and Founder of Satyam; henceforth called "Raju"), who has been arrested and has confessed to a \$1.47 billion (or Rs. 7800 crore) fraud, admitted that he had made up profits for years. According to reports, Raju and his brother, B. Rama Raju, who was the Managing Director, "hid the deception from the company's board, senior managers, and auditors". The case of Satyam's accounting fraud has been dubbed as "India's Enron". In order to evaluate and understand the severity of Satyam's fraud, it is important to understand factors that contributed to the "unethical" decisions made by the company's executives. First, it is necessary to detail the rise of Satyam as a competitor within the global IT services market-place. Second, it is helpful to evaluate the driving-forces behind Satyam's decisions: Ramalinga Raju. Finally, attempt to learn some "lessons" from Satyam fraud for the future.

Emergence of Satyam Computer Services Limited

Satyam Computer Services Limited was a "rising-star" in the Indian "outsourced" IT-services industry. The company was formed in 1987 in Hyderabad (India) by Mr. Ramalinga Raju. The firm began with 20 employees and grew rapidly as a "global" business. It offered IT and business process outsourcing services spanning various sectors. Satyam was as an example of "India's growing success". Satyam won numerous awards for innovation, governance, and corporate accountability. "In 2007, Ernst & Young awarded Mr. Raju with the 'Entrepreneur of the Year' award. On April 14, 2008, Satyam won awards from MZ Consult's for being a 'leader in India in CG and accountability'. In September 2008, the World Council for Corporate Governance awarded Satyam with the 'Global Peacock Award' for global excellence in corporate accountability" [26]. Unfortunately, less than five months after winning the Global Peacock Award, Satyam became the centerpiece of a "massive" accounting fraud.

By 2003, Satyam's IT services businesses included 13,120 technical associates servicing over 300 customers worldwide. At that time, the world-wide IT services market was estimated at nearly $400 billion, with an estimated annual compound growth rate of 6.4%. "The markets major drivers at that point in time were the increased importance of IT services to businesses worldwide; the impact of the Internet on eBusiness; the emergence of a high-quality IT services industry in India and their methodologies; and, the growing need of IT services providers who could provide a range of services". To effectively compete, both against domestic and global competitors, the company embarked on a variety of multi-pronged business growth strategies.

From 2003-2008, in nearly all financial metrics of interest to investors, the company grew measurably. Satyam generated USD $467 million in total sales. By March 2008, the company had grown to USD $2.1 billion. The company demonstrated "an annual compound growth rate of 35% over that period". Operating profits averaged 21%. Earnings per share similarly grew, from $0.12 to $0.62, at a compound annual growth rate of 40%. Over the same period (2003-2009), the company was trading at an average trailing EBITDA multiple of 15.36. Finally, beginning in January 2003, at a share price of 138.08 INR, Satyam's stock would peak at 526.25 INR—a 300% improvement in share price after nearly five years. Satyam clearly generated significant corporate growth and shareholder value. The company was a leading star—and a recognizable name—in a global IT marketplace. The external environment in which Satyam operated was indeed beneficial to the company's growth. But, the numbers did not represent the full picture. The case of Satyam accounting fraud has been dubbed as "India's Enron".

Mr. Ramalinga Raju and the Satyam Scandal

On January 7, 2009, Mr. Raju disclosed in a letter (see Annexure) to Satyam Computers Limited Board of Directors that "he had been manipulating the company's accounting numbers for years". Mr. Raju claimed that he overstated assets on Satyam's balance sheet by $1.47 billion. Nearly $1.04 billion in bank loans and cash that the company claimed to own was non-existent. Satyam also underreported liabilities on its balance sheet. Satyam overstated income nearly every quarter over the course of several years in order to meet analyst expectations. For example, the results announced on October 17, 2009 overstated quarterly revenues by 75 percent and profits by 97 percent. Mr. Raju and the company's global head of internal audit used a number of different techniques to perpetrate the fraud. "Using his personal computer, Mr. Raju created numerous bank statements to advance the fraud. Mr. Raju falsified the bank accounts to inflate the balance sheet with balances that did not exist. He inflated the income statement by claiming interest income from the fake bank accounts. Mr. Raju also revealed that he created 6000 fake salary accounts over the past few years and appropriated the money after the company deposited it. The company's global head of internal audit created fake customer identities and generated fake invoices against their names to inflate revenue. The global head of internal audit also forged board resolutions and illegally obtained loans for the company" [27]. It also appeared that the cash that the company raised through American Depository Receipts in the United States never made it to the balance sheets.

Greed for money, power, competition, success and prestige compelled Mr. Raju to "ride the tiger", which led to violation of all duties imposed on them as fiduciaries—the duty of care, the duty of negligence, the duty of loyalty, the duty of disclosure towards the stakeholders. "The Satyam scandal is a classic case of negligence of fiduciary duties, total collapse of ethical standards, and a lack of corporate social responsibility. It is human greed and desire that led to fraud. This type of behavior can be traced to: greed overshadowing the responsibility to meet fiduciary duties; fierce competition and the need to impress stakeholders especially investors, analysts, shareholders, and the stock market; low ethical and moral standards by top management; and, greater emphasis on short-term performance" [28]. According to CBI, the Indian crime investigation agency, the fraud activity dates back from April 1999, when the company embarked on a road to double-digit annual growth. As of December 2008, Satyam had a total market capitalization of $3.2 billion dollars.

Satyam planned to acquire a 51% stake in Maytas Infrastructure Limited, a leading infrastructure development, construction and project management company, for $300 million. Here, the Rajus's had a 37% stake. The total turnover was $350 million and a net profit of $20 million. Raju's also had a 35% share in Maytas Properties, another real-estate investment firm. Satyam revenues exceeded $1 billion in 2006. In April, 2008 Satyam became the first Indian company to publish IFRS audited financials. On December 16, 2008, the Satyam board, including its five independent directors had approved the founder's proposal to buy the stake in Maytas Infrastructure and all of Maytas Properties, which were owned by family members of Satyam's Chairman, Ramalinga Raju, as fully owned subsidiary for $1.6 billion. Without shareholder approval, the directors went ahead with the management's decision. The decision of acquisition was, however, reversed twelve hours after investors sold Satyam's stock and threatened action against the management. This was followed by the law-suits filed in the US contesting Maytas deal. The World Bank banned Satyam from conducting business for 8 years due to inappropriate payments to staff and inability to provide information sought on invoices. Four independent directors quit the Satyam board and SEBI ordered promoters to disclose pledged shares to stock exchange.

Investment bank DSP Merrill Lynch, which was appointed by Satyam to look for a partner or buyer for the company, ultimately blew the whistle and terminated its engagement with the company soon after it found financial irregularities [29]. On 7 January 2009, Saytam's Chairman, Ramalinga Raju, resigned after notifying board members and the Securities and Exchange Board of India (SEBI) that Satyam's accounts had been falsified. Raju confessed that Satyam's balance sheet of September 30, 2008, contained the following irregularities: "He faked figures to the extent of Rs. 5040 crore of non-existent cash and bank balances as against Rs. 5361 crore in the books, accrued interest of Rs. 376 crore (non-existent), understated liability of Rs. 1230 crore on account of funds raised by Raju, and an overstated debtor's position of Rs. 490 crore. He accepted that Satyam had reported revenue of Rs. 2700 crore and an operating margin of Rs. 649 crore, while the actual revenue was Rs. 2112 crore and the margin was Rs. 61 crore". In other words, Raju: 1) inflated figures for cash and bank balances of US $1.04 billion vs. US $1.1 billion reflected in the books; 2) an accrued interest of US $77.46 million which was nonexistent; 3) an understated liability of US $253.38 million on account of funds was arranged by himself; and 4) an overstated debtors' position of US $100.94 million vs. US $546.11 million in the books.

Raju claimed in the same letter that "neither he nor the managing director had benefited financially from the inflated revenues, and none of the board members had any knowledge of the situation in which the company was placed". The fraud took place to divert company funds into real-estate investment, keep high earnings per share, raise executive compensation, and make huge profits by selling stake at inflated price. The gap in the balance sheet had arisen purely on account of inflated profits over a period that lasted several years starting in April 1999. "What accounted as a marginal gap between actual operating profit and the one reflected in the books of accounts continued to grow over the years. This gap reached unmanageable proportions as company operations grew significantly", Ragu explained in his letter to the board and shareholders. He went on to explain, "Every attempt to eliminate the gap failed, and the aborted Maytas acquisition deal was the last attempt to fill the fictitious assets with real ones. But the investors thought it was a brazen attempt to siphon cash out of Satyam, in which the Raju family held a small stake, into firms the family held tightly". Table 1 depicts some parts of the Satyam's fabricated 'Balance Sheet and Income Statement' and shows the "difference" between "actual" and "reported" finances.

Fortunately, the Satyam deal with Matyas was "salvageable". It could have been saved only if "the deal had been allowed to go through, as Satyam would have been able to use Maytas' assets to shore up its own books". Raju, who showed "artificial" cash on his books, had planned to use this "non-existent" cash to acquire the two Maytas companies. As part of their "tunneling" strategy, the Satyam promoters had substantially reduced their holdings in company from 25.6% in March 2001 to 8.74% in March 2008. Furthermore, as the promoters held a very small percentage of equity (mere 2.18%) on December 2008, as shown in Table 2, the concern was that poor performance would result in a takeover bid, thereby exposing the gap. It was like "riding a tiger, not knowing how to get off without being eaten". The aborted Maytas acquisition deal was the final, desperate effort to cover up the accounting fraud by bringing some real assets into the business. When that failed, Raju confessed the fraud. Given the stake the Rajus held in Matyas, pursuing the deal would not have been terribly difficult from the perspective of the Raju family. Unlike Enron, which sank due to agency problem, Satyam was brought to its knee due to tunneling. The company with a huge cash pile, with promoters still controlling it with a small per cent of shares (less than 3%), and trying to ab- sorb a real-estate company in which they have a majority stake is a deadly combination pointing prima facie to tunneling [30]. The reason why Ramalinga Raju claims that he did it was because every year he was fudging revenue figures and since expenditure figures could not be fudged so easily, the gap between "actual" profit and "book" profit got widened every year. In order to close this gap, he had to buy Maytas Infrastructure and Maytas Properties. In this way, "fictitious" profits could be absorbed through a "self-dealing" process. The auditors, bankers, and SEBI, the market watchdog, were all blamed for their role in the accounting fraud.

Table 1: Fabricated balance sheet and income statement of Satyam: as of September 30, 2008.

Items Rs. in crore	Actual	Reported	Difference
Cash and Bank Balances	321	5361	5040
Accrued Interest on Bank Fixed Deposits	Nil	376.5	376
Understated Liability	1230	None	1230
Overstated Debtors	2161	2651	490
Total	Nil	Nil	7136
Revenues (Q2 FY 2009)	2112	2700	588
Operating Profits	61	649	588

Table 2: Promoter's shareholding pattern in Satyam from 2001 to 2008.

As on	Promoter's holding in %
March 2001	25.6
2002	22.26
2003	20.74
2004	17.35
2005	15.67
2006	14.02
2007	8.79
2008	8.74
Dec. 2008	2.18

The Auditors Role and Factors Contributing to Fraud

Global auditing firm, PricewaterhouseCoopers (PwC), audited Satyam's books from June 2000 until the discovery of the fraud in 2009. Several commentators criticized PwC harshly for failing to detect the fraud. Indeed, PwC signed Satyam's financial statements and was responsible for the numbers under the Indian law. One particularly troubling item concerned the $1.04 billion that Satyam claimed to have on its balance sheet in "non-interestbearing" deposits. According to accounting professionals, "any reasonable company would have either invested the money into an interest-bearing account, or returned the excess cash to the shareholders. The large amount of cash thus should have been a 'red-flag' for the auditors that further verification and testing was necessary. Furthermore, it appears that the auditors did not independently verify with the banks in which Satyam claimed to have deposits".

Additionally, the Satyam fraud went on for a number of years and involved both the manipulation of balance sheets and income statements. Whenever Satyam needed more income to meet analyst estimates, it simply created "fictitious" sources and it did so numerous times, without the auditors ever discovering the fraud. Suspiciously, Satyam also paid PwC twice what other firms would charge for the audit, which raises questions about whether PwC was complicit in the fraud. Furthermore, PwC audited the company for nearly 9 years and did not uncover the fraud, whereas Merrill Lynch discovered the fraud as part of its due diligence in merely 10 days. Missing these "red-flags" implied either that the auditors were grossly inept or in collusion with the company in committing the fraud. PWC initially asserted that it performed all of the company's audits in accordance with applicable auditing standards.

Numerous factored contributed to the Satyam fraud. The independent board members of Satyam, the institutional investor community, the SEBI, retail investors, and the external auditor—none of them, including professional investors with detailed information and models available to them, detected the malfeasance. The following is a list of factors that contributed to the fraud: greed, ambitious corporate growth, deceptive reporting practices—lack of transparency, excessive interest in maintaining stock prices, executive incentives, stock market expectations, nature of accounting rules, ESOPs issued to those who prepared fake bills, high risk deals that went sour, audit failures (internal and external), aggressiveness of investment and commercial banks, rating agencies and investors, weak independent directors and audit committee, and whistle-blower policy not being effective.

Aftermath of Satyam Scandal

Immediately following the news of the fraud, Merrill Lynch terminated its engagement with Satyam, Credit Suisse suspended its coverage of Satyam, and Price water house Coopers (PwC) came under intense scrutiny and its license to operate was revoked. Coveted awards won by Satyam and its executive management were stripped from the company. Satyam's shares fell to 11.50 rupees on January 10, 2009, their lowest level since March 1998, compared to a high of 544 rupees in 2008. In the New York Stock Exchange, Satyam shares peaked in 2008 at US $ 29.10; by March 2009 they were trading around US $1.80. Thus, investors lost $2.82 billion in Satyam. Unfortunately, Satyam significantly inflated its earnings and assets for years and rolling down Indian stock markets and throwing the industry into turmoil [31]. Criminal charges were brought against Mr. Raju, including: criminal conspiracy, breach of trust, and forgery. After the Satyam fiasco and the role played by PwC, investors became wary of those companies who are clients of PwC, which resulted in fall in share prices of around 100 companies varying between 5% - 15%. The news of the scandal (quickly compared with the collapse of Enron) sent jitters through the Indian stock market, and the benchmark Sensex index fell more than 5%. Shares in Satyam fell more than 70%. The chart titled as "Fall from grace", shown in Exhibit 1 depicts the Satyam's stock decline between December 2008 and January 2009.

Immediately after Raju's revelation about the accounting fraud, "new" board members were appointed and they started working towards a solution that would prevent the total collapse of the firm. Indian officials acted quickly to try to save Satyam from the same fate that met Enron and WorldCom, when they experienced large accounting scandals. The Indian government "immediately started an investigation, while at the same time limiting its direct participation, with Satyam because it did not want to appear like it was responsible for the fraud, or attempting to cover up the fraud". The government appointed a "new" board of directors for Satyam to try to save the company. The Board's goal was "to sell the company within 100 days". To devise a plan of sale, the board met with bankers, accountants, lawyers, and government officials immediately. It worked diligently to bring stability and confidence back to the company to ensure the sale of the company within the 100-day time frame. To accomplish the sale, the board hired Goldman Sachs and Avendus Capital and charged them with selling the company in the shortest time possible.

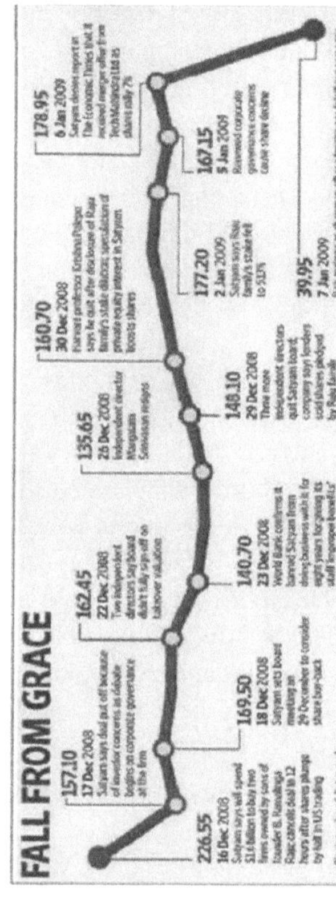

Exhibit 1: Stock Charting of Satyam from December 2008 to January 2009.

By mid-March, several major players in the IT field had gained enough confidence in Satyam's operations to participate in an auction process for Satyam. The Securities and Exchange Board of India (SEBI) appointed a retired Supreme Court Justice, Justice Bharucha, to oversee the process and instill confidence in the transaction. Several companies bid on Satyam on April 13, 2009. The winning bidder, Tech Mahindra, bought Satyam for $1.13 per share—less than a third of its stock market value before Mr. Raju revealed the fraud—and salvaged its operations [32]. Both Tech Mahindra and the SEBI are now fully aware of the full extent of the fraud and India will not pursue further investigations. The stock has again stabilized from its fall on November 26, 2009 and, as part of Tech Mahindra, Saytam is once again on its way toward a bright future.

Investigation: Criminal and Civil Charges

The investigation that followed the revelation of the fraud has led to charges against several different groups of people involved with Satyam. Indian authorities arrested Mr. Raju, Mr. Raju's brother, B. Ramu Raju, its former managing director, Srinivas Vdlamani, the company's head of internal audit, and its CFO on criminal charges of fraud. Indian authorities also arrested and charged several of the company's auditors (PwC) with fraud. The Institute of Chartered Accountants of India [33] ruled that "the CFO and the auditor were guilty of professional misconduct". The CBI is also in the course of investigating the CEO's overseas assets. There were also several civil charges filed in the US against Satyam by the holders of its ADRs. The investigation also implicated several Indian politicians. Both civil and criminal litigation cases continue in India and civil litigation continues in the United States. Some of the main victims were: employees, clients, shareholders, bankers and Indian government.

In the aftermath of Satyam, India's markets recovered and Satyam now lives on. India's stock market is currently trading near record highs, as it appears that a global economic recovery is taking place. Civil litigation and criminal charges continue against Satyam. Tech Mahindra purchased 51% of Satyam on April 16, 2009, successfully saving the firm from a complete collapse. With the right changes, India can minimize the rate and size of accounting fraud in the Indian capital markets.

Corporate Governance Issues at Satyam

On a quarterly basis, Satyam earnings grew. Mr. Raju admitted that the fraud which he committed amounted to nearly $276 million. In the process, Satyam grossly violated all rules of corporate governance [34]. The Satyam scam had been the example for following "poor" CG practices. It had failed to show good relation with the shareholders and employees. CG issue at Satyam arose because of non-fulfillment of obligation of the company towards the various stakeholders. Of specific interest are the following: distinguishing the roles of board and management; separation of the roles of the CEO and chairman; appointment to the board; directors and executive compensation; protection of shareholders rights and their executives.

Lessons Learned from Satyam Scam

The 2009 Satyam scandal in India highlighted the nefarious potential of an improperly governed corporate leader. As the fallout continues, and the effects were felt throughout the global economy, the prevailing hope is that some good can come from the scandal in terms of lessons learned [35]. Here are some lessons learned from the Satyam Scandal:

- Investigate All Inaccuracies: The fraud scheme at Satyam started very small, eventually growing into $276 million white-elephant in the room. Indeed, a lot of fraud schemes initially start out small, with the perpetrator thinking that small changes here and there would not make a big difference, and is less likely to be detected. This sends a message to a lot of companies: if your accounts are not balancing, or if something seems inaccurate (even just a tiny bit), it is worth investigating. Dividing responsibilities across a team of people makes it easier to detect irregularities or misappropriated funds.
- Ruined Reputations: Fraud does not just look bad on a company; it looks bad on the whole industry and a country. "India's biggest corporate scandal in memory threatens future foreign investment flows into Asia's third largest economy and casts a cloud over growth in its once-booming outsourcing sector. The news sent Indian equity markets into a tail-spin, with Bombay's main benchmark index tumbling 7.3% and the Indian rupee fell". Now, because of the Satyam scandal, Indian rivals will come under greater scrutiny by the regulators, investors and customers.
- Corporate Governance Needs to Be Stronger: The Satyam case is just another example supporting the need for stronger CG. All public-companies must be careful when selecting executives and top-level managers. These are the people who set the tone for the company: if there is corruption at the top, it is bound to trickle-down. Also, separate the role of CEO and Chairman of the Board. Splitting up the roles, thus, helps avoid situations like the one at Satyam.

The Satyam Computer Services' scandal brought to light the importance of ethics and its relevance to corporate culture. The fraud committed by the founders of Satyam is a testament to the fact that "the science of conduct" is swayed in large by human greed, ambition, and hunger for power, money, fame and glory.

CONCLUSIONS

Recent corporate frauds and the outcry for transparency and honesty in reporting have given rise to two outcomes. First, forensic accounting skills have become very crucial in untangling the complicated accounting maneuvers that have obfuscated financial statements. Second, public demand for change and subsequent regulatory action has transformed CG scenario across the globe. In fact, both these trends have the common goal of addressing the investors' concerns about the transparent financial reporting system. The failure of the corporate communication structure, therefore, has made the financial community realize that "there is a great need for skilled professionals that can identify, expose, and prevent structural weaknesses in three key areas: poor corporate governance, flawed internal controls, and fraudulent financial statements [36]. In addition, the CG framework needs to be first of all strengthened and then implemented in "letter as well as in right spirit". The increasing rate of white-collar crimes, without doubt, demands stiff penalties and punishments.

Perhaps, no financial fraud had a greater impact on accounting and auditing profession than Enron, WorldCom, and recently, India's Enron: "Satyam". All these frauds have led to the passage of the Sarbanes-Oxley Act in July 2002, and a new federal agency and financial standard-setting body, the Public Companies Accounting Oversight Board (PCAOB). It also was the impetus for the American Institute of Certified Public Accountants' (AICPA) adoption of SAS No. 99, "Consideration of Fraud in a Financial Statement Audit" [37]. But it may be that the greatest impact of Enron and WorldCom was in the significant increased focus and awareness related to fraud. It establishes external auditors' responsibility to plan and perform audits to provide a reasonable assurance that the audited financial statements are free of material frauds.

As part of this research study, one of the key objectives was "to examine and analyze in-depth the Satyam Computers Limited's accounting scandal by portraying the sequence of events, the aftermath of events, the key parties involved, major reforms undertaken in India, and learn some lessons from it". Unlike Enron, which sank due to "agency" problem, Satyam was brought to its knee due to "tunneling". The Satyam scandal highlights the importance of securities laws and CG in emerging markets. There is a broad consensus that emerging market countries must strive to create a regulatory environment in their securities markets that fosters effective CG. India has managed its transition into a global economy well, and although it suffers from CG issues, it is not alone as both developed countries and emerging countries experience accounting and CG scandals. The Satyam scandal brought to light, once again, the importance of ethics and its relevance to corporate culture. The fraud committed by the founders of Satyam is a testament to the fact that "the science of conduct is swayed in large by human greed, ambition, and hunger for power, money, fame and glory". All kind of scandals/frauds have proven that there is a need for good conduct based on strong ethics. The Indian government, in Satyam case, took very quick actions to protect the interest of the investors, safeguard the credibility of India, and the nation's image across the world. Moreover, Satyam fraud has forced the government to re-write CG rules and tightened the norms for auditors and accountants. The Indian affiliate of PwC "routinely failed to follow the most basic audit procedures. The SEC and the PCAOB fined the affiliate, PwC India, \$7.5 million which was described as the largest American penalty ever against a foreign accounting firm" [38]. According to President, ICAI (January 25, 2011), "The Satyam scam was not an accounting or auditing failure, but one of CG. This apex body had found the two PWC auditors prima-facie guilty of professional misconduct". The CBI, which investigated the Satyam fraud case, also charged the two auditors with "complicity in the commission of the fraud by consciously overlooking the accounting irregularities".

The culture at Satyam, especially dominated by the board, symbolized an unethical culture. On one hand, his rise to stardom in the corporate world, coupled with immense pressure to impress investors, made Mr. Raju a "compelled leader to deliver outstanding results". On the contrary, Mr. Raju had to suppress his own morals and values in favor of the greater good of the company. The board connived with his actions and stood as a blind spectator; the lure of big compensation to members further encouraged such behavior. But, in the end, truth is sought and those violating the legal, ethical, and societal norms are taken to task as per process of law. The public confession of fraud by Mr. Ramalinga Raju speaks of integrity still left in him as an individual. His acceptance of guilt and blame for the whole fiasco shows a bright spot of an otherwise "tampered" character. After quitting as Satyam's Chairman, Raju said, "I am now prepared to subject myself to the laws of land and face consequences thereof". Mr. Raju had many ethical dilemmas to face, but his persistent immoral reasoning brought his own demise. The fraud finally had to end and the implications were having far reaching consequences. Thus, Satyam scam was not an accounting or auditing failure, but one of CG. Undoubtedly, the government of India took prompt actions to protect the interest of the investors and safeguard the credibility of India and the nation's image across the world. In addition, the CG framework needs to be strengthened, implemented both in "letter as well as in right spirit", and enforced vigorously to curb white-collar crimes.

REFERENCES

1. ACFE, "Report to the Nation on Occupational Fraud and Abuse," The Association of Certified Fraud Examiners, 2010. www.acfe.com
2. COSO, "Fraudulent Financial Reporting: 1987-2007," Committee of Sponsoring Organizations of the Treadway Commission, 2010. http://www.coso.org
3. KPMG Fraud Survey 2009, 2003, 1998, 1994. www.kpmginstiutes.com
4. Deloitte Forensic Center, "Fraud, Bribery and Corruption Practices Survey," 2011. http://www.deloitte.com.
5. National Fraud Authority, "Annual Fraud Indicator," 2012. www.homeoffice.gov.uk
6. W. K. Black, "Epidemics of Control Fraud Lead to Recurrent, Intensifying Bubbles and Crises," University of Missouri, Kansas City, 2010.
7. Ernst & Young, "Detecting Financial Statement Fraud: What Every Manager Needs to Know," E & Y LLP, London, 2009, pp. 1-8. www.ey.com
8. A. R. Reuber and E. Fischer, "Organizations Behaving Badly: When Are Discreditable Actions Likely to Damage Organizational Reputation?" Journal of Business Ethics, Vol. 93, No. 1, 2009, pp. 39-50. doi:10.1007/s10551-009-0180-3
9. D. L. Crumbley, L. E. Heitger and G. S. Smith, "Forensic and Investigative Accounting Chicago: CCH Incorporated," 2003.
10. C. E. Crutchley, M. R. H. Jensen and Marshall, "Climate for Scandal: Corporate Environments that Contribute to Accounting Fraud," The Financial Review, Vol. 42, No. 1, 2007, pp. 53-73.
11. R. Jeffords, "How Useful Are the Treadway Risk Factors?" Internal Auditor, Vol. 49, No. 3, 1999, pp. 12-30.
12. E. R. Smith, "A Positive Approach to Dealing with Embezzlement," The White Paper, August/September 1995 pp. 17-18.
13. D. E. Ziegenfuss, "State and Local Government Fraud Survey for 1995," Managerial Auditing Journal, Vol. 11, No. 9, 1996, pp. 50-55. doi:10.1108/02686909610150395
14. S. Haugen and J. R. Selin, "Identifying and Controlling Computer Crime and Employee Fraud," Industrial Management & Data Systems, Vol. 99, No. 8, 1999, pp. 340- 344.doi:10.1108/02635579910262544
15. Sharma, S. and Brahma, "A Role of Insider in Banking Fraud," 2000. http://manuputra.com
16. Harris and William, "The Two Faces of the Transgender Fraudster Who Made Thousands of Pounds in Scams Posing as Both Sexes," 2004.
17. J. L. Beirstaker, R. G. Brody and C. Pacini, "Accountants' Perceptions Regarding Fraud Detection and Prevention Methods," Managerial Auditing Journal, Vol. 21. No. 5, 2006, pp. 520-535. doi:10.1108/02686900610667283
18. R. Willison, "Understanding the Offender/Environment Dynamic for Computer Crimes," Information Technology & People, Vol. 19, No. 2, 2006, pp. 170-186. doi:10.1108/09593840610673810

19. F. Choo and K. Tan, "An American Dream Theory of Corporate Executive Fraud," Accounting Forum, Vol. 31, No. 2, 2007, pp. 203-215. doi:10.1016/j.accfor.2006.12.004

20. Schrand and Zechman, "Executive Overconfidence and the Slippery Road to Fraud," 2007. http://faculty.chicagobooth.edu

21. M. L. Bhasin, "Corporate Governance and Role of the Forensic Accountant," The Chartered Secretary Journal, Vol. 38, No. 10, 2008, pp. 1361-1368.

22. S. Chen, "The Role of Ethical Leadership Versus Institutional Constraints: A Simulation Study of Financial Misreporting by CEOs," Journal of Business Ethics, Vol. 93, No. 1, 2010, pp. 33-52. doi:10.1007/s10551-010-0625-8

23. M. Cecchini, H. Aytug, G. J. Koehler and P. Pathak, "Detecting Management Fraud in Public Companies," Management Science, Vol. 56, No. 7, 2010, pp. 1146-1160.doi:10.1287/mnsc.1100.1174

24. E. Basilico, H. Grove and L. Patelli, "Asia's Enron: Satyam," Journal of Forensic & Investigative Accounting, Vol. 4. No. 2, 2012, pp. 142-160.

25. T. Ahmad, T. Malawat, Y. Kochar and A. Roy, "Satyam Scam in the Contemporary Corporate World: A Case Study in Indian Perspective," IUP Journal, 2010, pp. 1-48. www.ssrn.com/abstract=1460022

26. S. Agrawal and R. Sharma, "Beat This: Satyam Won Awards for Corporate Governance, Internal Audit," VCCircle, 2009. www.vccircle.com/news

27. S. Ramachadran, "Raju Brings Down Satyam, Shakes India," Asia Times Online Ltd., 2009. www.a.times.com

28. M. Damodaran, "Listed Firms to Get New Conduct Code," Financial Chronicle, 2009. http://wrd.mydigitalfc.com.

29. R. M. Bowen, A. C. Call and S. Rajgopal, "WhistleBlowing: Target Firm Characteristics and Economic Consequences," The Accounting Review, Vol. 85, No. 4, 2010, pp. 1239-1271.doi:10.2308/accr.2010.85.4.1239

30. S. Shirur, "Tunneling vs. Agency Effect: A Case Study of Enron and Satyam," Vikalpa, Vol. 36, No. 3, 2011, pp. 9-20.

31. H. Timmons and B. Wassener, "Satyam Chief Admits Huge Fraud," New York Times, 8 January 2009. www.nytimes.com

32. S. S. Dagar, "How Satyam Was Sold the Untold Story: How the IT Services Major Was Rescued against all Odds. Business Today Reconstructs the Events of the 14 Crucial Weeks that Led up to the Sale," Business Today, 2009, pp. 25-42.

33. ICAI, "ICIA Finds ex Satyam CFO, Price Waterhouse Auditors Guilty," Outlook, 2009.

34. R. Chakrabarti, W. Megginson and P. K. Yadav, "Corporate Governance in India," Journal of Applied Corporate Finance, Vol. 20, No. 1, 2008, pp. 59-78. doi:10.1111/j.1745-6622.2008.00169.x

35. B. Behan, "Governance Lessons from India's Satyam," Business Week, 16 January 2009.

36. Z. Rezaee and B. L. Kedia, "Role of Corporate Governance Participants in Preventing and Detecting Financial Statement Fraud," Journal of Forensic & Investigative Accounting, Vol. 4, No. 2, 2012, pp. 176-205.

37. AICPA, "SAP-99: Consideration of Fraud in a Financial Statement Audit. Auditing Standard Board," 2002. http://www.aicpa.org

38. F. Norris, "Indian Accounting Firm Is Fined $7.5 Million over Fraud at Satyam," The New York Times, 5 April 2011.

CHAPTER 17 QUALITY ENHANCEMENT OF CORPORATE MANAGEMENT SYSTEMS

Giron Kamonja, Yan Liang, Muhammad Tayyab Sohail, and Shahzad Ahmad Khan

Keywords: Management, Training, Quality, Management Practice

INTRODUCTION

Senior Managers' Role

Based on Malcolm Baldrige National Quality Award (MBNQA) deep lying analysis, Easton [1] , in capturing the state of leadership of top management in the Baldrige applicants, states that senior management is committed to quality. Senior managers are actively involved in promoting the importance of quality and customer satisfaction and they devote a substantial part of their time to quality-related issues. Their involvement includes activities such as meeting with employees, meeting with customers, giving formal and informal recognition, and receiving training and training others. Senior management also develop and communicate key company quality values which place emphasis on the importance of the customer, process orientation, continuous improvement, teamwork, management-by-fact, mutual respect and dignity, and value of individual employees and their contributions. They ensure that the entire workforce understands its role in satisfying the customer. To support and promote the quality process of the organization, senior management develops and puts in place elements of quality management structure. These include a senior management TQM council or division and departmental councils (Figure 1).

Discussions of implementation case studies in the literature are also unanimous in reinforcing this reality. The examples range from large to small companies, service to manufacturing, multinationals to family business, and government to non-profit agencies [2] . At ICL Product Distribution UK, the chief executive and senior executives spearheaded the company-wide quality drive; while at Ciba Geigy Italy, the total quality initiative was led by the group chief executive, with the active support and involvement of senior executives [3] . It is the same for CCTEC metallurgical company in China (Wuhan).

Senior Management's Specific Mission

First and foremost in the quality evolution process, senior management must start by understanding what TQM really means [4] . They must be well aware of the benefits to the organization and acknowledge the fundamental change which will bring in the running of that organization. It is critical that they build the requisite commitment before getting the rest of the staff involved. There must be consensus among them regarding what the organization needs to achieve its quality goal.

At the Aluminum Company of America (Alcoa), it was the chief executive officer who initiated the quality initiative. The directors and senior managers then labored over six months to identify the challenges and opportunities, and then to design and begin the total quality process there. During this period, the top management team, including the CEO, spent many hours in quality education, training, visiting and benchmarking companies that had acquired reputations as leaders in quality management. All these helped form a consensus among top management about why were they interested in quality and what they need to get done to achieve the goals [5] .

Seniors Executives' Behavior

One of the precepts of TQM is employees' greater involvement and commitment to the process and its goal. It is through the

Citation: Kamonja, G. , Liang, Y. , Sohail, M. and Khan, S. (2014) Quality Enhancement of Corporate Management Systems. Journal of Service Science and Management, 7, 302-312. doi: 10.4236/jssm.2014.74027.

actions and behavior of the management that employees identify with the goals of the company and extend their commitment towards its success [6] . Ramirez and Loney's[7] study also highlighted the fact that it is not sufficient for management just to be committed, but they must also be obvious [8] . Bertsch and Williams' [9] study also found that senior executives see being visible in their commitment to quality sends strong signals about what is expected and desired from the staff. It is through their demonstrated actions and behavior that management can harness the involvement of employees corresponding to the necessary skills, and thence their commitment to the quality goals of the company not only will be assured but also will achieve as the senior executives might be expected [10] . Johnston and Daniel [11] in relating Fuji Xerox experiences, stress that if top management command employees to improve but are not themselves constantly seeking ways to improve systems, continuous improvement initiatives will fail. In describing the experiences of TQM implementation at Johnston Matthey plc, UK, George [12] emphasizes that senior management demonstrating involvement in the quality process is just as critical as commitment. There were initial hiccups in the implementation process when staff felt that senior executives were not committed [12] . This experience represents tangible proof, it is imperative to respect the hierarchy provided in the command structure. The violation of the commandment line either horizontal or vertical can harm mutual respect between subordinate and hierarchical superior and ultimately will lead to the disobedience leader in question.

Figure 1: Senior managers'activities and role.

The CEO of Alcoa stressed the need for his directors and senior managers to be visible in terms of their commitment in the eyes of the staff involved [5] . The findings of a survey carried out among employees at two Hewlett-Packard factories in the UK, disclosed the degree of buy-in amongst the respondents was favorable amongst those who saw their management staff using the TQM techniques themselves to improve processes [13] .

Relationship of the Tasks between CEO and Senior Executives

Some of the ways CEOs and senior executives of best companies make this commitment evident is by leading quality initiatives and investing the requisite time and effort. A study found that most of the CEOs of the 62 major US-based companies spend at least 10 percent of their time in quality improvement efforts [6] . At Southern Pacific Lines, leadership meant role modelling. This involved leaders being out on the "track and yards" with the employees to demonstrate and speak about the quality-driven approach to doing business [14] . The CEO of Motorola spent a significant amount of time explaining the corporate vision to enable every employee to translate it into personal work goals [15] . The president and his senior executives at Shorts Brothers were the first to be trained in the theory, practice and tools of quality improvement [16] . The managing director of Rockware Glass Ltd. UK meets every employee in a series of TQM-related sessions at various locations and times convenient to the workers [17] . A high-powered steering committee to manage the TQM process at Paul Revere Insurance Group is a visible sign of top-level commitment to the process[18] . The vice-president at Philips Electronics personally leads a company-wide task force on quality improvement of software development, while at Ericsson Sweden; a top executive took ownership of analyzing and improving the order-make-market system [9] .

Role and Responsibilities of Chief Executive Officer (CEO)

The Chief Executive Officer ("CEO") is responsible for leading the development and execution of the Company's long term strategy with a view to creating shareholder value. The CEO's leadership role also entails being ultimately responsible for all day-to-day management decisions and for implementing the Company's long and short term plans. The CEO acts as a direct liaison between the Board and management of the Company and communicates to the Board on behalf of management. The CEO also communicates on behalf of the Company to shareholders, employees, Government authorities, other stakeholders and the public.

The Main Task of the Responsible CEO

According to Juran [19] , there are seven steps that a responsible CEO must take to achieve quality in any organization:

1) Set up and serve on the company's quality council.
2) Establish corporate quality goals and make them a part of the business plan.
3) Make provision for training the entire company hierarchy in managing for quality.
4) Establish the means to measure quality results against quality goals.
5) Review results against goals on a regular basis.
6) Give recognition for superior quality performance.
7) Revise the reward system to respond to the changes demanded by world class quality.

Oakland [20] lists the five requirements for effective leadership:

1) Clear beliefs and objectives in the form of a mission statement.
2) Clear and effective strategies and supporting plans.
3) The critical success factors and critical process.
4) The appropriate management structure.
5) Employee participation through empowerment, the EPDCA (Evaluate, Plan, Do, Check, Amend) helix.

Specifics Responsibilities of the CEO

More specifically, the duties and responsibilities of the CEO include the following:

1) to lead, in conjunction with the Board, the development of the Company's strategy;

2) to lead and oversee the implementation of the Company's long and short term plans in accordance with its strategy;
3) to ensure the Company is appropriately organized and staffed and to have the authority to hire and terminate staff as necessary to enable it to achieve the approved strategy;
4) to ensure that expenditures of the Company are within the authorized annual budget of the Company;
5) to assess the principal risks of the Company and to ensure that these risks are being monitored and managed;
6) to ensure effective internal controls and management information systems are in place;
7) to ensure that the Company has appropriate systems to enable it to conduct its activities both lawfully and ethically;
8) to ensure that the Company maintains high standards of corporate citizenship and social responsibility wherever it does business;
9) to act as a liaison between management and the Board;
10) to communicate effectively with shareholders, employees, Government authorities, other stakeholders and the public;
11) to keep abreast of all material undertakings and activities of the Company and all material external factors affecting the Company and to ensure that processes and systems are in place to ensure that the CEO and management of the Company are adequately informed;
12) to ensure that the Directors are properly informed and that sufficient information is provided to the Board to enable the Directors to form appropriate judgments;
13) to ensure the integrity of all public disclosure by the Company;
14) in concert with the Chairman, to develop Board agendas;
15) to request that special meetings of the Board be called when appropriate;
16) in concert with the Chairman, to determine the date, time and location of the annual meeting of shareholders and to develop the agenda for the meeting;
17) to sit on committees of the Board where appropriate as determined by the Board; and 18) to abide by specific internally established control systems and authorities, to lead by personal example and encourage all employees to conduct their activities in accordance with all applicable laws and the Company's standards and policies, including its environmental, safety and health policies.

INTERNAL STAKEHOLDERS' MANAGEMENT

Employee Involvement

While top management involvement and leadership are essential for TQM success, they are not sufficient on their own [21] . TQM succeeds only with employees' involvement in the TQM process and their commitment to its goals [8] [18] [22] . In 1979, when the founder president of Matsushita Japan spoke of how Japanese products swept aside Western products in the world market, he attributed it to the involvement of everyone in the company in the quest for quality [18] . This fact was also captured in a study which found that organizations with a high level of employee involvement stand a greater chance of success [23] . Crosby [24] talks about the need for every individual in the organization to understand his or her role in making quality happen. In fact, the need to maximize the involvement of all employees is one of the basic principles of change implementation in an organization. It involves the employees having a common understanding of quality and the importance of their involvement to maintain the quality momentum.

Importance of Labor in Quality Process

According to the chief executive of Federal Express, the foundation for the success of the quality improvement process at this company is the involvement of every employee in that process [25] . He calls it the "human side of quality". LeaRonal (UK) believes that "for a quality improvement program to be successful, the commitment to total quality must encompass a whole workforce who must be encouraged to participate actively in the search for continuous improvement" [26] . The success of the quality improvement process at Mitel Telecom Ltd. UK is attributed to the total involvement of the workforce [27] . In implementing the quality process, Shorts Brothers views greater involvement of its workforce as important evidence that the company is progressing in the right direction [16] .

The critical importance of employees' involvement in the quality process of an organization is based on the belief that the best process innovation ideas come from the people actually doing the job[21] . The quality reputation of Japanese companies is mainly credited to their great success in this area.

Labor Empowerment Result

A total quality environment demands that people participate in continuous improvement activities in an unhindered manner, that pushing decision making to the lowest practical level is the way. In TQM terminology, this is called "empowerment". Deming [28] and Juran [29] also stress the importance of empowerment or giving employees the authority and autonomy to do their job when they talk about "pride of workmanship", "self-improvement", "self-control" and "self-inspection" respectively. At Tioxide Group Limited, empowerment to enable its employees to participate in continuous improvement activities was seen as a key element in the development of its total quality strategy [16] .

Zink [30] emphasizes that employee empowerment is an important area of assessment of major quality awards around the world. Empowered employees go by many labels: self-managing teams, self-directing teams, autonomous groups. Zink [30] even includes participation in employee suggestion schemes.

Advantages of Labor Conscientious

Promoting employee involvement by operating employee

suggestion schemes is common in the majority of the 158 US companies in the Fortune 1000 surveyed (Conference Board in Olian and Rynes [6]). While such schemes are also common in non-TQ organizations, enthusiasm is often stifled due to poor follow-up from management. TQ organizations, however, generally design schemes that are responsive and user-friendly. Employees who wish to make a suggestion at Thomas Interior Systems simply fill out a half-page pre-printed form and drop it in a designated suggestion box [11] . Response to the suggestions is ensured within 72 hours. At Thomas, ideas are submitted at an average monthly rate of 40, with an implementation at 80 percent.

At Milliken, which received 262,000 ideas in 1989, suggestions are acknowledged within 24 hours and acted on within 72 hours, while at Globe Metallurgical, ideas discussed at the weekly quality circle meeting are implemented the same day where possible [31] . However, at Eastman Chemical Company, the suggestion system was eliminated because it was found to impede teamwork [32] .

Greater employee involvement in quality efforts can only come about when the employees know that the organization cares for them [25] . Baldrige winners treat their employees as partners rather than hired hands [31] . The chief executive of Wainwright Industries, the 1994 winner of the Baldrige Award, sums up this point well when he said: "An internal customer (employee) will treat the external customer the way he or she is treated by the company" [33] . This message is echoed by Townsend and Gebhardt [25] , "Without the co-operation of the latter group (employees), the loyalty of the former (external customers) is always in jeopardy".

MIDDLE MANAGEMENT ROLE

The act of maximizing employee involvement in the quality process requires middle managers within the organization to make major adjustments. They must give up some authority as power and control are pushed to lower levels in the organization. In addition, managing according to the philosophy of TQM requires new attitudes and skills from middle managers [34] . The transition towards TQM can be an uncertain and troubling process for middle managers [25] [35] . Only when middle managers are convinced that the transition process that may cost them in status, power and recognition leads to a better world, can the implementation of TQM be smooth. If they do not see it, they may react with suspicion, uncertainty and resistance [17] [34] [36] . Crosby [24] says "It is hard to get people interested in improvement of any kind if they perceive it is a threat to their authority or life style." Unless there is a middle management buy-in, they soon become barriers to rather than champions of the new system. According to Manz and Sims [35] , "On the road to a total quality culture, the biggest obstacle to success is the middle management brick wall".

Middle Manager's Functions

It is in this sense that Saritha Pujari tried to define the main functions of Middle Managers, namely:

1) Interpreting Policies:

At this level, policies framed by top-level managers are interpreted. Like the marketing manager introduces his salesmen to the sales policy of the company that at no cost credit sales will be made.

2) Preparing Organizational Set-Up:

Every middle-level manager prepares outline of his respective department in accordance with the objectives of the organization.

3) Appointing Employees:

Every departmental manager appoints employees to fulfill the activities of his department.

4) Instructor:

Departmental managers direct their subordinates about what to do and how they have to do it. Needful resources are made available to subordinates so that they can do the assigned jobs uninterrupted.

5) Motivating Employees:

Middle-level managers motivate their employees by various means so that they work most efficiently to achieve organizational objectives.

6) Cooperation with Employee:

Cooperation among different divisions is required to successfully achieve company's objectives and this is done by middle level managers.

This fact was also reflected in a survey of 161 organizations. It was established that one of the elements that differentiated the successful TQ organizations from the less than successful ones was middle management support. A survey concluded that without middle managers' committed support for the quality process, the process will be derailed.

Specific Function of Middle Managers

Another survey reported in Quality Progress [37] , which examined 536 organizations using TQM, returned similar findings. The study, which aimed to identify specific practices that have contributed to or detracted from TQM success, revealed that middle management are the main roadblocks to successful TQM. The study recommends that senior management should work hard to understand and involve middle managers in TQM efforts such as involvement in designing and promoting TQM, creating different but meaningful roles for them in supporting widespread quality improvement initiatives, and providing training and development not only in TQM concepts and practices, but also in new leadership skills.

In this sense, getting middle managers to buy-in and be involved in a positive manner is viewed as key to the success of TQM [6] [24] [38] [39] . Ishikawa [38] says that middle management can contribute greatly to quality improvement but conventional organizational arrangements do not encourage their contributions. He calls for senior management to provide greater attention to encourage new roles for middle managers.

At Norand Corporation, management discovered that without middle management's committed support, the total quality process can fail. Middle management training and acceptance were made a priority. Training was created for middle managers to show them how to manage empowered employees and to become facilitators of quality improvement initiatives and coaches of employee development [36] .

At Charrette Corporation, it was recognized at the outset that the new role of middle managers, especially in the transition stage, would be critical to achieving a successful implementation [35] . At Nissan UK, the supervisors have a wide range of responsibilities where people management skill features prominently. For example, supervisors are involved in staff selection, developing and training their staff and motivating and maintaining morale. They are also the channel for all communications to manufacturing staff.

TRAINING AND EDUCATION

TQM Training

Introducing new systems such as TQM when people do not have the fundamental skills to work in the new system is a prescription for disaster [40] . There should be no doubt that for TQM to succeed, the entire workforce must acquire new knowledge, skills and abilities. Training and education based on total quality must be planned and provided if this is to be realized. Oakland[20] stresses that training strategy should be addressed early alongside other strategies within the qualitypolicy. He goes on to say that training is the single most important factor in improving quality once the necessary commitment has been assured.

TQM Training's Repercussion

The importance of training and education is also echoed by other quality gurus. Ishikawa [38] says "Quality begins and ends with training" (also Imai, in Clemmer [41]). Crosby [24] , Juran [42] and Feigenbaum [43] also emphasized the need for organization wide education and quality awareness programs. Top management of best organizations, recognizing the link between education and successful TQM, also focus their implementation process around it. This point is well summed up by Durrant [44] in discussing TQM initiatives at Rockware Glass Ltd., UK; "There would be more training for all in one year than the previous ten years". At Shorts Brothers, training is a number one priority [23] . Some 400 training sessions were conducted, catering for the president, the management committee and the shop floor workers. Rank Xerox has had a comprehensive training program for all its employees since the beginning of its TQ initiatives. It considers training to be an essential element in developing the TQ process throughout the company [45] . AT & T Istel UK and Mitel Telecom Ltd. UK have also ensured that all employees are provided with formal and rigorous education at the outset of the TQM process [27] [46] . Both organizations believed that education provides a firm foundation for a common language and for understanding the organization's quality aspirations. Best companies do not just confine education and training to their shop floor employees and managers. Top executives are actively involved in the learning process themselves. Wallace Company's five top leaders each underwent more than 200 hours of intensive training in the methods and philosophy of continuous improvement. The managing director of Grundos spends an average of 30 days a year sitting in seminars with all levels of managers [3] .

Training and Education Evaluation

It is critical for training and education programs to be linked explicitly to implementation if they are to have maximum effectiveness. Management should not assume that the new knowledge from such programs will be applied when trainees return to their workplaces. Management should have in place a system to ensure employees follow through what they have learnt when they return to their jobs after training. For example, the management at GTE (company) has put in place a system whereby employees know that they will be evaluated on the implementation of the new knowledge acquired during training. Organizations such as Honda, Corning and General Electric are other examples where new knowledge had been effectively translated into new ways of behaving. These companies actively manage the training process to ensure that it occurs by design rather than by chance.

Best Time for Training

Maximizing the impact of training by the correct timing of training programs was highlighted in a recent study of 536 TQM organizations in the USA [47] . Hence, conducting organization-wide training in TQM before the need or desire for TQM is created could have a negative impact in the TQM implementation process. Employees unable to apply their knowledge forget the details by the time they encounter a real need, and thence lose enthusiasm in the quality initiative. As training and education prepare employees for greater involvement in the organization's quality process, providing them with the right type of training is crucial. Generally, leading organizations ensure their education and training programs include both the basics of quality and TQM and the set of skills for continuous quality improvement.

Training Contents

Kano [3] stresses the importance of adapting training programs to the company's workplace. At British Steel, top management spent considerable time defining the challenges to be faced by the organization and clarifying their vision and values before embarking on training. In designing their training courses, they matched the methodologies and content to the specific culture and values of their organization [11] . At Rank Xerox, a task force was set up to develop a training curriculum to support the implementation plan. On the same note, Oakland [20] cautioned that training for quality is too important to be totally left to the so-called external quality professionals [26] . Bought-in training courses may not be compatible with the philosophies and culture of the company. In fact, some TQ organizations perceive the generic nature of off-the-rack education and training materials as a barrier to steady progress in the quality drive [48] . GPT Ltd. is one such organization. The literature gives a good degree of indication of the type of new skills best organizations provide for their workforce to nurture a quality ethic [11] [14] [18] [49] -[51] . A study in the USA reported that training in continuous improvement skills, interpersonal skills and leadership skills is common amongst 536 TQM organizations [47] . It is also evident from the studies that organizations are emphasizing both interactive and technical skills. According to a survey, good communication skills are one of the two employee characteristics most valued by quality-driven organizations [52] . British Airways' training for its crew is a 50-50 split between the technical and the behavioral. The latter type of training includes treating customers as individuals and taking ownership of their problems. At Charrette Corporation, training for supervisors and managers to develop the necessary facilitator skills and behavior was essential to overcome the initial uncertainty and suspicion amongst middle managers [35] . Only with a considerable amount of suitable training and education can this be achieved.

Impact of Training and Education

Facility in Communication between the Work-force

Organizations such as Fuji Xerox commence training for all employees immediately on hiring. They believe that putting everyone through the same TQM training provides the employees across the organization with a common language of quality and a shared way of thinking. TQM concepts are generally understood and used, making communication much easier [11] .

TQM is a leadership issue at all levels. Middle managers become leaders of empowered employees, facilitators of the new management system, and coaches of new methods. Only with a considerable degree of training and education can this changed role be assumed [25] . Organizations are investing a significant amount of resources in preparing their managers to be different types of leaders. Based on a survey among UK managers [34] , it was concluded that the effective training of managers may be an important factor in the success of TQM implementation.

At Nissan UK where supervisors are empowered to recruit their own staff and people management skills feature prominently in their functions, the company puts a great deal of emphasis on training and developing supervisors as leaders. In addition to standard training elements, professional programs conducted cover personal effectiveness and impart knowledge required by a supervisor in one function which is different from that needed by his or her peer in another function [53] .

Training of Trainer

It produced its own education package comprising a work book, manual and videos. In many TQ organizations that conduct internal training, cascading of training is common [54] . This basically involves a number of managers and supervisors who, after undergoing training and education themselves, are selected to be trained as course instructors for internal training. These trainers then develop their own training package best suited to their team's needs. In some organizations, the process starts at the top [9] . The CEO, who is trained first, trains managers who report to him or her, and who in turn teach their immediate staff and so forth.

By accepting responsibility for and conducting training courses themselves, managers are seen as visible supporters and get buy-in from their "students". Training will have more impact as a result as employees, seeing that management is committed; will also be more willing to get involved. In the process, managers also develop self-discipline and expertise in promoting TQM within the organization [55] .

GPT Ltd. UK, call such training "family group training" [48] . The majority of its training workshops were designed and run by line managers. The cascading approach was used at Ilford Ltd. to great effect [56] . A top management committee delivered the training, starting with themselves and followed by the next level. This level then trained their reporting managers. At Southern Pacific Lines, internal staffs deliver most of the formal quality training for the company's 23,000 employees [14] . Rank Xerox Limited, whose first-line managers also worked with their staff during training, sees the line management ownership of the training process as critical to effective continuing implementation [57] .

In some TQ organizations, however, training is led by employees who are recognized by the management as having particular interpersonal skills. This is done without reducing or compromising the role of the work group leader in any way. At LeaRonal (UK), training achieved a high degree of success using dedicated in-house trainers [4] .

Effect of Training Quality

Protect Training Materials

Before they develop tailor-made training packages, some organizations start by using training materials put together by external consultants, gradually reducing their involvement. BP Chemicals UK, started by using the Crosby program [58] . While they retained Crosby's key principles and philosophy, the training materials are now their own. After getting training help externally in the initial years, Paul Revere Insurance Group has now taken responsibility for its own training [18] . At Shorts Brothers, the training was initially consultant-led [16] . In the later stages, the employees took ownership of all courses. The three organizations view the ownership of the training process as an important factor in their quality initiatives.

In almost all the 20 best companies surveyed in the USA, Europe and the Far East, Bertsch and Williams [9] found that quality training is frequently conducted by line managers with consultants used sparingly and for specific short-term assignments. The use of cascade systems is common.

Reward of Training Employees

In TQ organizations, most employees receive a substantial amount of annual training. Employees of Baldrige applicants receive 40 to 80 hours of training per year [59] . At Grundos, an average of 4 percent of employees' working time is devoted to training [3] . In terms of training expenditures, top American organizations, Baldrige applicants included, commit 2 - 5 percent of total corporate payroll.

In the USA, several top companies is recognizing the importance of training and education and have come together to form a cooperative venture to identify training's best practices and generate comparative data to set a standard for their individual efforts. The American Society for Training and Development's Benchmarking Forum is represented by

37 companies, and includes many Baldrige winners. One of their motives is a desire to learn how to adopt or adapt training practices that clearly provide a competitive advantage [60] .

CONCLUSION

For the smooth run of any institute and organization we need a path and guidance, which path we can follow and that guidance can provide us a clear path to achieve our goals, my paper described that path as well as the management system. It was concluded that the effective training of managers might be an important factor in the success of TQM implementation. After my study, I can conclude that training is the back bone for the improvement of management system; training is not only for lower employees but also for the high ranking employees. Leadership managers also need training for the smooth running of any organization. Secondly, cooperation is also necessary among all employees between the same level staffs as well as cooperation between leadership and lower level employees.

ACKNOWLEDGEMENTS

This research is intended to International Education College, China University of Geosciences (Wuhan) as thanks from Madagascar community.

REFERENCES

1. Easton, G.S. (1993) The 1993 State of US Total Quality Management: A Baldrige Examiner's Perspective. California Management Review, 35, 32-54.http://dx.doi.org/10.2307/41166742
2. Powers, V. (1994) The Sweet Smell of Success. Continuous Journey, October/November, 18-24.
3. Binney, G. (1992) Making Quality Work: Lessons from Europe's Leading Companies. The Economist Intelligence Unit, London.
4. Smith, S. (1994) The Quality Revolution. Management Books Ltd., Didcot.
5. Kolesar, P.J. (1993) Vision, Values, Milestones: Paul O'Neill Starts Total Quality at Alcoa. California Management Review, 35, 133-165. http://dx.doi.org/10.2307/41166748
6. Olian, J.D. and Rynes, S.L. (1991) Making Total Quality Work: Aligning Organizational Processes, Performance Measures, and Stakeholders. Human Resource Management, 30, 303-333. http://dx.doi.org/10.1002/hrm.3930300303
7. Ramirez, C. and Loney, T. (1993) Baldrige Award Winners Identify the Essential Activities of a Successful Quality Process. Quality Digest, January, 38-40.
8. Bertram, D. (1991) Getting Started in Total Quality Management. Total Quality Management, 2, 279-282. http://dx.doi.org/10.1080/09544129100000032
9. Bertsch, B. and Williams, R. (1994) How Multinational CEOs Make Change Programme Stick. Long Range Planning, 27, 3-11. http://dx.doi.org/10.1016/0024-6301(94)90223-2
10. Barker, R.L. (1991) Basic Improvement Tools and Total Quality Management. In: Oakland, J.S., Ed., Total Quality Management, Proceedings of the 4th International Conference, Warwick, IFS Ltd, Bedford.
11. Johnston, C.G. and Daniel, M.J. (1991) Customer Satisfaction through Quality: An International Perspective. The Conference Board of Canada, Ottawa.
12. George, D. (1990) The Routine Involvement of Senior Managers in the Quality Improvement Process. In: Oakland, J.S., Ed., Proceedings of the 3rd International Conference on Total Quality Management, Warwick, IFS Ltd., Bedford.
13. Browning, S.A. and Shaw, W.N. (1990) Employees' Views of TQM at Two Hewlett-Packard Manufacturing Plants. In: Oakland, J.S., Ed., Proceedings of the 3rd International Conference on Total Quality Management, Warwick, IFS Ltd., Bedford.
14. Carman, J.M. (1993) Continuous Quality Improvement as a Survival Strategy: The Southern Pacific Experience. California Management Review, 35, 118-132.http://dx.doi.org/10.2307/41166747
15. Wiggenhorn, W. (1990) Motorola U: When Training Becomes an Education. Harvard Business Review, 68, 71-83.
16. Oakland, J.S. and Porter, L. (1994) Cases in Total Quality Management. Butterworth-Heinemann, Oxford.
17. Durrant, P.W. (1990) TQM and The Cultural Changes Required. In: Oakland, J.S., Ed., Proceedings of the 3rd International Conference on Total Quality Management, Warwick, IFS Ltd., Bedford.
18. Bank, J. (1992) The Essence of Total Quality Management. Prentice-Hall, London.
19. Juran, J.M. (1993) Made in USA: A Renaissance in Quality. Harvard Business Review, 71, 42-50.
20. Oakland, J.S. (1993) Total Quality Management. Butterworth-Heinemann, Oxford.
21. Haksever, C. (1996) Total Quality Management in the Small Business Environment. Business Horizons, 39, 33-40.http://dx.doi.org/10.1016/S0007-6813(96)90021-X
22. Reeves, C.A. and Bednar, D.A. (1993) What Prevents TQM Implementation in Health Care Organizations? Quality Progress, 26, 41-44.
23. Quality Progress (1994) Companies That Link Quality to Reward Program Report Success. Quality Progress, 27, 15, 18.
24. Crosby, P. (1989) Let's Talk Quality: 96 Questions That You Always Wanted to Ask Phil Crosby. McGraw-Hill, New York.
25. Townsend, P.L. and Gebhardt, J.E. (1992) Quality in Action. John Wiley & Sons, New York.
26. Smith, P.K. and Tee, M.R. (1990) Total Quality—The Issues and Realities for a Leading Supplier of Advanced Surface Treatment Technology. In: Oakland, J.S., Ed., Proceedings of the 3rd International Conference on Total Quality Management, Warwick, IFS Ltd., Bedford.
27. Boyer, S.M. (1991) Total Quality Management and New Product Development. Total Quality Management, 2, 283-290. http://dx.doi.org/10.1080/09544129100000033
28. Deming, W.E. (1986) Out of the Crisis. MIT Centre for Advanced Engineering Study, Cambridge.

29. Juran, J.M. (1991) Juran on Quality by Design. Free Press, New York.

30. Zink, K.J. (1995) Total Quality Management and People Management. In: Kanji, G.K., Ed., Total Quality Management: Processing of the 1st World Congress, Chapman & Hall, London.

31. Nadkarni, R.A. (1995) A Not-So-Secret recipe for Successful TQM. Quality Progress, 28, 91-96.

32. Bemowski, K. (1992) Carrying on the P&G Tradition. Quality Progress, 25, 21-25.

33. Bemowski, K. (1994) Baldrige Award Recipients Share Their Expertise. Quality Progress, 28, 35-40.

34. Wilkinson, A., Redman, T. and Snape, E. (1994) Quality Management and the Manager. Employee Relations, 16, 62-70. http://dx.doi.org/10.1108/01425459410054934

35. Manz, C.C. and Sims, H.P. (1993) Business without Bosses. John Wiley, New York.

36. Wacker, K.A. (1993) Uncommon Common Sense. Quality Progress, 26, 97-100.

37. Quality Progress (1993) Middle Managers Can Inhibit TQM. Quality Progress, 26, 16,18.

38. Ishikawa, K. (1985) What Is Total Quality Control? The Japanese Way. Prentice-Hall, Englewood Cliffs.

39. McDermott, L. (1993) Jump-Starting Managers on Quality. Training & Development, 47, 37.

40. Dumas, R. (1989) Organizational Quality: How to Avoid Common Pitfalls. Quality Progress, 22, 41-44.

41. Clemmer, J. (1990) Firing on All Cylinders. Judy Piatkus Publishers, London.

42. Juran, J.M. (1974) Quality Control Handbook. McGraw-Hill, London.

43. Feigenbaum, A.V. (1961) Total Quality Control. McGraw-Hill, London.

44. Durrant, P.W. (1990) TQM and The Cultural Changes Required. In: Oakland, J.S., Ed., Proceedings of the 3rd International Conference on Total Quality Management, Warwick, IFS Ltd., Bedford.

45. Cullen, J. and Hollingum, J. (1987) Implementing Total Quality. IFS Ltd., Bedford.

46. Hutt, G. (1990) Quality—The Proper Way of Managing. In: Oakland, J.S., Ed., Proceedings of the 3rd International Conference on Total Quality Management, Warwick, IFS Ltd., Bedford.

47. DDI (1994) TQM: Forging Ahead or Falling behind—A Study of Quality Practices. Development Dimensions International Inc., Bridgeville.

48. Cashbourne, B.R. (1991) Organizing for Total Quality Management. In: Oakland, J.S., Ed., Proceedings of the 4th International Conference on Total Quality Management, Warwick, Bedford, UK, IFS Ltd.

49. Sanford, R.L. (1992) Baxter Healthcare Uses Its Own Quality Award to Help Achieve Excellence. National Productivity Review, 12, 37-43.http://dx.doi.org/10.1002/npr.4040120106

50. Oakland, J.S. and Beardmore, D. (1995) Best Practice Customer Service. Total Quality Management, 6, 135-148.http://dx.doi.org/10.1080/09544129550035486

51. Westbrook, R. and Barwise, P. (1995) Total Quality Management in Leading Fast-Moving Consumer Goods Companies. Total Quality Management, 6, 365-382. http://dx.doi.org/10.1080/09544129550035314

52. Quality Progress (1995) Workforce Study Identifies Most Valued Employee Characteristics. Quality Progress, 28, 14.

53. Vallely, I. (1993) Why Supervisors Can with Nissan. Works Management, 18-21.

54. Bendell, T., Boulter, L. and Kelly, J. (1993) Benchmarking for Competitive Advantage. Pitman Publishing, London.

55. Kanji, G.K. and Asher, M. (1993) Total Quality Management Process—A Systematic Approach. Advances in Total Quality Management Series. Carfax Publishing, Abingdon.

56. Hunt, W. and Hillman, G.P. (1990) Achieving the Real Culture Change Necessary for TQM. In: Oakland, J.S., Ed., Proceedings of the 3rd International Conference on Total Quality Management, Warwick, IFS Ltd., Bedford.

57. Wright, J. (1988) Rank Xerox Approach to Implementation. In: Oakland, J.S., Ed., Proceedings of the 1st International Conference on Total Quality Management, Warwick, IFS Ltd., Bedford.

58. Stark, J.A.L. (1990) Experience of TQM at BP Chemicals. In Oakland, J.S., Ed., Proceedings of the 3rd International Conference on Total Quality Management, Warwick, IFS Ltd., Bedford.

59. Easton, G.S. (1993) The 1993 State of US Total Quality Management: A Baldrige Examiner's Perspective. California Management Review, 35, 32-54.http://dx.doi.org/10.2307/41166742

60. Kimmerling, G. (1993) Gathering Best Practices. Training & Development, 47, 29-36.

CHAPTER 18

ASSESSMENT OF AUDITING IN DATABASE SYSTEMS

Olumuyiwa O. Matthew and Carl Dudley

Keywords: Auditing, Techniques, Security, Framework, Procedure

INTRODUCTION

Database Auditing allows security personnel to ascertain who did what to which data, when and how [1]. It is a mechanism used to monitor the actions of every user in a database [2]. Database auditing helps strengthen the security of the database by keeping logs of the activities performed on a database. It can be used to confirm that data or information is not accessed by those without permission and that they do not go beyond the privileges granted to them by the database administrator.

The security mechanism must not only prevent attacks but also detect potential attacks. After all, the best security policy is still not going to stop every attacker. This is where auditing helps in monitoring the environment and identifying potential attacks [3]. Lu et al [4] describe auditing operations as critical processes for identifying malicious behaviour, maintaining data quality and improving system performance. Mullins [5] said database auditing is the process of monitoring access to and modification of selected database objects and resources within operational databases and retaining a detailed record of the access where said record can be used to proactively trigger actions and can be retrieved and analysed as needed. This means with auditing records, a database administrator can carry out analysis on the trend of events in a database system.

Database auditing is an increasingly important aspect of database security. The implementation of user identification, authentication and access control are part of the security measures, but with all of these in place, database is still not fully secured. None of these measures are capable of monitoring and logging database activities, to allow subsequent detection of security breaches [2]. To manage access to sensitive data, a user can be subjected to a variety of authentication and access control mechanisms which implement rules and controls for known and acceptable data access behaviours. But to protect against and discover unknown or unacceptable behaviours always requires a need to monitor data access. To assist in this task, a database system that provides an audit facility must be used.

The level of security that a database system offers is, at least in part measured by the level of auditing that can be implemented with the system. Yang [6] explains that there is no security without auditing; therefore security and auditing should be implemented in an integrated fashion. Auditing database activity and access can help identify security issues and resolve them quickly. Auditing as a function needs to play a central role in ensuring compliance with regulations because an audit produces documentation of actions, practices and conduct of a business or individual. It can be used to measure compliance to policies, procedure, process and law. So, it helps measure the compliance of both the developers and users to the business ethics.

This paper has been divided into different sections. Section 1 is a brief introduction to the subject of database auditing. Section 2 gives an overview of existing techniques, models and architectures. Section 3 has the finding from the research and proposed algorithm for the auditing procedure. Section 4 is about the risk assessment. Section 5 concludes the paper focusing on recommendation.

RELATED WORKS

Database auditing is now seen as a major factor in determining the security level of a database system. It is proven that no

Citation: Olumuyiwa O. Matthew and Carl Dudley, Assessment of Auditing in Database Systems, DOI:10.5121/csit.2015.50801.

system or database can be one hundred per cent secured but the ability of it to recover from attack as quickly as possible with the help of auditing facilities provided by the DBMS is of paramount importance. Liu and Huang [7] said that all architects must bolster policies by using database auditing in addition to other security features built into all major database platforms. This is an indication that security measures alone cannot ensure security without auditing. Different actions are performed on a database ranging from logging, deletion, update, and privilege control. All these actions contributes to the security of a database depending on the basis to which they are carried out.so auditing is used to check for the genuineness of every actions performed on a database. Huang and Liu [7] put it that database auditing involves observing a database so as to be aware of the actions of the database users, to help ensure that information is not accessed by those without the correct permissions.

Looking at the concept from the field of telecommunications industry, the term data audit was explained by Bagchi et al [9] as a broad range of custom and ad hoc, application- level techniques for detecting and recovering from errors in a switching environment. Elshiekh and Dominic [10] looked at auditing in terms of a statistical database used as a mechanism for keeping up-to-date logs of all queries made by each user and constantly checking for possible compromise whenever a new query is issued. Kogan and Jajodia [11] put it that auditing capability is one of the requirements for secure databases and that a secure database management system, among other things, has to provide not only facilities for recording the history of all updates but high-level support for querying this history as well. This is an indication that this concept at any time can query i.e. audit any update done to the system to ascertain the quality of information in the database.

Database efficiency improvement

Wentian and Miklaus [12] point out that auditing the changes to a database is critical for the identification of malicious behaviour, maintenance of data quality and improving system performance. Waraporn [13] gives two major reasons for database auditing which are to have data log files which helps in the recovery of transactions and also in the investigation of transactions. This is true because information security in term of authentication and authorisation can help protect information but does not provide help in investigating transaction activity. Therefore, the efficiency of the system can also be improved with the use of auditing techniques. Every system should have self-check facilities to improve its quality and efficiency.

Database auditing for compliance

Database auditing has also helped to improve the compliance of organisations to the different acts and regulations concerning data privacy from both the customer's and the organisation's points of view. When databases are audited, data integrity is maintained. Due to the high rate of information and financial fraud, several laws and regulations were propounded by different governments to militate against this trend. Hasan and Winslett [14] historically informed that the drumbeat of financial accounting scandals, from ENRON in 2000 to Satyam InfoTech in 2008, has prompted the introduction of regulations intended to guarantee the integrity of business records. This gives room for companies to have control over their sensitive data. Organisations that handle sensitive data are now held to a much higher standard of data access accountability [15]. This arises from the different regulatory compliance laws enforced by different countries and regions. Yang [6] explain that auditing as a function needs to a play a central role in ensuring compliance because an audit documents actions, practices and conduct of a business or individual. It then measures their compliance to policies, procedure, process and law. Regulations such as the following have common auditing-related requirements: Sarbanes-Oxley Act, Health Insurance Portability and Accountability Act (HIPAA), International Convergence of Capital Measurement and Capital Standards- a Revised Framework (Basel II), Japan Privacy Law and European Union Directive on Privacy and Electronic Communications.

Database auditing methods

There are different auditing techniques and methods depending on what type of auditing to be carried out or what data is to be audited. According to Mullins [5] database auditing can be categorized into three major types. Namely:

- Authorization Auditing - Who can do what?
- Access Auditing - Who did what, Modifications?
- Replication Auditing - Who copied which data where.

While Noreen et al [8] itemized the following as different methods

- *Triggers* - Set of procedures that automatically executes in response to a certain event.
- *Transactional Log* - A log maintained by SQL Server to store information of almost any activity taking place on the database Server.
- *C2 Auditing* - It records the database information that goes beyond server level events.
- *Default Trace* - It runs as a background service of MS SQL Server 2005 and assists the database administrator (DBA) to check the database users' activities.

While according to Srivastava [16] said auditing techniques are divided into the following types:

- *Statement Auditing*- The auditing of selective SQL statements irrespective of the schema object on which they are fired is Statement auditing. For example, auditing on the DDL statement fired by a user.
- *Privilege Auditing*- Privilege auditing is nothing but the audit of the usage of selective privileges like the Create Table privilege by a user. Privilege auditing can be done on any user or on all users.
- *Schema Object Auditing* - Auditing on specific schema objects is met by schema object auditing. All DML activities, Grant and Revoke performed on a specific table or all tables within a schema can be captured.
- *Fine Grained Auditing*-Fine grained auditing provides auditing on data access based on the data content.

Dudley [17] itemized the different types of auditing techniques that can be used on the Oracle database including the default System-based auditing, fine-grained auditing, trigger-based auditing, flashback techniques and flashback data archive. Each of the authors prove and explain all the techniques with examples to show the impact on security.

Database auditing models, framework etc

There are few open source projects or publication in this area. However, the following related publications in database auditing derive frameworks, algorithms, architectures, techniques, or models for carrying out database auditing.

Bagchi et al [9] came up with an audit subsystem architecture that shows the design of the database audit process and its interaction with other system components. The proposed audit framework provides audit functionality and consists of the top-layer shell (the audit interface) and the individual elements that implement specific audit triggering, error detection and recovery techniques.

Bottcher and Steinmetz [18] proposed another system architecture for a privacy audit system of any XML database, extended by a middleware that consists of a query log and a backlog. These two above architecture were proposed as a solution to carry out basic audit in a system.

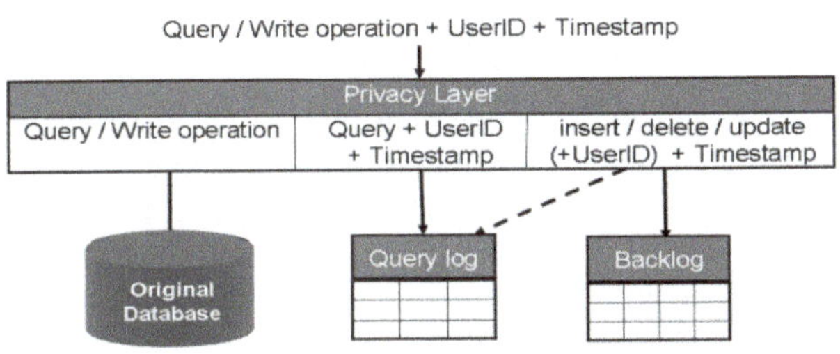

Figure 1: system architecture [18]

Another architecture was shown in Woo et al [19] which has three main components for auditing a database system. The logger, analyzer and notifier.

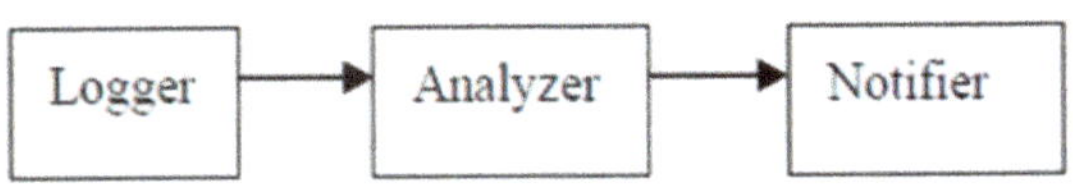

Figure 2: Anatomy of Auditing System (Bishop 2003) in Woo et al [19]

Woo et al produce this architecture in order to verify every access made into the system. The analyser does this by analysing every query and update activity on the system and comes up with authorizations which the notifier will further send to the appropriate session as the case may be.

Agrawal et al [20] have developed an architecture for their Sarbanes-Oxley solution which consists of four main components: (i) workflow modelling, (ii) active enforcement, (iii) workflow auditing, and (iv) anomaly detection. Agrawal solution was designed for compliance purposes and incorporates the work process into the system.

Johnson and Grandison [21] also proposed an architecture based system called Hippocratic Database(HDB) which enables compliance with security and privacy regulations without impeding the legitimate flow of information.

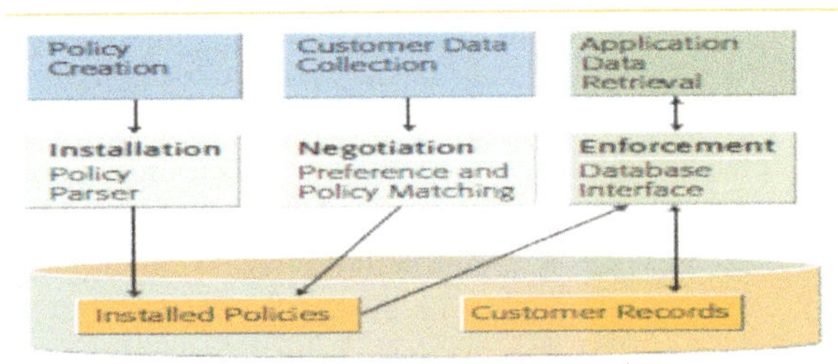

Figure 3: HDB active enforcement architecture [21]

Yangquig et al [22] produced an audit model that set up traces through database stored procedures to collect audit data The audit module stored and transported audit data in standard XML format to the audit server.

Noreen et al [8] proposed a system architecture for a target database on which auditing is to be performed. It is mounted on an instance of Microsoft SQL Server (MS SQL 2005).

Zonnone et al [23] also proposed an approach that will verify the compliance of user behaviour with data protection policies. The introduction of all these architectures only serves to emphasise the importance of auditing to any database environment. Security is not complete until there is an effective and efficient auditing system in place.

Database Audit and Protection (DAP) versus Database Activity Monitoring (DAM)

DAP — a term Gartner has developed to replace the earlier DAM concept — refers to suites of tools that are used to support the identification of and reporting on inappropriate, illegal or otherwise undesirable behaviour in RDBMSs, with minimal impact on user operations and productivity. These suites have evolved from DAM tools (which offered analysis of user activity in and around RDBMSs) to encompass a more comprehensive set of capabilities, including:

- Discovery and classification
- Vulnerability management
- Application-level analysis
- Intrusion prevention
- Support for unstructured data security
- Identity and access management integration

DAP provides better auditing and monitoring support than native logging, which can add significant overhead and does not provide the same level of granularity as DAP tools. DAP, moreover, provides comprehensive cross-platform support in heterogeneous database environments, and can serve as an effective addition to identity and access analytics [24].

DISCUSSION OF FINDINGS

Database auditing is a recognised technology used to determine if security and other policies are being violated. It is used in obtaining details about system usage, data modification and to help in the detection and recovery of database systems from system failure or human errors. Therefore the implementation and management of this technology is critical to the efficiency and performance of the system.

Auditing procedures and techniques

The auditing procedures in most environments start with logging activities (i.e when and how logging was done). This includes the logon and logoff records with failed and successful ones. Every environment provides this. The second stage is to check for privileges, user's definitions and other security attributes like role definition, password changes, deletion and addition of users. The third stage is to check for changes made to the database schema such as data being copied from one table to an additional table thereby changing the schema. The fourth stage is the auditing of the use of sensitive data. The fifth stage is concerned with auditing the changes made to stored procedures or codes. Other auditing stages that can be carried out involve the audit of database errors because attackers tend to make several erroneous attempts before making head way. Also, auditing any changes made to the definition of what is to be audited. These identified procedures were proposed in the framework for auditing shown below.

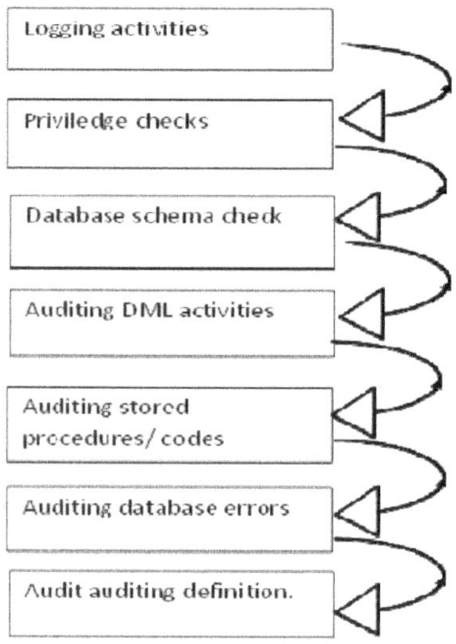

Figure 4: A framework for auditing procedure

Impact of auditing on security

Auditing activities within a database can help identify security issues and also resolve those issues. In fact it can be said that there is no security without auditing. The following are areas identified in which auditing impacts greatly on the security of a database.

- Auditing activities enable future accountability for current actions.
- Auditing activities can help deter users and even intruders from inappropriate actions based on that accountability.
- These activities also help in investigating suspicious activity.
- It helps Notify an auditor of actions by an unauthorized user.
- Also helps detect problems with an authorization or access control implementation.
- Auditing activities also address auditing requirements for compliance.

Impact of government policies and regulations on auditing

There exist today numerous policies and regulations which have been put in place because increasing numbers of organisations are faced with sensitive information protection difficulties. These policies have stringent requirements on the collection, processing and disclosure of personal data. Now because of the difficulties associated with companies coping and enforcing these laws, there is a new trend to adopt a database compliance auditing system. It is obvious that without a compliance auditing system in place it is very difficult for organisations to monitor and enforce compliance with the policies and regulations.

Johnson and Grandison [21] give an example of a company called BankCo which uses HDB active enforcement to operate as a middleware layer above the database enforcing fine-grained policies. These policies are advised to be built into the database which gives the organisation a control measure over who has access, when the access occurs and where the access took place.

How to handle audit trail size

The database auditors are responsible for monitoring access to the database and tracking malicious actions after they have occurred [4]. When auditing is enabled in any DBMS, the audit output is recorded in an audit trail. The size of this trail can grow out of control when database activity increases. This will lead to issues such as how to keep it to a manageable size. Nando [25] explains the solution could be to relocate the audit trail to a different tablespace (Oracle) and set up an automatic purge process to keep its size under control. Nando [25] pointed out that this is one of the new features in Oracle Database 11g release2. This enables the database administrator to move audit trails from the SYSTEM tablespace to a different area of choice, allowing better management of the audit trail and to minimise the performance impact and disk space management.

Well-kept audit trail involving sensitive data should be part of any database deployment [26]. This helps in keeping track of malicious activity on the database. The failure to get this detailed audit records of database activity represents a serious organizational risk on many level. Many enterprises will turn to native audit tools provided by their database vendors or rely on ad-hoc and manual solutions. These approaches do not record details necessary to support auditing, attack detection, and forensics. Furthermore, native database audit mechanisms are notorious for consuming CPU and disk resources forcing many organizations to scale back or eliminate auditing altogether. Finally, most native audit mechanisms are unique to a database server platform. For example, Oracle logs are different from MS-SQL, and MS-SQL logs are different form DB2.

RISK ASSESSMENT

Based on nCircle [27] survey data breaches increased by 95% in 2010. The survey also shows that audit cost in 2008 to 2009 increased by 45%, while from 2009 to 2010 it increased to 47% (nCircle 2010 p4). Also from the nCircle [27] survey, meeting security compliance requirements was the biggest security concern in 2010 with 30% among other areas of concern. The PWC [28] survey, shows that there are two major factors acting as the driver for information security expenditure which are protecting customer information (34%) and complying with laws/regulations (17%).

Therefore, organisations should have a database compliance auditing system which has in place all the policies and laws applicable to their operations. This incorporates enforcement compliance with internal security policies and the ability to demonstrate continuous compliance.

CONCLUSION

In this paper, a critical assessment of auditing has been performed and an auditing procedural framework was developed. The rationale of the work presented here is to review some existing auditing techniques and architectures to bring out major benefits, in order to produce a framework which will effectively facilitate the database auditor to perform the intricate task of auditing. This procedure must be customized to the processes and operations already in place, and the relevant policies and regulations. This will allow organisations to enforce automated security and privacy controls that will align with existing laws and regulations to facilitate cross-border information transfers. The adoption of a particular architecture or model for auditing activities has strategically placed organisations in a high level of effective security.

The work done on the auditing procedural framework can be enhanced in future by the inclusion of other stages of auditing not identified here and other functionalities. Firstly, each stage can be expanded by splitting it into sub-stages which will make it a more comprehensive system. Secondly, the entire proposed framework could be incorporated into a DBMS for adoption by organisations as part of their process.

Recommendation is also made to organisations to adopt a compliance auditing system which has policies and regulations inbuilt. This provides a control measure over those that have access, when and where access is made and also allows the demonstration of continuous compliance.

REFERENCES

1. Dudley, C. (2012) Database Auditing. Lecture 14: 7C1006L14 [online]. [Accessed 17 May 2012]. Available at http://wolf.wlv.ac.uk/stech/68343/Slides/7CI006.
2. Qiang, H. and Lianzhong, L. (2009) A Logging Scheme for Database Audit, Computer Science and Engineering, 2009. WCSE '09. Second International Workshop on 2009, pp. 390-393.
3. Baccam, T (2010) Oracle database security: what to look for and where to secure. SANS analyst Program, April 2010. [Online]. London. [Accessed 23 may, 2012]. Available at: http://download.oracle.com/doc
4. Lu, W., Miklau, G. and Immerman, N. (2013) Auditing a database under retention policies. The VLDB Journal—The International Journal on Very Large Data Bases [online], 22(2), pp. 203-228 .
5. Mullins, C. (2008) Database Auditing. NEON enterprise software. Texas. [Accessed 24 July, 2012]. Available at: <http://www.neonsoft.com.
6. Yang, L. (2009) Teaching database security and auditing. In Proceedings of the 40th ACM technical symposium on Computer science education (SIGCSE '09). ACM, New York, NY, USA,241- 245. DOI=10.1145/1508865.1508954 http://doi.acm.org/10.1145/1508865.1508954
7. Liu, L. and Huang, Q. (2009) A Framework for Database Auditing, Computer Sciences and Convergence Information Technology, 2009. ICCIT '09. Fourth International Conference on 2009, pp. 982-986.
8. Noreen, Z. Hameed, I. and Usman, A. (2009) Development of database auditing infrastructure. In Proceedings of the 7th International Conference on Frontiers of Information Technology (FIT '09). ACM, New York, NY, USA, Article 78, 6 pages
9. Bagchi, S., Liu, Y., Whisnant, K., Kalbarczyk, Z., Iyer, R., Levendel, Y. and Votta, L.(2001) A framework for database audit and control flow checking for a wireless telephone network controller, Dependable Systems and Networks, 2001. DSN 2001. International Conference on 2001, pp. 225- 234.
10. Elshiekh, A. and Dominic, P. (2008) A new auditing scheme for securing statistical databases Information Technology, 2008. ITSim 2008. International Symposium on. [Online]. pp.1-5.
11. Kogan, B. and Jajodia, S. (1991) An audit model for object-oriented databases Computer Security Applications Conference, 1991. Proceedings., Seventh Annual. [Online]. pp.90-99.
12. Wentian, L. and Miklau, G. (2009) Auditing a Database under Retention Restrictions, Data Engineering, 2009. ICDE '09. IEEE 25th International Conference on 2009, pp. 42-53.
13. Waraporn, N. (2010) Database Auditing Design on Historical Data. In Proceedings of the Second International Symposium on Networking and Network Security (ISNNS '10). Jinggangshan, China, April. 2010, pp. 275-281
14. Hasan, R and Winslett, M. (2011) Efficient audit-based compliance for relational data retention. In Proceedings of the 6th ACM Symposium on Information, Computer and Communications Security (ASIACCS '11). ACM, New York, NY, USA, 238-248.
15. Mazer, M. (2006) Auditing Databases for Compliance and Risk Management, DM Review, vol. 16(3), pp. 18-19
16. Srivastava, M. (2009) Fine Grained Auditing in Oracle 10g [online]. [Accessed 28th July, 2012]. Available at: < http://hosteddocs.ittoolbox.com/ms080609.pdf>
17. Dudley, C. (2012) Auditing techniques for oracle database 11g. Lecture delivered during oracle conference 2012, Texas, USA.
18. Bottcher, S. and Steinmetz, R. (2006) Finding the Leak: A Privacy Audit System for Sensitive XML Databases, Data Engineering Workshops, 2006. Proceedings. 22nd International Conference on 2006, pp. 100-100.
19. Woo, J., Lee, Sael. And Zoltowski, C (2007) Database Auditing [online]. [Accessed 24th July, 2012]. Available at :http://www.citeseerx,ist,psu.ed
20. Agrawal, R., Johnson, C., Kiernan, J. and Leymann, F.

(2006) Taming Compliance with SarbanesOxley Internal Controls Using Database Technology Data Engineering, 2006. ICDE '06. Proceedings of the 22nd International Conference on. [Online]. pp.92-92.

21. Johnson, C. and Grandison, T. (2007) Compliance with data protection laws using Hippocratic Database active enforcement and auditing [online].

22. Yangqing, Z., Hui, Y., Hua, L. and Lianming, Z. (2009) Design of a New Web Database Security Model, Electronic Commerce and Security, 2009. ISECS '09. Second International Symposium on 2009, pp. 292-295.

23. Zannone, N., Petkovic, M. and Etalle, S. (2010) Towards data protection compliance [online]. IEEE, pp.1-4Available at: http://wlv.summon.serialssolutions.com/

24. Wheatman, J. (2012) Database Auditing Monitoring is evolving into Database Audit and protection. Gartner Incorporation [online] February, 2012, [Accessed 22 September,2012]. Availableat:http://www.gartner.com/technology/

25. Nando, A. (2010) managing Audit trails. Oracle Magazine [online] November 2010, [Accessed 19 September 2012].Available at:http://www.oracle.com/technetwork....

26. Akanji, A. and Elusoji, A. (2014) A Comparative Study of Attacks on Databases and Database Security Techniques. [online].

27. Ncircle (2010) information security and compliance trend study: Technical report [online]. California. [Accessed 03 August 2012]. Available at <:http://www.inteco.es/file/us>

28. PWC (2012) Information security breaches survey: Technical report [online]. London. [Accessed 03 August 2012]. Available at :< http://www.pwc.co.uk/.../uk-information-security-breaches-surveytechnica>

CHAPTER 19

INTERNAL AUDITING AND QUALITY OF FINANCIAL STATEMENT

Maryam Abulghasemi Komeleh and Mansour Garkaz

INTRODUCTION

Internal auditing is considered as an independent, objective assurance and consulting activity designed to add value and to improve firms' operations. It assists firms to accomplish their objectives by bringing a systematic, disciplined method to assess and to improve the effectiveness of risk management, control, and governance processes (Fama & French, 1993; Raghunandan et al., 2001). Internal auditing is a catalyst for improving firms' governance, risk management and management controls by giving insight and recommendations based on analyses and evaluations of data and business processes (Healy & Palepu, 2001). With commitment to integrity and accountability, internal auditing gives value to governing bodies and senior management as an objective source of independent advice. The scope of internal auditing within firms is extensive and may include topics such as an organization's governance, risk management and management controls (Krishnan, 2005). Internal auditing may also include conducting proactive fraud audits to determine potentially fraudulent acts; participating in fraud investigations under the direction of fraud investigation professionals, and conducting post investigation fraud audits to detect control breakdowns and to establish financial loss.

Doyle et al. (2007) investigated the relationship between accruals quality and internal controls using 705 firms that disclosed at least one material weakness from August 2002 to November 2005 and reported that weaknesses were generally associated with poorly estimated accruals, which were not realized as cash flows. They reported that this relation between weak internal controls and lower accruals quality was driven by weakness disclosures, which was associated with overall company- level controls, which could be more difficult to "audit around." They also reported no such relationship for more auditable, account-specific weaknesses. Nevertheless, they reported similar results using four additional measures of accruals quality: discretionary accruals, average accruals quality, historical accounting restatements, and earnings persistence.

THE PROPOSED STUDY

This paper presents an empirical investigation to study the relationship between internal auditing and quality of financial statements on selected firms listed on Tehran Stock Exchange. The proposed study selects 140 firms over the period 2008-2012. To select the firms, only firms whose financial statements were available were selected and there should not be any three-month-long interruption on their shares activities. In addition, no financial or holding firm was permitted to this study. The accruals (Accri,t) is calculated as follows,

$$Accr_{i,t} = \alpha_0 + \alpha_1(1/TA_{i,t-1}) + \alpha_2\Delta REV_{i,t} + \alpha_3 PPE_{i,t} + \alpha_4 ROA_{i,t} + \varepsilon_{i,t} \quad (1)$$

where $Accr_{i,t}$ is estimated as follows,

$$\frac{\Delta CurrentAssets - \Delta Cash - \Delta CurrentLiabilities - Depreciation}{TotalAssets} \quad (2)$$

Let $\Delta REV_{i,t}$ be the ratio of net revenue divided by total assets, $PPE_{i,t}$ be the ratio of net equipment divided by total assets and ROA_t be the return on assets. Discretionary accruals (DisTA) is calculated by measuring the absolute values of residuals in Eq. (1) and then we multiplying by negative one. The more negative value represents better quality of financial

Citation: Maryam Abulghasemi Komeleh and Mansour Garkaz, Internal auditing and quality of financial statement, DOI: 10.5267/j.msl.2014.8.028.

statements. We may also use the method suggested by Dechow and Dichev (2002) to calculate the quality of earnings as follows,

$$WCA_{i,t} = \alpha_0 + \alpha_1 OCF_{i,t-1} + \alpha_2 OCF_{i,t} + \alpha_3 OCF_{i,t+1} + \alpha_4 \Delta \mathrm{Rev}_{i,t} + \alpha_5 PPE_{i,t} + \alpha_6 DOCF_{i,t} + \alpha_7 OCF_{i,t} \times DOCF_{i,t} + \varepsilon_{i,t} \quad (3)$$

where WCA_{it} is the working capital accruals, which is calculated as follows,

$$\frac{\Delta CurrentAssets - \Delta Cash - (\Delta CurrentLiabilities - \Delta CurrentDebt - \Delta TaxPayables)}{TotalAssets}$$

In addition, in Eq. (3), OCF represents operating cash flow, Rev states the total revenue, DOCF is a dummy variable, which is one if money is going out and zero, otherwise. The residuals of Eq. (3) is multiplied by negative one and it yields DisWCA as discretionary working capital accruals. The last model was originally developed by Wallman (1996) and is as follows,

$$\Delta AR_{i,t} = \alpha_0 + \alpha_1 \Delta \mathrm{Rev}_{i,t} + \varepsilon_{i,t} \quad (4)$$

where $\Delta AR_{i,t}$ represents the change in receivable accounts and $\Delta Rev_{i,t}$ represents the change in net profit divided by total assets and the procedure of calculating discretionary accruals is the same as the previous models. To examine the main hypothesis of this paper we use the following model,

$$(DisTA, DisWCA, Dis\mathrm{Rev}, AccrCash)_{i,t} = \alpha_0 + \alpha_1 IAQ_{i,t} + \alpha_2 BODQ_{i,t} + \alpha_3 CG_{i,t} + \alpha_4 AQ_{i,t}$$
$$+ \alpha_5 LASSET_{i,t} + \alpha_6 INV_{i,t} + \alpha_7 LEV_{i,t} + \alpha_8 CFO_{i,t} + \alpha_9 LAGE_{i,t} + \alpha_{10} SGROWTH_{i,t} + \varepsilon_{i,t} \quad (5)$$

where

$$AccrCash_{i,t} = -\ln\left(\frac{|Accr|}{|OCF|}\right). \quad (6)$$

In addition, $IAQ_{i,t}$, is one if firm has signed a contract for internal auditing and zero, otherwise, $BODQ_{i,t}$ is one if there is a person with the financial background in board of directors and zero, otherwise, and finally $CG_{i,t}$ is one if the average number of corporate governance is greater than an average number and zero, otherwise. Table 1 demonstrates the summary of some basic statistics.

Table 1: The summary of some basic statistics for the first model

Variable	First model					Second model	
	ROA_t	$PPE_{i,t}$	$\Delta REV_{i,t}$	$1/TA_{i,t-1}$	$Accr_{i,t}$	$\Delta REV_{i,t}$	$\Delta AR_{i,t}$
Number	700	700	700	700	700	700	700
Mean	0.156	0.236	0.144	0.000	0.099	0.144	0.010
Median	0.131	0.196	0.110	0.000	0.069	0.110	0.020
Mode	0.320	0.180	0.000	0.000	0.030	0.000	0.000
Standard deviation	0.116	0.158	0.130	0.000	0.106	0.130	0.392
Skewness	1.212	0.700	1.736	34.539	2.574	1.736	-1.283
Kurtosis	1.532	-0.374	4.106	1225.000	9.981	4.106	316.573
Range	0.650	0.690	0.920	0.000	1.000	0.920	16.000
Min	0.000	0.000	-0.020	0.000	-0.090	-0.020	-8.000
Max	0.660	0.700	0.890	0.000	0.910	0.890	8.000
Q25	0.072	0.105	0.053	0.000	0.029	0.021	0.053
Q50	0.131	0.196	0.110	0.000	0.069	0.098	0.110
Q75	0.211	0.351	0.198	0.000	0.133	0.185	0.198

THE RESULTS

Table 2 demonstrates the results of regression analysis for Eq. (5). The table shows the implementation of four regression models where dependent variables are DisTA, DisWCA, DisRev and AccrCash.

Table 2: The summary of regression analysis

	AccrCash			DisRev			DisWCA			DisTA		
	P-value	t	β_i	P-value	t	β_i	P-value	t	β_i	P-value	t	β_i
α_0	0.330	0.975	1.731	0.011	-2.538	-0.772	0.827	-0.219	-0.030	0.480	0.707	0.199
IAQ	**0.000**	**3.081**	**1.010**	**0.000**	**3.486**	**0.910**	**0.000**	**3.129**	**1.001**	**0.000**	**3.455**	**1.009**
BODQ	0.887	0.142	0.018	0.761	-0.304	-0.007	0.492	-0.687	-0.007	0.784	-0.275	-0.005
CG	0.443	0.767	0.096	0.186	1.324	0.028	0.138	1.486	0.014	0.847	-0.193	-0.004
AQ	0.397	-0.848	-0.108	0.444	0.767	0.017	0.828	-0.217	-0.002	0.526	-0.635	-0.013
LASSET	0.534	-0.622	-0.030	0.836	0.207	0.002	0.898	0.128	0.000	0.613	-0.506	-0.004
INV	0.111	-1.595	-0.805	0.510	0.659	0.057	0.996	-0.005	0.000	0.931	0.087	0.007
LEV	0.801	-0.252	-0.102	0.000	4.030	0.278	0.076	1.775	0.055	0.623	-0.492	-0.031
CFO	0.601	-0.524	-0.002	0.262	1.124	0.001	0.652	0.452	0.000	0.540	0.614	0.000
LAGE	0.854	-0.184	-0.113	0.265	1.115	0.117	0.557	-0.587	-0.028	0.316	-1.004	-0.097
SGROWTH	0.243	-1.170	-0.155	0.748	0.321	0.007	0.274	-1.096	-0.011	0.003	-3.000	-0.063
Durbin-Watson		2.062			2.027			1.995			2.132	
F-value		3.633			2.708			3.812			3.206	
P-value		0.000			0.003			0.000			0.000	
Adjusted R^2		0.005			0.024			0.003			0.003	
R		0.095			0.194			0.108			0.131	

As we can observe from the results of three regression models, Durbin-Watson values for all models are within an acceptable level. Therefore, we can conclude that there was no auto-correlation among residuals. In addition, F-value is statistically significant, which means the relationship was linear. The sign of IAQ variable is positive and t-student values for all models are statistically meaningful when the level of significance is one percent. Therefore, we can confirm the main hypothesis of the survey and conclude that there was a positive and meaningful relationship between the quality of financial statements and having internal auditing.

CONCLUSION

In this paper, we have presented an empirical investigation to study the relationship between the quality of financial statements and having internal auditing services in selected firms listed on Tehran Stock Exchange. The proposed study of this paper has implemented various models and the results have confirmed that there was a positive and meaningful relationship between the quality of financial statement and helping some external agencies on having internal auditing

ACKNOWLEDGEMENT

The authors would like to thank the anonymous referees for constructive comments on earlier version of this paper.

REFERENCES

1. Dechow, P. M., & Dichev, I. D. (2002). The quality of accruals and earnings: The role of accrual estimation errors. The accounting review, 77(s-1), 35-59.
2. Doyle, J. T., Ge, W., & McVay, S. (2007). Accruals quality and internal control over financial reporting. The Accounting Review, 82(5), 1141-1170.
3. Fama, E. F., & French, K. R. (1993). Common risk factors in the returns on stocks and bonds. Journal of financial economics, 33(1), 3-56.
4. Healy, P. M., & Palepu, K. G. (2001). Information asymmetry, corporate disclosure, and the capital markets: A review of the empirical disclosure literature. Journal of Accounting and Economics, 31(1), 405-440.
5. Krishnan, J. (2005). Audit committee quality and internal control: An empirical analysis. The Accounting Review, 80(2), 649-675.
6. Raghunandan, K., Rama, D. V., & Read, W. J. (2001). Audit committee composition, "gray directors," and interaction with internal auditing. Accounting Horizons, 15(2), 105-118.
7. Wallman, S. M. (1996). The future of accounting and financial reporting part II: the colorized approach. Accounting Horizons, 10, 138-148.

INDEX

Q

R

S

T

U

W